investment in

JAPAN

basic information

for United States businessmen

GREENWOOD PRESS, PUBLISHERS
NEW YORK

Originally published in 1956
Washington, D.C.

First Greenwood Reprinting 1969

SBN 8371-2267-8

PRINTED IN UNITED STATES OF AMERICA

Foreword

This handbook, designed primarily to serve the needs of potential investors, is one in a series of country studies issued by the U. S. Department of Commerce. The basic economic, commercial, and legal information brought together here will also be of interest to exporters and importers trading with Japan.

Japan, not unlike many countries, has experienced a shortage of domestic capital and has turned to foreign capital to bridge the gap. Over the years there has been a moderate flow of equity capital into Japan. However, by and large the Japanese have given preference to loans and indirect types of investments, especially technological arrangements.

During the past few years the Japanese Government and business community have given special emphasis and inducements to arrangements involving the introduction of technical knowledge. This has resulted in a substantial number of such arrangements, which in a significant number of cases have been accompanied by direct investments and loans. There is every indication that, as in the past, indirect investment will be preferred but greater selectivity will be exercised as to types. American businessmen have shown, and continue to show, active interest in current conditions in Japan and the outlook for the future.

This volume describes factors which the American businessman will wish to consider in evaluating Japan as a field for investment and trade. Partial or full texts of pertinent Japanese laws and regulations and United States-Japanese treaties affecting private investment and trade are included.

Requests for additional information and assistance may be addressed to any Field Office of the Department of Commerce or to the Far Eastern Division, Bureau of Foreign Commerce, Washington 25, D. C.

It is planned to keep the basic information contained in this handbook up to date through our World Trade Information Service. Reference should be made to parts 1, 2, and 3 of that publication series for information on subsequent economic, administrative, and legal developments affecting private foreign investment. Current developments are reported in Foreign Commerce Weekly.

Both Foreign Commerce Weekly and World Trade Information Service reports may be purchased from any Field Office of the Department of Commerce or from the Superintendent of Documents, U. S. Government Printing Office, Washington 25, D. C.

The information furnished in this study is not intended to serve in lieu of the legal, financial, or business surveys which businessmen customarily make before investing abroad.

This handbook was prepared under the supervision of Eugene M. Braderman, Director of the Far Eastern Division, by Saul Baran, Chief of the Japan-Korea Section, primarily while he was Assistant Commercial Attache of the American Embassy, Tokyo.

Many individuals contributed in varying degree to preparation of the handbook, especially the officers in the Economic Division of the American Embassy in Tokyo. Credit is due particularly to Ralph J. McGuire, Second Secretary, for his work on chapter III, and to James W. Wescott, Assistant Treasury Representative of the Embassy, for his assistance in the preparation of chapter V.

American and Japanese businessmen and Japanese Government officials also contributed in many ways. Their help and cooperation are appreciated.

H. C. McClellan
Assistant Secretary for International Affairs
U. S. Department of Commerce

January 1956.

IV

Contents

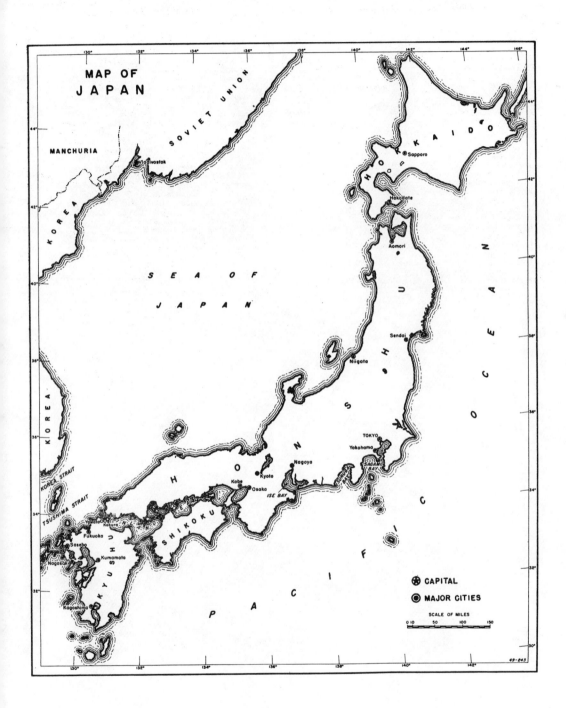

MAP OF
JAPAN

SOVIET UNION

MANCHURIA

Vladivostok

KOREA

HOKKAIDO

Sapporo

Hakodate

SEA OF
JAPAN

Aomori

HONSHU

Sendai

Niigata

TOKYO
Yokohama

OCEAN

Nagoya

Kyoto
Kobe
Osaka
ISE BAY

TOKYO BAY

HONSHU

KOREA

SHIKOKU

Moji
Kokura
Fukuoka
Sasebo
Kumamoto
Nagasaki

KYUSHU

Kagoshima

PACIFIC

KOREA STRAIT

TSUSHIMA STRAIT

⊛ CAPITAL

◉ MAJOR CITIES

SCALE OF MILES

0 10   50   100   150

49-243

The Climate for Foreign Investment

Foreign capital has historically played an important role in the economic development of Japan. This role has not been a decisive one, however. During the approximately 100 years since the opening of Japan to Western civilization, the flow of foreign capital in the aggregate has been relatively small compared with Japan's total investment requirements, except in certain periods and in specific sectors of the economy, when it was of singular significance.

Traditionally, the Japanese have favored foreign investment in the form of loans and technological assistance agreements on a royalty basis, which, unlike equity arrangements, enables the Japanese to retain control of enterprises. Thus, quantitatively, the greater proportion of the foreign capital which entered the Japanese economy has been principally in the form of public loans and through arrangements involving licensing of patents and transfer of technical information and know-how.

The Japanese have been determined and show every evidence of continued determination to prevent foreigners from obtaining a significant degree of ownership and control, particularly in important sectors of the economy. Moreover, Japanese Government officials find that loans, again unlike equity capital, provide a vehicle through which they can exercise quantitative and qualitative control over the country's investment program. In the early days of Japan's industrialization and during other periods as well, this control was considered essential in order to direct the country's economic development along predetermined lines. Since the end of World War II, but more particularly during the past 5 years, a considerable number of foreign companies have entered into technological arrangements with Japanese firms, granted sizeable loans, and found a limited market for equity investments.

EXTENT AND KINDS OF INVESTMENT

As of December 1954, the estimated aggregate value of foreign investment from all sources was $948 million. Approximately 53 percent of this total consists of a prewar investment of $501 million, most of which (about $376 million) is the funded amount of bonds (dollars and sterling) of the Japanese Government.[1] The total value of postwar investment is estimated at $447 million, with the major portion consisting of the capitalized value of technological assistance contracts ($293 million) and loans ($101 million). Of the $101 million in postwar loans, $40 million is a public loan from the International Bank for Reconstruction and Development (IBRD) for electric power development;[2] of the $61 million in private loans, almost 45 percent ($27.3 million) represents loans to the petroleum industry. Only $53 million, or slightly less than 12 percent of postwar investment, is made up of equity investments—$37 million in stocks and proprietary interest and $16 million is real estate.

American companies account for the largest portion of the total value of postwar foreign investments in Japan. United States corporations are involved in 71 percent of the technological assistance contracts approved by the Japanese Government in the postwar period (307 of a total of 431) and 62 percent of the capitalized value of such contracts.[3]

Of the $61 million in private loans outstanding at the end of 1954, all but $3 million came from the United States. Slightly less than one-half of the $58 million ($27.3 million) in loans from the United States went to Japan's petroleum-refining industry. Other major recipients were the electric power industry, $10 million; the construction industry, $9 million; and transportation, $10 million. United States investors owned almost 68 percent (about $23 million) of the total amount of stocks and proprietary interest in the hands of foreigners as of December 1954. Of this amount, $16.5 million involves participation in management.

A substantial portion of the stock obtained by Americans and other foreigners was in connection with technological assistance agreements through the issuance of new shares of stock by joint Japanese-American or other foreign companies. In some cases the shares issued to the foreign

---

[1] See appendix A, table IX, footnote 3.
[2] For further information on electric power development see chapter III, Resources and Industry.
[3] Table X of appendix A provides a breakdown of the capitalized value of technological assistance contracts by country. Table XIV of appendix A lists the foreign companies which have concluded technological assistance contracts with Japanese firms, giving date when each contract was concluded, the name of the Japanese recipient, and a brief description of the technology involved. Table XI of appendix A contains data on the number of technological assistance contracts approved by the Japanese Government classified by major industry groups.

company covered payment of a part or the whole of the agreed value of the technology or know-how. There have been instances where Americans and other foreigners have obtained majority ownership in Japanese companies or where wholly owned foreign companies have been established; notable examples are found in the oil-refining industry and in foreign trade.[4]

Many aspects and factors must be considered in explaining the present level of foreign investments in Japan and the prospects for the future. This report provides basic information on, and an evaluation of, Japan as a field for private foreign investment, which this chapter attempts to highlight for the prospective investor.

SOCIAL AND POLITICAL FACTORS

The population of Japan is and has been for many centuries among the most homogenous of any in the world. For many hundreds of years Japan has had a centralized government, and its people have had a deep sense of law and order. The paternalistic relationship which characterizes most of Japanese society tends to stress essentially personal loyalties (a relic of feudalistic social patterns) and often results in rigidity and stratification. In the business world, these factors have a bearing on the rate of economic growth.

Japan today has a relatively stable government which has avowed its friendship for, and cooperation with, the United States and other countries of the free world. The two major conservative parties, which merged into one party in November 1955 and which control approximately two-thirds of the votes in the lower House of the legislative branch, are committed to the maintenance of a comparatively free enterprise system. There is no indication that the Government intends to nationalize industries or establish Government enterprises to compete with private industry.

The present Constitution and Government organization patterned on those of the United States and Great Britain guarantees to the people basic rights in political, social, and economic affairs. Under it and other basic laws, foreign nationals appear to have substantially the same rights and privileges in nonpolitical fields as Japanese nationals and the sanctity of private property is explicitly recognized, i. e., private property may not be taken by the Government for public use without compensation. This and other aspects of United States–Japan commercial relations are given further recognition in the Treaty of Friendship, Commerce and Navigation (FCN) which has been in effect since October 30, 1953. Through a Mutual Defense Assistance Agreement, a Security Treaty and implementing Administrative Agreement, and an Investment Guarantee Agreement, and in numerous other ways, Japan

[4] Appendix A, table XIII.

and the United States have cemented their relations in recent years.

Japan's population today is greater than in prewar years, and it is both the country's major resource and biggest problem—social, political, and economic. The large population provides a plentiful supply of labor which is diversified and skilled, particularly in comparison with labor in other Far Eastern countries. Workers generally are industrious and can be trained relatively quickly. An illiterate adult Japanese is a rarity. Compulsory education has been in effect for at least 80 years and many Japanese attend higher institutions of learning, thus creating a pool of trained engineers, technicians, and potential managers and executives.

On the other hand, the efficiency of labor is, on the average, lower than in most Western countries, particularly the United States. Many Japanese contend that labor's inefficiency is attributable to overpopulation and too few resources. Since labor is plentiful, underutilization of workers is not uncommon. Management will keep workers on the payroll at low wages during periods of low business activity on the usually sound assumption that finding other employment will be difficult— an example of the paternalistic attitude prevailing in Japanese society. This practice obviously is related to the population problem, but it also constitutes the modern version of an original feudal pattern under which the employer assumed responsibility for his employees in return for faithful service.

The paternalistic attitude has been modified to some extent in recent years, but it still exerts considerable influence on management-labor relations and other aspects of Japanese life. However, both employers and the unions have mixed feelings about it. For example, even the less important aspects of paternalism, such as management's general practice of paying midyear and year-end cash bonuses and providing housing at cost or less than prevailing rates, have become accepted by labor as a right and are often a major point of issue between management and labor.

Some observers recently have shown apprehension over the increased strength of the trade unions, particularly those which are dominated by the left-wing parties. They contend that the union leadership has little understanding and appreciation of business unionism, being more inclined toward furthering leftist political objectives than in undertaking sound and realistic economic negotiations. On the other hand, there is a growing awareness among certain relatively important segments of the labor movement of the need for sound business unionism.

There is a strong desire among large and influential groups to revert to what are described as more essentially Japanese concepts and practices. This inclination is found in all segments of the

Japanese society and in all areas of activity—social, political, and economic—and is exemplified by the proposals to change the local autonomy and election laws and regulations, the education system, labor legislation, and the antimonopoly and related business legislation. Some changes have already been effected and it is likely that others will be translated into legislation and put into practice within the near future.

ECONOMIC CONSIDERATIONS

The nature of Japan's economy and economic position does not lend itself to simple generalization. For some years, Japan has had the most highly developed economy of any Far Eastern country and it compares favorably in several important respects with the more advanced industrial nations of the West.

Resources

The small mountainous area comprising Japan is poorly endowed with many of the more important natural resources required for industrial production and most of those present are being fully exploited. However, some key resources are available, most significantly a large and skilled labor force, water power for hydroelectric development, and coal—although the last-named is of a generally poor quality and, to a considerable degree, is not suitable for metallurgical purposes. Japan's population density per square mile of cultivated area is among the highest in the world. Limited expansion of cultivable area is possible and is being explored by the Japanese Government. Plans also are being considered for expansion of electric power. Possibilities may exist for increasing the recovery of other resources, but the extent of such expansion is circumscribed by the natural environment.

Barring a major scientific revolution, Japan's resources will be insufficient for its needs. Consequently, it will have to depend on utilizing imports, as it has for nearly a century, for the production of semimanufactures and manufactures to provide sufficient earnings to maintain a reasonable level of living for its large and growing population. In 1953, per capita national income was about $160, one-fourth that of the United Kingdom and France, less than one-third that of West Germany, and only about one-eleventh that of the United States. However, it is considerably higher than that of most Far Eastern countries.

Industrialization

Japan has the most highly developed and diversified industrial complex of all the Far Eastern countries. In 1953, manufacturing accounted for 24 percent of the country's national income. Japan is anxious to maintain and, if possible, expand its position as a processing nation, for thus only can its chief resource—a skilled labor force—be fully utilized in gainful employment.

Significant strides in this direction have been taken in recent years. By mid-1955 the index of industrial production was about 78 percent greater than the average of 1934–36, indicating the extent to which Japanese industry has recovered from the effects of World War II. Limited progress also has been recorded in effecting shifts in lines of activity and in increasing the diversification of industry and raising its technical standards. A program was devised to encourage the introduction of advanced technology centered around the Foreign Investment Law and special tax inducements to engineers and technicians. This gave rise to the 431 technological assistance agreements which foreign corporations had concluded with Japanese firms by the end of 1954. Also, it was the single most important factor in providing a sizable market for loans and a much more limited market for foreign equity capital.

Notwithstanding the progress to date, there are still large and important segments of Japanese industry in need of technical improvement, and even larger segments require modern management practices. Low productivity of labor and other factors, such as power shortages and high power costs, high interest rates, and relatively high material costs, all combine to result in high production costs in several important industries, particularly capital goods and heavy chemicals. Consequently, Japan finds it difficult to compete against other major trading countries in the commodities which appear most promising as important exchange earners. Thus, the greatest opportunities for foreign investment are in manufacturing, particularly in lines requiring advanced technology for the production of goods for export or products which would reduce Japan's dependence on imports.

Foreign Trade and Balance of Payments

Foreign trade has been and will continue to be the mainstay of Japan's economy. As a matter of fact, its importance to Japan is greater today than prior to World War II, owing to the country's substantial population increase since the 1930's. Nevertheless, the basic maladjustments in Japan's foreign trade have limited foreign investment and are cited as justification for continued restrictions on the entry of private foreign capital.

Since the end of World War II, Japan has experienced difficulty in balancing its merchandise account. In all postwar years, Japan's import balance has been much greater than prewar. Moreover, the loss of its prewar colonies, as well as other factors, has necessitated greater de-

3

pendence on the dollar area for raw materials, whereas purchases of Japanese goods by the United States and other dollar countries were far less than their sales to Japan. Since for some years currencies have been inconvertible, Japan has been unable to use its export surpluses with some soft-currency countries to partially offset imbalances in trade with other countries.

Aggravating Japan's balance-of-payments problems have been the substantial outpayments of foreign exchange for ocean freight and certain other invisibles; in many prewar years, earnings from invisibles compensated for the merchandise trade deficit. Other important foreign exchange burdens on the Japanese economy are payments for reparations and repayment of postwar United States aid.

The postwar trade gap was filled first by direct United States aid and in more recent years by earnings from procurement of a large variety of Japanese goods by United States Government agencies and expenditures in Japan by United States Security Forces. As a matter of fact, over the past several years Japan has been able to accumulate substantial dollar reserves.

Since it is generally recognized that special dollar earnings will not continue indefinitely, Japan must expand its sales abroad to pay for the food and raw materials required to support its large and growing population. However, Japan faces many serious internal handicaps and external obstacles in expanding and achieving a balanced trade. Important export industries are high-cost producers, resulting in inability to compete abroad. Some progress has been recorded in mitigating the handicaps through improvement of technology and factory management practices. In 1954 the Government took several steps to control the inflation which followed the outbreak of the Korean War. Much still could be done, including further fiscal and monetary measures to reduce inflationary pressures—and thereby help reduce export prices—and additional efforts to increase production efficiency.

Improvement of product quality and better service will need to be emphasized as will market surveys. In addition, Japan will require equal opportunity to trade in major markets. During the past few years Japan has faced quota restrictions and other barriers in several important areas. Furthermore, a reduction in import duties by Japan's principal trading partners would help to expand Japan's exports.

Some foreign investors have found that Japan's dearth of natural resources and great dependence on foreign trade, and its all-encompassing system of trade and exchange controls (which may be expected to continue at least as long as Japan is faced with serious balance-of-payments problems), are major deterrents to investment. Others, although recognizing these problems, have found

that through investment arrangements they are able to maintain and expand the market for their products in Japan and various Asian and other soft-currency countries, from which otherwise they would be barred or severely limited because of restrictions against dollar imports. Moreover, Japan's proximity to and experience in the vast Asian market are favorable factors for some foreign investors since the former eliminates or at least reduces shipping costs and the latter results in savings of marketing and certain other expenses.

Taxation

Many investors believe that the level of taxes in Japan provides no encouragement for investment and in certain instances may actually deter the entry of capital. In principle, foreign nationals and Japanese are treated equally under Japanese tax laws. However, during the past few years, certain foreign taxpayers have been permitted a special deduction of 50 percent of their taxable income. There is no well-established, authoritative body of rules and procedures governing the administration of the tax system. It is not uncommon, therefore, for the tax liability, especially in the case of the individual income tax, to be based on administrative decisions of a tax official and subject to negotiation.

Business profits are subject to national, prefectural, and municipal taxes. The aggregate burden on net profits, exclusive of taxes on income, is about 60 percent for the first year of doing business in Japan and approximately 54 percent for successive years, since the prefectural tax is an allowable business expense when computing the corporation tax. It is not an uncommon practice for Japanese corporations to deduct as business expenses various welfare, entertainment, and other payments made to employees (which in many cases are substantial), thereby reducing the net profit figure subject to taxation.

Individual income tax rates for foreign nationals are higher in Japan than in the United States on comparable salaries, particularly at the middle or slightly higher income brackets. On a net income of 2.5 million yen (equivalent to about $7,000), the rate is 55 percent; on 3 million to 5 million yen (approximately $8,333 to $13,900), the rate is 60 percent; and on an income of more than 5 million yen, the rate is 65 percent. The tax is computed on a sliding-scale basis, starting at 15 percent, with each rate applying only to that portion within each bracket. Employers customarily pay low cash wages and provide various special benefits to employees in lieu of cash, which minimizes the tax burden. The special tax exemptions which have been extended during the past few years to foreigners employed in designated corporations or engaged in specified activities expired on December 31, 1955.

4

Individuals also are subject to other taxes which in the aggregate are significant. These include municipal and prefectural inhabitants taxes and a municipal property tax. Noncorporate business profits are subject to the same taxes as individual incomes. However, unlike corporations, all income accruing in Japan is subject to taxation irrespective of source of such income.

With the ratification of the Convention for the Avoidance of Double Taxation, American investors will not be subject to the 10-percent income tax levied at the source in Japan on dividends from Japanese firms. Moreover, under the Convention, the tax rate on income from bonds, securities, royalties, and similar earnings received by residents is not to exceed 15 percent.

Financial Organization

For some years, Japan has had a relatively well developed and well organized financial system, which has been fostered and controlled by the Government. In the 1930's the Government centralized the financial organization and exercised greater control and the banking system became an important instrument of the Government's policy of deficit financing. The banks were also directed to assist in the financing of specified war industries.

Following the end of World War II, the financial system was reorganized along with other measures taken by the Occupation to democratize Japan's economy. As an integral part of the dissolution of the Zaibatsu (financial, industrial, and trading combines), the Zaibatsu banks and the Zaibatsu-controlled banks underwent some reorganization. In recent years there has been a noticeable revival of the trend toward close relations between successor Zaibatsu manufacturing and trading companies and the increasingly powerful successor Zaibatsu banks.

Today, the financial system generally shows an unusually high volume of Government loans and investments, great dependence of commercial banks on the central bank (Bank of Japan), extended lending by the commercial banks, extended borrowing by business, high interest rates, and a shallow market for securities. Before the war, the banks largely performed the functions of security exchanges; the prewar stock market was principally for speculators' activities, rather than a vehicle through which to attract investment capital. At present, exchanges deal only in corporate stocks; there are no transactions in corporate or Government bonds, but it is anticipated that a debenture market will be opened soon. Purchases of stock on the stock exchanges by foreigners are permitted under certain conditions which are of a complicated nature. To date, the volume of such purchases has been relatively small.

Service Industries

With the exception of shipping (the merchant fleet is about one-half its prewar size), Japan's transportation and communications systems have recovered from the effects of the war and are currently able to provide adequate service. The railroad system is by far the most highly developed but it is the most overburdened, presently operating at one of the highest train-densities in the world. Efforts are being made to extend and improve the railroad system; any significant expansion involves additional double tracking, which, with the bridges and tunnels required because of the topography, would be costly. Only 15,000 miles of Japan's 86,000 miles of roads are improved and only a few sections can be classified as first-class roads. Nevertheless, the road system is extensively used by trucks on short hauls.

Ports, storage, refrigeration, and similar facilities also are being expanded throughout the country; there is no indication that present facilities are a serious limiting factor, at least for the near future. Other basic facilities are generally adequate. However, it has not been possible to satisfy the demand for telephone service, and a 5-year plan has been formulated for the improvement and expansion of the telephone system.

Business Operations

There is evidence of a substantially greater interest in scientific management principles and practices today than in earlier years. However, Japanese businessmen generally give greater emphasis to personal factors and less consideration to scientific management principles and practices than do American businessmen. This is a manifestation of the essentially paternalistic nature of Japanese society to which reference already has been made. In business operations this results in uneconomic utilization of labor and management personnel, continued use of older accounting methods, purchase of materials and supplies at higher prices than may be necessary because of long and close personal relations with a particular supplier, and various other practices which increase costs.

Moreover, there is a trend toward reconcentration of business. The banks are now the center of power, a circumstance directly related to the general financial weakness of industry and trade. There are also mounting pressures for cartels and similar arrangements.

Notwithstanding, there is much more competitiveness in Japanese business today than prior to World War II, and a greater awareness of economic factors in conducting business. And postwar business legislation continues to act as a deterrent to a return to the prewar business organi-

5

zation of centralized control by a few over the important sectors of the economy. There are some investors who believe that some reconcentration, if limited, is beneficial, since it will result in stronger business organizations, which will enhance possibilities of sound investment arrangements.

Prospective investors occasionally find that Japanese businessmen are disinclined to make decisions rapidly. This desire to engage in prolonged negotiations is a reflection of a thorough and cautious attitude. Also, it is indicative of a basic conservatism, centralization of authority, and disinclination by subordinates to assume responsibilities. Once a decision is made and a program adopted, however, progress normally is rapid, particularly in adopting and integrating new technologies to existing operations.

GOVERNMENT AND BUSINESS POLICIES

Japanese Government officials and business leaders have made positive efforts to encourage technological assistance arrangements involving transfer of patent rights, technical processes, and specialized industrial techniques. The greatest encouragement is given to straight royalty agreements, but favorable consideration is given to equity investments when necessary to obtain the desired technology. There is widespread recognition in Japan of the need for foreign capital, but there is definite and outspoken preference for such capital in the form of loans rather than equity capital; and generally neither Japanese Government officials nor industrial and financial leaders favor the introduction of equity capital, particularly if it involves management control.

This policy of preference for highly selective investments is implemented through the Law Concerning Foreign Investment (No. 163 of 1950 as amended), hereinafter referred to as the Foreign Investment Law. Under this law, investments approved by the Government's Foreign Investment Council carry a guaranty of subsequent remittance of income and principal and prompt compensation in foreign exchange in the event of expropriation.

On the other hand, the Foreign Investment Law is used by the Japanese Government to limit the magnitude of equity investments. In this respect, the law specifically states that its purpose "is to create a sound basis for foreign investment in Japan, by limiting the introduction of foreign investment to that which will contribute to the self-support and sound development of the Japanese economy and to the improvement of the international balance of payments. . . ."

Thus, in theory one of the basic reasons for screening applications for foreign investment is to protect Japan's balance-of-payments position. As a matter of fact, the law states that preference is

to be given to those investments which are likely to contribute to the improvement of Japan's international-payments position. According to many observers, however, the screening procedure in operation often reflects what is considered to be a longstanding and strongly negative attitude on the part of responsible Government officials and businessmen toward equity capital. This attitude has been especially evident in instances involving majority ownership and control. It stems from the fear that the unrestricted introduction of foreign capital will result in both competition which will be detrimental to domestic companies and an undesirable degree of alien management control over Japanese industry and trade.

Some Japanese take issue with the contention of prospective investors that the Japanese Government through the screening procedures of the Foreign Investment Law restricts the entry of foreign capital. They point out that the limitations or restrictions are imposed only where the investor desires to obtain a Government guaranty for remittances of earnings and principal and an assurance of compensation in foreign currency in the event of expropriation. The Japanese claim that, if such guaranties are not sought, the Government does not screen investments and no restrictions exist in Japanese law on the free entry of foreign capital. The only exception is the purchase of outstanding stock in Japanese corporations.[5] In such an instance, the investor obtains no guaranty of remittance of earnings, repatriation of capital, or compensation should the Government take over his business; permission to remit is subject to case-by-case approval of the Ministry of Finance.

Naturally, foreign investors generally have chosen to avail themselves of the guaranties provided under the Foreign Investment Law in the light of Japan's difficult economic and foreign exchange problems and its all-inclusive foreign exchange controls. The Japanese contend that, as long as it is necessary for Japan to place restrictions on foreign exchange payments and specifically on capital movements, the exemptions to such restrictions provided by the Foreign Investment Law for approved investments protect Japan against overextending itself and increase the confidence of the foreign investor (who has availed himself of the guaranties under the Law) in Japan's ability to meet its obligations. These same considerations are given as justification for not extending, at present, the right of remittance to firms which were established prior to the enact-

---

[5] Licensing by, or registration with, the appropriate Government agency is required in any case. Moreover, in actual practice foreign equity investments in Government-owned enterprises would in all probability not be permitted. Additionally, the Treaty of Friendship, Commerce and Navigation between Japan and the United States gives each party the right to limit the extent to which aliens may make investments in public utilities, shipbuilding, air or water transport, banking involving depository and trust functions, and the exploitation of natural resources. It also recognizes the right of Japan, until October 22, 1956, to restrict the purchase by Americans, with yen, of outstanding stock in Japanese companies.

6

ment of the Foreign Investment Law and limiting the withdrawal of capital for approved investments to an amount not exceeding 20 percent annually, after a 2-year waiting period.

The prevailing view among foreign investors is that the Japanese want foreign capital—but on Japanese terms, which is generally defined to mean that preference will be given to public loans. This indirect type of investment has the obvious advantage of permitting the Japanese Government to exercise the widest possible latitude as regards use of the investment, and precludes foreign management participation in the economic life of the country. There is every indication, according to foreign investors, that the direct type of investment will continue to be largely in the form of technological assistance agreements, and that the most favorable consideration will be given to straight royalty arrangements for the transfer of patent rights and industrial know-how for a stipulated period. Investors report that the Government is likely to give much closer scrutiny not only to the rate of royalties, but also to the duration of a contract; and that its attitude toward purchases of stock will become less liberal, with such transactions being permitted only to the extent necessary to obtain a desired technology.

Many Japanese believe that the Government has been too liberal since the enactment of the Foreign Investment Law in approving investment proposals and that it is necessary to be more cautious because the arrangements (1) did not produce the foreign exchange predicted by the foreign investors; (2) show little prospect of doing so in the future; (3) have not significantly reduced expenditures for imports; (4) have not made, and show no real evidence of making, an important contribution to the improvement of essential industries; and (5) have placed too great a foreign exchange burden on Japan.

With respect to the last-named, reference is made to the level of remittances on investments approved under the Foreign Investment Law, which rose from $501,000 in fiscal year 1950 (ending March 31) to about $17.9 million in fiscal 1953 and, on the basis of the first 9 months of fiscal year 1954, is running at the rate of $21 million. As a consequence, it may be expected that Japanese businessmen will find it more and more difficult to convince Government officials of the need for certain types of foreign technology and, more particularly, the level of payment therefor.

Where direct investments are permitted they are likely to be confined to minority interests obtained by the issuance of new shares of stock and largely as part of a technical assistance arrangement. Undoubtedly, however, some purchases of stock also will be permitted in other instances, partly because of the prestige value to Japan of investments by prominent foreign companies and partly to create a favorable atmosphere for future sales of Government bonds abroad.

Majority control in Japanese corporations will be discouraged in the future even more than in the past. As a matter of fact, some investors believe that the Japanese Government has adopted an unwritten 51-percent rule with respect to majority control. Their opinion is based on the fact that majority control by foreigners is granted rarely, and then only when the benefits to Japan of the enterprise are demonstrated to be exceptionally great and foreign control is necessary to insure its success.

Many foreign investors have attempted to avoid the difficulties involved in making an equity investment by effecting technological arrangements on a straight royalty basis. Others have found it desirable to obtain minority control, particularly when the Japanese companies and/or businessmen involved are well known, influential, and reliable.

7

CHAPTER II

Geography, People, Government

THE PHYSICAL ENVIRONMENT

Japan is an island country situated off the eastern coast of Asia between latitudes 31° and 46° N. and longitudes 128° and 146° E. Before World War II, Japan's territory totaled more than 263,000 square miles and included Korea, Taiwan (Formosa), the Kwantung Leased Territory in China, the Kurile Islands, and the Japanese Mandated Islands. The country now comprises 4 large islands and approximately 1,000 small islands, whose total area is about 147,000 square miles, less than one-twentieth the area of the United States. The largest island is Honshu, located in the center of the island archipelago and by far the most important economically. To the south and southwest lie Kyushu and Shikoku and on the north Hokkaido, the least developed of the islands, sometimes referred to as Japan's frontier.

Japan's terrain is very rugged, more than 75 percent of the total area being too mountainous for permanent cultivation; and mountains or sea are visible from virtually every location. Because the mountain ranges rise precipitously from unusually narrow coastal plains and because of other important factors, such as sandy soils, undrainable areas, and erosion, only about 15 percent of Japan's total area is presently under cultivation.

The climate of Japan is a compromise between continental and maritime types and, in general, may be described as mild and humid. Conditions vary greatly, however, from region to region. Because of the country's topography, the influence of monsoons, and the effects of the warm Japanese current and the cold Okhotsk current, there are marked contrasts in temperatures.

No part of Japan is deficient in precipitation but the amount of rainfall varies considerably from place to place. The distribution of precipitation is influenced largely by monsoons as is indicated by the abundant summer rains. Over much of the country rains are lightest during the winter months. Snow is a possibility in all parts of Japan, particularly in regions fronting on the Japan Sea. However, snow cover for lengthy periods is characteristic only of Hokkaido, northern and western Honshu, and the higher mountain regions in other parts of Japan. High humidity prevails in most of Japan; readings range from 71 to 86 percent, with the humidity being greatest during the summer months. Typhoons and earthquakes are not uncommon and occasionally result in loss of life and property damage.

THE POPULATION

Japan is one of the most densely populated areas in the world, particularly if population is related to arable land. In 1953, Japan had a population density of 4,286 persons per cultivated square mile.

The ratio of population to land and other national resources makes the Japanese economy highly dependent on foreign trade and, consequently, very sensitive to international economic conditions. These are the touchstones for a realistic assessment of the country's present and future economic position and prospects. Japan's total population exceeded 88 million in 1954 and the population continues to increase at the rate of about 1.2 million per year.

The birth rate declined significantly from 34.3 per thousand in 1947 to 21.4 in 1953, a rate appreciably lower than the 30.8 per thousand in 1937 and 27.1 in 1938, and the lowest rate since the turn of the century. The death rate in Japan, however, dropped from about 17 per thousand during the 1930's to slightly less than 9 in 1953. Thus, a further considerable decline in the rate of population growth in the foreseeable future seems unlikely, particularly in view of the population's age structure, which has a high proportion of children and young people. According to projections by the Population Problems Research Institute of the Government's Ministry of Welfare, the population of Japan will total 95 million in 1960 and reach 100 million about 5 years later.[1]

Despite the fact that Japan often has been described as essentially a composite of small villages and towns, it is probably one of the most highly urbanized countries in the Far East. In 1954, about 23 percent of the nation's approximately 88 million people lived in 34 of the larger cities (table 1). The major concentrations of population, as would be expected from the geography of the country, are in the narrow plains, the valleys, and the coastal areas. Nearly three-fifths of the total population live in about one-fifth of the total area of the country.

[1] *On the Latest Trend of Japanese Population*, Institute of Population Problems, Ministry of Welfare, August 15, 1951.

Japan is divided into 10 geographic regions with 46 administrative areas called prefectures. Population density is greatest in the Kanto, Kinki, and Tokai regions, which are in the main central island of Honshu and contain the six most densely populated cities—Tokyo, Osaka, Kyoto, Nagoya, Yokohama, and Kobe. These cities have a combined population of nearly 13 million, or about 15 percent of the total for all of Japan (table 1).

Table 1.—Population of Major Cities, 1940, 1950, and 1953

City	October 1, 1940	October 1, 1950	March 31, 1953
Total for Japan	72,539,729	83,199,637	[1] 88,100,000
Honshu			
Tokyo	6,778,804	5,385,071	6,409,638
Osaka	3,252,340	1,956,136	2,188,565
Kyoto	1,089,726	1,101,854	1,152,524
Nagoya	1,328,084	1,030,635	1,183,694
Yokohama	968,091	951,189	1,048,387
Kobe	967,234	765,435	1,004,386
Sendai	223,630	341,685	347,177
Kawasaki	300,777	319,226	377,908
Hiroshima	343,968	285,712	323,018
Amagasaki	181,011	279,264	320,024
Kanazawa	186,297	252,017	259,108
Yokosuka	193,358	250,533	267,213
Shizuoka	212,198	238,629	259,927
Niigata	150,903	220,901	229,949
Sakai	182,147	213,688	231,308
Himeji	104,259	212,100	219,248
Gifu	172,340	211,845	233,435
Shimonoseki	196,022	193,572	208,437
Wakayama	195,203	191,337	200,880
Kure	238,195	187,775	197,120
Okayama	163,552	162,904	209,375
Kyushu			
Fukuoka	306,763	392,649	426,961
Kumamoto	194,139	267,506	276,573
Nagasaki	252,630	241,805	274,978
Kagoshima	190,257	229,462	251,489
Yawata	261,309	210,051	235,213
Kokura	173,639	199,397	220,607
Sasebo	205,989	194,453	228,132
Omuta	124,266	191,978	198,281
Shikoku			
Matsuyama	117,534	163,859	175,313
Kochi	106,644	161,640	169,492
Hokkaido			
Sapporo	206,103	313,850	351,232
Hakodate	203,862	228,994	234,069
Otaru	164,282	178,330	184,750

[1] Estimate as of August 1954.

Source: For 1940 and 1950, Population Census, by Bureau of Statistics, Prime Minister's Office; for 1953, Registration of Inhabitants, Ministry of Justice.

Hokkaido, the northern island, which is both a region and a separate prefecture, has the lowest population density—142 people per square mile. It comprises one-fifth of the total area of Japan but has only one-twentieth of the country's inhabitants, of which about 45 percent are rural. It is to Hokkaido that the Japanese people must look for any substantial increase in cultivable areas. Various plans are under consideration for reclamation and improvement of land and other types of economic development in that area.

Females outnumber males in Japan. As of 1951, when the total population was estimated at 84,573,000, approximately 43 million were females and 41,573,000 were males. In the same year, approximately 63 percent of the population were under 30 years of age, the heaviest concentration of both sexes being in the age groups under 15 years.

Unlike many countries in Asia, Japan today consists of an essentially homogenous people. From the earliest period of its history, Japan has been influenced by the peoples and cultures of other countries, which over the years have been blended together to form the nation's unique culture. Present-day Japan is probably the most Westernized country in the Orient, but the centuries' old and revered cultures have not been uprooted by the introduction of Western processes. The traditions still are shared by all Japanese, with little variation in the basic cultural pattern throughout the various parts of the country.

The Japanese language is the only official language, and it is spoken with only slight variations in dialects throughout the country. English—which for some time has been the accepted language of foreign commercial intercourse and widely used in commercial circles and by a substantial number of educated people—has become more popular since the end of World War II. English is taught in many schools, colleges, and universities and it is being recognized increasingly as the second language of the country.

The Japanese are among the most literate peoples of the world; it has been estimated that approximately 98 percent of the population between the ages of 15 and 64 can read and write. Compulsory elementary education in Japan dates from 1872, the fifth year of the Meiji era.[2] A national education system, patterned after the French system, operated in Japan until the end of World War II. In 1947, in line with the new Constitution, a basic education law was passed by the Diet. This law provides for 9 years of compulsory, free education; the elimination of political and religious activities in schools; and the decentralization of educational authority—greater responsibility and freedom than ever before was given to the prefectural and other local authorities.

In the school year 1951–52, 20,035,657 students were attending classes in about 45,000 schools. Nearly 11.5 million were enrolled in elementary schools, more than 7.3 million in secondary schools, and 422,000 in 425 colleges and universities; the others were in various special schools, such as teacher training schools, kindergartens, and schools for the deaf or otherwise handicapped. According to the Ministry of Education, Japan in 1951 had 1,550 libraries, of which less than 1,000 were public libraries and only about 290 had more than 3,000 volumes. All of the libraries, combined, had more than 9 million books which were used by approximately 11 million people.

[2] The period of the reign of Emperor Meiji, 1868–1912. His accession to the throne in 1868 marks the beginning of modern Japan, and it was during this period that Westernization progressed rapidly.

These data do not adequately reflect the extent of the usage of books in Japan, inasmuch as there is a large sale of new and used books and magazines in all parts of the country and among all educational levels. In recent years, upwards of 10,000 new book titles have been published annually, with the number of copies sold running into the millions; and there are many magazines, the combined circulation of which aggregates tens of millions. In addition, magazines and books are imported in sizable volume. Furthermore, in 1953, 180 daily newspapers were published with a total circulation of more than 35 million—the equivalent of one copy per 2.5 persons.

More than one-half of the Japanese people adhere to Shintoism, which, unlike other religions, has no doctrine or creed other than imperial and ancestor worship. Before World War II, the Shinto religion was accorded a privileged position by the Japanese Government and was in effect the national religion. Following World War II it was given equal status with other religions. Many Japanese combine Shintoism with another religion, such as Buddhism; in 1953, there were reportedly about 415,000 Christians.

THE GOVERNMENT

The Constitution

A new Japanese Constitution was promulgated on November 3, 1946, and became effective on May 3, 1947. This Constitution was modeled on the basic laws of Great Britain and the United States, and provided for basic changes in the prewar Japanese political system. Under its terms, sovereignty is vested in the people; the Emperor is deprived of executive powers, retaining only ceremonial functions; the peerage is abolished; suffrage is granted to women; the voting age is lowered from 25 years to 20; a bill of rights is outlined; and social standards are set.

The present Japanese Constitution guarantees civil liberties and defines the basic rights of the people. Basic rights in social, political, and economic fields are guaranteed and equality of all persons under law is assured. Workers may form unions and bargain collectively and the people are free to choose their work and worship as they wish. Freedom of speech, press, and assembly also is guaranteed to all citizens. Where the exercise of police power is necessary, it must be in accordance with established procedures and subject to judicial processes. Individuals have the right of redress against the state and to choose and dismiss public officials.

An interesting feature of the Constitution is the provision which recognizes the right of the people "to maintain the minimum standards of wholesome liberty" and enjoins the state to take appro-priate measures to assure "the promotion and extension of social security, and of the public health." Moreover, the provision of compulsory, free education is considered to be a fundamental obligation of the state.

Of interest to American businessmen contemplating investment in Japan is the fact that, under the new Japanese Constitution and applicable laws, foreign nationals appear to have substantially the same rights and privileges in nonpolitical fields as do Japanese nationals. In this connection, the Constitution specifically states that "the right to own or to hold property is inviolate" and that "private property may be taken for public use upon just compensation therefor." With respect to foreign investment, this is of significance particularly in view of the additional legal protection against expropriation, with due compensation provided for approved investments under Japan's Foreign Investment Law and the Treaty of Friendship, Commerce and Navigation between Japan and the United States (see chapter VIII).

National Government Organization

Legislative power in Japan is presently vested in a bicameral body called the Diet; in the words of chapter 4 of the Constitution, "The Diet shall be the sole lawmaking organ of the state." The Diet consists of a House of Representatives of 467 members elected for not more than 4 years and a House of Councillors of 250 members, one-half of whom are elected every 3 years for 6-year terms. Ultimate legislative power rests with the House of Representatives. Legislation passed in the House of Representatives and disapproved in the House of Councillors becomes effective if passed again by the House of Representatives by a two-thirds majority. In the event of a difference between the two Houses as regards the budget or treaties, a majority vote of the House of Representatives only is necessary.

The Executive power in Japan is vested in the Prime Minister chosen by the Diet from among its own members. The Prime Minister nominates the Cabinet, a majority of whom must be members of the Diet, and all of whom must be civilians. The Cabinet is collectively responsible to the Diet; on a vote of nonconfidence, the Cabinet must resign or dissolve the House of Representatives and call for a new general election.

The new Constitution provides for an independent judiciary. Judicial power is vested in a Supreme Court and in lower courts established by special legislation.[3] The Supreme Court is composed of 1 Chief Justice and 14 associate judges. The Chief Justice is appointed by the Emperor following designation by the Cabinet, and the other judges of the Supreme Court are

---

[3] Court Organization Law, law No. 59 of April 16, 1947.

appointed by the Cabinet. The judges of the lower courts also are appointed by the Cabinet from a list submitted by the Supreme Court. Supreme Court appointments are reviewed in a special referendum held at 10-year intervals with general elections.

The new Constitution specifically provides that the Diet is the responsible body in all matters relating to national finances. No money can be expended or obligated except as authorized by the Diet. The power to institute new taxes or modify existing tax laws resides in the Diet. The Cabinet is responsible for the preparation of the national budget, but to assure that the public has adequate control over the nation's purse strings, the Constitution requires that the Diet approve the budget, postapprove all deficiency appropriations, have a complete audit every fiscal year, and have annual financial reports submitted by the executive.

Amendments to the Constitution must be initiated by the Diet, concurred in by at least two-thirds of the members of each House, and approved by a majority of popular votes at a special referendum or election.

Local Government

As of late 1954 Japan was subdivided into 46 prefectures, 543 rural districts, 248 seats, 871 towns, and 8,295 villages. The Constitution and the Local Autonomy Law, both of which went into effect on May 3, 1947, guarantee the principle of local autonomy and provide for the direct popular election of the executive officials of local government entities and all members of the legislative bodies (assemblies). Unlike the National Government, the local assemblies are unicameral. The powers and responsibilities of the assemblies have been greatly expanded compared with prewar years; their authority is wide and varied, ranging from traffic regulation to the levying and collection of taxes.

Political Parties

As a result of the general election of February 27, 1955, the Democratic Party gained the largest number of seats in the Diet. This party was formed during 1954 following the defection of some members from the Liberal Party and their joining forces with the Progressive Party. Prior to that time the Liberal Party was the majority party in the Diet and except for periods in 1947 and 1948 had been in control of the Government since 1946.

Distribution of 467 seats in the lower House of the Diet at the opering session following the February 27, 1955, election was as follows: Democrats, 185; Liberals, 112; Left-wing Socialists, 89; Right-wing Socialists, 67; Labor-Farmers, 4; Communists, 2; and others, 7. No

party has a majority; the present Cabinet was formed by the Democrats. Like the Liberals, the Democratic Party is a moderately conservative party. Both parties advocate a relatively free enterprise system and cooperation with the United Nations and the United States. The Democrats campaigned on a pledge of expanded trade with Communist China and Soviet Russia and "normalization" of relations with the latter, but gave assurance that Japan will maintain its policy of close cooperation with the United States.

Following a long period of negotiations the two Socialist parties merged on October 13, 1955, under the name of Japan Socialists. About a month later the two conservative parties also effected unification. As of the end of November 1955 the Japan Socialists had 154 seats in the lower House of the Diet and the new conservative (Liberal-Democratic) party, 300 seats; minor parties and vacancies account for the remaining seats.

The conservative parties have indicated a desire to amend the Constitution to remove the uncertainty regarding the right of Japan to maintain defense forces. They also wish to effect changes in certain other provisions of the Constitution, as well as other basic legislation enacted during the occupation. The Socialists have expressed opposition to the program of the conservative parties to amend the Constitution and effect changes in the education, labor, and other social legislation. Since a two-thirds majority vote is necessary to amend the Constitution, the opposition parties for the present can block such action.

INTERNATIONAL RELATIONS

Since the Peace Treaty, which became effective April 28, 1952,[4] Japan has entered a new phase in its international relations, and its foreign policy has been based on close cooperation with the United States and other nations of the free world in conformity with the principles of the Charter of the United Nations.

The framework of the United States-Japan relationship includes a Security Treaty signed at San Francisco on the same day as the Peace Treaty (September 8, 1951), and an Administrative Agreement signed at Tokyo on February 28, 1952, implementing the Security Treaty. The Security Treaty provides for the maintenance of United States armed forces in and about Japan for the preservation of Japan's security and as a contribution to the peace and stability in the Far East "with the hope and expectation that Japan will itself increasingly assume its own defense against direct and indirect aggression. . . ." The Administrative Agreement is the basic instrument governing the conditions under which the United

---

[4] Signed by 48 nations at San Francisco on September 8, 1951.

States security forces are maintained in Japan and sets forth the rights, privileges, obligations, and responsibilities of both countries.

Japan's first commercial postwar treaty was concluded with the United States on April 2, 1953 (see especially chapter VIII for a discussion of the Treaty of Friendship, Commerce and Navigation). Another postwar first was the Civil Air Transport Agreement between Japan and the United States, signed on August 11, 1952. On March 8, 1954, as part of the Mutual Defense Assistance Agreement, Japan agreed to participate in the United States Government's Investment Guaranty Program (see chapter VIII). Since the end of the war the United States has tried to assist Japan in many other ways, including (1) the provision of direct civilian aid in the form of food, medical supplies, and other basic necessities and the furnishing of raw materials to stimulate recovery of Japan's war-torn economy during the early postwar years; (2) the extension of technical assistance; and (3) sponsorship for Japan's admittance to the membership of the United Nations,[5] the General Agreement on Tariffs and Trade (GATT),[6] and various other international organizations.

With the resumption of sovereignty Japan has expanded significantly its participation in international affairs. Among important international organizations, in addition to those already mentioned, in which Japan has full membership are the International Monetary Fund (IMF), the International Bank for Reconstruction and Development (IBRD), the Food and Agriculture Organization (FAO), and the Economic Commission for Asia and the Far East (ECAFE). Japan has also participated in the International Materials Conference and various other international commodity agreements and conferences. It is a contributor to the Colombo Plan and attended the Afro-Asian Conference in Indonesia in April 1955.

There is every reason to believe that Japan will continue to maintain cordial relations with the United States and simultaneously pursue a foreign policy of closer cooperation with all Asian countries. In this connection, Japan recently concluded a reparations agreement with Burma and hopes that it may soon find a way to reach agreements on reparations with Indonesia, the Philippines, and the former Associated States of Indochina (now Viet-Nam, Laos, and Cambodia). Moreover, Japan has recently accepted a proffer from the U. S. S. R. to conduct negotiations looking toward an agreement to end the state of war and expand commercial relations.[7]

It is also evident that Japan will increase its efforts to expand trade relations with communist China, an important prewar market for Japanese products and the source of supply for several important raw materials, notably iron ore, coking coal, salt, and soybeans. As noted above, the present Government may be expected to seek a rapprochement with communist China and the U. S. S. R. The left parties (Japan Socialists and the Communists) advocate establishment of full diplomatic relations with communist China and the U. S. S. R. and either the renunciation of the Security Treaty and the Administrative Agreement with the United States or significant revisions.

---

[5] Were it not for repeated vetoes by the U. S. S. R. Japan would today have full membership in the United Nations; at present it has only a permanent observer status.

[6] In 1953, Japan succeeded in obtaining provisional accession; the contracting parties held negotiations in Geneva in the spring of 1955 for the purpose of bringing Japan into the GATT as a full member and Japan became a full member on September 10, 1955.

[7] The U. S. S. R. did not sign the San Francisco Peace Treaty and, therefore, a technical state of war still exists between Japan and the U. S. S. R. The two countries have no official diplomatic relations, but the U. S. S. R. maintains an unofficial mission at Tokyo.

CHAPTER III

Resources and Industry

Japan is, in general, poorly endowed with natural resources. The nation's prewar colonial raw material sources have been lost, and most of the basic raw materials now must be purchased abroad. Among the few key resources domestically available are water power for hydroelectric development and coal, although the latter is of a generally poor quality. In addition, Japan has important resources in the diligence, skill, and manual dexterity of its people, and in the industrial experience and tradition the country has acquired in the past.

Japan is a processing nation—an importer of foodstuffs and raw materials and an exporter of finished products. Because of its large and expanding population and limited arable land, Japan must export and import to survive.

Japan is the most highly industrialized nation in Asia and it is the only nation in that area capable of exporting machinery and capital goods. Its industrialization began with the Meji restoration in 1868. Through an intensive program of importing Western technology and a high rate of Government-induced capital formation, Japan was transformed in less than a century from a predominantly feudal and agricultural economy to a highly industrialized capitalist economy with a large export trade in manufactured and semimanufactured goods.

World War II deprived Japan of a vast colonial and controlled area which had provided that country with both a ready source of many industrial raw materials and a sheltered market. Furthermore, a large portion of Japan's industrial complex was destroyed and another large portion became obsolete. At the close of the war, therefore, Japan was faced with the very formidable task of reconstructing and rehabilitating its industry to a point sufficient to support a large population on a much smaller land base. In addition, Japan had to find new markets for its products and to change the composition of its exports to meet the needs and demands of those new markets.

Japan's success in this endeavor has been noteworthy. In 1953, real national income was 6 percent above the 1934–36 average. By June 1955 the manufacturing index stood at 186 (1934–36=100). In 1954, mining, construction, and manufacturing combined accounted for 31.4 percent of the total national income, virtually the same level as during 1934–36. However, significant alterations in the composition of Japan's production have taken place. Textiles, for example, which in 1934 accounted for 23 percent of total industrial output, had declined to about 8 percent in 1954. On the other hand, the percentage of total production represented by mining, machinery, and chemicals increased. The result has been that Japan's production pattern has become more diversified and consequently more resilient than in the prewar era. Nonetheless, Japan is still facing serious difficulty. The volume of exports is still well below that of prewar years, and Japan is in many fields a high-cost producer.

AGRICULTURE

Agriculture ranks second only to manufacturing in importance in Japan's economic life. At the end of 1954, approximately 40 million people were classified as rural. This agricultural population earned slightly more than 20 percent of the country's national income.[1]

At least 70 percent of the area of Japan is presently unsuitable for cultivation because it is too mountainous or because the soil is too poor for economic operation. However, 80 percent of the country's food requirements are produced on the less than 16 million acres under cultivation. Cultivated areas are found principally along the coastal plains and in the valleys. Since the need for land is so great, slopes greater than 15 degrees and some as steep as 30 degrees are under cultivation. Moreover, the Japanese Government is constantly trying to develop new areas which will be suitable for cultivation and agricultural output in an effort to meet the food requirements of a population growing at the rate of about 1.2 million annually. The alternative to increased agricultural production is food imports—in 1954, the Japanese imported grains, flour, soybeans, and sugar valued at $710 million.

All arable land is intensively cultivated; in many parts of the country double cropping is the rule and in some parts multiple cropping is practiced. The soil in Japan is not naturally fertile, but heavy application of fertilizers and very close attention

[1] In Japanese fiscal year 1952 (April 1952–March 1953), as estimated by the Economic Counsel Board (now the Economic Planning Board) of the Japanese Government.

15

to the requirements of the soil result in crop yields which are among the highest in the world.

Food crops take precedence over all industrial crops, and grains dominate food production. However, the varied topography and climate of Japan make it possible, and profitable, to grow a wide variety of crops. Data on acreage and production of principal crops in the years 1953 and 1954 are shown in table 2. As noted, rice is the most important crop; wheat, barley, naked barley, sweet potatoes, and white potatoes constitute other staple crops. Raw silk and tea are the two most important export agricultural products; exports of these products in 1954 were valued at $46.9 million and $13.6 million, respectively.

Table 2.—*Planted Area, Yield, and Production of Specified Crops, 1953–54*

Crop	Planted area (1,000 acres)		Indicated yield per acre (kilograms)[1]		Indicated production (1,000 metric tons)	
	1953	1954	1953	1954	1953	1954
Grains:						
Rice	7,449	7,539	1,106	1,209	8,239	9,113
Wheat	1,696	1,660	810	913	1,374	1,516
Barley	1,000	1,108	1,099	1,143	1,099	1,268
Naked barley	1,276	1,398	778	941	992	1,316
Oats	218	223	666	732	146	163
Corn	173	168	573	352	99	59
Buckwheat	130	125	322	224	42	28
Potatoes:						
White	492	514	4,850	5,270	2,386	2,714
Sweet	895	876	6,020	5,960	5,391	5,226
Pulses:						
Soybeans	1,062	1,082	413	355	438	384
Kidney beans	168	212	386	345	65	73
Broad beans	60	52	413	484	25	75
Peas	24	31	444	480	11	15
Fruits:						
Oranges	113	[2]118	7,990	[2]10,730	419	[2]642
Apples	103	[2]110	4,640	4,090	476	[2]451
Pears	24	25	4,000	n. a.	94	[2]97
Oilseed:						
Rapeseed	605	431	478	509	289	220
Sesame	24	22	224	n. a.	5.3	n. a.
Flaxseed	43	42	86	80	3.7	3.4
Other crops:						
Tea	82	87	[3]688	[2][3]770	[2]56	[2][3]67
Tobacco	160	172	637	677	102	117
Sugar beets	38	38	8,560	8,910	322	340
Mulberry	429	446				
Cocoons					[2]69	[2]66

n. a.—Data not available.
[1] 1 kilogram equals 2.2046 pounds.
[2] Preliminary.
[3] Dried leaves.

Source: Ministry of Agriculture and Forestry, except for tobacco and sugar beets, the sources for which are the Monopoly Corporation and the Sugar Refiners' Association, respectively.

Since land is so scarce, very little is devoted to the production of animal feed. For this reason, as well as because the average Japanese farmer has small landholdings, the livestock industry is relatively small. The average Japanese farmer seldom has more than two of each kind of animal. Nearly 40 percent of the farmers have draft animals and 16 percent have horses. An estimated 200,000 dairy cattle are distributed among some 133,000 farm families; and the number of hogs, sheep, and goats is small. Pasturing generally is not practiced, animals being barn-fed throughout the year. Poultry raising is widespread, with

more than one-half of all farmers raising chickens. However, holdings are small, averaging about five chickens per farmer.

The use of dairy products and meat in the Japanese diet is very limited; fish is the main source of protein for the vast majority of the people.

Maximizing food production is one of Japan's most important problems. For some years this has been high on the list of policy programs of the Japanese Government. Extensive plans have been formulated for the irrigation and reclamation of land, the improvement of farm techniques, expansion of multiple cropping, and pest and disease control. The Government has set aside substantial funds to support this program, and significant progress has been recorded.

It is difficult at this time to estimate the extent to which food production can be increased. Some improvement probably can be made, but at great cost, since all of the better land is already under intensive cultivation. Perhaps the most promising prospects for land reclamation are in Hokkaido, where there are extensive peat bog and marshland areas; the Japanese Government has formulated plans for the development of such areas for which it hopes to obtain a $10-million loan from the World Bank. Self-sufficiency is impossible, barring revolutionary scientific developments. The most that can be anticipated is a gradual increase in domestic production, perhaps at a level sufficient to keep up with the growth of population. A reasonable assumption, therefore, is that Japan will continue to import foodstuffs at about the level of recent postwar years.

Per capita food grain consumption has reached the prewar level. However, there has been a shift from rice to other grains, mainly wheat, imports of which have increased far beyond prewar levels. Output of rice in Japan has risen to the prewar totals, but production has not kept up with the increase in population. The precarious nature of Japan's food position was vividly illustrated in 1953, when rice production was considerably below normal because of adverse weather conditions. As a consequence, an additional 1.3 million tons of food grains were imported during the food year 1953–54 at a cost of $150 million.

FISHERIES

Historically, Japan has been the foremost fishing nation in the world, producing as much as 50 to 70 percent of the total world catch. The Japanese islands are advantageously situated in a zone of convergence and mixing of two great water masses—the cold waters of the northwestern Pacific and the warm-surfaced water of the Japanese current—a situation which produces abundant resources. This natural productivity of the waters surrounding Japan, a long coastline, and the urgent need to exploit all available sources of food have combined to encourage an active fishing industry.

Fishing is of major importance to Japan both as a source of domestic food supply and as a prime factor in the country's export trade. Despite the fact that the fishing industry suffered heavily as a result of the war and postwar restrictions upon fishing areas, the total catch in 1952 and 1953 exceeded the prewar peak. In 1953, the total catch of fish, shellfish, other marine animals, and seaweed (but excluding whales) amounted to 9,330 million pounds, only slightly less than the catch in 1952.

Exports of marine products in 1954 totaled $74.2 million, an increase of approximately $14 million over exports in the preceding year, and in quantity were more than equal to the prewar level.

Principal species in the Japanese catch are, in the northern cold-water mass, herring (one of the largest herring runs in the world), salmon, crab, cod and related fishes, and cold-water seaweed; and in the warm-surfaced Japan-current mass, sardines, mackerel, tuna and tunalike fish, and seabreams. Near the shore there are also a sizable shellfish industry and thousands of acres of seaweed.

The area in which Japan now fishes is smaller than that fished prior to World War II (for example, the waters around Korea, the U.S.S.R., and the mainland of China are at present closed to Japanese fishing), but the total catch compares very favorably with the prewar averages. The use of marine radar and sonar and electronic aids to navigation, all introduced largely through licensing and technical assistance agreements between Japanese and American firms, has been an important factor in facilitating deep-sea fishing and locating schools.

FORESTRY

Japan's mild climate and its geographical location together constitute a favorable condition for the growth of plants and trees. Roughly one-half of the total area of Japan can be considered forest land. Wood is by far the most important building material in Japan, partly because of its availability and partly because of a lack of other building materials. Ninety-nine percent of the people live in houses built of wood, and wood is utilized to a much greater extent than in America and Europe to make household and other articles.

As a result of the dependence of the Japanese economy on wood material, the wartime demand, followed by the acute need for reconstruction at the close of the war, resulted in heavy overcutting of Japanese forests. In addition, the loss of Formosa, Korea, and South Sakhalin at the end of the war reduced the forest reserves available to Japan 45 percent by area and 30 percent by amount of standing timbers. Because of the increased demands placed upon a diminished supply, standing timber reserves since the close of the war have been reduced at a rate far exceeding new growth. The Japanese Government, in an attempt to retard this reckless exploitation of the country's timber resources, has promulgated a series of laws aimed at timber conservation, reforestation, and afforestation. The Government also has recognized the need to conserve the use of wood products for construction and fuel through employment of substitute materials and wood preservatives, more efficient processing methods, and maximum utilization of waste.

According to the agriculture census of 1949, the total forest area of Japan was approximately 51.1 million acres, with standing timber amounting to an estimated 483,440 million board feet. About 25 percent of this area is in Hokkaido, but forest land is found in every prefecture in Japan. Approximately 10 percent of the total forest area is unexploited, largely because of inaccessibility. However, the construction of new roads is reducing the extent of the unexploited forest land.

A wide variety of woods is produced in Japan ranging from subtropical forest woods through broad-leaved evergreens in Shikoku and Kyushu and deciduous broad-leaved woods in northern Honshu and southern Hokkaido to coniferous woods in northern Hokkaido, with the latter being the most important. *Sugi* (Japanese redwood) and four species of pine are the principal woods, followed by firs, spruces, hemlock, and various other types. Beech and several species of oak are the dominant broad-leaved trees, and there are also extensive stands of maple, birch, chestnut, and larchwood.

Production of logs in 1953 totaled 7,154,796,000 board feet, a postwar peak. Lumber production during the same year totaled almost 6,625 million board feet, an alltime high.

In spite of Japan's high production of timber in relation to the size of the country, annual growth is not sufficient to meet the country's needs, and a small percentage—but significant in terms of foreign exchange—of Japan's consumption must be imported. In 1954, imports of wood (including logs) totaled 1,869,020 cubic meters, valued at $48,044,000. A sizable proportion of such imports is composed of lauan logs from the Philippines and British North Borneo which are used in Japan's rapidly growing plywood industry and reexported.

Japan's dependence upon wood for construction would be even greater, with a consequent greater need for imports, were it not for the wide use of bamboo, straw, and grass. Bamboo has literally hundreds of uses, and it is estimated that in

1946 bamboo was utilized as a substitute for 14,270,000 cubic feet of construction lumber.

OTHER BASIC RESOURCES

Electric Power

In general, coal and water power are the main power and fuel sources of Japan. In view of Japan's comparatively favorable endowment of natural resources for hydroenergy production, and the relatively difficult conditions under which coal is mined, electric power is produced primarily by hydroelectric facilities and secondarily by supplemental thermal plants using coal. The mountainous topography and plentiful rainfall, averaging about 70 inches a year, have encouraged the development of water power for electricity.

Most of the hydroelectric plants in Japan are small, about 59 percent of them having a capacity of less than 2,000 kilowatts, and only about 10 percent of the plants are of the reservoir type. As a result, the typical hydroelectric generating plant depends upon stream flow, and water storage capacity is insufficient to avoid seasonal reduction of output or even to meet daily load fluctuations during low or medium stream stages. A subsidiary supply from thermal power plants is necessary, therefore, during the dry winter months and periods of peak load.

Thermal power generation in Japan is markedly more expensive than hydropower, owing in part to the high prices and relatively low calorific value of indigenous coal and in part to the inefficiency of obsolescent equipment. In 1952, for example, the average calorific value of coal for thermal power generation was 5,510 kilo calories per kilogram and the average thermal efficiency was 19.4 percent—the highest being 24.5 percent and the lowest, about 10 percent.

Prior to World War II, Japan's electric power system was sufficient generally to meet the demands placed upon it. During the war, however, overutilization, obsolescence, lack of maintenance and replacement, and war destruction all adversely affected the industry's productive capacity. At the close of the war, demand for electricity rose

Table 3.—*Electric Power Companies and Generating Capacity, March 31, 1954*

[In thousands of kilowatts]

Company	Capacity
Hokkaido	437
Tohoku	1,061
Tokyo	1,392
Chubu	1,219
Hokuriku	576
Kansai	2,365
Chugoku	727
Shikoku	349
Kyushu	1,254
Total	9,380

Table 4.—*Electric Power Plants, Capacity, and Output, as of December 31, 1953*

[Capacity and output in thousands of kilowatts]

Item	Hydro-electric	Thermal	Total
Total:			
Number of plants	1,444	300	1,744
Capacity	7,454	4,501	11,955
Generated	41,397	13,620	55,017
Electric power companies:			
Number of plants	1,307	89	1,396
Capacity	6,683	3,160	9,843
Generated	37,161	9,933	47,094
Private plants:			
Number of plants	137	211	348
Capacity	771	1,341	2,112
Generated	4,236	3,687	7,923

sharply with the progress of industrial rehabilitation and increased residential use resulting from the high prices of other fuels and Japan's expanding population. In December 1953, there was a shortage estimated at about 1.5 million kilowatts or 18.4 percent from peak load. To meet this shortage, a number of firms have constructed their own generating plants.

Electric power is produced and distributed commercially by nine companies, established on a regional basis (see table 3). At the end of 1953, these companies represented 82.3 percent of the country's generating capacity and 85.6 percent of the power generated, with private plants for self-consumption comprising the remainder.

The total capacity at the end of 1953 was about 11,955,000 kilowatts, of which about 7,454,000 represented hydropower generation and about 4,501,000 represented thermal power generation (see table 4).

The frequencies of power supplied are generally 50 cycles in the eastern part of the country and 60 cycles in the western part; however, in central Honshu and parts of Kyushu the generating capacity can operate at either frequency. Electric power companies in all districts except the islands of Hokkaido and Shikoku have concluded power accommodation contracts to eliminate extreme unbalances of power supply. The distribution system for large customers is chiefly an alternating current 6.6-kilovolt or 3.3-kilovolt, three-phase, three-wire system, and for electric lighting it is a 100-volt, single-phase, two-wire system.

Rates for electricity are higher during the dry winter months, when the hydroelectric power shortage is supplemented with expensive thermal power, than during the summer months. The establishment of rates is subject to Government authorization, which is preceded by public hearings. At the present time there are separate rates for lighting and power; and lighting rates may be on either a flat or a meter rate basis. The rates for both lighting and power rise sharply for consumption exceeding a standard volume. During Japanese fiscal year 1952 (April 1, 1952–

March 31, 1953), the average unit price for lighting was ¥969 ($2.69) per kilowatt-hour and, for electric energy, ¥352 per kilowatt-hour. In view of the deficits now being incurred by the electric companies and the added costs of the present construction programs, rates may be raised in the near future.

Consumption of electric power in 1953 totaled 43,700 million kilowatt-hours, of which 36,300 million kilowatt-hours, or 83 percent, were supplied by electric power companies and 7,400 million were supplied by private plants for self-consumption. Of the power consumed, 6,700 million kilowatt-hours were supplied for electric lighting and 37,000 million were used for electric energy. Indicative of the pattern of large-scale consumption of electric power is the following list of industries which were the largest consumers in 1953:

Billion kilowatt-hours

Iron and steel	4
Sulfate of ammonia	3
Coal mining	2.7
Calcium cyanamide and carbide	2.4
Paper and pulp	1.9

In 1953, about 15 million houses, or 98 percent of the total number in Japan, were equipped with electric lights, but the annual average per capita consumption for lighting was only 77 kilowatt-hours and the average per capita consumption of electric power was about 500 kilowatt-hours. The consumption of electric power over the past several years has shown an average annual increase of about 10 percent.

To meet the needs of Japan's expanding industrial complex and increasing population, the Japanese Government in 1952 prepared a 5-year power development plan aimed at increasing existing electric power generating capacity by 5,120,000 kilowatts by the end of the Japanese fiscal year 1957 (March 31, 1958). This total includes about 3.7 million kilowatts of water power and more than 1.4 million kilowatts of thermal power. Upon completion of the plan, Japan will have a capacity of approximately 16 million kilowatts, consisting of about 11 million kilowatts of hydroelectricity and about 5 million kilowatts of thermal electricity, to meet the nation's power consumption in 1957 roughly estimated at 53,400 million kilowatt-hours.

Under the development plan, emphasis has been placed upon the construction of large reservoirs to avoid the results of the seasonal variations in stream flow in hydroelectric facilities. The Government also hopes, by constructing new thermal power plants particularly during the first half of the 5-year plan, to be able gradually to retire super-annuated and inefficient existing thermal power stations. The development plan envisages the utilization of about one-half of the nation's estimated hydraulic power reserves of 21,830,000 kilowatts.

The authors of the 5-year plan have recognized the possibility that opportunities may present themselves, as the plan progresses, to negotiate loan agreements to assist in the financing of the program in order to introduce superior machines and equipment, as well as more advanced engineering techniques. In fact, in 1953 the International Bank for Reconstruction and Development granted a loan of $40.2 million for the construction of thermal power facilities, and in the same year the Bank of America granted a loan of $9 million to the Electric Power Development Company for the development of hydropower generation. In addition, a large American electrical equipment firm has granted a long-term credit for the purchase of electrical generating machinery. In spite of the magnitude of this program, however, it is estimated that the maximum capacity of supply at the completion of the plan will show a deficit of more than 10 percent under estimated peak loads.

Coal

Japan is adequately, but not abundantly, supplied with certain types of coal. The most recent estimate (1947) of proved, probable, and possible reserves was somewhat more than 17.8 billion tons, exclusive of lignite. Of the estimated reserves, approximately 75 percent are judged to be bituminous, about 20 percent subbituminous, and less than 5 percent anthracite or natural coke.

Japanese coal mines are for the most part high-cost producers, in part as a result of a lack of mechanization, in part because of a surplus of underemployed labor, and in part because of the structure of the deposits. Coal seams are generally thin, compared with the deposits of other coal-producing countries; in most fields the seams are broken and discontinuous, and some of the important mines must contend with large amounts of ground water.

The quality of Japanese coals is generally low. Most indigenous coals have a low heat value and a high ash content; comparatively little is suitable for coking and virtually none produces coke suitable for large blast furnaces. Some of the best Japanese coals yield slightly above 13,000 British thermal units per pound, but the average good coal produces about 11,000 units per pound, and the ash contents are high, being 20 percent or more for some mines. Thus, while the cost of production of a given quantity of coal is high, the cost per unit of heat is even higher. As a result, Japan finds it expedient to import between 5 and 10 percent of its annual coal requirements, and the figure probably would be even higher were it not for the restrictions placed upon coal imports by the Government. Not only is Japan lacking in adequate supplies of coking coal, but, because of high production costs, the consumer price of imported coal frequently is lower than that of domestic coal. For example, the consumer price of Japanese high-grade coking coal in March 1954 was about $20 a ton, while the c. i. f. price of coking coal imported from America was about $18.50 a ton.

The bulk of Japanese coal production comes from two regions—northern Kyushu and central Hokkaido; minor amounts are derived from fields in eastern and southeastern Honshu. In recent years, about 55 percent of the output has come from Kyushu, and 25 to 30 percent from Hokkaido. At least 80 percent of mine capacity is distant from the largest industrial centers and the main concentrations of population, but virtually all fields are relatively near to water transportation and thus are accessible to all parts of the country at relatively low cost differentials.

Coal production in 1954 totaled 42.7 million metric tons, a slight decrease from output in the preceding 2 years. The decrease occurred as a result of a decline in domestic demand as industrial firms tended to shift to petroleum fuels or imported coal because of the high prices of the domestic product. Of the 1954 production, standard coal accounted for 74.4 percent, coking coal for 18.2 percent, anthracite for almost 3 percent, and other coals for 4.4 percent.

Approximately 90 percent of Japan's coal and coke imports in 1954, totaling 3.4 million metric tons, consisted of bituminous coal for coking, of which more than 90 percent came from the United States. Anthracite coal, principally from North Viet-Nam, Korea, and the Union of South Africa, and noncoking bituminous coal, from Australia, India, and Formosa, accounted for most of the remainder of Japan's imports.

In 1953, there were 993 coal mines in Japan, operated by about 600 companies, but 10 companies operating 68 mines produced 53 percent of total national output.

Because the high cost of Japanese coal contributes to the high cost of Japanese iron and steel products, which in turn precludes a reduction in the export prices of many Japanese manufactures, the Government is making efforts to mechanize the coal-mining industry and increase labor productivity. Primarily this modernization involves shifting from the present inclined-slope method to the vertical-shaft method of mining, which requires the introduction of modern machinery and techniques, involving sizable capital expenditures. Since it is doubtful that sufficient funds can be raised internally, outside assistance will be required if existing goals for the mechanization and rationalization of the Japanese coal industry are to be achieved.

Petroleum

Japan's indigenous oil resources are meager, and the production activity of the petroleum industry has been concerned chiefly with the intensive development of deposits which are lean, scattered, and of a geologically complex character. Consequently, Japan is dependent upon imports for approximately 90 percent of its petroleum requirements.

The present producing districts are located in northern Honshu and northern Hokkaido, but there are stratigraphic conditions widely distributed throughout Japan which give sufficiently favorable indications to encourage exploration. However, the past records of producing districts do not suggest the probability of major discoveries in the future, and it does not seem likely that Japan's petroleum production will increase appreciably as a result of the opening of new fields.

The Japanese refining industry has made a marked recovery from the wartime destruction. At present, there are nine operating petroleum refining companies with a daily capacity of about 139,700 barrels. Of this total, three companies having an aggregate daily capacity of 22,500 barrels, refine domestically produced crude oil, and seven companies, having a daily capacity of 117,200 barrels, refine imported crude oil, with one using both imported and domestic crude.

The postwar reconstruction of Japan's refining industry has developed with substantial financial assistance from foreign oil companies. Of the nine refining companies, only three have no capital tieups with foreign firms, and one of the three has a technical assistance agreement with an American company. None of the five foreign companies with equity investments in refining companies have less than 50 percent equity ownership, and four of them also have made substantial loans.

Because of the meagerness of Japan's indigenous oil resources, most of the industries were originally established on the basis of other sources of power and the domestic demand for petroleum products has been low in comparison with that in other industrialized countries. Because of the greater efficiency of petroleum-fueled plants, as compared with coal-fueled plants, an industrial shift from coal to petroleum has taken place in recent years which has had adverse repercussions upon the hard-pressed Japanese coal industry. The Japanese Government, in an attempt both to aid the coal industry and conserve foreign exchange, has administratively restricted imports of petroleum products. However, the pressure for increased use of petroleum at the expense of coal continues and will undoubtedly increase with any improvement in Japan's foreign exchange position.

Iron Ore

Indigenous iron ore sources in Japan are deficient in both quantity and quality. The latest (March 1954) estimate of proved, probable, and possible reserves of 52 major producing localities totaled 55 million long tons, but only 3 mines had reserves of as much as 1 million tons each. The iron content of the ore is low, averaging roughly 50 percent, and the sulfur content is relatively high. Magnetite, limonite, and hematite constitute the major forms of ore, and deposits of these ores are scattered widely. Iron sand deposits are found in northern Honshu and southern Hokkaido.

Because of limited iron ore resources, 70 percent of the total supply of 5.6 million tons of iron ore, including iron sand, available in 1953 was imported. Principal sources of Japan's imports of iron ore are Malaya, the Philippines, India, the United States, and Canada; and Japan is in the process of establishing capital investments in iron mines in the Philippines and Malaya. Japanese production of iron ore is shown in table 5.

Table 5.—*Production of Metallic Ores, 1952–54 and January–June 1955*

[Quantity in units indicated]

Product [1]	1952	1953	1954	1955 (Jan.–June)
Copper_____metric tons__	53,600	58,400	65,199	33,580
Lead_____do____	17,490	18,520	22,899	12,013
Zinc_____do____	82,480	96,100	109,320	50,359
Tin_____do____	648	744	727	441
Antimony_____do____	204	324	265	125
Chromium [2]_____do____	47,200	37,600	32,497	12,044
Manganese [2]_____do____	207,200	187,500	163,877	87,914
Iron ore [2]_____do____	1,071,648	1,102,752	1,121,377	416,236
Iron sand [2]_____do____	322,008	437,868	509,490	238,600
Gold_____kilograms___	6,264	7,080	7,381	3,513
Silver_____do____	161,100	187,400	187,893	86,661
Mercury_____do____	107,200	128,200	149,667	83,312
Molybdenum [2]_____do____	166,600	334,000	380,607	187,413
Tungsten [2]_____do____	590,000	1,003,000	1,101,536	505,404

[1] Metal content except as noted.
[2] Concentrates.

Nonferrous Metals

Japan traditionally has been a copper-producing country, and until about 1920 was an exporting country. Its domestic copper supply still is substantial, but a major portion of presently known reserves consists of marginal or submarginal ores. Therefore, primary domestic production is insufficient to meet domestic demand, and the deficiency is offset by the use of scrap copper, both imported and domestic, and imported ores.

Japan is a net exporter of zinc. Zinc is produced by both the electrolytic refining process and distillation, with the former method comprising about 70 percent of total production. The use of the more efficient distillation process is increasing, however.

Most of the lead in Japan is found in conjunction with zinc, in sulfide ores, in a ratio of about 1 to 5. Japan produces only about 20 percent of its lead requirements from domestic sources.

Japan also produces gold and silver in amounts more than sufficient for domestic needs, and lesser amounts of antimony, mercury, chromium, manganese, molybdenum, and tungsten.

Research is progressing in the recovery of titanium from iron slag and from iron sand. In fact, production started in 1953 and a small amount of titanium sponge was exported during 1954. Indications are that titanium recovery may develop into a major metallurgical industry in Japan.

Nonmetallic Minerals

Japan is favorably supplied with many basic nonmetallic construction substances (see table 6). Supplies of limestone, clay, and gypsum are sufficient to assure the manufacture of any quantity of cement likely to be needed in the country for many years. Construction sand and gravel, building stone, and the more common clays are adequate to meet anticipated needs indefinitely. The most important lacks are high grades of high-refractory clays, kaolin and china clay, gypsum, and glass sand. Glass can be produced from Japanese materials, but its quality is low and the cost high; and the lack of glass sand partly accounts for the absence of glass in much of Japanese construction.

Table 6.—*Production of Nonmetallic Minerals, 1952–54 and January–June 1955*

[Quantity in metric tons]

Product	1952	1953	1954	1955 (Jan.–June)
Asbestos_____	3,060	3,864	6,052	3,221
Gypsum_____	200,640	264,600	329,466	160,430
Graphite_____	4,624	4,008	4,050	1,453
Talc_____	10,572	10,560	14,798	10,710
Barite_____	14,232	17,244	13,042	4,263
Alunite_____	2,618	4,272	5,864	2,666
Dolomite_____	667,104	593,136	599,265	345,268
Limestone_____	15,572,000	17,466,000	20,713,800	10,094,000
Refined sulfur_____	180,000	187,000	187,200	95,000

Japan is less favorably situated with respect to certain other nonmetallic minerals. The country must import all or most of its requirements of salt, phosphate, potash, borax, barite, and fluorites. Japan has no nitrate deposits, but nitrogen is obtained from domestic sources through atmospheric fixation. As regards various other items, Japan can produce sufficient arsenic, iodine, and bromine for its own needs.

INDUSTRY

The average yearly indexes of industrial production as a whole (1934–36=100) have risen steadily—from 126.4 in 1952 to 166.9 in 1954 and to 169.9 in the first 6 months of 1955 (see table 7).

Iron and Steel

The iron and steel industry in Japan is of primary importance, not only from the standpoint

21

Table 7.—Indexes of Industrial Production, 1952–54 and January–June 1955

[1934–36=100]

Item	1952	1953	1954	1955 (Jan.–June)
Industrial activity	131.8	161.2	173.5	176.8
Utilities	201.2	220.7	236.9	251.8
Industrial production	126.4	155.1	166.9	169.9
Mining	114.2	122.6	117.0	113.2
Manufacturing	128.2	159.7	173.8	177.6
Durable manufacturing	171.8	209.9	213.2	209.3
Metals	154.2	183.5	192.3	211.3
Machinery	205.1	266.5	257.4	225.5
Ceramics	138.2	156.0	175.3	166.5
Lumber and wood products	158.0	169.8	177.0	185.5
Nondurable manufacturing	104.5	131.8	150.3	157.2
Textiles	66.2	76.5	81.9	83.0
Chemicals	168.5	216.6	267.2	299.6
Rubber and leather	131.6	172.1	170.8	168.5
Foods and tobacco	114.6	161.7	191.8	170.6
Printing	78.4	106.5	109.6	122.6

Source: Economic Planning Board of the Japanese Government.

Table 8.—Production of Leading Manufactures, 1952–54 and January–June 1955

[Quantity in units indicated]

Item	1952	1953	1954	1955 (Jan.–June)
Textiles:				
Raw silk_____metric tons__	12,303	12,068	12,159	5,431
Rayon staple_____do____	118,926	162,175	203,238	117,127
Yarn:				
Cotton_____do____	353,137	414,464	464,491	217,543
Rayon filament_____do____	64,497	74,054	83,846	43,325
Spun rayon_____do____	93,876	113,543	146,715	88,996
Spun silk_____do____	2,149	2,033	1,729	970
Woolen_____do____	35,765	42,860	33,760	17,675
Worsted_____do____	32,720	41,793	42,826	22,582
Fabrics:				
Cotton_____1,000 sq. meters__	1,871,599	2,349,642	2,661,451	1,268,977
Woolen and worsted____do____	126,045	140,104	128,772	70,295
Rayon filament_____do____	415,622	481,014	551,386	308,026
Spun rayon_____do____	386,133	421,414	544,640	356,155
Silk filament_____do____	144,488	123,450	134,630	76,385
Spun silk_____do____	18,046	18,670	18,378	9,607
Fish nets, total_____metric tons__	9,165	9,867	11,082	5,669
Cotton_____do____	7,540	7,494	8,355	3,598
Others_____do____	1,625	2,373	2,727	2,071
Chemicals:				
Sulfuric acid (50° Be [1])				
1,000 metric tons__	4,009	4,296	4,871	2,599
Finished soda ash____metric tons__	200,400	274,800	306,000	157,000
Caustic soda_____do____	268,800	372,000	445,200	237,400
Salt [1]_____1,000 metric tons__	434	461	430	195
Ammonium sulfate [2]_____do____	1,953	2,038	2,186	1,133
Calcium cyanamide [2] metric tons__	525,780	525,468	519,890	281,634
Calcium superphosphate [3]				
1,000 metric tons__	1,346	1,516	1,854	994
Calcium carbide_____metric tons__	595,351	596,200	572,759	361,060
Urea_____do____	56,416	77,932	124,836	82,108
Ammonia_____do____	567,249	608,604	693,822	372,404
Bleaching powder_____do____	54,708	49,031	38,534	17,341
Ammonium nitrate_____do____	27,319	32,804	37,782	14,882
Soap_____do____	150,243	191,878	233,777	131,407
Photographic film 1,000 sq. meters__	3,709	4,970	6,013	3,712
Coal tar_____metric tons__	386,042	432,915	428,201	252,542
Toluene, pure_____do____	4,289	6,717	6,685	3,746
Phenol, crude_____do____	4,652	4,818	5,312	2,655
Aniline_____do____	3,768	5,016	4,393	2,729
Synthetic dyestuffs, total___do____	13,944	19,572	17,484	9,818
Direct colors_____do____	3,228	4,176	3,528	1,807
Acid colors_____do____	565	768	770	403
Basic colors_____do____	506	612	720	444
Mordant and acid mordant colors_____metric tons__	523	924	516	246
Sulfur colors_____do____	6,468	8,724	7,488	3,695
Vat and sulfo-vat colors__do____	804	2,052	1,452	1,012
Naphthol and other colors_____do____	1,850	2,316	3,010	2,211
Camphor, crude_____do____	1,517	1,305	1,312	920
Industrial explosives_____do____	26,267	29,161	27,879	12,412
Petroleum products, total 1,000 kiloliters__	3,507	6,069	7,373	3,944
Gasoline_____do____	1,389	1,707	2,009	1,127
Kerosene_____do____	111	359	486	266
Gas oil_____do____	424	457	663	340
Diesel oil_____do____	578	472	609	291
Fuel oil_____do____	552	2,424	2,963	1,575
Lube oil_____do____	233	317	341	170
Other_____do____	220	293	302	175
Coke_____1,000 metric tons__	5,876	6,912	6,595	3,473
Iron and steel products:				
Pig iron_____do____	3,474	4,518	4,608	2,511
Crude steel (ingots and castings) 1,000 metric tons__	6,989	7,662	7,750	4,557
Finished steel and secondary products_____1,000 metric tons__	5,112	5,776	5,918	3,586
Ordinary steel_____do____	4,638	5,184	5,357	3,308
Special steel_____do____	227	304	294	143
Steel wire_____do____	420	454	506	293
Galvanized iron sheet___do____	475	539	654	326
Steel pipe_____do____	294	409	380	175
Rubber goods:				
Truck tires_____1,000 units__	455	558	454	135
Balloon tires_____do____	557	858	1,162	665
Bicycle tires_____do____	11,726	14,815	13,483	7,043
Truck tubes_____do____	413	513	393	130
Balloon tubes_____do____	580	858	1,138	591
Bicycle tubes_____do____	12,132	15,581	14,563	7,731
Rubber soled canvas shoes 1,000 pairs__	37,559	43,988	46,940	29,452
Rubber boots and shoes___do____	26,951	34,328	33,267	13,927
Leather footwear_____do____	3,408	3,900	3,952	2,172
Wheat flour_____1,000 metric tons__	1,481	1,799	2,039	1,081
Tobacco, fine cut_____metric tons__	8,804	9,691	6,454	3,091
Cigarettes_____millions__	81,193	87,096	96,295	49,703
Lumber_____million board feet__	6,354	6,627	6,661	3,274

See footnotes at end of table.

of its relative size within the industrial complex of the country, but also because of its position as a primary determinant of the export prices of a substantial proportion of Japan's industrial exports. In addition to the prices of primary products, such as galvanized sheets, plates, bars, and pipes, of secondary products, such as various kinds of rods, wires, and polished straps, and of such materials as pig iron, ferroalloys, and semi-finished products, the world competitive position of manufactured and industrial capital machinery is in large part determined by the production cost of steel.

Japan has become one of the world's major producers of iron and steel, but its iron and steel industry is dependent upon oversea sources for virtually all major component materials, such as iron ore, scrap iron, coking coal, and alloys for special steel products. The problem of cost reduction is thus not completely within Japan's control.

Japan's pig iron production in 1954 totaled 4,608,000 metric tons (see table 8), 96 percent of which was produced in blast furnaces and most of the remainder in electric furnaces. Total crude steel production (ingots and castings) in 1954 was 7,750,000 metric tons, of which 5,357,000 represented ordinary steel.

Japanese iron and steel prices are generally above world prices, as a result of wartime damage to production facilities, high prices of imported and domestic components, and relatively inferior production techniques. In an attempt to reduce costs, the Japanese iron and steel industry has undertaken two plans for the modernization and rationalization of the industry. The first plan, begun in 1951, was aimed at the reconstruction of the industry. It has been implemented by the reconstruction of blast furnaces and coke ovens and the installation of iron sand refineries for pig iron; the enlargement of melting pots; and the acceleration of production by the adoption of the

Table 8.—Production of Leading Manufactures, 1952–54 and January–June 1955—Continued

[Quantity in units indicated]

Item	1952	1953	1954	1955 (Jan.–June)
Plywood_____million sq. feet [4]__	802	1,099	1,439	906
Pulp_____1,000 metric tons__	1,240	1,508	1,632	914
Paper_____do__	1,342	1,761	1,922	1,058
Cement_____do__	7,131	8,768	10,675	4,952
Sheet glass				
1,000 cases of 100 sq. feet, 2 mm. thick__	5,415	5,826	6,165	3,020
Railway rolling stock:				
Steam locomotives_____number__	43	33	70	79
Electric locomotives_____do__	32	43	53	19
Diesel locomotives_____do__	35	40	24	6
Passenger and electric cars__do__	613	819	1,159	359
Freight cars_____do__	3,951	2,747	3,428	940
Industrial rolling stock:				
Steam locomotives_____do__	10	19	_____	_____
Battery locomotives_____do__	109	112	129	41
Gasoline locomotives_____do__	349	413	324	85
Freight cars, steel_____do__	12,536	11,316	7,588	2,511
Electric locomotives_____do__	63	31	28	5
_____do__	308	336	338	238
Vessels, steel_____{gross tons__	517,137	756,013	444,537	235,408
100 gross tons and {__number__	129	165	217	105
over_____{gross tons__	510,597	749,411	438,758	230,262
99 gross tons and {__number__	179	171	121	133
under_____{gross tons__	6,540	6,602	5,904	5,146
Motor vehicles:				
Standard size:				
Trucks and buses___number__	23,844	27,720	34,099	13,224
Small size:				
Passenger cars_____do____	4,668	7,044	8,497	6,175
Trucks_____do____	10,524	11,652	18,086	9,654
Three-wheeled vehicles__do____	62,256	98,352	101,902	44,506
Motorcycles_____do____	45,108	111,228	120,796	48,887
Motorscooters_____do____	30,528	53,532	48,732	24,861
Bicycles_____thousands__	1,019	1,217	1,087	572
Sewing machines:				
Household_____do____	1,260	1,318	1,372	776
Industrial_____do____	62	76	66	54
Watches and clocks:				
Watches_____thousands of units__	1,217	1,617	2,002	1,065
Clocks_____do____	2,576	3,054	3,596	1,761
Cameras, excluding X-ray and motion picture_____thousands__	401	608	981	504
Binoculars and opera glasses____do____	274	286	284	167
Microscopes_____number__	20,400	22,800	24,400	12,900
Radio receivers_____thousands__	939	1,410	1,423	866
Electric light bulbs, standard___do____	127,188	140,280	149,421	73,344
Bearings:				
Ball bearings_____do____	16,144	23,618	26,756	9,746
Roller bearings_____do____	3,659	5,953	6,630	2,857
Machine tools, total_____number__	11,587	18,722	18,124	8,408
Lathes_____do____	986	1,215	1,427	508
Drilling machines_____do____	6,688	12,460	11,876	5,307
Boring machines [5]_____do____	534	772	900	454
Milling machines [6]_____do____	67	274	269	123
Grinding machines_____do____	1,611	2,452	2,213	1,218
Gear-cutting machines____do____	104	143	180	70
Other [7]_____do____	1,697	1,406	1,259	728
Textile machinery:				
Silk:				
Manufacturing machines number	2,933	3,402	1,859	1,273
Preparing machines____do____	4,590	4,509	3,806	2,810
Looms_____do____	9,162	12,489	11,050	7,066
Cotton and staple fiber:				
Carding engines_____do____	6,337	3,959	5,418	1,174
Ring spinning frames____do____	3,564	2,410	3,386	766
Looms_____do____	24,540	23,385	32,323	11,247
Woolen and worsted:				
Carding machines_____do____	252	295	153	57
Ring spinning frames____do____	84	575	56	25
Looms_____do____	3,747	3,104	1,676	1,448
Dyeing and finishing:				
Dyeing_____do____	400	630	643	316
Others [8]_____do____	1,728	797	956	447
Spindles_____thousands__	3,077	2,579	2,335	863

[1] Production in Government-licensed plants only.
[2] Converted to 20 percent N_2 content.
[3] Converted to 16 percent P_2O_5 content.
[4] Converted to 4 mm. thickness.
[5] Includes vertical turning and boring mills beginning April 1953.
[6] Excludes vertical turning and boring mills beginning April 1953.
[7] Includes shapers, slotters, and sawing machines.
[8] Includes starching machines and cloth-handling machines.

oxygen process for open hearths, converters, and electric furnaces for the manufacture of steel.

Partially as a result of these measures, costs for certain iron and steel products dropped in varying degrees during 1954.

A second plan, for improving quality and techniques, has now been developed which will require a substantial investment in equipment. In view of present financial conditions in Japan, raising the amount of capital required is likely to prove difficult and, consequently, foreign capital will be needed either in the form of equity investment or as loans. Japan is seeking financial assistance from the International Bank for Reconstruction and Development to provide part of the capital requirements for this program. One such loan amounting to $5.3 million was granted on October 25, 1955.

Since 1951, several Japanese steel companies have entered into technical assistance agreements with foreign firms, and it is likely that further opportunities exist for investments of this nature.

Shipbuilding

Japan has long been one of the major shipbuilding countries of the world. Immediately before World War II, Japan vied with Germany for second place in world shipping construction, and Japan's merchant fleet was the third largest in the world.

Japan's shipbuilding facilities were not seriously damaged during the war. However, by the end of the war, the effects of bombing and the choking off of raw material supplies had reduced ship construction virtually to the vanishing point. In the early postwar years several factors inhibited any significant revival of the industry; prior to 1950, therefore, many shipbuilding companies engaged in the manufacture of farm implements, rolling stock, and mining machinery in order to maintain their existence.

Beginning in 1950, orders for a wide variety of vessels were placed with Japanese shipyards, and in that year, for the first time since the war, the construction of large oceangoing diesel-powered vessels was begun. Each succeeding year has shown a substantial increase in tonnage constructed in an effort to develop Japan's merchant marine to the point where the country will not be so dependent on foreign-flag vessels for its oversea trade.

Exports of ships are large, but have not reached prewar levels; in 1953, ships accounted for more than 80 percent of Japan's heavy industry exports. In the years 1950–53, a total of 59 ships, aggregating 579,000 gross tons and valued at $174 million, were exported. This export activity largely reflected the worldwide demand for tankers, and the fact that European shipyards were working at capacity, rather than any cost differential favorable to Japan. In fact, Japanese shipbuilding costs are high, and the Japanese Government has resorted to various types of indirect export subsidies to bring export prices down to competitive levels.

Equipment and techniques in the shipbuilding industry have been markedly improved, but further modernization of the industry is required and, particularly, new and more efficient machine tools are needed.

Motor Vehicles

The first automobile produced in Japan appeared in 1907. Prior to World War II, automobile production for commercial use was small, virtually all capacity being used to meet the needs of the military. Trucks and buses were produced in quantity, but again largely for the armed forces. Both Ford and General Motors established assembly plants in Japan in the 1920's, but the majority of passenger vehicles were imported. The production of small, three-wheeled, truck-type motor tricycles became well established before the war, and provided the Japanese with a serviceable and economical means of transport. Since the war, however, with the motor vehicle industry being freed from military demands, production has increased rapidly, and in 1953 motor vehicles constituted about 20 percent of total major production. The annual value of motor vehicle production in Japan at the present time is estimated at $400 million.

Postwar passenger automobile design in Japan is far behind that of other countries. Furthermore, the demand for domestically produced automobiles is not sufficient to sustain assembly-line production, and the cost of Japanese produced vehicles is substantially above that of foreign vehicles of comparable quality and size. The condition of Japan's highway system and the high cost of gasoline have encouraged the use of light-weight, small vehicles and directed domestic passenger automobile demand toward the lighter cars.

Recognizing their deficiency in modern production techniques, at least four Japanese firms have concluded technical assistance agreements with foreign firms. All of these agreements have been for light, small cars and only one of them has been with an American company. American producers of standard size automobiles have attempted to conclude agreements with Japanese companies, but have not been able to obtain Government consent. The principal reasons advanced for the reluctance to permit such agreements are that American automobiles in general are not suited to the Japanese economy because of their size and cost of operation, and that the country cannot economically absorb more cars than are being produced with existing facilities.

Before the war a large number of trucks and buses were exported to China and Manchuria, and the loss of those markets has sharply reduced vehicle exports. Southeast Asia, Korea, Formosa, and Okinawa now constitute a market for Japanese trucks and buses, but total exports of such vehicles are only a fraction of the prewar level. Japanese exports of passenger vehicles are negligible. The price factor appears to be the major deterrent to an expansion of Japanese vehicle exports, but quality and design also are important considerations.

Optical Goods and Related Products

The manual dexterity and capacity for painstaking work that characterize the Japanese people have been an important influence in the production of optical goods and precision instruments.

The Japanese optical goods industry received a great impetus from the requirements of the war, and Japan at the end of the war had a large reservoir of skilled labor and a well-developed optical industry whose facilities were readily and rapidly converted to peacetime production. Japan's output of cameras, binoculars, and microscopes has increased rapidly and the growth of exports to world markets of these items has been impressive. The quality of Japanese cameras and optical equipment is high and the cost comparatively low, largely because nearly all raw materials are domestically available.

The major problem confronting optical goods manufacturers, particularly those making cameras and binoculars, is the proliferation of small-scale producers making low-quality goods, who have injected a note of cutthroat competition into the industry. In the fear that these producers, with the uneven and often low quality of their products, will have a deleterious effect upon the reputation of Japanese products in its export markets, the Government has established rigid quality inspection of export production. In view of the active measures being taken to maintain quality standards, as well as to encourage exports, the future of this industry would appear to be good.

Japan also has a well-developed precision measuring instrument and surveying instrument industry. Exports of these items have been inhibited, however, by the fact that the quality of the Japanese product—which is still suffering the effects of its prewar reputation of being poor and uneven in quality— has not yet been established in oversea markets. The industry is aware of these adverse factors and is taking measures to overcome them.

A number of technical assistance agreements have been concluded between American and Japanese firms for the manufacture of such items as radar, sonar, and radio-navigation equipment— both marine and airborne—and aircraft and marine instruments. Also, a number of contracts for the repair of such equipment have been concluded, which will provide Japan with the necessary skills and know-how for the further development of these industries. In addition to creating possibilities for the export of these items, the development of such industries provides domestic support for Japan's shipbuilding industry and its growing aircraft industry.

Chemicals and Chemical Fertilizers

Japan has a highly developed chemical industry for which most of the basic raw materials, such as salt, potassium salt, phosphate ore, and oils and fats, must be imported. Certain key resources, such as pyrite ore and limestone, however, are available in Japan. Despite the high level of development of the industry, chemical exports have been retarded by relatively high prices, particularly of heavy chemicals, largely as a result of the present high electric power rates.

At the end of World War II, Japan's chemical industries were generally in poor condition. However, numerous technical assistance agreements and capital investment arrangements have been concluded with foreign firms; and priority in reconstruction and substantial financial aid were given by the Government to certain chemical industries, most notably chemical fertilizers, to support a badly needed increase in food production. Thus, the industry as a whole has rapidly recovered to its prewar activity and in most cases has far outstripped its prewar production level.

Chemical fertilizers.—The chemical fertilizer industry has a long history in Japan. Ammonium sulfate was first produced, as other than a by-product, in 1923. Calcium cyanimide was produced in 1909, and calcium superphosphate was in production during the Russo-Japanese War.

Ammonium sulfate, the most important source of nitrogenous fertilizer, reached a level of output in 1954 of 2,186,000 metric tons, the highest production on record, and more than the estimated domestic requirements of about 1.7 million metric tons. Because of the importance placed upon the production of ammonium sulfate by the Government at the end of the war, about $22 million was spent on reconstruction of the industry, the major portion of this sum being provided by the Government. Nonetheless, in spite of an estimated capacity, as of April 1953, of about 2,892,000 metric tons, production has not been sufficient to meet both domestic and export requirements. Electrolysis-process facilities account for about 763,000 metric tons of total capacity, and gas-process facilities for about 2,128,500 metric tons. A shortage of electric power is the principal factor retarding full production, and recently the Government has announced that it intends further to encourage the production of this commodity by

making additional quantities of electric power available to the industry.

Exports of ammonium sulfate in 1953 and 1954 averaged 481,908 metric tons, most of which went to Formosa and South Korea, and lesser amounts to India and southeast Asian countries.

Calcium cyanamide production also has increased every year since the war's end, and the quality has been improved, the nitrogen content now averaging about 20 percent. As Japan is comparatively rich in limestone, the raw material for this commodity is plentiful. The improvement of this industry is due largely to the introduction through technical assistance agreements of foreign techniques, such as the use of a large closed-type carbide furnace. The present annual production capacity of the calcium cyanamide industry is about 520,000 metric tons, and production in 1954 totaled about 520,000 metric tons. Again, a shortage of electric power is the principal deterrent to full production.

Urea, ammonium chloride, and ammonium nitrate have developed since the war as new nitrogenous fertilizer industries. Urea was produced on a limited scale before the war for the production of urea resin and medicine, and only since the war has it come to the fore as a fertilizer. Present production capacity is somewhat more than 103,000 metric tons—making Japan one of the leading urea-producing countries in the world—and capacity is being expanded to a goal of 273,000 metric tons by 1956.

Calcium superphosphate production depends upon imported phosphate rock as the basic raw material and adequate supplies of sulfuric acid. The industry has made an excellent recovery since the end of the war, but production, totaling 1,854,000 metric tons in 1954, has not yet reached the prewar peak. Output has been limited by a shortage of sulfuric acid, in spite of a record production of that commodity. The present annual production capacity of calcium superphosphate is 2,840,000 metric tons.

Fused phosphate has recently become an important commodity, production reaching 263,000 metric tons in 1953, as compared with only 61,000 metric tons in 1952. Ammonium phosphate and triple phosphate are being produced on a small scale, and there is every prospect of increased output in the future.

Calcium carbide production in 1954 reached 573,000 metric tons, and with Japan's adequate supplies of limestone and potentially cheap electric power, the prospects for this commodity appear to be excellent. Present capacity is in the neighborhood of 1 million metric tons, and a program for increasing production of synthetic resins and fibers should bring about a substantial increase in domestic demand.

Sulfuric acid.—Sulfuric acid output has increased rapidly since the close of the war as a result of the priority given to the production of chemical fertilizer and the increased production of pyrites, and in 1954 reached an alltime peak of 4,871,000 metric tons. This volume was not sufficient, however, to meet the demand resulting from the increased production of the chemical fertilizer industry, which consumes about 80 percent of sulfuric acid production, the remainder being used for synthetic fibers. About 57 percent of 1954 output was produced by the contact process and the remainder by the chamber process; most of the new facilities under construction are contact.

Other chemicals.—Japan produces sufficient soda for its own uses, principally in the ceramics, chemicals, and foodstuffs industries, and has a small surplus for export. Soda production is dependent upon salt, however, and Japan's domestic production of the latter commodity is far below its needs. Soda production in 1954 totaled 306,000 metric tons of soda ash and 445,000 metric tons of caustic soda, better than 50 percent of the prewar production peak. About 55 percent of Japan's soda is produced by the electrolytic process and the remainder by the Solvay process. Approximately 58 percent of electrolytic output is presently produced by the more efficient mercury process and the remaining diaphragm plants are being converted.

With respect to synthetic organic chemicals, acetic acid and acetone of the acetylene derivatives and methanol and formalin of the methanol derivatives are the principal ones produced in Japan.

Synthetic dyestuffs.—The output of synthetic dyestuffs, comprising more than 800 items, has increased rapidly since the end of the war, and in 1954 totaled 17,486 metric tons, a decline from the 1953 total of 19,572 metric tons. Prior to the war, a substantial portion of synthetic dyes were exported, but exports have not recovered to the same extent as production. The failure of the export trade in dyestuffs to revive has been due in part to the increasing demands of the Japanese textile industry, and in part to the lower quality of the postwar product.

Plastics and resins.—Production of plastics is proceeding apace, and the number and variety of items made from plastics is growing rapidly. Certain plastics, such as Bakelite and various urea resins, have long been produced in Japan, but the full commercial production of other plastic materials did not begin until after the war; in fact, the most rapid development has occurred since the beginning of 1952. Vinyl resins particularly, such as polyvinyl chloride and polyvinyl acetate, silicon resin, fluorine resin, polyethylene, and polyester, are now being produced in commercial quantities by a number of large and small firms.

The synthetic resin industry is suffering from the effects of high prices of raw materials and outmoded techniques. In an attempt to overcome the technological handicap, a significant number of technical assistance contracts have been concluded with foreign firms, particularly American. There is little doubt but that there is room for further technological improvement, as well as for modernization of production equipment.

Pharmaceuticals

Japan produces a wide range of pharmaceutical products, of particular importance being sulfa drugs, antibiotics, and vitamin preparations. Because of the domestic demand for these items and the resulting high profit margins immediately following the war, a number of Japanese pharmaceutical manufacturers have entered into technical assistance or licensing agreements with foreign firms. Competition in the pharmaceutical field is intensifying and there are indications that the industry is beginning to feel the effects of overproduction. Undoubtedly, therefore, concentration of the industry through a reduction in the number of competing firms—a process which already has become noticeable—will continue.

Exports of pharmaceuticals are still well below prewar levels, but there were slight increases in 1952 and 1953; in 1954 exports of vitamins, vitamin preparations, penicillin, streptomycin, and other antibiotics advanced sharply over the average for the years 1952–53. The major markets for Japan's pharmaceutical products—principally penicillin, household remedies, vitamins, and sulfa preparations—are Taiwan, South Korea, Okinawa, Hong Kong, and India. Japan imports substantial quantities of pharmaceuticals, primarily antibiotics, from the United States and Western Germany, and lesser amounts from other European countries.

Machinery

Japan's machinery industry suffered heavily during the war, but recovery and conversion to peacetime production has been rapid, as evidenced by the production index for the industry which stood at 257.4 in 1954 (1934–36=100).

Japan is the only country in Asia which produces machinery for export, and it is relying heavily upon such exports to assist in rectifying the existing imbalance in its international merchandise trade accounts. Japan is successfully attempting to expand machinery exports in southeast Asia, and the Near and Middle East and Latin America also are becoming important markets as a result of the present industrialization programs of those areas.

Machine tools.—In Japan, the machine tool industry is relatively small, accounting in 1954 for not more than about 5 percent of total machinery production. Because of the drive toward industrial rationalization, the demand for machine tools has increased at a more rapid rate than the industry itself has been able to expand, with the result that Japan is heavily dependent upon imports—about one-fourth of all of the machine tools used in Japan are imported. Imports of machine tools in 1953 were valued at about $6,261,000. In an attempt to stimulate the industry and reduce Japan's deficiency in machine tools, the Japanese Government granted subsidies amounting to about $700,000 in 1952 for the import of machine tools and about $300,000 in 1953 for experimental manufacturing.

Textile machinery.—Textile machinery is one of the major machinery items produced in Japan. Prior to World War II, Japan ranked second only to Great Britain in output of spinning and weaving machines, but plant destruction and a radical decline in export markets during and immediately after the war dealt a serious blow to the industry. Domestic demand revived rapidly after the close of the war, and production in 1951 reached 432,196 units valued at slightly more than $147 million. With completion of the rehabilitation of the domestic textile industry, however, the production of textile machinery declined sharply and, despite an expanding export market in southeast Asia, 1953 output fell to 128,110 units valued at only slightly more than $75 million. The quality of Japanese textile machinery is high and the industry, in general, is optimistic over its future, particularly with respect to exports of machinery for synthetic textiles. In recent postwar years, a number of technical assistance and licensing agreements have been concluded between Japanese and American textile machinery firms.

Japan's sewing machine industry was well established before the war, with an annual output slightly higher than 150,000 machines, and in the postwar period the industry has made vast advances in both volume and quality of machines. In 1954, for example, a total of approximately 1,438,000 machines were produced, including 66,000 industrial machines. Sewing machines have become one of the leading machinery exports; in 1954, approximately 1,215,058 machines valued at $28.2 million were exported. The United States has become the principal market for Japanese sewing machines, receiving approximately 20 percent of exports in terms of value (1954); significant quantities also are exported to the sterling area and various countries in southeast Asia and Latin America.

Exports of Japanese sewing machines have been somewhat limited by the lack of a well-developed marketing system, and the Japanese have been reluctant to conclude agreements with foreign firms in this field. One American sewing machine manufacturer has been attempting for some time to negotiate an agreement with one of the large Japanese manufacturers, but has not yet been successful in overcoming the objections of the Japanese Government and competing sewing machine producers.

Rolling stock.—The manufacture of rolling stock is one of Japan's leading heavy industries. Prior to World War II, the industry had substantial export markets in China, Manchuria (Manchukuo), Formosa, and Korea, all areas under Japanese control, and exported also to Thailand and Malaya. The prosperity of the industry was more dependent, however, upon the demand from the Government-controlled Japan National Railway. The loss of Japan's controlled Asian markets, as a result of the war, has intensified this dependence.

The postwar recovery of the rolling-stock industry was rapid; facilities suffered relatively moderate war damage, and the Government gave priority and special incentives to rolling-stock production for the reconstruction of Japan's war-shattered transportation system. Consequently, freight-car production in 1948 was almost at the wartime peak, passenger- and electric-car production was very high, and production of locomotives, although considerably below the wartime level, was substantial. Since 1948, production has fallen, as reconstruction approaches completion, and export demand has failed to rise to prewar levels. However, the industry has undergone a process of rationalization and modernization, and at the present time it is relatively stable.

Japan's exports of rolling stock since the war have been limited by high prices, resulting from the high cost of raw materials, which constitute a major part of the production expense of rolling stock. However, despite the fact that Japan has been underbid on several occasions by Western European manufacturers of rolling stock, it is becoming increasingly successful in developing southeast Asia as a market, partly because of an advantageous position with respect to shipping costs and partly because of familiarity with the area. Various Latin American countries also are indicating an interest in purchasing Japanese heavy transportation equipment.

Japanese rolling stock is considered to be of good quality and modern design. However, the industry is not experienced in the production and design of diesel locomotives, and in 1951 a Japanese manufacturer concluded a technical assistance agreement with a large American firm to obtain up-to-date know-how.

Textiles

Japan long has been one of the world's leading textile producers, and prior to World War II it was first in the production and export of cotton textiles and silk; its synthetic fiber industry also was of major importance. The war dealt a severe blow to the industry, and the restrictions placed upon its development during the occupation prevented a rapid recovery. After the restrictions

27

were lifted, however, rehabilitation in all fields of textile production was rapid.

Textiles have been Japan's leading export, both before the war and at the present time. Their relative importance has decreased, however, as the proportion of total exports represented by textiles has fallen from 52 percent during the 1934–36 period to 36 percent in 1953 and 40 percent in 1954.

Japan's imports of raw cotton and raw wool are greater than the overall value of the nation's textile exports. Despite the fact that cotton is the largest item of textile exports, and the most inportant single commodity in Japan's export trade, virtually all of the raw cotton for the industry is imported. Nearly all of the raw wool for Japan's woolen industry also is imported. The raw materials for Japan's synthetic fiber and silk industries for the most part are produced domestically.

Cotton.—The cotton textile industry recovered rapidly from the effects of the war, but production today is considerably below the prewar level and below capacity. Despite the fact that only about 30 percent of total cotton textile production is exported, Japan in 1953 was the world's leading cotton textile exporter. At present, owing to the development of the cotton textile industry in many countries which traditionally were markets for Japan, exports are below the prewar level.

There are approximately 122 cotton mills and textile factories in Japan, many of which have been established since the war, but 10 old-line firms account for approximately 75 percent of all yarn production.

Because of the dependence of the Japanese cotton textile industry upon imports of raw cotton, financial assistance was sought from the United States and several loans for the purpose of importing American cotton have been granted by the Export-Import Bank.

Japan's cotton textile industry has been seriously affected by the growth of textile manufacturing in several countries which before the war were important markets and the restrictive actions taken by some countries against Japanese textiles. In an effort to stabilize the industry Japanese manufacturers have voluntarily curtailed production.

In 1955, because of the increase in imports of textiles from Japan, American textile producers complained that they were being injured. The Japanese industry and Japanese Government, fearing restrictive action on the part of the United States against Japanese textiles, imposed additional production cuts and, effective January 1, 1956, exports of fabrics and cotton blouses to the United States will be subject to quota limitations.

As announced by the Japanese Government in late December 1955, the volume of fabric exports in 1956 will be restricted to 150 million square yards. This total includes those quantities for which export contracts were concluded in 1955 but not filled prior to the November 9, 1955, action by the Japanese Government suspending the acceptance of new orders. Within the 150-million-square-yard total, exports of grey goods will be limited to 20 million square yards and certain other items will also be quantitatively controlled. In addition, exports of women's blouses will be limited to 2.5 million dozen. Although quantitative controls were not announced at that time on other types of made-up goods it was understood that the Japanese Government planned to use its export control authority to maintain current information on the movement to the United States of such products as underwear and outerwear, pillowcases and bedsheets, and woolen cardigans.

The Japanese Government also planned to strengthen its quality regulations and price controls on various textile products, particularly those which are most directly competitive with United States manufactured items.

It was also reported at the time the quotas for the United States were announced that the Japanese Government intended, in the near future, to establish quotas for exports of textiles to Canada. Furthermore, although it was not intended that quotas would be established for other areas, the Japanese Government was expected to exercise close control over exports of cotton fabrics and made-up goods, particularly to Latin American and other nearby countries, in order to prevent transshipment to the United States.

Silk.—Japan produces more than 60 percent of the world's raw silk, and before the war silk was the most important textile export from Japan. The development of synthetic fibers and the consequent decline in the oversea demand for natural silk have seriously reduced the relative importance of this commodity in Japan's export trade, and in 1954 exports of raw silk constituted 2 percent of Japan's total exports.

In an attempt to keep the price of natural silk competitive with prices of synthetic products and to maintain the position of the silk industry, the Government has resorted to various types of export subsidies to offset losses incurred as a result of the industry's high costs.

Synthetic and chemical textiles.—In 1936 and 1937, Japan was the world's leading producer of rayon and other synthetic textiles. The development of nylon in the United States at about that time jarred both the Japanese silk and rayon industries but also stimulated research in synthetic fibers. As a result, two polyvinyl alcohol fibers, "vinylon" and a polyamide synthetic "amilan" of the same type as nylon, were developed. Other synthetic fibers also were developed but, with the approach of the war, synthetic fiber manufacturers converted to war production.

Production of all synthetic fibers dropped sharply during and immediately after the war. However, Japan's domestic demand for textiles, as well as a recognition of the suitability of synthetic textiles as export commodities, soon stimulated a rapid advance in production.

The recovery and development of the synthetic and chemical fibers industry have been remarkable. The output of synthetic fibers, such as nylon, vinylon, and saran, totaled approximately 21 million pounds in 1954, compared with 7 million pounds in 1951, placing Japan second only to the United States in the production of such fibers. Exports of these fibers are relatively small, but domestic uses are numerous and include utilization for knitted goods, broad-width textiles, and fishnets and various industrial purposes.

A 3-year plan for the development of synthetic fibers envisages a production of 79 million pounds during 1956, but whether this goal will be attained is questionable. However, two factors favor the development of the industry: (1) An abundant domestic supply of raw materials, and (2) relatively stable prices. Further, as increased output brings about lower unit costs, it seems probable that Japanese exports of synthetic fibers will increase. Two technical assistance agreements for the manufacture of nylon and saran have been concluded with American firms.

Japan's production of rayon and staple fiber has shown a rapid postwar increase. In 1954, Japan ranked first in the world in the production of chemical staple fiber, with an output of 448,065,000 pounds, and third in production of rayon, with an output of 184,852,000 pounds. Exports of chemical fibers have been increasing steadily, and during 1954 accounted for 10 percent by value of total exports. The quality of Japanese rayon has improved as a result of research in spinning and weaving and in dyeing and resinification.

Wool.—Japan also has an important woolen industry, which is dependent almost entirely upon imports of raw wool. Postwar woolen production for the most part has exceeded prewar levels, but exports have been retarded because of high prices of raw wool imports and consequent high export prices. However, various measures have been adopted to promote the export of woolen products, such as a raw wool import quota linked to exports of woolen products.

Fibers.—Hard and bast fiber production in Japan is based chiefly upon flax, ramie, and jute. These raw materials must be imported, however, as Japan has insufficient domestic supplies. Production techniques are improving with the use of new modern machinery imported from the United States and Great Britain.

Other Industries

Japan has a wide variety of secondary and less important, but promising, industries. Traditionally, the nation has been a producer of cheap toys, but recently it has turned to the manufacture of higher quality and ingenious mechanical toys which give every indication of becoming an increasingly important export item. Japanese chinaware has long been famous, and the Government is taking steps to improve and maintain the quality of china exports. The electrical equipment, television, radio, and high-fidelity equipment industries are expanding, and there appear to be no deterrents to the development of a high degree of skill and technical proficiency in these fields.

Japan's aviation industry is beginning to revive, at present, through the utilization of American knowhow and designs, but Japanese designers are at work and indications are that aircraft designed and produced in Japan will be flying soon. Japanese paper, plywood, and other wood products industries are flourishing. In brief, Japan, as an industrial nation, produces virtually every product common to such an economy, and if the basic problems of increasing labor productivity, reducing costs, and maintaining sound business practices can be successfully surmounted, the future of Japanese industry would seem to be assured.

CHAPTER IV

Transportation and Communications

SHIPPING

Maritime losses during World War II reduced the Japanese merchant marine from the 1941 high of almost 6 million tons to a low in 1945 of about 1 million tons, mostly old and small ships. Before the war, earnings from shipping services made a significant contribution to balancing the country's trade account, but since the end of the war, Japan has made substantial outpayments of foreign exchange for ocean freight.

Between 1945 and 1949 the Occupation authorities permitted Japan to construct only steamers of less than 5,000 gross tons for coastwise and nearby trade. In 1949, this restriction was lifted and Japan began a program of rebuilding its merchant marine. Because Japanese companies had lost both their ships and a large part of their liquid assets during the war, capital was borrowed. The growth of the oceangoing merchant fleet has been slow. As shown in table 9, by the middle of 1954 tonnage had been restored to a little more than 3 million tons, of which the oversea fleet comprised about 2.5 million tons. It should be noted that the relatively little change in number of vessels despite the increase in tonnage is the result of continued replacement of small, old ships with large, new ones.

The Japanese Government does not subsidize shipping in the strict sense of the word, i. e., by giving a direct grant of money. Rather, it advances a substantial amount of the first cost of new ships on a loan basis and absorbs part of the high rate of interest charged for commercial

loans.[1] Theoretically, the steamship company is obligated to repay such advances with interest.

Japan imports mainly foodstuffs and raw materials and exports manufactured articles. Tonnagewise, its import movement is about six times the volume of its export cargo—in 1954, imports were 33,528,000 metric tons and exports 5,712,000 tons. Consequently, a great majority of imports are tramp or tanker cargo rather than liner cargo.

Since the end of the war, a substantially greater proportion of Japan's foreign trade has been carried in foreign bottoms. For instance, in 1953, about 41 percent of Japan's foreign trade was handled by the Japanese merchant fleet, compared with 52 percent of imports and 61 percent of exports carried in Japanese vessels before the war.

Table 10.—Ratio of Foreign Trade Carried by Japanese Vessels,[1] Average 1930–34 and 1952–54

[In percentages]

Period	Imports	Exports
1930–34 (average)	51.8	61.4
1952	45.5	31.6
1953	45.8	35.8
1954	49.0	43.9

[1] In terms of metric tons; includes dry and tanker cargo.

Virtually all of the lines serving Japan—including both foreign and Japanese companies—are members of 15 steamship "conferences" or mutual associations which maintain uniform rates and usually regulate the tonnage placed in the trade. The growth in the number and net registered tonnage of commercial vessels entering Japanese ports during the period 1952–54 was as follows:

	Number	Net tonnage
1952	5,753	17,833,000
1953	7,453	22,347,000
1954	7,516	22,821,000

In 1954, Japanese-flag vessels reportedly accounted for about 38 percent, United States-flag vessels 17 percent, and United Kingdom vessels

Table 9.—Postwar Growth of Japan's Merchant Shipping,[1] 1950–54

Year[2]	Number	Gross tons
1950	949	1,754,000
1951	1,019	2,319,000
1952	1,094	2,851,000
1953	1,086	3,173,000
1954	1,066	3,288,000

[1] Steel vessels of 100 gross tons and over.
[2] As of December 31.

[1] It is not unusual for the rates for the so-called blue ribbon companies to be between 8 and 12 percent, with others running considerably higher.

15 percent of the tonnage of ships which entered Japanese ports.

The expansion of Japan's cargo liner fleet required participation in trade routes dominated by the shipping conferences. In some instances, participation was granted on a limited basis; in others, it was opposed and the Japanese vessels operated as outsiders. The worldwide shipping slump of 1952–53 resulted in depressed rates and some criticism of Japanese practices.[2] The improvement noticeable in the last half of 1954 has opened the way to Japanese admission to most of the conferences and to improved rate structures.

RAILWAYS

The first railway in Japan was constructed by the Government in 1872, between Tokyo and Yokohama. Construction continued both privately and by the Government until 1906 when the major private railways were nationalized. In 1949, the Japanese National Railways (JNR) was created as a public corporation to administer the state railway system, under the Ministry of Transportation. The JNR, in addition to its railway activities, operates ferries, buses, coal mines, powerhouses, transmission lines, and telecommunications systems, all ancillary to its primary responsibility. Private lines continue to operate, but the JNR controls the trunklines.

Since the greater part of Japan's raw materials derive from Hokkaido and Kyushu, and the manufacturing and consuming centers are located in the densely populated Tokyo-Yokohama and Osaka-Kobe regions, there are an inward flow of raw materials by rail to the center of Honshu and an outward flow of manufactured goods. Coastal shipping once carried much of the coal, gravel, and timber, but even these commodities now are largely hauled by rail.

As noted in chapter II, the four main Japanese islands are generally mountainous and the railways tend to follow the seacoast where possible. In the interior the rights-of-way are winding and require grades as steep as 6 percent. Along the coast the mountain spurs project into the sea and must be tunneled through. The small streams of Japan are subject to spring freshets which swell them to rivers of one-half mile width and which must be bridged.

Consequently, of the nearly 12,000 miles of main track, 449 miles are carried on bridges, 521 miles are in tunnels, 9,000 miles are on a gradient, and only a small proportion of the system is double tracked.

Since 1936 until the present, the working trackage has been increased 14 percent, and the ton-

kilometers of freight moved has increased 152 percent. The Japanese gage is 42 inches; because of this narrow gage and the grade and curve limitations, most Japanese freight trains have a maximum individual weight limit of 1,200 tons. Increased demands, on existing trackage, can be met only by the use of additional trains, but this would constitute a severe strain on a railroad system which is presently operating at one of the highest train-densities in the world. On the other hand, further double tracking, in view of the bridge and tunnel requirements, would be both difficult and costly.

Honshu and Kyushu are connected by twin tunnels between Shimonoseki and Moji. The tunnels were built in sequence and were placed in service in 1942 and 1944, respectively. An average of 55 trains per day pass through the tunnels in either direction. Honshu is connected with Hokkaido by car ferry service across the Tsugaru Straits, between the terminal points of Hakodate and Aomori; and with Shikoku by car ferries and smaller-type passenger ferries.

As of March 1954, JNR possessed 5,035 steam locomotives, 448 electric locomotives, and 3 experimental diesel electric locomotives. In addition, it had 2,762 electrically driven passenger cars for commuter service and 458 diesel-driven passenger cars for light traffic lines. Passenger coaches numbered 11,596, including 83 diners, 224 sleepers, and 949 baggage and mail cars. Passenger and freight cars are being scrapped and replaced at the rate of almost 2 percent per year. Freight cars number 106,732, consisting of 53,864 gondolas, 47,428 boxcars, 2,793 refrigerator cars, 338 tank cars, and 2,259 miscellaneous. At any given time about 95 percent of these cars are available for service. The Japanese boxcar is a small, two-axle car of 15 tons capacity, generally similar to the European "goods-wagon." The gondolas are of 25 to 35 tons capacity.

For the year ending March 1954, JNR transported 159 million tons of freight at an average haul of 151 miles per ton. Coal accounted for 41 million tons and lumber for 15 million tons; sand and gravel, cement, fertilizer, and limestone were in excess of 5 million tons per year. The JNR is one of its own best customers and uses large quantities of coal and construction materials.

Because of the small size of Japanese boxcars, more shipments can be made as carloads than would be the case if cars were larger. Freight rates are based upon a rate per kilometer which decreases with length of haul. For a commodity in class 5, for example, the rate per ton-mile is the equivalent of 1.87 cents for a 100-mile haul, 1.09 cents for 500 miles, and 0.95 cent for 1,000 miles. Carload freight rates also are based upon classification of the commodity. For a given distance, class 1 rates are about 2½ times class 12 rates. There is no classification for less-than-

---

[2] For example, the Japanese shipping companies were accused of competing unfairly by granting secret rebates to shippers and cutting established conference rates.

carload shipments, but these are subject to certain special charges.

Passenger cars generally follow the United States design rather than the European. There are first-, second-, and third-class coaches. Third-class cars, which are used by about 90 percent of the traffic, are of two types: (1) Those similar to day coaches; and (2) those equipped with back-to-back seats facing each other—these being older cars used on short runs. The second-class cars have adjustable, individual day-coach seats which are available at an extra charge. The first-class cars, which are very limited in number, are similar to Pullman club cars. Sleeping accommodations generally are patterned after the United States Pullman, having both open sections and compartments.

Dining cars are similar to United States equipment and serve fixed-price meals at a comparatively low cost. To encourage tourism, major railway stations have a special ticket office and waiting room for "westerners," the principal trains have English-speaking attendants, and nearly all railway station and train signs are in the English language as well as in Japanese.

Passenger fares are based on a tapering rate per kilometer, adjusted for class, type of train, and accommodations. The second-class fare is double the third-class rate, and the first-class fare is double that for second. An extra charge is made for travel in coaches with reclining seats, as well as for travel on "express" and "limited express" trains. An overall surcharge of 20 percent has been applied since 1953 to all transportation charges, except the basic third-class fare, to meet the increasing costs of materials and wage demands of railway employees. Consideration is being given to eliminating the first-class coach service, which is little used.

As is the case with freight, the volume of passenger traffic has increased very significantly—estimates place the increase at 219 percent since 1936. The postwar trend toward concentration of the working population in the industrial cities and the housing shortages which have forced many workers to reside at greater distances from such cities have resulted in a serious commuter problem, since few Japanese own automobiles. Commuter traffic has increased by 271 percent since 1936. The traffic load occurs in two short periods of the day and, since expansion of station trackage is even more difficult than expansion of line trackage, the problem of accommodation is very acute.

Japanese families also travel extensively for purposes of recreation or to make religious pilgrimages. To accommodate such travel, there are 12 privately owned electric interurban railways which supplement the service of the JNR. These lines primarily serve populous regions—Tokyo, Osaka, Kobe, Nagoya, and Fukuoka—and, in addition to absorbing part of the commuter load,

are intended to handle much of the traffic to pilgrimage points such as Nikko, Kyoto, Nara, and Ise. They carry about 2.4 billion passengers annually.

HIGHWAYS

The geographical factors which make railway building expensive in Japan have even greater significance in connection with highway construction. Horse-drawn vehicles were never utilized in any great degree, and early roads were required only to accommodate pack animals and foot passengers. Consequently, roads were built with the minimum amount of excavation and they encircled, rather than crossed, elevations; and their width, through villages, scarcely permitted two vehicles to pass. These two factors hinder widening or straightening existing highways. Japan's present road system totals nearly 86,000 miles, of which about 15,000 miles are classed as improved roads and the remainder as unimproved.

The major highway systems in general follow the pattern of railway systems in running along the coasts to reduce grades and curves, and they connect the major cities, which for the most part are on or near the coast. However, other than a few sections of highway built chiefly after the war for the use of the United States Occupation Forces, none of the highways could be considered first-class roads.

Since the termination of the war, there has been an eightfold increase in the number of vehicles registered in Japan. There is no heavy "weekend" recreational use of the highways, since both automobiles and gasoline are luxury items in Japan, but the overloading of the railway system has led to extensive use of motor vehicles as supplementary transportation for both passengers and freight, particularly freight. Trucks carry a large volume of freight on short hauls in and near the larger cities but are not generally used elsewhere.

As of June 1954, the slightly more than one-half million trucks (including more than 300,000 small three-wheel and nearly 64,000 slightly larger four-wheel trucks) conveyed 456,000 tons of various types of commodities or more than twice the prewar volume. Truck freight tonnage is more than double that of rail; however, according to unofficial reports, ton-miles of freight carried by the railways far exceed truck ton-miles. Buses are employed extensively for service to outlying villages not adequately served by train. They are utilized also for group transportation, such as visits of school children to the capital, pilgrimages to shrines, and outings of associations or guilds.

There is little or no "over-the-road," common-carrier trucking in Japan but manufacturing establishments employ their own trucks for handling raw materials or finished articles within a reasonable radius of the plant. Weight limits are not rigorously enforced and overloaded trucks and buses hasten the progressive deterioration of surfaced highways.

Paved roads in Japan customarily are surfaced with cement. Roadbuilding is done by means of many small subcontracts with resultant lack of adequate supervision of materials and workmanship. Consequently, hard-surfaced roads quickly deteriorate and, in many places, insufficient foundation causes serious cracking of the entire roadway. Secondary roads are of gravel construction not suitable for heavy traffic. Since roadbuilding is primarily a function of the prefectures, it is not uncommon to find a recently completed section of highway in one prefecture while the approaches on either side, and in other prefectures, are virtually impassable.

Various roadbuilding projects are in the discussion stage. One involves construction of a toll highway between Tokyo and Kobe; it is being held in abeyance, however, because of divergent opinions as to the route to be followed. A second project under discussion calls for a toll highway across central Kyushu, to open up less accessible parts of that island. Financing these projects would be difficult for present-day Japan, and some circles favor the Government's seeking a foreign loan to improve the country's highway system, and particularly for the construction of a superhighway connecting Tokyo and Osaka and Kobe. The need for improvement and expansion of Japan's highway system is widely recognized. The highway system suffered neglect during the war period, and the deterioration continued for some years during the postwar era. The country lacks particularly cross-country (east-to-west) roads and there is a great shortage of farm-to-market roads as well as access roads to existing rail terminals. However, in view of the country's present financial position, it is unlikely that a major roadbuilding program will be initiated in the near future, since there is a more urgent need to improve and expand industrial plant, increase power facilities, and reclaim land for greater food production.

AIR TRANSPORTATION [3]

Japan is the natural Asian abutment of the Pacific air bridge. It is an important terminal point for airlines serving southeast Asia—either direct or en route from Europe—including the Philippines, Taiwan, Okinawa, and South Korea.

Japan is at present served by the following foreign airlines, in addition to the international services of its own national line, Japan Air Lines [4] (the point of origin and routes follow the names of the carriers):

Air France—Paris, Rome, Karachi, Saigon, Tokyo.

Air India International—Bombay, Calcutta, Bangkok, Hong Kong, Tokyo.

British Overseas Airways Corporation—London, Rome, Karachi, Hong Kong, Tokyo.

Civil Air Transport Co., Ltd.—Taipeh, Okinawa, Iwakuni, Tokyo, Seoul.

Canadian Pacific Airlines—Vancouver, Tokyo, Hong Kong.

KLM—Royal Dutch Airlines—Amsterdam, Rome, Karachi, Bangkok, Tokyo.

Northwest Airlines—(1) Seattle, Anchorage, Tokyo, Okinawa, Manila, (2) Tokyo, Seoul (Pusan), and (3) Tokyo, Okinawa, Taipeh.

Pan American World Airways—San Francisco, Los Angeles, Honolulu, Wake Island, Toyko, Hong Kong, Bangkok, Karachi.

Qantas Empire Airways—Sydney, Darwin, Manila, Iwakuni, Tokyo.

Scandinavian Airlines System—Stockholm, Copenhagen, Rome, Karachi, Bangkok, Toyko.

Thai Airways Co., Ltd.—Bangkok, Hong Kong, Taipeh, Tokyo.

A number of nonscheduled flights operate to Japan, principally to transport ships' crews from the United States or special recreation parties from Guam or other United States-held islands. Special, nonscheduled flights also are made by commercial airlines to take care of heavy movements of military mail or excess cargo above the capacity of the Military Air Transport Service.

In view of the limited highway system and relatively slow railway service, air travel should be a preferred form of transport between important cities of Japan. However, the cost of air travel is a deterrent to Japanese citizens not traveling on business, and the foreign tourist normally has sufficient time available and prefers to see the country from a train.

The Japan Air Lines maintains service between Sapporo in Hokkaido and Fukuoka in Kyushu, via intermediate points, the heaviest travel being between Tokyo and Osaka. Service to Nagoya, Misawa, and other points of lesser importance has been reduced since the traffic failed to justify four-engined equipment. This traffic has been taken over by two privately owned airlines—the Japan Helicopter Company and the Far East Airlines.

Many airfields are in use in Japan, most of them being of wartime origin. The great majority are now being used by the United States Far East Air Force.[5] Tokyo International Airport, which is located at Haneda, about 12 miles from the

[3] See report in the World Trade Information Service, Part 4, No. 55–15, *Japanese Civil Aviation*, for further information on this subject.

[4] Japan Air Lines is a quasi-Government corporation in which the Government owns 60 percent of the stock. It was constituted in its present form in 1953. Service to the United States was instituted in February 1954.
[5] Under the terms of the Security Treaty between Japan and the United States.

34

business center of Tokyo, is the principal port of entry for international flights. Iwakuni, located between Hiroshima and Fukuoka in Kyushu, is the only other official port of entry. This terminal is used by 2 international lines (Qantars Empire Airways and Civil Air Transport) and by 1 domestic line (Far East Airlines).

The Tokyo airport is located on made ground in Tokyo Bay and offers a reasonably unobstructed approach from any direction. A modern terminal building, three stories high with floor space aggregating 252,000 square feet, was put into service in May 1955.

COMMUNICATIONS FACILITIES

Since their inception, Japan's telephone, telegraph, and postal systems have been wholly under public ownership, and all postal and telecommunications are under the general supervision of the Ministry of Postal Services. The communications system was rehabiliated rapidly after World War II. In August 1952, the Nippon Telegraph and Telephone Public Corporation was established; and in April 1953, a separate corporation, the Kokusai Denshin Denwa Company (International Telegraph and Telephone Corporation), was set up to administer the international services. The capital of these monopolies was fully paid up by the Government at the time of formation.

Telephone and Telegraph

Telephone service has improved considerably during the past few years following the rehabilitation of war-damaged facilities and some expansion in the number of line stations and total length of telephone circuits. The number of telephones in use in Japan rose from 1,192,000 in 1947 to 2,727,000 in September 1954. As of January 1953 it was estimated that there were 2.6 telephones per 100 persons in Japan; this was below the world average of 3.4 but considerably higher than the average in any other Asian country. There are automatic exchanges in most of the principal cities in Japan; and at the beginning of 1953, 40 percent of all telephones in service were the dial type. Since January 1954, "no hang-up" service (relatively rapid service) has been in operation between Tokyo and Nagoya and Tokyo and Osaka. Long-distance service is available to all parts of Japan, but the placing of calls may be delayed from 30 to 90 minutes. By the end of 1953 radiotelephone service was available between Japan and most countries.

An official charge is made for initial provision of the service equivalent to approximately $12 for installation, $83 for the instrument, and $166 for

the posting of a bond. The purchase price of the instrument may be reclaimed within 5 years, and the bond is redeemable or negotiable after a period of 7 to 10 years.

Despite the rapid expansion in telephone facilities and service since the termination of the war, it has not been possible in recent years to supply more than about 30 percent of the demand, and during the past few years foreign businessmen have experienced difficulty in obtaining a sufficient number of telephones for the efficient conduct of their business activities.

The Nippon Telephone and Telegraph Corporation has formulated a 5-year plan for the improvement and expansion of the telephone system which involves the construction of 10 telephone exchanges provided with cross-bar dial switching equipment in Tokyo and other major cities. The Government is seeking a World Bank or other foreign loans amounting to $20 million to be used for the importation of equipment. Production of instruments, which has increased significantly following the Government assistance extended to producers in 1951, is expected to continue to expand, and there is no indication that the Government plans to import instruments.

Telegraph facilities and service are nearly "normal" as compared with the prewar level. In 1953, the approximately 2,300 circuits in use for domestic service handled more than 400 million messages, or slightly more than 4 messages per person a year. Average time from acceptance to delivery in domestic service had declined from nearly 2½ hours in 1949 to less than 1 hour by mid-1954, slightly better than the prewar average. International telegraph service has been restored and expanded; 30 radiotelegraph circuits now connect Japan directly or indirectly with virtually all parts of the world. The number of international messages sent rose from a monthly average of 95,000 in 1949 to 295,000 in 1953 and the number of words transmitted, from 1.8 million to about 7.3 million

Postal Service

As of April 1, 1954, Japan had approximately 15,600 post offices, with a total of 255,224 employees, under the jurisdiction of the Ministry of Postal Services, and upwards of 2 billion pieces of mail and 48 million packages were handled. The Japanese postal system provides ordinary surface and airmail service, as well as special facilities, such as registered- and special-delivery mail service. The postal offices also operate extensive life insurance and savings accounts systems, receive various types of taxes, and pay certain kinds of pensions and annuities on behalf of the Treasury.

Mail moves rapidly throughout the country and service is very good. Ordinary mail is delivered and collected 5 or 6 times daily in Tokyo, Osaka, and Kyoto, 4 or 5 times daily in other large cities, 3 or 4 times in the smaller cities, and twice a day in towns and villages. International postal service between Japan and other countries is operating normally and in accordance with the Universal Postal Union Convention and Agreements and other international bilateral postal agreements. Airmail and air parcel-post, as well as surface-mail, service is available between Japan and the United States and other principal nations of the world. Money-order service is available to Japan from the United States, and to the United States from Japan subject to license by the Bank of Japan as agent for the Ministry of Finance.

Radio

The Broadcasting Corporation of Japan (NHK), a quasi-governmental corporation, conducts a noncommercial broadcasting service, with two major radio networks having 164 stations. It is authorized by the Government to charge fees for the use of receiving sets, the quarterly fee being 200 yen per household. The number of licensed receiving sets in 1954 was reported as 12,248,648. NHK also operates an oversea broadcasting service. Under the radio regulatory legislation of 1950, broadcasting ceased to be a monopoly and commercial broadcasting began, and, by 1954, 56 commercial radio stations were broadcasting in Japan. The largest and most influential of the commercial stations is Radio Tokyo, which began broadcasting in early 1952. It is owned and operated jointly by the three leading newspaper companies in Japan.[6]

Television

Television broadcasting, which was inaugurated in Japan early in 1953, is still in its infancy, and neither the Government-subsidized station (NHK) nor the commercial station (NTV) has adequate facilities. The growth of television has been slow. At the end of 1954 there were about 40,000 receivers in operation throughout the country, of which 40 percent were in Tokyo; virtually all of the others were in Osaka and Nagoya. Both networks broadcast only about 5 hours a day. However, neither the small number of sets in operation nor the length of the broadcast day is an adequate measure of the popularity of television. In Tokyo, Osaka, and Nagoya, the only cities which had broadcasting stations in early 1955, it was not uncommon to see large crowds of people congregated before shop windows which displayed television sets.

Operation of Japan's first long-distance microwave circuits connecting Tokyo and Osaka via Nagoya was inaugurated on April 16, 1954. The Japan Telegraph and Telephone Corporation currently uses 2 routes, 1 for television and the other for telephone.

---

[6] The Mainichi, Asahi, and Yomiuri. These three newspapers, all of which have morning and afternoon editions, had an estimated circulation in 1954 of nearly 9.5 million.

CHAPTER V

Financial Organization and Policy

HISTORICAL BACKGROUND

Banking, in the modern terminology, has been developed in Japan only since the Meiji Restoration (reign of Emperor Meiji, 1868–1912)—much later than in Western countries—but the system has moved forward relatively fast. In 1882, the Bank of Japan was created to centralize the activities of the various monetary exchange companies, which had been set up by the Government in 1869 to advance necessary funds to Government trading corporations, commercial establishments, and individuals. As a result of strong backing, protection, and prodding by the Government and the central bank, a private banking system, patterned somewhat after the Western concept, was developed. In this connection, it is important to note that private capital accumulation was not the major force; in the past, as today, Japan was severely handicapped by a lack of private capital.

The rapid industrialization of the Japanese economy under Government direction and supervision likewise advanced the banking system. To offset the power rapidly being acquired by the private banks, certain "special" financial institutions were formed. In 1879, the Yokohama Specie Bank was organized to resolve some of the difficulties encountered by foreign trade in financing and foreign exchange transactions. Industrial modernization brought a need for low-interest, long-term credit, and other special banks were formed by the Government to meet this need.

In 1896, the Hypothec Bank, a debenture-issuing institution, was created to supply long-term loans with real property as collateral, primarily for agricultural development. In 1899, the Hokkaido Colonial Bank was established, which collected deposits and issued debentures to supply funds necessary for the development of the northern island of Hokkaido. In 1902, the Industrial Bank of Japan, also a debenture-issuing bank, was formed to extend long-term (in Japan, 5 years is considered long-term) industrial loans, with movable assets as collateral. By the turn of the century, the industrialization of Japan had shown considerable progress, largely owing to assistance from a relatively well organized financial system, under which funds were made available to commerce and industry through the cooperative efforts of the private and special banks.

The use of checks and bills developed slowly in Japan principally because of low incomes and the slow accumulation of capital. As late as 1936, deposit currency and cash currency in Japan were about equal, as compared with a ratio of nearly 5 to 1 in the United States and about 3 to 1 in Great Britain. Investments in stocks or corporate debentures by the public were negligible, and there was no stock market in the true Western sense, the existing stock market being utilized primarily by speculators rather than by real investors.

Most of the corporate debentures that were issued were handled by banks. The banks were reluctant to issue or subscribe to stocks, but on a limited scale they extended loans on stocks as collateral, and today they hold a majority of corporate stocks and bonds. Traditionally, the Bank of Japan (the central bank) has made direct loans to private banks, because the banks lacked sufficient capital to meet the needs of a rapidly developing economy; and most of the Bank's loans were channeled direct to financial institutions, with Government bonds, stocks, corporate debentures, and other securities as collateral.

Because the Government played such an important role in the development and promotion of industry, a close relation existed between banking and public finance. As noted, the special banks were organized and aided by the Government to facilitate economic development and expansion. The Ministry of Finance played an active role in the monetary field. Through its Deposit Bureau it obtained funds largely through the accumulation of postal savings. These funds were invested primarily in National and local government bonds; but they were used also to purchase debentures of the special banks and corporations sanctioned and aided by the Government, and the Government made loans to these institutions.

In the early 1930's significant changes began to take place in the financial system. To provide the materials needed by an economy mobilizing for war, the Government's fiscal policy was directed to the issuance of Government bonds, most of which were absorbed by the banks; and the banks were forced to go along with the Government's policy of deficit financing. In 1936, a new policy was instituted permitting one bank in each prefecture, and soon thereafter the needs of a wartime economy made bank mergers virtually compulsory. In 1941, the Bank of Japan was basically reorganized to fit the wartime situation and the Wartime Finance Bank was formed by the Government to supply funds for essential war industries. In 1944, specific commercial banks were designated to assist in the financing of specified war industries. This, in effect, gave the Government complete control over the banking business and relegated the banks to a position of serving the needs of wartime industry.

Following the cessation of hostilities in 1945, the financial system of Japan underwent some reorganization. Almost all the special banks, which had received preferential treatment in the past, were abolished. The Yokohama Specie Bank was reorganized and in 1947 began functioning as an ordinary city bank (the Bank of Tokyo), using its domestic assets to capitalize the new bank. In 1948, the Hypothec Bank, the Industrial Bank, and the Hokkaido Colonial Bank were reorganized into ordinary banks. The Reconversion Finance Bank was organized in 1947 to assist in the rehabilitation of the war-ravaged economy, but it was dissolved in 1951 and succeeded by the Japan Development Bank.

The dissolution of the Zaibatsu combines at the order of the Occupation authorities brought with it some reorganization of the Zaibatsu-controlled banks. The intricate interlockings of these banks and their affiliated companies were somewhat weakened, and the pressing need for funds coupled with the postwar inflation made it necessary at times for several banks to join in extending a loan to one large corporation—a practice which further weakened the relations between individual banks and companies. In recent years, however, there has been a noticeable trend toward revival of the close relationship between individual banks and specific large corporations.

MONETARY POLICY

The Bank of Japan, as the central bank, is the only one permitted by the Government to issue banknotes. It regulates the currency and controls credit in line with the established policies of the Government.

Non-interest-bearing current deposits are received from financial institutions, but there is no reserve requirement system. The perennial dearth of accumulated capital and the great need for additional capital resulting from wartime destruction have brought about heavy borrowings by commercial banks from the Bank of Japan, causing what is known as the "overloan" situation. Because of these large borrowings, deposit balances with the Bank are very small. Most of the bond holdings of the Bank of Japan are Government

bonds, and the small amount of buying and selling of Government bonds is carried out directly and individually with the financial institutions. There are at present no open market operations.

The Bank acts as a depository, without interest, of Government funds. At the discretion of the Minister of Finance, certain deposits are "designated" to be made with financial institutions, which deposits are interest-bearing and provide loanable funds. Deficit financing of the Government can be carried out by issuance of bonds. These bonds are relatively short term (5 years at 5.475 percent per annum), and the Bank is the only buyer because of their unattractive interest rates in a country where the cost of money usually begins at 8 percent or higher The buying and selling of Government bonds already issued are carried out between the Bank of Japan and the Ministry of Finance's Trust Fund Bureau, successor to the Deposit Bureau.

Credit control at present is based on a complicated classification of money rates. Commercial banks are able to profit from borrowing funds from the Bank of Japan at an official rate that is lower than their own lending rates. To offset this factor, the Bank sets a borrowing ceiling for each bank, and loans in excess of this borrowing limit are penalized by assessment of higher interest rates. Such control obviously can operate only as long as the demand for funds is high. A revision of the interest rate structure, aimed possibly at a unified rate system, as well as other refinements in the banking system, is under consideration by the Government.

The balance sheet of the Bank of Japan, as of December 31, 1954, is as follows, in thousands of yen (360 yen equal US$1):

Assets:	*Thousand yen*
Gold	447, 581
Cash	3, 845, 573
Bills discounted	53, 560, 024
Loans	189, 824, 222
Loans in foreign exchange	21, 864, 437
Loans to Government	1, 283, 350
Government bonds	483, 573, 195
Interbank remittance account	36, 211, 413
Agencies' accounts	8, 433, 694
Other accounts	62, 002, 479
Total	861, 045, 968
Liabilities:	
Bank notes issued	622, 061, 025
Financial institutions' deposits	1, 761, 123
Government deposits	55, 804, 206
Other deposits	52, 031, 848
Interbank remittance deposit account	30, 636, 750
Contingency reserves	21, 047, 746
Other accounts	67, 660, 614
Capital	100, 000
Surplus	9, 942, 656
Total	861, 045, 968

Until the latter part of 1953, the Government and the banks followed a relatively easy monetary policy. This was permissible only because of the large amount of special dollar earnings coming into Japan as a result of special procurement and expenditures for and by United States troops in the area. Imports rose steadily and Bank of Japan credit expanded accordingly.

In October 1953, an attempt at financial retrenchment was begun which necessitated action with respect to both public finance and monetary policy.

On the monetary side, action consisted of restrictions on the preferential treatment formerly given to import financing and an increase in the cost of money to borrowers by revising upward the secondary higher interest rates of the Bank of Japan. These measures were instituted primarily in the period October 1953–March 1954. The strongest measures affecting imports occurred in March 1954 when the special foreign exchange loan system of the Bank of Japan, as well as the application of most stamp bills, was abolished. These "tight money" measures brought an immediate decline in loans and bank deposits, and caused a substantial increase in the number of dishonored bills and business failures, particularly among the smaller enterprises.

Despite these consequences, the Bank of Japan did not ease its financial retrenchment policy, but rather increased somewhat the cost of money. Wholesale prices, in general, declined in 1954 owing to deflationary influences. Monetary retrenchment was reflected in note issue of the Bank of Japan. From August 1954 onward, the amount of banknotes in circulation at the end of each month was less than the amount outstanding on the same date of the preceding year. Loans and discounts at the end of 1954 were 55.4 million yen less than at the end of 1953. Outstanding foreign exchange loans of the Bank of Japan decreased substantially in 1954 as a result of the abolishment of the special foreign exchange loan system.

Table 11.—Principal Accounts of the Bank of Japan, by Month, 1953–54

[In billions of yen]

Month	Banknote issue		Loans and discounts		Loans in foreign exchange	
	1953	1954	1953	1954	1953	1954
January	519.8	566.2	233.6	254.4	96.2	84.8
February	521.1	549.6	274.7	386.0	91.3	78.1
March	516.0	534.6	291.2	417.3	96.3	68.5
April	517.7	544.0	272.7	379.3	91.5	59.7
May	501.1	522.6	290.1	359.1	92.2	53.4
June	516.4	534.2	326.2	399.6	93.8	45.0
July	512.8	524.0	326.2	394.8	95.3	35.8
August	527.0	521.7	361.6	406.3	97.2	29.5
September	520.9	515.3	350.0	389.8	96.1	26.1
October	533.6	529.8	349.6	356.7	96.7	24.1
November	547.3	542.1	315.0	298.9	95.7	22.6
December	629.9	622.1	298.8	243.4	92.3	21.9

Source: Bank of Japan.

FOREIGN EXCHANGE BUSINESS

The Minister of Finance has the power to authorize any bank to engage in foreign business in Japan, such as the buying and selling of foreign currency and the issuance of letters of credit. There are two types of foreign exchange banks in Japan: Class A and class B. The former are banks which are authorized to conclude correspondent contracts with foreign banks, and in this category are 12 Japanese banks and 13 foreign banks with branch offices in Japan. In the class B category are 21 Japanese banks which are not authorized to conclude correspondent contracts with foreign banks, but may conduct various activities in connection with foreign exchange business. See chapter VII for a listing of class A and class B banks.

On April 3, 1954, the Diet passed the Foreign Exchange Bank Law (effective April 10, 1954), which authorized the Minister of Finance to license a bank, or banks, to specialize in foreign exchange transactions and foreign trade financing. The law did not specifically limit exclusive international banking operations to the Bank of Tokyo, but there were many who believed this was the intent. On August 2, 1954, the Bank of Tokyo was reorganized as a specialized foreign exchange bank under the terms of the Foreign Exchange Bank Law. The Bank of Tokyo is in no sense as powerful a financial organ as was the prewar Yokohama Specie Bank. It is substantially smaller than a number of the largest Japanese city banks, and its authorized capital at present is the equivalent of only $10 million. However, it probably will receive preferential treatment from the Government in the field of foreign exchange.

DOMESTIC FINANCING

Ordinary Banks

Japan's ordinary banks correspond in general to commercial and savings banks in the United States and Europe. More than one-half of all loan and deposit business is conducted by 10 large banks—Fuji, Mitsubishi, Sanwa, Sumitomo, Tokai, Kyowa, Dai-ichi, Teikoku, Daiwa, and Kobe. The Hypothec Bank of Japan and the Hokkaido Colonial Bank also are now considered to be ordinary banks; they no longer issue debentures, but they still maintain balances of debentures previously issued.

Total deposits of all banks in Japan rose from 145 million yen in 1946 to 2,708 million yen in 1953. Loans increased in approximately the same magnitude, from 146 million yen in 1946 to 2,671 million yen in 1953; the ratio of loans to deposits was 101.1 percent in 1946 and 98.7 percent in 1953. These figures support the observation made earlier in this study that there is an extreme shortage of capital in Japan and that, to satisfy the demand, the Bank of Japan in general has followed an easy money policy by making it possible for commercial banks to borrow quite freely with the result that commercial banks have become precariously overloaned. Financial officials in the Government recognize the seriousness of the situation and are giving consideration to ways and means of correcting it.

The banks are required to set aside as legal reserves 10 percent of their profits before dividends are declared, but there is no reserve arrangement comparable with the reserve requirements under the Federal Reserve System in the United States. Hence, the Bank of Japan lacks this specific tool for the control of credit.

Debenture-Issuing Banks

Debenture-issuing banks supply relatively long term funds for plant and equipment or long-term working funds. Several quasi-governmental banks are in this category. Among them are the Industrial Bank of Japan, formerly a special bank, which elected to remain a debenture-issuing bank in 1948—the year that the Hypothec Bank of Japan and the Hokkaido Colonial Bank became deposit (ordinary) banks—and the Long-Term Credit Bank of Japan, which was established in 1952. The Government may invest in the Long-Term Credit Bank, but investment must be in the form of subscriptions to preferred stocks which do not carry voting rights.

The Central Bank for Commercial and Industrial Cooperatives, established in 1936, is a debenture-issuing bank that receives deposits from small business cooperatives and their members and from Government sources, and issues long-term loans to small enterprises. At the end of Japanese fiscal year 1952 (March 31, 1953), the paid-in capital of this bank amounted to 1,463 million yen and it had bonds outstanding aggregating 17,860 million. Its deposits for the same period totaled 13,646 million yen, with loans almost three and one-half times greater than deposits (35,944 million yen).

The Central Cooperative Bank of Agriculture and Forestry receives deposits from and makes loans to subsidiary agricultural credit cooperatives. About two-thirds of its capital is derived from investments by the Government.

The basic difference between the long-term banks and the ordinary banks is that the former are permitted to accept deposits only from Government sources, local public organizations, and their clients. Consequently, the main source of their funds, exclusive of their own capital, is from debentures. Under present regulations, this type

of bank may issue in debentures up to 20 times the total of its capital and reserves, except during the first 5 years following its establishment when the permissible limit is 30 times the total.

Credit Associations and Cooperatives

A number of nonprofit small business credit associations accept deposits from members and the general public and make loans to members, which are small and medium-sized enterprises in specified small areas. Operating on a somewhat larger scale are the mutual loan and savings banks, a few of which are comparable in size with local banks. Each member of such an organization is required to make periodic payments on an installment basis, and the funds thus accumulated are loaned to other members of the group who, in turn, repay in installments. Generally, these transactions are relatively small. These banks also are authorized to accept deposits and extend loans to nonmembers.

Nonprofit agricultural credit cooperatives have been established in every town and village to assist in financing the farmers. Their primary function is to finance the payments for deliveries of rice to the Government, and they accept deposits from and extend loans to members. Each prefecture also has a federation of agricultural credit cooperatives, and above the federations is the Central Cooperative Bank of Agriculture and Forestry. The three types of agricultural financing organizations are integrally related, and the lower groups make deposits with or borrow from the higher groups when necessary. It is the practice in Japan for farmers to deliver to the Government each year, through the cooperatives, a specified portion of the rice crop, which is then rationed to the public. The Government deposits funds for payment with the Central Cooperative Bank, which passes the money down through the federations to the credit cooperatives, and the farmers withdraw their deposits from the credit cooperatives as needed.

Insurance Companies

All insurance companies in Japan are regulated by the Ministry of Finance. Japanese insurance laws provide for deposit, reserve, and investment requirements. There are 40 Japanese insurance companies, made up of 20 life and 20 nonlife. There are 34 foreign insurance companies licensed to write nonlife business (23 British, 8 American, 1 Dutch, 1 Indian, and 1 Philippine).

Life insurance companies.—Prior to World War II, life insurance companies ranked only behind the commercial banks and the Ministry of Finance's Deposit Bureau (now the Trust Fund Bureau) in importance in the financial field. After World War II life insurers suffered great losses through depreciation of their assets, but have enjoyed relatively prosperous conditions in recent years. About 40 percent of life insurance is sold by the Government Post Office Life Insurance System and 60 percent by the 20 private insurers. About two-thirds of the privately written business is done by the 7 leading life insurance companies. Total assets of life insurance companies as of December 1954 amounted to 128,847 million yen. Of these assets, loans accounted for 64,550 million yen and securities for 39,438 million. Real estate made up a substantial portion of the balance. About 88 percent of securities held by life insurance companies (34,680 million yen) consists of shares of stock.

Nonlife insurance companies.—In the nonlife field, fire and marine insurance are the most important branches. Casualty, other than automobile, is little developed. Foreign nonlife insurers write only about 1 percent of direct business, although they also provide reinsurance cover for large Japanese risks. Total assets of nonlife insurance companies as of December 1954 amounted to 84,087 million yen. Of this total, holdings of securities were 26,196 million yen; deposits with other financial institutions, 20,636 million; loans, 11,276 million; and real estate holdings, 11,074 million.

CAPITAL FACILITIES

Securities Market

As noted earlier in this chapter, the securities market developed slowly, since investments in stocks or corporate debentures by the public were not plentiful. In Japan, the banks traditionally performed the functions which in Western countries are handled by the securities market.

During the war, the issuance of and transactions in securities were discouraged by the Government, so that banks were the source of all funds for business. The securities exchanges in Japan ceased to operate at the termination of the war, and under the guidance of the Occupation authorities, attempts were made to develop a true securities market. As a result of the enactment of the Securities and Exchange Law in 1948, the securities exchanges were reopened in May 1949, but at present they handle only corporate stocks. At first, stocks were purchased and sold only through spot transactions, but since May 1951 margin transactions have been permitted.

The largest securities exchange is the Tokyo Stock Exchange; others are located in Osaka, Nagoya, Kobe, Fukuoka, Kyoto, Hiroshima, and Niigata. In December 1954, the daily turnover of stocks in Tokyo averaged about 5.5 million shares

valued at about 688 million yen ($1.9 million equivalent).

No transactions are conducted in Government bonds or corporate debentures but there is a move toward the establishment of a modified debentures market. Since the demand for debentures is small, Japanese companies encounter considerable difficulty in having a debenture issue underwritten. Some businessmen and bankers believe that one step in the right direction would be to reduce underwriting charges, thus lowering the burden on issuing companies. Another widely held opinion is that the term of debentures should be lengthened; there are those who favor abolishing present restrictions on direct purchases of debentures by commercial banks.

The establishment of a modified debentures market would, according to many foreign and Japanese businessmen, bring numerous favorable results, including (1) less dependence on short-term, high-priced loans; (2) more effective use of the banks' surplus funds; and (3) less dependence by the commercial banks upon borrowings from the Bank of Japan.

The stock exchanges are regulated by the Securities and Exchange Law, which was based in many important respects on the comparable United States law. It is administered by a special Securities Section established in the Ministry of Finance. The more important features of the law are as follows:

1. A corporation must make certain basic information available through a registration system when securities are to be offered for sale to the public.

2. Securities dealers must meet certain financial requirements, including the deposit of guaranty funds, before being permitted to register—this is designed to protect the customer, who has a prior claim against these funds. (There are other provisions for the protection of the purchaser including the requirement that the dealer must make known to a prospective customer whether he is the agent of the broker or the principal, and the dealer may not act in both capacities in any one transaction.)

3. Dealers may not pledge shares without delivery of title or possession or combine shares owned by customers unless specifically authorized in writing and, if such permission is obtained, the dealer is not permitted to use any amount exceeding that which was extended as credit to the customer.

4. Fraudulent methods of conducting securities business, or making false or misleading statements or false quotations, are punishable—another protection afforded the customer against unfair methods to induce sales.

5. All security exchanges must register with the Ministry of Finance and their operating rules and regulations must be approved, the general criteria

being that operating procedures be adequate to assure that trading will be conducted in a generally fair and equitable manner.

As of February 1955, there were 770 registered securities dealers in Japan with capital averaging about 14 million yen ($38,556) each. These dealers not only buy and sell securities but are authorized by the Securities and Exchange Law to underwrite various types of corporate securities, subject to the requirement that issuers and underwriters register the securities offered to the public and issue a prospectus. The principal securities dealers are the Yamaichi Securities Co., Nikko Securities Co., Daiwa Securities Co., and Nomura Securities Co.

Government Financing Agencies

Nonjuridical financial organs.—Several financial institutions under the jurisdiction of the Ministry of Finance which are nonjuridical in character play an important role in the conduct of business in Japan. They are the Trust Fund Bureau, the Industrial Investment Special Account, and the Foreign Exchange Fund Special Account. Of these, the Trust Fund Bureau is the most important. The Bureau receives its funds primarily from postal savings and reserves of post office life insurance and postal annuities, and the funds may be used only to purchase Central and local government bonds and bank debentures and extend loans to Government institutions. The amount of funds at the command of the Trust Fund Bureau is second only to bank funds.

The Industrial Investment Special Account was established in August 1953, superseding the Special Account for U. S. Aid Counterpart Funds. The latter used the proceeds from the sale of United States aid goods—until such aid terminated in 1951—to redeem Government bonds and to supply funds to important industries. The assets remaining from the earlier special account, plus funds obtained through the sale of special tax reduction bonds, are used to supply industrial funds where needed.

Because the Government holds most of the country's foreign currencies, the Foreign Exchange Fund Special Account was set up to deal in the buying and selling of foreign exchange. Minor holdings are found in the Bank of Japan and in foreign exchange banks, but consideration is being given to a plan to make the Central Bank the depository of the Government's foreign exchange. When there is a shortage of Government funds for the purchase of foreign exchange, the Special Account is authorized to make temporary borrowings or issue short-term bills, which are absorbed by the Bank of Japan.

Juridical financial institutions.—Japan also has a number of juridical Government financial institutions, all of which are forbidden to accept deposits or issue debentures, but may borrow from the Government. These institutions are described in following paragraphs.

Upon the termination of United States aid in 1951, the Japan Development Bank was established in May of that year with Government funds for the purpose of furnishing long-term loans for plant and equipment for industry. In addition to its capital, which was 246,200 million yen as of December 1954, the Bank is permitted to borrow from Government agencies. Also as of December 1954, such borrowings amounted to 117,786 million yen. The Bank not only extends loans (355,744 million yen as of December 1954), but also subscribes to corporate debentures and takes over certain commercial bank loans. It is the primary organ through which the Government's funds are invested in Japanese industry.

In January 1951, the Export Bank of Japan was established for the purpose of assisting in financing exports of capital goods and heavy equipment. In April 1952, when the Bank's functions were expanded to include the financing of imports of raw materials essential to the manufacture of export commodities, the Bank's name was changed to Export-Import Bank of Japan. The Bank is capitalized at 21,000 million yen, but it is expected that this amount will be increased substantially. As of the end of 1954, borrowings amounted to 6,000 million yen.

In 1951, a Special Account for Agriculture, Forestry and Fishery Finance was instituted to supply long-term funds for the development of these fields of enterprise. It was replaced in April 1953 by the Agriculture, Forestry and Fishery Finance Corporation. This Corporation differs from the Japan Development Bank and the Export-Import Bank of Japan in that its loans are extended through either the Central Cooperative Bank of Agriculture and Forestry or ordinary banks. As of December 1954, the Corporation's capital amounted to 41,607 million yen.

Established in August 1953, the Small Business Finance Corporation has the function of supplying long-term funds to small businesses which have difficulty in obtaining funds through regular commercial channels. The maximum amount of loans to any one enterprise is limited to 10 million yen ($27,778 equivalent). For working funds, the Corporation had received up to the end of 1954 investments amounting to 16,726 million yen from the Government's General Account. It has also taken over a number of Japan Development Bank loans and other Government loans falling within its terms of reference. The Corporation's loans are made through financial institutions having small business connections.

The Housing Loan Corporation was established in 1950 to supply funds for the construction of dwellings which would help to ease the severe housing shortage in Japan. Its capital amounted to 41,800 million yen as of December 1954. The long-term, low-interest funds of this Corporation are available not only to individuals for construction of their own houses but also to companies intending to construct housing for personnel in their employ.

The only prewar Government financial institution still in existence is the People's Finance Corporation. Originally known as the People's Bank, this organization was established by the Government in 1938 for the purpose of making small loans to individuals. It became the People's Finance Corporation in 1949. As of December 1954, the Corporation's capital amounted to 19,500 million yen.

CREDIT AND INTEREST

Both the Government and the banks rely heavily for funds on the Bank of Japan. The banks and the securities markets are unable to meet the demands for credit at any time of the year even with the assistance of substantial Government financing—a situation that has caused heavy overborrowing by commercial banks as well as excessive note issues by the Bank of Japan. The general shortage of credit has resulted in high interest rates, with more than 60 percent of bank loans carrying interest rates of 8.8 percent or higher. The effective rates are even higher than the published rates, since it is common practice for the banks to collect the interest in advance.

The demand for loans is much greater now than before the war because of the weak financial condition of many companies, largely owing to loss of assets during the war. Consequently, banks are exercising greater selectivity with the result that the larger, well-known firms—many of which are former Zaibatsu affiliates—receive preference for the limited supply of available funds. The ex-Zaibatsu banks, which comprise most of the 11 commercial banks, particularly follow this credit policy. Since these 11 banks account for about 50 percent of total national bank deposits and credit and have more than 50 percent of the assets of all commercial banks in Japan, the smaller companies have found it difficult to obtain credit during the postwar period.

The Government has attempted to provide special assistance to small and medium-sized companies, but its efforts have been inadequate. Consequently, such firms must still for the most part rely on the smaller banks, which have a more limited supply of loanable funds and generally charge higher interest rates; or resort to borrowings from nonbanking sources at even higher rates (some American businessmen report that rates for such loans run as high as 3 to 4 percent per month). The chronic shortage of owned capital and the difficulty of getting loans at less than 8-percent interest is considered by businessmen to be a major deterrent in effecting foreign investment arrangements—because of the difficulties involved in raising the required yen—as well as in reducing costs and prices.

Interest rates of the Bank of Japan provide the key to the overall interest rate structure in Japan, because commercial banks depend heavily upon it, as the central bank, for loanable funds. As noted earlier in this chapter, the Bank of Japan operates under a multiple-rate structure, i. e., official rate and primary and secondary rates. The secondary rate is considered to be a penalty rate and by its use the Bank exercises some quantitative control over credit since this rate is higher than the lending rate of commercial banks. Toward the end of 1954, the Finance Minister recommended that the interest rate structure be revised in both the city banks and the Bank of Japan with the desirable objective of reducing the high rates as one means of lowering business costs, since a substantial proportion of short-term loans have been made under the secondary higher rate.

As noted in chapter VI, during the second half of calendar year 1954 there was an improvement in Japan's balance-of-payments position which had a significant effect on bank loans. During that period large payments of yen funds from the Foreign Exchange Special Account gave many banks the wherewithal to repay obligations to the Bank of Japan and reduce their dependence on that Bank. Loans at secondary higher interest rates, which amounted to 109.2 billion yen on March 31, 1954, declined to about 77.2 billion yen by the end of the year. Loans and discounts by the Bank of Japan, which totaled 417.3 billion yen on March 31, 1954, reportedly declined 243.4 billion yen by December 31, 1954.

PUBLIC FINANCE

National Government

Under the Constitution the Cabinet is charged with the responsibility of preparing the national budget, which must be submitted to the lower House of the Diet (House of Representatives); the legislature is the only body which can authorize the expenditure of funds by the National Government. Moreover, as indicated in chapter II taxes can be imposed or modified only as prescribed by laws enacted by the Diet, or, with respect to local taxes, by the local legislative bodies. The upper House (House of Councillors) considers the budget, but even if it does not agree with the decision of the House of Representatives, the budget automatically becomes effective.

The Constitution further provides that the budget be formulated on a fiscal-year basis and the Japanese fiscal year traditionally has extended from April 1 to March 31. Actual preparation of the budget in the administrative branch of the Government is vested in the Budget Division of the Ministry of Finance. In both prewar years and some postwar years, the executive branch generally has found it necessary, toward the end of the fiscal year, to submit supplementary budgets to the Diet.

The center of the Government's budget system is the General Account, which theoretically includes all revenue and expenditures directly applicable to the overall fiscal operation of the National Government. The Japanese Government also uses a Special Account system in its budgeting. This portion of the budget includes a large number of special accounts for the operation of various Government enterprises and other special aspects of Government finance. Theoretically, each special account is self-balancing, but in actual practice there have been substantial deficits in these accounts in both prewar and postwar years which have been covered by direct Government appropriations, borrowings, and transfers of funds from one account to another.

The postwar fiscal policy of the Japanese Government has been characterized by large deficit financing. Unbalanced budgets and expansion of banknote issue by the Bank of Japan were the principal underlying factors in the postwar inflation. In the early postwar years there were enormous claims on a depleted national income, among the more important being the large amount of war bonds and war indemnity claims, and the need to assist private enterprise. With economic activity at a very low level during the first 3 years after the war's end, revenues were woefully insufficient to cover expenditures; in fiscal years 1945 and 1946, revenues were less than 60 percent of expenditures.

In fiscal year 1949, the principle of a balanced budget was introduced by the Occupation authorities. With expanding economic activity, efforts were made to improve revenues and to hold expenditures to the minimum essentials, and the ratio of revenues to expenditures rose to approximately 109 percent. This was achieved principally by increased corporation taxes (personal income taxes were reduced) and by reductions in subsidies. By fiscal year 1952, subsidies were down to about 27 billion yen, compared with nearly 180 billion yen in 1949.

Nevertheless, the budget continued to increase and by fiscal year 1953 had reached 1,027.2 billion yen, compared with 741 billion yen in fiscal year 1949. The increases in 1951 and 1952 were attributable largely to the heavy fiscal requirements attendant with the resumption of sovereignty, rise in cost of general government operations, and expansion in social welfare programs.

The budget for fiscal 1953 was set originally at 965 billion yen, but it was expanded to 1,027.2 billion by supplementary appropriations to pay for disaster relief (flood damages to farmers), larger food imports because of a poor harvest, salary increases to Government employees, expansion in Government investments and public works, and larger payments for war pensions. In late 1953, the Government, alarmed by a deterioration in the country's external payments position (see chapter VI), adopted a budgetary retrenchment policy for fiscal year 1954, together with a generally more restrictive credit policy. The total General Account budget was limited to 1,000 billion yen and actually was held to 999.9 billion—27.3 billion yen less than the preceding year's budget. There was a noticeable reduction in Government investment in fiscal year 1954.

In the postwar years, and particularly in more recent years, national taxes have provided the bulk of Government revenue. For example, in 1954 taxes accounted for 778.3 billion yen of the total budgeted revenue of 999.9 billion yen. Of the tax revenue, it was estimated that the individual income tax provided 288 billion yen; the corporation tax, 203 billion; and the liquor tax, 141 billion. Another very significant revenue producer is the income from the Government monopolies—tobacco, salt, and camphor, with tobacco accounting for the largest proportion.

In prewar years, emphasis was placed on indirect taxes, and there are indications of a reversion to increased indirect taxes and decreased direct taxes.

The substantial carryover of General Account expenditures from the preceding fiscal year, a better crop in 1954 than in 1953, and a favorable turn in the international accounts after the middle of the year to a large extent offset the disinflationary measures. The balance of the Treasury account with the public registered excess payments amounting to 116.2 billion yen during the April–December 1953 period, but there were excess payments of 295.3 billion yen during the comparable period in 1954—an increase of 179.1 billion yen.

On July 1, 1955, 3 months after the beginning of Japan's fiscal year, a 991.5-billion-yen budget for fiscal year 1955 (April 1, 1955–March 31, 1956) was approved. During the April–June hiatus the Government was forced to improvise on provisional budgets. On the receipts side, this budget takes into account a reduction of 6.7 billion in taxes (both personal income and corporate rates were reduced in 1955). Increases in expenditures were budgeted for various types of public welfare activities, including social insurance, veterans' pensions, and education. Approximately 133 billion yen are budgeted for defense purposes; the Japanese defense budget has been relatively small since the resumption of sovereignty in 1952, averaging about 13 percent of the total budget and slightly more than 2 percent of total national income.

Local Government

Despite the fact that retrenchment is being encouraged in National Government finance, no concerted effort has been made as yet to reduce local government expenditures. In fiscal 1954, local government expenditures approached the 1,000-billion-yen level, only slightly below National Government expenditures.

It is true that many of the democratic principles instituted under the Occupation, particularly in the field of education, have increased local government expenditures, but greater freedom on the part of local governments has resulted in further increases. For example, the number of local government employees has increased substantially in the postwar period.

Lack of control by the National Government has permitted a high degree of local patronage with respect to both the administrative and financial operations of the local governments. As a result, local government offices are generously staffed and salaries of personnel are generally higher than those of National Government civil servants. Deficit financing has been practiced to permit ambitious public works programs which, in some instances, have been uncoordinated or competitive with Central Government expenditures for public works. There has been considerable recognition by the administration of the need to straighten out local government finance, but little progress has been made to date.

CHAPTER VI

Foreign Trade and Commercial Policy

RECEIPTS AND PAYMENTS

Basic maladjustments have been evident in the foreign trade of Japan since the end of World War II. In every year since 1945 imports of merchandise have greatly exceeded exports. There has been also a heavy additional burden on Japan's external payments since the war for ocean freight and other invisibles; in some prewar years invisible receipts had offset the merchandise imbalance.

During the early postwar years Japan was able to accumulate foreign exchange because of the approximately $2 billion in aid extended by the United States.[1] This aid was terminated officially on July 1, 1951, but some goods already contracted for continued to enter Japan for several months after that date. Since mid-1950, when Korean hostilities began, and through 1952, special procurement for United States forces in Japan and Korea and related income accruing to Japan (special dollar earnings) exceeded the trade deficit by such magnitude that foreign exchange reserves increased to approximately $1.2 billion by the end of 1952.

In 1953, however, with a record merchandise trade imbalance amounting to $1,135 million, the level of special dollar income was insufficient to offset this large deficit and Japan's net foreign exchange holdings declined by almost $194 million. In 1954 there was a moderate decline in imports and an expansion of dollar receipts, compared with the previous year, and the balance of international payments registered a surplus of $100 million. Total receipts came to $2,309.3 million and payments were $2,209.3 million. There was a further improvement in 1955; for the period January–September receipts exceeded payments by $315.2 million.

The overall improvement in Japan's balance-of-payments position in 1954 and 1955 obscures the fundamental problem in the country's postwar trading relationships. In every postwar year the

[1] This is the so-called Government and Relief in Occupied Areas (GARIOA) funds appropriated by the U. S. Government principally for food and other necessities required for Japan's civilian economy. Japan is expected to repay at least a portion of this aid; the precise amount is still subject to negotiation.

dollar area, particularly the United States, has supplied Japan with the major portion of its imports, but purchases by the dollar-area countries were only about one-third of the value of their sales to Japan. Trade with the sterling area and the countries with which Japan trades on an open-account basis under bilateral arrangements fluctuated between export and import surpluses (further information on Japan's trade and payments agreements is contained in another section of this chapter and in appendix B).

Except under special circumstances and to a very limited extent, Japan has been unable to utilize earnings from trade with any country in the soft-currency area to buy from any other area. Thus, Japan is faced with the problem not only of eliminating the overall gap in its balance of payments, but also of balancing its trade with the various currency areas. Japan's receipts and payments for merchandise trade and invisible transactions for 1953, 1954, and January–September 1955 by currency areas, are given in table 12.

NATURE AND DIRECTION OF TRADE

In every postwar year the value of imports increased more rapidly than that of exports. By 1950 imports totaled $974 million whereas exports totaled $820 million. The outbreak of hostilities in Korea in June 1950 stimulated Japan's imports greatly, purchases aggregating nearly $2 billion; exports, on the other hand, rose to only $1.4 billion.

In 1952 and 1953 imports continued to increase, totaling $2 billion and $2.4 billion, respectively. Exports during those 2 years averaged slightly less than $1.3 billion per year. Thus the excess of imports in calendar year 1952 was $755 million and in 1953 it reached an alltime high of $1,135 million, the latter figure being roughly equal to 89 percent of the value of exports. In 1954 the trend of previous years was reversed—imports declined to $2,399 million and exports expanded to $1,629 million, resulting in a deficit for the year of $770 million. Continued improvement was recorded for the first half of 1955, with the import balance totaling $330 million primarily because of a rise in exports (see table 13).

Table 12.—Receipts and Payments, by Currency Area, Calendar Years 1953–54 and January–September 1955

[In millions of dollars]

Item	All areas			Dollar areas			Sterling area			Open-account area		
	1953	1954	1955 (Jan–Sept)	1953	1954	1955 (Jan–Sept)	1953	1954	1955 (Jan–Sept)	1953	1954	1955 (Jan–Sept)
Receipts:												
Merchandise	1,156.4	1,582.5	1,402.7	481.4	486.2	527.0	314.0	507.7	537.2	361.0	538.6	338.5
Invisibles	963.6	776.8	519.2	889.0	711.9	478.6	55.2	37.7	23.9	19.4	27.2	16.7
Total	2,120.0	2,309.3	1,921.9	1,370.4	1,198.1	1,005.6	369.2	545.4	561.1	380.4	565.8	355.2
Payments:												
Merchandise	2,101.0	1,961.7	1,374.3	1,019.2	1,129.6	643.3	617.2	351.9	387.1	464.6	480.1	343.9
Invisibles	212.7	247.6	232.4	142.2	160.4	133.1	56.5	69.1	77.1	14.0	18.2	22.2
Total	2,313.7	2,209.3	1,606.7	1,161.4	1,290.0	776.4	673.7	421.0	464.2	478.6	498.3	366.1
Balance:												
Merchandise	−944.6	−429.2	+284.0	−537.8	−643.5	−116.4	−303.2	+155.7	+150.1	−103.6	+58.5	−5.3
Invisibles	+750.9	+529.1	+286.8	+746.8	+551.3	+345.5	−1.3	−31.3	−53.2	+5.4	+9.1	−5.5
Total	−193.7	+100.0	+315.2	+209.0	−92.2	+229.1	−304.5	+124.4	+96.9	−98.2	+67.6	−10.8

Source: Ministry of Finance.

Note: Figures may not add because of rounding.

Table 13.—*Value of Merchandise Imports and Exports, Calendar Years 1930–34 Average and 1946–55* [1]

[In thousands of dollars]

Year	Imports	Exports	Excess of imports
1930–34, average	752,675	686,981	−65,694
1946 [2]	305,611	103,292	−202,319
1947	523,542	173,568	−349,974
1948	684,220	258,271	−425,949
1949	904,845	509,700	−395,145
1950	974,339	820,055	−154,284
1951	1,995,039	1,354,520	−640,519
1952	2,028,163	1,272,915	−755,248
1953	2,409,830	1,274,945	−1,134,885
1954	2,399,596	1,629,367	−770,229
1955 (January–June)	1,222,167	892,187	−329,980

[1] Based on customs data of actual receipts and shipments of goods and therefore differs from table 12.
[2] September 1945–December 1946.

Note.—Conversion from yen to dollars for 1930–34 made at the prevailing average exchange rates. Data for those years also include trade with Korea and Formosa.

Trade by Commodities

Japan is a heavy importer of food and industrial raw materials and an exporter of manufactured goods, semimanufactured products, raw silk, and certain food products, notably tea and fish.

Imports.—The basic pattern of postwar merchandise imports has not changed from that of prewar years, with foodstuffs and raw materials continuing to comprise the bulk of the country's imports. However, in the period 1946–50, foodstuffs constituted a much larger proportion of total imports than before the war, owing to the critical shortage of food and the economic dislocations caused by the war which resulted in a low level of industrial activity. In subsequent years Japan's import trade reverted substantially to the prewar pattern. However, the proportion of industrial materials and mineral fuels to total imports increased slightly; and in the most recent postwar years imports of specialized machinery and equipment were significantly larger than in many prewar years.

In terms of value, approximately 92 percent or $2,207 million of Japan's imports in 1954 consisted of foodstuffs, raw materials, industrial chemicals, drugs, and some capital goods. The remaining $193 million was used primarily to purchase a wide variety of luxuries and semiluxuries. Japan's food bill for that year amounted to $643 million, nearly 27 percent of total imports and equal to almost 40 percent of the value of exports.

As noted in chapter III, Japan is poorly supplied with most of the raw materials needed for its industrial complex. It must import all of its requirements of raw cotton, wool, bauxite, and crude rubber; about nine-tenths of its crude oil; three-fourths of its iron ore, tin, and salt; and smaller but substantial quantities of other raw materials. Imports of these commodities in 1954 aggregated as follows, in millions of dollars: Textile raw materials (raw cotton, raw wool, hemp, jute, flax, ramie, and manila fibers), 576; iron ore, 66; petroleum and petroleum products, 294; bituminous coal for coking, 54; nonferrous metal scrap, 36; nonmetallic mineral ores (principally potash salts, other salt, and phosphate rock), 70; crude rubber, 38; wood (mostly logs and apitongs), 48; drugs and chemicals, 64; and hides and skins, 20. Japan's foreign exchange expenditures for specialized machinery and equipment needed to modernize its industrial plant amounted to $99 million in 1954.

The volume of imports also has increased during recent years, but it is still below that of prewar years, having risen to approximately 77 percent of the prewar average by 1954. The larger volume resulted in a greater output of manufactured goods which, through calendar year 1953, was absorbed mainly by significantly increased domestic consumption. As a matter of fact, the attractiveness of the domestic market militated against more active efforts to promote exports. During 1954, there was a moderate decline in imports owing to a general contraction of the economy as a result of the Government's deflationary measures.

Exports.—Exports have risen at a far slower rate than imports. The volume of exports in 1953 was only 35 percent of the prewar volume; but, with the marked increase recorded in 1954, it increased to 46 percent of prewar. Merely to attain the prewar volume, however, would not restore exports in per capita terms because of Japan's increased population. It is estimated that, to regain the prewar per capita export level, Japan would have to expand its exports three and a half times—from the 1954 postwar peak of $1.6 billion to $5.5 billion.

As in prewar years, textiles and textile products represent the bulk of Japan's income from exports; but the importance of these products and other light manufactures has been declining and that of metal products, machinery, and chemicals has grown. Exports of textiles and textile products during the years 1953–54 averaged $559 million, or better than 38 percent of the value of all exports. However, this share was significantly lower than the prewar ratio of more than 50 percent, the decline being due very largely to the large reduction in sales of raw silk.

The second most important foreign exchange earner in 1953–54 was metals and metal products, shipments of which averaged $218 million, or about 15 percent of the total; in 1934–36 the ratio was less than 4 percent. Machinery exports also have advanced sharply in recent years as compared with prewar. Shipments of machinery, including ship exports, rose from $110 million in 1952 to $189.5 million in 1953, and by 1954 had attained the record total of $202 million. The 1954 figure was slightly more than 12 percent of the year's exports; in 1934–36, such exports were less than 2 percent.

As in prewar years, exports of fresh, frozen, and processed foods continue to be significant. In 1953–54, sales of fish and fish products, tea, and other food items averaged $128 million, about 52 percent of which was accounted for by the first-named group. Sales of various sundries also continue to loom large in the country's postwar export trade. For example, in 1954 export sales of pottery and porcelainware were valued at nearly $35 million and toys at $32 million. Relative newcomers as important export items are lumber and plywood, the latter going principally to the United States; the total export sales of these two products in 1954 stood at nearly $47 million.

Geographic Composition

Prior to World War II, Japan traded primarily with other countries of Asia, including its former empire areas, and maintained a rough balance in its trade with various currency areas. In sharp contrast, during the postwar period Japan has relied heavily on the dollar area, particularly the United States, for its imports and there has been a decided imbalance in its trade with that area. In the past 4 years, however, the trend has been toward a wider dispersion of suppliers and customers, and Asian countries are becoming increasingly important in Japanese trade.

In 1954, Asian countries supplied about 31 percent of Japan's imports and provided an outlet for nearly 49 percent of its exports, with South and Southeast Asian countries accounting for the larger part of this trade.

Despite the greater diversification of Japan's trade in recent postwar years, the countries of North America in 1954 supplied Japan with 46 percent of its imports, the United States and Canada being the leading suppliers. However, the North American countries purchased only about 21 percent of Japan's exports in that year. The following 14 countries listed in order of importance, with their relationship to total imports shown in percentages, supplied 77 percent of Japan's import requirements in 1954: United States, 35.3; Canada, 5.1; Australia, 4.9; Saudi Arabia, 4.6; Mexico, 3.8; Brazil, 3.1; Thailand, 2.9; the Philippines, 2.8; Burma, 2.6; Argentina, 2.5; Indonesia, 2.5; Formosa, 2.4; Malaya, 2.4; and India, 2.1.

In order of value, Japan's 14 best customers in 1954, with their standing among total exports shown in percentages, were: United States, 17; Indonesia, 7.3; Brazil, 4.8; Hong Kong, 4.7; Republic of Korea, 4.2; Formosa, 4; Thailand, 4; Pakistan, 3.4; United Kingdom, 3.1; Argentina, 3; Burma, 2.8; India, 2.7; Ryukyu Islands, 2.6; and Singapore 2.3.

Trade With the United States

Japan's trade with the United States has been considerably larger in the postwar years than prewar. The United States has been the principal postwar supplier of imports into Japan, but at a lower percentage in recent years than in the earlier postwar years; and it has been the major market for Japanese exports. Most striking, however, is the fact that Japan's import balance with the United States has been larger than with any other country. In 1953 and 1954, Japan's imports from the United States averaged $802 million, compared with sales of Japanese products in the United States market averaging $252 million, and the average import balance of $550 million was almost 58 percent of Japan's total merchandise trade deficit for those years.

Table 14.—Leading Japanese Imports From the United States, 1953–54 and January–June 1955

Commodity	Value (thousands of dollars)			Percent of Japan's total imports of listed commodities			Percent of total imports from the United States		
	1953	1954	1955 (Jan.–June)	1953	1954	1955 (Jan.–June)	1953	1954	1955 (Jan.–June)
Wheat, unmilled	77,332	83,082	34,900	55.6	49.4	48.5	10.2	9.8	8.9
Rice, unmilled	38,874	68,123	19,872	18.1	27.2	19.0	5.1	8.0	5.1
Barley, unmilled	16,889	13,648	8,336	27.9	26.7	42.2	2.2	1.6	2.1
Maize (corn), unmilled	12,832	5,799	11,423	87.7	40.4	80.7	1.7	.7	2.9
Soybeans	49,929	56,232	40,855	89.7	84.6	69.3	6.6	6.6	10.4
Hides and skins, undressed	16,242	12,557	8,042	53.0	63.4	75.1	2.1	1.5	2.1
Cotton, raw, including linters	122,009	170,527	81,845	32.6	41.7	39.4	16.0	20.0	20.9
Iron ore	8,699	6,345	1,045	14.2	9.6	3.6	1.1	.7	.3
Coal	65,750	52,422	21,626	73.2	83.1	83.0	8.6	6.1	5.5
Phosphate rock	7,033	13,481	8,470	39.3	55.1	56.0	.9	1.6	2.2
Gas oil, diesel oil, and other fuel oils	25,942	15,947	13,871	47.8	34.6	49.1	3.4	1.9	3.5
Automobiles, passenger	27,753	14,367	3,497	78.2	79.0	91.5	3.6	1.7	.9
Total, leading commodities	469,284	512,530	253,782	----------	----------	----------	61.6	60.2	64.8

An increase in exports in 1954 was more than offset by the rise in imports so that the imbalance for the year was $570 million. However, some of the imports from the United States in late 1953 and 1954 did not require payments of foreign exchange since they represented sales of surplus agricultural commodities for yen.

The bulk of Japan's imports from the United States in 1953–54 and the first half of 1955 consisted of foodstuffs, raw materials, and capital goods; as shown in table 14, these comprised 62 percent of Japan's total purchases from the United States in 1953, 60 percent in 1954, and 65 percent in the first half of 1955. The United States was Japan's leading supplier of soybeans, corn, wheat, hides and skins, coal, phosphate rock, and automobiles. It was an important contributor also to Japan's import requirements of raw cotton, rice, fuel and diesel oil, iron ore, animal oil, fats and greases, and industrial chemicals and drugs. In 1954 there was a sharp decline in passenger-car imports from the United States as well as from other countries as a consequence of the Government's policy to reduce imports of luxury and semiluxury goods.

Japan's exports to the United States by principal commodities in 1953–54 and January–June 1955 are included in table VIII of appendix A. The composition of its sales to the United States in 1953–54 differs in several respects from that of the 1930's. In the prewar period raw silk was the largest single dollar earner; in the postwar years exports of raw silk have been relatively small. Exports of sewing machines, optical goods, and plywood have provided Japan with a substantial amount of dollars in recent years, but in the prewar period these items were not produced for export and, as a matter of fact, the market for plywood in the United States was very small, if even existent.

On the other hand, there are many similarities. The United States continues to be an important market for Japan's fish and fish products, tea,

pottery and porcelainware, miscellaneous textile products, pearls, imitation jewelry, toys and games, ornamental flowers, and carpets and rugs. Japan may be expected to increase its sales to the United States of light consumer goods; and the recent trend toward greater use of silk for clothing offers promise of a significantly expanded market for this item in the next few years.

PROBLEMS IN INCREASING EXPORTS

Because of extraordinary receipts, Japan has been able to accumulate sizable foreign exchange holdings in the postwar years.[2] Since such income cannot be expected to continue indefinitely, Japan is faced with the necessity of expanding its exports to pay for the foodstuffs and raw materials it needs to feed, clothe, provide useful jobs, and maintain a decent standard of living for its large and increasing population. Many factors affect the expansion of Japan's trade and the achievement of a balance in its international accounts, however. For instance, there has been a serious deterioration in its source of international income from invisibles, principally shipping (see chapter IV).

Japan is handicapped also by several internal factors, including technological obsolescence in basic industries, a serious power shortage, high interest rates, and relatively high raw-material costs. Contrary to popular belief, Japan is not a low-cost producer in such important fields as capital goods and heavy chemicals, which appear more promising than many light industries as a means of expanding Japan's export volume. Some progress toward rationalization has been made in

---

[2] According to the Japanese Ministry of Finance, such holdings amounted to $1,131 million on June 30, 1955. The net amount is considerably less, however, since these holdings include sizable open-account debts owed by Indonesia and Korea (estimated in June 1955 to have totaled at least $200 million) and certain short-term liabilities, such as credits from the U. S. Export-Import Bank for raw cotton and imports financed by usances and other short-term credits; as of the first half of 1955 these latter aggregated upwards of $108 million.

these industries largely through capital and know-how obtained from abroad, particularly from the United States, since the end of the war (see chapter VIII and table XIV of appendix A).

Deficit financing and other inflationary fiscal policies following the outbreak of Korean hostilities stimulated consumer demand and resulted in high prices for Japanese export products. Thus, Japan found it difficult to sell abroad and Japanese businessmen had little incentive to export since, by and large, it was more profitable to channel goods into the domestic economy. Alarmed over the deterioration in its balance-of-payments position, the Government in late 1953 and early 1954 announced several measures designed to cope with the problem, the most significant elements of which were a balanced national budget, curtailment of imports, tightening of credit, reduction of Government investment, and the adoption of special measures to promote exports.

Undoubtedly, this so-called austerity program was partly instrumental in arresting the course of inflation, reducing imports, and increasing exports in 1954 and 1955. The favorable turn in Japan's export trade, however, may be attributed also to various temporary and fortuitous factors, such as generally favorable world economic conditions, the pressure from surplus inventories, reduction in import restrictions by sterling-area countries, intensified use of various export promotion measures (including the link system and dual pricing) during 1954, and greater reliance on barter transactions. According to estimates, 30 to 40 percent of Japan's exports in 1954 were made under arrangements not related to the commercial exchange rate.

Failure to control domestic inflation effectively could largely offset the benefits derived from rationalization of industry, since, if Japan's domestic price structure continues to be higher than that of its major competitors, the country will find it difficult to compete internationally.

In addition to improvement of industrial plant and management practices, a program for expansion of exports involves emphasis on consistent high-quality production at competitive prices, adequate inspection facilities, other quality-control measures, and export promotion. In recent years Japan has made greater efforts to increase exports through more extensive and intensive sales promotion along the lines employed by other major exporting countries.

Since 1953 trade missions have been sent to various countries; the number of commercial representatives in Japan's diplomatic establishments has been increased; commercial firms have established offices in key countries; trade centers displaying Japanese export products have been established in New York and San Francisco and in Cairo, Egypt; machinery consultant centers

have been set up in important South Asian and South and Central American countries; and Japan has participated in several international trade fairs. In April 1953, the first international trade fair in Japan's history was held in Osaka, and it reportedly resulted in sizable orders for Japanese firms and should result in future business.

Japan must continue its efforts, however, to meet the intensified international competition. As the Japanese Government's Ministry of International Trade and Industry (MITI) observed in reviewing Japan's trade results in 1953, the performance of Japanese businessmen "compares unfavorably with major European nations, and it is ironic that it is left for our competitors themselves to often point to the lack of publicity given to products sold abroad by Japan." [3] The MITI concludes that this is due to some extent to the dearth of Government assistance and to inadequate efforts by manufacturers and traders, which are attributed in part to the financial weakness of many companies.

Additionally, the MITI points out that less than satisfactory service was rendered in connection with capital goods exports. Moreover, it advises businessmen to devote more attention to market surveys, by noting that "potential and economic conditions, changes in the demand and supply situation and shifts in taste and designs should all be studied and analyzed. In this respect, too, Japan has lost much ground to major American and European countries." [4]

In pursuance of the vital objective of expanding exports, the MITI cautions Japanese businessmen to "guard against any unfair competition, e. g., violation of foreign industrial property rights or export of low-quality products which are inferior to samples." [5]

The loss of its colonies as a result of the war and the changed political situation in nearby areas have forced Japan to turn to the dollar and sterling areas for coking coal, iron ore, salt, and soybean and other products, thus substantially increasing production costs. Some of these countries buy much less from, than they sell to, Japan; therefore, Japan has attempted to expand its sales to such areas but has been faced with quota restrictions and discriminatory tariffs.

In this connection, Japan considered that one of its greatest handicaps in the past was its inability to gain full membership in the General Agreement on Tariff and Trade (GATT). Japan was admitted provisionally in 1953 and became a full member on September 10, 1955. Fourteen of the 34 Contracting Parties to the GATT have since invoked article 35 against Japan. The invocation of this article means that the agreement is not in effect as between them on the one hand and Japan

---

[3] *Foreign Trade of Japan, 1954*, Ministry of International Trade and Industry.
[4] Ibid.
[5] Ibid.

on the other, i. e., benefits resulting from adherence to the agreement may be withheld without constituting a violation by the contracting parties to the agreement.

Recognizing the need for obtaining a larger portion of its raw-material requirements from nearby areas, the Japanese Government and Japanese businessmen are anxious to increase trade with and investment in South and Southeast Asia. Many Japanese believe that increased trade with the countries in those regions could go a long way toward offsetting the loss of China and Manchuria as relatively cheap sources of food and raw materials. Because of the limitations on trade with communist China which Japan has imposed for security considerations in concert with other free world countries and the restrictions instituted by communist China itself, Japan's trade with that area has been low in recent years.

The South and Southeast Asian countries are considered to have important potentialities for supplying Japan with foodstuffs and raw materials in exchange for Japanese manufactures. However, political instability in some of the countries; inability to reach agreement with the Philippines, Indonesia, and Indochina on reparations; and lingering animosity against the Japanese dating from the war, all militate against the highest possible level of trade. Some progress has been made and further improvement is expected in the not distant future. In 1954 a reparations agreement was concluded with Burma and by the spring of 1955 the agreement was showing salutary results for both countries.

As an integral part of Japan's activities to boost exports, Japanese businessmen, actively backed by Government financial institutions, are exploring the possibilities of investment abroad. However, because of the acute shortage of domestic capital, great reliance is placed on investment in kind—the Japanese supplying the machinery and technical services. This procedure provides Japan with a market for its capital goods and it is likely to result in increased availabilities of raw materials at lower prices. A recent example is a joint undertaking by the three largest Japanese steel producers and Philippine mineowners. The Japanese companies will furnish mining equipment and services in return for a substantial quantity of iron ore supplies on a continuing basis. Other similar arrangements already have been effected and still others are under study.

COMMERCIAL POLICY

Trading Practices

During the first few years following the end of World War II, Japan's foreign trade was on a government-to-government basis. By early 1950 foreign trade had been restored to private hands, subject to a comprehensive and complex system of trade and exchange controls (see chapter VII). Following the transfer of trade to private channels and a greatly expanded industrial production, Japan's exports increased.

Japan's re-entry into international trade aroused the fear that Japan would again engage in the unfair trade practices, such as dumping, subsidization of exports, unfair pricing and sales techniques, violation of foreign industrial property rights, and improper labeling and marks of origin, which gave the country its unfortunate reputation in prewar years. The Japanese Government early recognized that such a resurgence of fear could seriously hamper Japan's export trade and retard or perhaps even prevent the achievement of a viable economy.

Various steps have been taken by the Japanese Government to protect foreign industrial property rights, to insure proper inspection of export products, and proper use of marks of origin, and to prevent dumping. An American businessman interested in investing in Japan should familiarize himself with the laws and regulations in force to accomplish these desirable objectives (see chapter X). The potential foreign investor should make certain that he deals only with reliable and experienced Japanese businessmen and that the investment contract clearly sets forth the rights, privileges, and obligations of both parties.

The Japanese contend that the specific anti-dumping legislation and the postwar labor laws (see chapter XI) have resulted in improved working conditions and various social benefits which would make it difficult for other countries to support an accusation of "social dumping." Moreover, it is agreed that large-scale dumping is precluded by the high cost-price structure of large segments of Japan's industry.

On the other hand, during 1953 and 1954 there were reports of the use of link arrangements, dual pricing, rebates, and similar trading methods to expand exports.[6] Under the link system, allocation of foreign exchange for raw materials is tied to exports of products containing the raw material. However, the link arrangement was used also to tie sugar imports to silk and ship exports.

In support of the raw material-finished goods link, Japanese Government officials claim that because of the more profitable domestic market, they could not otherwise induce manufacturers and trading companies to export. The link system has resulted in the adoption of dual prices—a certain volume of production is sold

---

[6] These practices met with disapproval by the International Monetary Fund, of which Japan is a member, as well as by various countries. At the end of 1954 responsible Japanese Government officials announced that the link system would be abolished in early 1955. It has been reported that all but the raw material-finished products link have been discontinued.

in the export market at lower than domestic prices, in some instances reportedly at prices below the cost of production, to enable the producer to qualify for a foreign exchange allocation. He can then sell the resulting imports in the domestic market at high prices, with the profits offsetting the possible losses incurred in selling abroad. This type of link in effect involves indirect subsidization for which the Japanese consumer bears the burden.

Tariffs and Commodity Excise Taxes

Japan completely revised its import tariff schedule in 1951, from a mixed schedule of specific and ad valorem rates to a schedule of ad valorem rates exclusively.[7] Modifications have been made in these rates since 1951, the most extensive of which resulted from Japan's negotiations for accession to the GATT in 1955. The current level of Japan's tariff is considered moderate but protective. The rates on many important manufactured products range between 15 and 50 percent. It is anticipated that further modifications in Japan's tariff will be made in 1956 as a result of the multilateral tariff negotiations scheduled for that time. No duties or levies are assessed on exports.

Since 1951, temporary exemptions or reductions of duties have been granted on a wide variety of commodities, mainly foodstuffs and industrial machinery and equipment, either because Japan's production is not large enough to meet its requirements or because some items required for modernization and expansion of industry, e. g., certain machinery, are not produced in Japan. The duty exemptions or suspensions have been changed from time to time as necessitated by changes in the domestic supply situation, the status of Japan's industrial progress, and other factors. Duties also have been reduced or suspended on imports of certain raw materials for the production of specific export items.

In addition to import duties, certain products are subject to commodity excise taxes which are assessed on the c. i. f. price plus import duty of the goods at the time of the importation. These taxes are payable also on domestic manufactures. The rates, which are the same for domestic and imported commodities, range from 5 to 50 percent, depending on the commodity; the higher rates are applicable to luxury and semiluxury goods.

[7] The currently effective tariff schedule is law No. 54 of April 15, 1910, as amended; the latest amendment was by law No. 42 of 1954. This and other laws relating to Japan's import tariff are contained in *The Import Tariff of Japan*, 1954, compiled by the Ministry of Finance and published by the Maruzen Co., Ltd., in cooperation with the Japan Customs Association of Tokyo (a private organization devoted to research and education in the fields of tariff and trade). Further information on Japan's tariff and customs laws may be obtained from the Far Eastern Division, Office of Economic Affairs, Bureau of Foreign Commerce, U. S. Department of Commerce, or from any of the Department's Field Offices.

The Customs Tariff Council was established in accordance with the provisions of the Customs Tariff Law and implementing regulations to conduct tariff investigations and make recommendations thereon to the Minister of Finance. The Council is composed of 45 members, including the Minister of Finance, who is its president. Members of the Council are appointed by the Minister of Finance, and presently comprise 18 persons from various Government agencies and 27 from trade associations, universities, and other groups directly interested in foreign trade matters. Members are appointed for 2-year terms and may be reappointed, and they serve only on a part-time basis.

Bilateral Trade and Payments Agreements

As of December 1955, Japan was a party to 25 bilateral trade and payments agreements. More than half of the agreements are dollar-expressed open-account arrangements and many include a trade plan specifying the commodities, by value, to be exchanged between Japan and the other participant. Except for most countries included in the dollar area, Japan's principal suppliers and customers are covered by trade agreements. (See appendix B for a list of these agreements, including their principal provisions.)

Japan's bilateral trade and payments agreement program was initiated by the Occupation authorities in 1948 as a temporary expedient to make possible the resumption of Japanese trade, after the complete paralysis occasioned by the war. The agreements had as their objective a balanced trade at the highest possible levels; and they assisted measurably in expanding and diversifying Japan's trade. Japan at that time, for all practical purposes, had no foreign exchange holdings; the country's gold reserve was put in escrow by the Occupation authorities against possible future reparation claims.

The most important agreement is the Anglo-Japanese Agreement covering trade with the sterling area. Unlike Japan's other agreements, it does not include a specific trade plan and there is no stipulation for balanced accounts between Japan and the various members of the sterling area. Until mid-1951 this agreement contained a dollar convertibility clause; since then transactions have been conducted only in sterling. Included under the sterling-area payment agreement are bilateral arrangements with Ceylon, Burma, and Pakistan; all stipulate that settlements are to be made in sterling. With respect to Ceylon and Burma, no specific trade plan is involved, since the estimates of total anticipated trade are included in the total figure for the sterling area; in effect, the agreements are merely understandings through which, it is hoped, trade

53

will be facilitated. The agreement with Pakistan, on the other hand, sets forth a trade plan and each party agrees to issue import licenses for the amounts specified.

The largest number of agreements are the bilateral agreements with settlement to be made in dollars. In some instances, payments provisions are included under which balances or amounts in excess of specified credits or "swing ceilings" are payable in dollars; many contain trade plans. These open-account arrangements have neither earned nor cost Japan any significant amount of dollars because the dollar-payment clauses generally have not been invoked—unpaid balances have been carried over with the hope of achieving a balance.

Some agreements do not fall within either of the foregoing categories, but may be categorized as payments agreements; most of these are based on dollar cash settlement with some having "swing" limits (see appendix B). They contain neither specific trade plans nor an overall target for two-way trade.

Japan's bilateral agreements served the purpose of restoring Japan's trading channels following the disruption of war, but there is evidence that they have a restrictive effect on trade, and tend to foster unorthodox trading practices and increase Government controls over private business.

Both parties to bilateral agreements, each unwilling to incur import balances, often negotiate with a conservative approach and in actual practice, in many instances, it has been found that the overall amounts expressed in the agreements have not been targets but upper limits; careful licensing controls have been exercised to insure that trade does not exceed the expressed amounts. Moreover, bilateralism has resulted in Japan's use of the following techniques to maintain a balanced trade: (1) Buying goods at higher than world market prices in order to sell at similarly high prices, (2) purchasing a greater volume of luxuries and semiluxuries than desired, and (3) channeling purchases of certain products from one country to the detriment of another country.

To fulfill these Government-negotiated trade agreements, the Japanese Government has exercised some control over private business activities. This has taken a variety of forms, including preferential exchange allocations, link arrangements, production controls, and barter arrangements. Some Japanese Government officials point to the continuing success of these trade agreements as justification for their continuation, particularly in the light of certain restrictions by several important trading countries against Japanese goods and the general inconvertibility of currencies. Recently, however, the Government has shown some indication of placing less reliance on bilateral and other special trading arrangements.

CHAPTER VII

Trade and Exchange Controls

TRADE CONTROLS

Trade controls were first instituted in Japan in 1937, when the nation began to tighten its economy for the prosecution of the war with China, and were intensified during World War II. In the early stages of the occupation of Japan all foreign trade was conducted on a government-to-government basis. The changeover to private trade was made gradually, and with the passage of the Foreign Exchange and Foreign Trade Control Law (law No. 228) on December 1, 1949, all foreign trade transactions were put under a unified system of controls which, in the words of the law, ". . . provide for the control of foreign exchange, foreign trade and other foreign transactions, necessary for the proper development of foreign trade and for the safeguarding of the balance of international payments and the stability of the currency, as well as the most economic and beneficial use of foreign currency funds. . . ."

The necessity for prudent use of Japan's foreign exchange assets is understandable and appreciated, in the light of Japan's continuing difficulty in achieving a balance in its merchandise trade accounts. Thus, the fundamental objective of Japan's import controls is to assure that food and raw materials have priority for allocations of foreign exchange.

Import Licensing

All commercial imports are subject to licensing. Food and basic raw materials are given first priority, followed by machinery and equipment required for modernization and expansion of industrial plant, particularly those which contribute to an improvement of exports. Licenses are granted also for a wide variety of consumer goods, but there is a tendency to reduce imports of such commodities, particularly from the dollar area.

In general, Japan's import controls are non-discriminatory, but they may operate to restrict imports from certain countries in favor of others, depending upon the state of Japan's exchange position at a given time. Such controls have handicapped the planning of prospective investors whose investment program requires the importa-tion of certain products, since they face the possibility of being denied sufficient exchange for their needs. Several investment projects have been discouraged because foreign exchange was not guaranteed for imported parts.

A businessman interested in effecting an investment arrangement which would entail importation of raw materials or parts from the United States or other countries should seek assurance from the Japanese Government that import permits will be granted. Moreover, he should become familiar with the provisions of Japan's Foreign Exchange and Foreign Trade Control Law (see appendix F).

In most instances, applications for import licenses are filed with an authorized foreign exchange bank (for a list of such banks see section on exchange controls in this chapter). However, for imports for which foreign exchange is not specifically set aside in the import budget and for those which do not involve payment of foreign exchange or are made under processing arrangements, i. e., import of raw materials and/or parts to be used in production of goods specifically earmarked for export, such applications must be filed with the Ministry of International Trade and Industry (MITI).

Foreign exchange for merchandise imports is budgeted semiannually. The import budget is compiled by the appropriate sections of the Ministries of Finance, International Trade and Industry, Agriculture and Forestry, and Transportation and by the Economic Planning Board. The responsibility for approval of the budget rests with the Ministerial Council composed of the heads of the above agencies and the Prime Minister, who is its chairman. Three types of import systems are provided under the import budget—the automatic approval (AA) system, the funds allocation (FA) system, and the global quota system.

The three systems have several things in common but differ in others. For instance, under all three systems, applicants for import licenses are required to deposit collateral varying from 1 to 35 percent of the value of the proposed import. This guaranty is forfeited in part—and in some cases in its entirety—if the applicant fails to import in accordance with the terms of the license. Second, under the three systems an import limit is established. This limit is the higher amount, in terms of value, for a particular commodity for which any applicant may obtain a license during the period specified in the import announcements made by the MITI under the commodity groups specified in the import budgets.

Also the same under the three systems is the principle of the import license. Issuance of the license gives the importer the right to pay the stipulated amount of foreign exchange to the seller without additional authorization by the Government. The validity period of a license is usually 6 months but it can be extended by the MITI through the authorized foreign exchange bank concerned.

Automatic approval system.—Under the AA system licenses for specified commodities are issued on application, with the amounts set aside for the goods included in the AA list for each currency area or open-account country. There is no value limitation set for each commodity and licenses are almost always approved.

It is customary under the AA system for the importer to conclude a contract with his foreign supplier before he applies to the foreign exchange bank for a license since (1) normally sufficient exchange is made available for the items included on the list, and (2) with limited exceptions, the recipient of the license is required to arrange for payment for 80 percent of the total value licensed within 10 days after obtaining the license.

Licenses for importation under the AA system generally are granted automatically. However, after the foreign exchange specifically allocated for a given area has been exhausted, imports from that area, or a country within the area, will be suspended. Suspension of applications for import licenses, for example, may apply to all items or to one commodity only. Notification of suspension of applications for import license under the AA system usually is made by the MITI and is likely to occur near the end of the 6-month budget period.

Occasionally, additional funds will be allocated from the Government's reserve fund to meet commitments made by importers with their foreign suppliers. However, there is no guaranty given by the Government that all commitments will be honored.

A special provision governing long-term contracts is included in the AA system and provides for a special budget. The license application procedure is the same as that for other AA listed items but the validity of the license is for a longer period.

Funds allocation system.—For imports programed under the foreign exchange allocation system (FA), an importer files his application with the MITI and receives a foreign exchange allocation certificate, which is presented to the foreign exchange bank together with the application for an import license. The bank issues the license without a case-by-case confirmation of the status of the foreign exchange budget since the allocation certificate insures that the amount applied for is within the limit of the budgeted amount for the particular commodity from the specified area. The allocation certificate is valid for 4 months from the date of issuance.

Unlike applications to import under the AA system, which may be made at any time during the 6-month budget period, applications for imports under the FA system must be made during specified periods. These periods are stipulated in notices issued by the MITI which detail the specific items permitted (the import budget lists the broad categories of the commodities), together with information with respect to the currency area from which the purchase may be made (presently divided into dollar area, sterling area, and open-account area), the opening and closing dates on which applications for license will be accepted[1], the import limit for each importer, and the amount of collateral required. Recipients of foreign exchange allocation certificates may apply personally for import licenses or engage a trading firm to do so and to handle all matters involved in the actual importation[2].

Global quota system.—Allocations under the global quota system are made by commodity only without any regard to the particular country of origin of the goods. This system was first introduced as a liberalization measure during Japanese fiscal year 1954 applicable only to wheat, barley, milk powder, synthetic resins, flaxseed, primary copper, and zinc and lead in pigs. It was subsequently expanded to include certain types of machinery and certain raw materials to be used for processing and reexported as well as some minor items.

Special import procedures.—Special procedures are in effect for imports (1) not involving payment of foreign exchange, such as imports of machinery or equipment in connection with a foreign investment plan; (2) made with foreign exchange earned as an incentive for exporting certain products (Special Foreign Exchange Allocation System); (3) effected under processing arrangements; (4) made on a consignment basis; and (5) intended for transshipment.

With respect to the first mentioned, it is necessary to obtain the approval of the Ministry of Finance or other Ministry having jurisdiction in the particular field; in most instances this agency will be the MITI, and investors who contemplate an arrangement involving necessary imports should notify the MITI of the details prior to shipment. There is no uniform procedure for the latter three special types of imports; however, for

---

[1] An allocation certificate must accompany the license application under the FA system.
[2] Consumers customarily employ a trading firm since most consumers are not experienced in handling foreign trade. Traditionally, in Japan trading companies have performed this function and consequently few manufacturing firms have trading departments.

each type application must be made on special MITI forms filed with the appropriate section of the MITI and each must receive prior approval from that agency.

Foreign businessmen often have faced difficulties in conducting their business under the system of trade controls in Japan, claiming that the administration of the control system is too restrictive, time-consuming, and expensive. In part, this is attributed to the nature of the controls. However, both foreign and Japanese businessmen have complained about the large number of Government employees who must be consulted and from whom approval must be obtained; the large amount of paper work required; and the discriminatory effect of exchange allocations and import licenses based on historical import experience. New companies find it difficult to enter a field in which there are well-established, experienced, and influential firms.

It has also been alleged that, in several indirect ways, the larger, well-known companies can obtain import licenses more readily than the smaller companies. In many instances this promptitude is due to the ability of the large companies to maintain more employees on the payroll to engage in negotiations with Government officials and follow through on involved and lengthy processing procedures.

The link system and other special methods of doing business devised by the Japanese Government to encourage exports also have received criticism from both foreign and Japanese businessmen, who claim that, when a company either cannot or does not desire to engage in these methods, it may find that an exchange allocation and an import license is much harder to obtain.

Export Controls

All exports from Japan are subject to registration with an authorized foreign exchange bank. The requirement that an export declaration must receive bank certification is imposed to assure surrender of all foreign exchange to the Government.

Moreover, individual licensing by the MITI is required for the export of (1) 32 groups of commodities covering hundreds of different products, which are considered to require control for price reasons, because of their strategic importance or because they are imported goods; (2) goods under a processing contract or merchandise to be compensated by imports specified in a barter contract; (3) goods under other than standard payment terms as specified by the Ministry of Finance; and (4) items which have been designated by the MITI under applicable regulations as likely to infringe on foreign industrial property rights in the country of destination.

Proceeds from exports must be surrendered within 10 days after acquisition. However, under a special Foreign Exchange Allocation System (formerly the Retention System), exporters are permitted to have credited to them 5 percent of their export proceeds which may be used for imports required for the promotion of exports and general economic development, expenses of oversea branches, travel and living expenses abroad for the purpose of promoting trade, and importation of samples, catalogs, and trade books and magazines.

Before a shipment can be cleared, the exporter must provide the customs authorities with a properly certified export declaration and, when applicable, a valid export license. After clearance, copies of the various documents are sent by customs to the Bank of Japan for a postreview. American importers customarily make payment for purchases from Japan by an irrevocable letter of credit, with the draft drawn at sight or within 3 months of sight.

EXCHANGE CONTROLS

Controls over foreign exchange transactions were first instituted in Japan in the mid-1930's. A basic foreign exchange control law was enacted in 1933 following devaluation of the yen and departure from the gold standard. Since then some form of exchange control has been in effect. The present system of controls is based on the Foreign Exchange and Foreign Trade Control Law, which has been amended several times.[3] Japan instituted exchange controls after World War II because of serious balance-of-payments problems and the extreme shortage of capital resources resulting from the disruption and dislocation of the war.

It may be assumed that Japan will continue to find it necessary to maintain foreign exchange controls for some time to come. It is likely that Japan will incur deficits in its merchandise trade account in the immediate future in view of the many internal and external difficulties involved in Japan's export trade, already detailed in chapter VI. Additionally, Japan is faced with heavy obligations, such as reparations to Burma, the Philippines, Indonesia, Laos, Cambodia, and Viet-Nam; repayment of postwar aid extended by the United States; and payment of prewar bonded indebtedness and the substantial loans from the International Bank for Reconstruction and Development (IBRD) for expansion of electric power facilities and modernization and some expansion of steel production.

However, the Government's stated policy is that controls will be relaxed as soon as conditions permit. In the words of the Foreign Exchange and Foreign Trade Control Law, the provisions

---

[3] For selected sections of this law see appendix F.

of the law ". . . shall be reviewed with the objective of gradually relaxing and eliminating restrictions . . . ." Japan also has signified its intention in this direction by becoming a member of the International Monetary Fund and the General Agreements on Tariffs and Trade (GATT). The extent to which Japan will relax its restrictions is dependent primarily on its ability to increase exports sufficiently to pay for essential food, raw materials, and fuel imports.

Transactions Subject to Controls

Japan's exchange control laws and regulations are all-encompassing in scope. A system of licensing is in effect for all transactions, both domestic and foreign, which involve foreign exchange payments or receipts. All foreign exchange must be surrendered to the Government and maintained in special accounts under Government control. The Minister of Finance administers the Government foreign currency accounts but the actual management and operation are delegated to the Bank of Japan, which acts as the agent of the Minister of Finance.

To facilitate the operation of Japan's foreign trade and foreign exchange control system, the Government has authorized various Japanese and foreign commercial banks to hold and deal in foreign currencies.[4] The 12 Japanese and 13 foreign banks listed below have been authorized as class "A" foreign exchange banks and as such are permitted to purchase, sell, or issue foreign means of payment; accept requests for payment or collection from foreign countries; and engage in other customary banking procedures incident thereto.

Japanese Banks
Dai-ichi Bank, Ltd.
Daiwa Bank, Ltd.
Fuji Bank, Ltd.
Industrial Bank of Japan, Ltd.
Bank of Kobe, Ltd.
Mitsubishi Bank, Ltd.
Nippon Kangyo Bank, Ltd.
Sanwa Bank, Ltd.
Sumitomo Bank, Ltd.
Teikoku Bank, Ltd.
Tokai Bank, Ltd.
Bank of Tokyo, Ltd.

Foreign Banks
American Express Co., Inc.[1]
Bank of America National Trust and Savings Association.[2]
Bank of China
Bank of India, Ltd.
Banque de l'Indochine

Chartered Bank of India, Australia & China
Chase Manhattan Bank, New York [3]
Hong Kong & Shanghai Banking Corp.
Bank of Korea
Mercantile Bank of India, Ltd.
First National City Bank of New York [4]
Nationale Handelsbank, N. V.
Nederlandsche Handel-Maatschappij, N. V.

---
[1] Branch in Tokyo.
[2] Branch offices in Tokyo, Yokohama, Kobe, and Osaka.
[3] Branch offices in Tokyo and Osaka.
[4] Branch offices in Tokyo, Yokohama, Osaka, and Nagoya.

There are also 21 class "B" Japanese foreign exchange banks. These banks, which are listed below, have received limited authorization from the Ministry of Finance to engage only in purchasing and selling foreign exchange and processing exchange transactions through class "A" banks.

Bank of Yamaguchi, Ltd.
Eighteenth Bank, Ltd.
Fukuoka Bank, Ltd.
Hokkaido Colonel Bank, Ltd. 4
Hokuriku Bank, Ltd.
Hyakugo Bank, Ltd.
Hyuga Kogyo Bank, Ltd.
Kagoshima Kogyo Bank, Ltd.
Kyowa Bank, Ltd.
Long Term Credit Bank of Japan
Mitsubishi Trust Bank, Ltd.

Mitsui Trust Bank, Ltd.
Nippon Trust Bank, Ltd.
Saitama Bank, Ltd.
Shiga Bank, Ltd.
Shinwa Bank, Ltd.
Shizuoka Bank, Ltd.
Sixteenth Bank, Ltd.
Sumitomo Trust Bank, Ltd.
Yasuda Trust Bank, Ltd.
Yokohama Koshin Bank, Ltd.

The official exchange rate for the yen is Y360 to one United States dollar. This rate applies to export, import, and all other foreign exchange transactions by the Government. Cross rates with other designated currencies, as well as buying and selling rates, also are set by the Government.

The Foreign Exchange Budget

The Japanese Government makes foreign exchange allocations for all transactions on the basis of special exchange budgets prepared semiannually. The foreign exchange budget is an estimate by the Government of receipts and payments of foreign currency from visible and invisible transactions. On the basis of this budget an import program is determined and exchange set aside for various commitments during the period, including remittances of profits and dividends on investments, interest on loans, and repatriation of foreign capital.

Remittances and Repatriation of Capital

As will be noted in the section dealing with the Foreign Investment Law, approved investments carry the right of remittances in foreign currency (see chapter VIII). It is important to note, however, that there is no provision in the Foreign Investment Law or any other Japanese law which automatically guarantees remittances. As a matter of fact, both the Foreign Investment Law (article 15, see appendix C) and the Foreign Exchange and Foreign Trade Control Law (article 27, see appendix F) specifically provide that prior approval must be obtained from the Japanese Government. It is essential, therefore, that the investor specify in the investment application whether remittances are desired, an estimate of the amount involved, the period covered, and other pertinent information. In validating the application, the Government stipulates the conditions upon which approval is based and these conditions are binding.

Under existing controls, no guaranty of remittances in foreign exchange is given to firms which made investments prior to the enactment of the Foreign Investment Law or to those for which

---
[4] The only currencies authorized by the Japanese Government's Ministry of Finance for international transactions are United States dollars, United Kingdom pounds sterling, Canadian dollars, Swiss francs, and, to a limited degree, German marks.

validation has not been obtained under the Foreign Investment Law. There is no general rule in effect covering remittability for those not covered by the Foreign Investment Law. Such firms must make application to the Ministry of Finance, which renders decisions on a case-by-case basis and whose general practice has been to allow only a portion, normally not more than 50 percent.

Similarly no provision is made under the Foreign Investment Law for remittances of profits of branch offices of foreign firms. Applications for such privileges also must be made on a case-by-case basis to the Ministry of Finance.

Withdrawal of capital of nonvalidated investments is not guaranteed but may be permitted under the Foreign Exchange and Foreign Trade Control Law upon application to the Ministry of Finance.

Invisibles

Individual licenses are required for invisible transactions involving foreign exchange, e. g., payment for freight, insurance, agent's commission, claims, and other matters connected with merchandise trade transactions, and for travel by Japanese on foreign carriers. The general practice of the Japanese Government has been to approve freely payments for various incidental costs involving authorized imports and exports. However, there have been some scattered reports that Government officials, particularly at the operation level, have attempted to influence businessmen to shift business from foreign companies to Japanese firms. There is evidence that this practice has been frowned on by policymaking officials of the Government.

CHAPTER VIII

Business Policy and Foreign Investment

Most business activities in Japan are privately owned and managed. Outstanding exceptions are salt, camphor, and tobacco manufacture, which have been Government monopolies for about 50 years, and alcohol production, which has been completely monopolized by the Government since 1937. In addition, the major portion of the railway system is owned and operated by the Government, which is also a competitor in the electric power field, a Government corporation having been established in 1953 to construct and operate electric power facilities and sell electric power. Quasi-governmental corporations compete with private business in radio and television broadcasting. Telephone and telegraph communications have traditionally been publicly owned and operated.

The Japanese Government has permitted foreign technological assistance arrangements and loans in these fields, but it is unlikely that foreigners will be allowed to obtain equity. Moreover, in accordance with provisions of the Treaty of Friendship, Commerce and Navigation between Japan and the United States, Japan has the right to limit the extent to which Americans may establish within its territory, or acquire interest in, public utilities, shipbuilding, air or water transport, or banking involving depository or trust functions, or the exploitation of land or natural resources.

There has been no indication recently that the Japanese Government proposes to establish and operate industrial plants in competition with private industry or to nationalize or expropriate existing facilities now under private ownership and management. Possibly, it may do so in the future, but safeguards are provided in the Japanese Constitution (see chapter II), the Foreign Investment Law, and the aforementioned treaty between Japan and the United States for compensation in the event of nationalization or expropriation (see sections following for discussion of the relevant provisions of the Foreign Investment Law and the treaty and see the text of the applicable sections thereof in appendixes C and E).

In view of the history of industrialism in Japan [1] and the extreme shortage of capital, it would not be surprising if the Government were to assist private industry more actively. In recent years Government assistance has been largely of an indirect nature, such as loans and preferential allocations of foreign exchange. However, such assistance could also take the form of outright subsidies and quasi-governmental corporations in which the Government would contribute a substantial portion of the capital—the methods used in the early days of Japan's industrialization and during the period of industrial expansion of the 1930's.

LICENSING AND REGISTRATION

Japanese law requires that all foreign nationals who desire to engage in business in Japan must obtain a license and register with the Government agency having jurisdiction over the particular business activity. For example, an insurance company must obtain a license from the Ministry of Finance, a producer or dealer in pharmaceuticals from the Ministry of Welfare, and an airline from the Ministry of Transportation. Under the provisions of the commercial code, trading firms engaged in general export-import business must be registered in the commercial register maintained in the city or prefecture in which the business is located.

Registration in no way obligates the Japanese Government to permit the remittance of profits, dividends, or other earnings or the repatriation of capital invested; only investments approved under the provisions of the Foreign Investment Law carry such rights.

THE FOREIGN INVESTMENT LAW

Japan's Foreign Investment Law was enacted on May 10, 1950 [2] (effective June 9, 1950). Its stated objective is to create "a sound basis for

[1] Authorities in general agree that much of Japan's industrial complex owes its existence to the stimulus given by the Japanese Government. In the past, once an enterprise became successful it was released to private ownership, generally to favored groups, such as the old Zaibatsu (see chapter X).
[2] Law No. 163 of 1950; this law has been amended six times, the latest amendment being in April 1954. Pertinent portions of the law, including the 1954 amendment, are given in appendix C.

foreign investment in Japan, by limiting the induction of foreign investment to that which will contribute to the self-support and sound development of the Japanese economy and to the improvement of the balance of international payments, by providing for remittances arising from foreign investment, and by providing for adequate protection for such investment."

If an investor meets the stipulated criteria and receives approval of the appropriate governmental authorities, then assurance is given for (1) remittance of dividends, profits, royalties, or other earnings; (2) repatriation of capital; and (3) protection of capital. Such assurance removes important elements of uncertainty regarding the future position of an approved investment. If an investment is not approved under the terms of the Foreign Investment Law, applications are subject to the uncertainties of case-by-case handling by the Ministry of Finance.

The Foreign Investment Law applies only to investments in Japanese corporations and covers the following types: (1) Technological assistance contracts; (2) purchases of stocks, bonds, and investment trust certificates; and (3) acquisition of debentures or claimable assets arising from loans.

The Foreign Investment Law does not cover branches of foreign corporations or investment in Japanese unincorporated businesses. It is expected, however, that the law will be amended to bring it into conformity with provisions of the Treaty of Friendship, Commerce and Navigation between Japan and the United States, which makes no distinction as regards types of business organizations that may be established.

The standards, or criteria, of validation for the investment of foreign capital carrying remittance rights are set forth in article 8 of the Foreign Investment Law. There are both positive and negative criteria. The positive criteria are the proposed investment's contribution, directly or indirectly, to the improvement of the balance of international payments [3] or to the development of essential industries or public enterprises, and the necessity for the continuation or modification of existing technological assistance contracts in essential industries or public enterprises.

The following negative standards are used, i. e., validation shall be denied, (1) in the event the provisions of the contract are unfair or contravene existing laws or regulations; (2) where contracts are entered into or altered because of fraud, duress, or undue influence; (3) where arrangements are deemed to have an adverse effect on the economy; and (4) where the intended acquisition of stocks, investment certificates, debentures, or other claimable assets resulting from a proposed loan is not made through the conversion of foreign currency

in accordance with applicable foreign exchange control laws and regulations or its equivalent.[4]

The technical administration of the law is the responsibility of the Foreign Investment Section, Foreign Exchange Bureau, Ministry of Finance and its counterpart in the Bank of Japan. However, the competent Minister [5] or the Minister of Finance is authorized to grant validation after consulting with the Foreign Investment Council, an advisory body established in the Ministry of Finance. This Council is composed of representatives from the various Government agencies, including the Ministries of International Trade and Industry (MITI), Agriculture and Forestry, Welfare, Transportation and Communication, and Foreign Affairs, and the Bank of Japan, Economic Counsel Board, Fair Trade Commission, and several representatives of the public. In actual practice investors have learned that, as is true in most matters of governmental administration in Japan, the technical officials wield a considerable amount of influence.

Types of Investment

Technical assistance contracts.—Technical assistance contracts are defined in the law to include licensing and other types of arrangements involving the transfer of industrial property rights; extension of technical assistance in various forms, including industrial and other types of management techniques; and such other arrangements as may be designated by an appropriate agency of the Government. For the guidance of Japanese companies and foreign investors, the Japanese Government, since the enactment of the law in 1950, has published from time to time lists of technologies in which investment is preferred.[6]

To illustrate the kinds of technologies included in such lists, the most recent of these announcements (issued in June 1955) is given in full in appendix G. This list differs from earlier lists in that in contains considerably fewer categories—an indication that the authorities consider that Japan has caught up in certain fields, at least to a level where special encouragement can no longer be justified in relation to other claims on Japan's foreign exchange assets.

According to some investors, another reason is the growing fear of competition. They contend that many Japanese Government officials and businessmen are fearful of the economic disadvantage to competing firms in many industries resulting from collaboration of one or more Japanese firms with a foreign company.

---

[3] This standard shall be given preference

[4] Article 8-2(4) of the law fully explains what are considered equivalents (see appendix C).
[5] This is dependent on the particular field in which the proposed investment is classified, e. g., for most industrial manufacturing it is the Minister of the MITI; for pharmaceuticals and drugs, the Minister of Welfare; and for food products, the Minister of Agriculture and Forestry.
[6] Seventeen such announcements have been made during the period May 1950-June 1955.

Many Japanese business and Government officials regard both the domestic and international markets as static, and believe that the entry of more competitors, particularly foreigners, in the field would result in less business for all. There is a fairly widespread belief that the foreigner with his more advanced technology and his scientific management techniques and skills would (1) cause the downfall of some companies (particularly the smaller ones), (2) obtain control of certain industries, and (3) increase the unemployment problem. This latter view is one of the basic reasons for the resistance of labor unions to the introduction of foreign capital.

During the past few years there has been a rather active demand in Japan for technological assistance from abroad, particularly from the United States, and many foreign companies have found it profitable to extend such assistance under the guaranties provided by the Foreign Investment Law. According to the Japanese Government, since May 1950, when the law became effective, through December 1954, 431 technical assistance contracts at an estimated total capitalized value of $293 million [7] have been approved. United States firms were participants in 307 or 71 percent of the contracts and represent 62.1 percent of the capitalized value, $181.9 million of a total of $292.9 million.[8]

A listing of the contracts, including name and nationality of the foreign company, a brief statement of the nature of the technology, the Japanese company involved, and the time period covered by each contract, is included as table XIV of appendix A.

These technological assistance agreements have been a principal vehicle in the postwar period by which Japan has raised its technical status to the present level. Consequently, it may be anticipated that Japan will continue to encourage investments involving certain types of technical know-how, particularly the licensing of patent rights which would make available to Japanese manufacturers the latest industrial techniques. The degree of encouragement undoubtedly will vary with the particular technology and the specific terms. There is increasing evidence that the Government will look more favorably on short-term arrangements and interpret more rigidly the Foreign Investment Law. Some Japanese and foreign businessmen are of the opinion that the sharp decline in the number of technical assistance contracts approved in 1954 (86) compared with 1953 (142) reflects in part a more conservative interpretation by Government officials.

Purchase of stocks, bonds, and investment certificates.—In general, purchases of stocks, bonds, or investment trust certificates require prior approval

[7] It is understood that calculation was made on the basis of an average royalty rate of 5 percent and the individual tenure of the contracts approved by the Japanese Government.
[8] See table X of appendix A.

by the Ministry of Finance if subsequent remittance of income or principal is desired. A distinction is made between the purchase of outstanding (old stock) and new stock, as well as between payment in Japanese currency (yen domestically acquired) and foreign currency (yen acquired from conversion of foreign exchange). Old stocks are defined as stocks the acquisition of which does not add to the assets of the company concerned. Purchases of old stock with yen domestically acquired generally are prohibited; an exception is the reinvestment of yen proceeds from the sale of stock originally purchased after validation under the Foreign Investment Law or of dividends therefrom.

Under terms of the Treaty of Friendship, Commerce and Navigation, the Japanese Government will continue until October 30, 1956, to apply existing restrictions on the purchase by Americans, with yen domestically acquired, of old stock in Japanese corporations. Purchase of old stock with foreign currency is permitted in principal but the procedure is cumbersome and time-consuming if the amount of the purchase exceeds 5 percent of the outstanding stock, all such purchases requiring the approval of the Foreign Investment Council, the Ministry of Finance, and the Bank of Japan. The yen used for purchase of stock must have been acquired in accordance with applicable regulations—for an American investor this means by the conversion of United States dollars.

New stock may be purchased with yen, with or without prior validation, but remittance guaranty is granted only with validation. A report of unvalidated purchases must be filed subsequently with the Ministry of Finance.

Approval of a stock purchase, whether outstanding or new stock, carries conversion rights of a portion of the yen proceeds of the investment and remittance of such proceeds. The conversion right is for a maximum of 20 percent per year, with a deferment period of 2 years during which no remittance may be made. Unremitted funds must be deposited in a special foreign investor's account in one of the foreign exchange banks.

Regulations concerning the purchase of bonds are similar to those for new stocks. If purchases are made with yen, no guaranty of remittance is granted; if purchases are made with foreign currency and validated by the Ministry of Finance, repatriation of interest and principal at maturity of the bonds is guaranteed, regardless of the date of acquisition.

Regulations concerning the purchase of investment trust certificates also are similar to those for new stocks. If investment trust certificates are acquired with yen, remittance of dividends is not guaranteed, but if purchased with foreign currency and validated by the Ministry of Finance, a guaranty is given for remittance of all dividends and the principal, not exceeding

63

20 percent annually, after 2 years. In Japan the life of an investment trust certificate customarily is 2 years.

Stocks, bonds, and other properties may be acquired also by payment in kind, for example, for the use of patents or other technical assistance, or in exchange for machinery or raw materials furnished by the foreign investor.

Acquisition of stock in Japanese companies by foreign investors has occurred largely through technical assistance contracts and has usually resulted in participation in management. From mid-1950 (the effective date of the Foreign Investment Law) through December 30, 1954, such investments amounted to $34.3 million, of which about 70 percent involved participation in management. However, there have been few instances where the extent of foreign ownership was more than 50 percent or the stock controlled by foreigners equaled 50 percent.

The Japanese Government seemingly has adopted an unwritten rule to limit the number of investment arrangements which involve majority ownership and/or control. Some observers of the investment scene maintain that this is a long-standing and basic attitude of the Japanese, and they believe that the Government will be more restrictive toward such investments in the future.

Since the opening of Japan to trade with the West, the Japanese have recognized the importance of foreign assistance in developing the country, but for the most part they have favored indirect aid, such as technical assistance, sale of Government bonds abroad, and debentures of private or semipublic corporations subscribed to or underwritten by foreign banks or investment houses. By these means the Japanese Government was able to channel foreign assistance in accordance with its predetermined national policy, which involved a strong determination to introduce modern industrialism and an equally strong resolve to maintain control in Japanese hands. The Japanese long have had an inherent fear that participation by foreigners in the management of their business enterprises would result in control of their economy and create a wedge for interference by foreigners in the political life of the nation.

Many Japanese feel that, by their own hard work and frugalness, plus indirect investment from abroad, they transformed their country from a feudal agricultural state to the major industrial power in Asia in less than a century. The Japanese take great pride in the fact that they have scrupulously honored their prewar bonded indebtedness. In this connection, it may be noted that on December 22, 1952, Japan resumed service on $430 million of prewar indebtedness to United States and British bondholders on original contractual terms, including all past-due interest, subject only to an extension of maturity date.

Loans.—Loans by foreign nationals which involve the right to claim assets of a Japanese juridical person require approval by the Ministry of Finance. Since the inception of the Foreign Investment Law (May 1950) through December 1954, private loans have aggregated $61 million. Of this total $27 million, or 44 percent, was extended to the petroleum industry. The next largest recipients were the electric power and transportation industries, which received loans of $10 million each, and the construction industry, which obtained a $9-million loan. Several of the loans have been made in connection with technological assistance contracts to cover importation of specialized machinery and equipment.

In addition to these private loans, a $40.2-million loan from the International Bank for Reconstruction and Development (IBRD) was extended to the Japan Development Bank, in accordance with the provisions of the Foreign Investment Law, on behalf of the three major electric power companies, to be used for expansion of electric power capacity. In October 1955, the IBRD, with participation by the Manufacturers Trust Company of New York, made a $5.3-million loan to the Japan Development Bank for relending to the Yawata Iron and Steel Company for modernization and some expansion of the company's steel-plate-rolling facilities.

Also, under U. S. Public Law 480 of the 83d Congress, $59.5 million of yen payments accruing from sales to Japan of United States surplus agricultural commodities in United States fiscal year 1955 will be loaned to the Japanese Government for purposes of economic development. According to an agreement between the United States and Japanese Governments, the loan in principle will be a dollar loan for 40 years with a 3-year moratorium on both interest and principal. Japan indicated its intention of repaying the loan in dollars, but under the terms of the agreement it reserved the right, for balance-of-payments considerations, to make periodic payments in dollars or yen. Both parties agreed that if payments are made in dollars the interest rate will be 3 percent; if in yen, the rate will be 4 percent.

Table XII, appendix A, provides a breakdown of the foreign loans obtained through 1954, by industry and by country, except the loan made pursuant to Public Law 480.

Remittances; Repatriation of Capital

Establishing a business in Japan, irrespective of the type (wholly owned subsidiary, joint Japanese-foreign firm, etc.), does not carry a guaranty of the remittance of profits, dividends, or any other earnings, or the repatriation of capital. According to current Japanese laws and regulations, such a guaranty can be obtained only under the provisions of the Foreign Investment Law, i. e., the particular investment plan or arrangement must have Government approval, and at present the Foreign Investment Law applies only to foreign investment in Japanese corporations.

Once a guaranty is obtained there is only one major limitation on the investor's freedom of action—repatriation of capital is permissible only after an investment has been held for 2 years, at the rate of 20 percent per year. The Japanese Government believes this restriction is necessary to protect Japan's foreign exchange assets, but investors consider it one of the deterrents to the flow of investment.

As already indicated, the Foreign Investment Law does not apply to branches of foreign corporations, individual proprietorships, and partnerships. Such enterprises must apply for remittance on a case-by-case basis to the Ministry of Finance. Approval by that Ministry is required also for reinvestment of nonremittable yen profits in industries other than those in which the original investment was made and for remittance of yen from prewar investments owned by companies or individuals whose prewar investments are not covered by the Foreign Investment Law.

Yen payments made to exchange nonresidents may be used for a limited number of purchases. In specific instances, such yen has been licensed for use in payment of taxes, for personal living expenses of employees of firms holding nonconvertible yen, and for the purchase of real estate. Dividends received must be remitted or reinvested within 3 months after their receipt. If the investor wishes to change his holding from one stock to another, Government approval again must be obtained. This does not involve sacrifice of the convertibility right, but the deferment period begins as of the date the changeover is approved.

Applications for Investment

Technical assistance.—Application for validation of technoligical assistance contracts must be made jointly by the foreign investor and the Japanese firm. Two copies of the application in Japanese must be submitted together with two copies of the contractual agreement, one copy of which must be in Japanese and the other in English. A facsimile of the application for validation of a technical assistance contract as published by the Japanese Government is included in appendix D. Applications are filed with the Foreign Exchange Control Section of the Bank of Japan.

The application for validation of a technological assistance contract must contain the following information, including signatures of the applicants: Name, address, nationality, and occupation of the contracting parties; description of the technological assistance to be provided; period of contract, amount and kind of compensation, and method of payment; benefits to the foreign investor and the Japanese economy, with special reference to expected increase in Japan's export earnings and improvement in balance of payments. The technologies included in the list of desired techniques, as set forth in appendix G, will be given preference, with more favorable consideration likely to be given to proposals offering the shortest term arrangements.

A certificate issued by a consul, a notary public, or other person of similar authority must be attached to the application authenticating the signature and nationality of the foreign investor. If the application is filed by an agent, a power of attorney must be attached to indicate the specific authority of the agent.[9]

Information furnished in technical assistance contracts must include a detailed description of the license or agreement covering the technical assistance to be granted, with particular reference to any patent rights involved, and the method of supplying the assistance (blueprints, technical personnel, inspection of manufacturing and research facilities, etc.).

Provisions may be made for the exchange of information relating to discoveries or new developments in the products or processes covered by the technical assistance Conditions should be stipulated in the contract governing sale of products manufactured by the techniques supplied, including any restrictions imposed on sales areas or the export of products. Some contracts state whether or not the licensor may grant the same license or technical assistance to persons other than the licensee residing in the same area. In some instances the licensee is authorized to grant sublicenses.

The duration of a contract may or may not be specified. Ten to 15 years has been the usual duration. License agreements usually are limited to a maximum of 15 years and are renewable if approved by the Japanese Government once only for a period not exceeding 10 years or not less than 3 years. These limitations are based upon the Japanese law. Many contracts stipulate that notification must be given over a stated period before the contract can be terminated. Provision for arbitration of disputes is sometimes made.

Various methods are used for computing royalties. Royalties may be based on a percentage of sales, and the percentage may remain fixed regardless of volume of sales, it may increase or decrease on an annual basis, or it may vary with change in volume of sales. They may be a fixed sum payable in a single payment or in fixed

---

[9] This is important since in some cases processing has been delayed owing to refusal of Japanese Government authorities to honor the right of agents to act on certain matters, particularly when revisions in the original application were involved, bcause the power of attorney did not specify such authority.

monthly or annual payments; or, they may be a percentage of profits.

Nearly all of the early contracts stipulated that the Japanese tax on royalties should be borne by the licensee. However, the Ministry of Finance has ruled that the licensor should bear the full tax in Japan when, as in the United States, he is granted tax exemption under the laws of his own country for taxes which he has paid abroad.

Licensors may agree to transfer trademark rights, in which case the licensor could not, under the Japanese Trademark Law, sell products bearing the same trademark in Japan.

Purchase of stocks, bonds, and investment trust certificates.—Application for validation of purchases of stocks, bonds, and investment trust certificates must be made in duplicate in the Japanese language. Applications must contain— in addition to name, address, nationality, and occupation of the foreign investor and Japanese investee—information concerning the company issuing the stocks or bonds, number and face value of the stocks or bonds, expected benefit to the issuing company, amount and kind of remittance desired, and other details relevant to the transaction.

As in the case of technological assistance, the Bank of Japan acts as deputy organ of the Ministry of Finance and accepts applications for validation of foreign purchases of stocks, bonds, or investment trust certificates. The Bank of Japan is authorized to process, at its own discretion, applications for purchases of stock, either through the securities exchange or outside the stock market, provided the stocks held by foreigners do not exceed 5 percent of the total stocks of the company in question; all others require prior approval of the Ministry of Finance.

Loans.—All loans resulting in acquisition of claimable assets require approval by the Ministry of Finance. The foreign investor who desires to obtain a guaranty of remittance must file two copies, in Japanese, of the application for validation, with copies of the loan contract between the Japanese and foreign firms attached.

TREATIES AND AGREEMENTS

Under the terms of the peace treaty, Japan signified its intention to enter into negotiations for the conclusion of commercial treaties with each of the Allied Powers and, pending the conclusion of such treaties, to extend national and most-favored-nation treatment to the extent that other countries reciprocate. The United States and Japan operated on this basis even before the peace treaty and the United States was the first country in the postwar period to enter into negotiations for the conclusion of a bilateral commercial treaty.

In addition to the Treaty of Friendship, Commerce and Navigation, the United States and Japan have entered into two agreements having a direct bearing on investment. These are (1) the Investment Guaranty Agreement (signed March 8, 1954) and (2) the Convention for the Avoidance of Double Taxation. The latter is discussed in the section dealing with taxation and that part of the Treaty of Friendship, Commerce and Navigation relating to employment is summarized briefly in chapter XI. The discussion which follows treats other important aspects of the Treaty of Friendship, Commerce and Navigation and summarizes the Investment Guaranty Agreement.

The FCN Treaty

This treaty provides for national and most-favored-nation treatment with respect to investment and the conduct of business in Japan by United States nationals, with the reservation that both countries may restrict investment in public utilities, shipbuilding, air and water transport, or banking involving depository or judiciary functions, or the exploitation of land or other natural resources.[10] This reservation is subject to the limitation that no new restrictions may be applied against enterprises already engaged in those activities at the time new limitations are adopted.

National and most-favored-nation treatment is granted with respect to the acquisition of property in Japan by United States nationals. Property of United States nationals in Japan may not be expropriated except for a public purpose, and just and effective compensation shall be made in dollars. In this connection, it should be noted that the Foreign Investment Law provides a guaranty of prompt remittances in the event of expropriation or compulsory purchase of property legally owned in Japan by a foreign investor, but it makes no provision as regards the adequacy of the payment. Moreover, article III also provides that reasonable provision be made for earnings on, and amortization of, investments in Japan by United States citizens.

The Treaty of Friendship, Commerce and Navigation recognizes one other qualification as modifying Japan's obligation to grant national and most-favored-nation treatment. This qualification is that either party may impose such restrictions on the entry of foreign capital as may be necessary to protect its monetary reserves.[11]

Exchange restrictions may be imposed only to prevent monetary reserves from declining to a very low level or to effect a moderate increase in exchange reserves. Should either country adopt such restrictions, the treaty provides that, after adequate exchange is made available for

---

[10] Article 7, paragraph 2. See appendix E.
[11] Paragraph 6 of the Protocol to the treaty, which is included in appendix E.

goods and services essential to the health and welfare of the people, reasonable provision shall be made for payment in foreign exchange of profits, interest, dividends, royalties, capital transfers, and similar payments.[12] The treaty also specifically provides that "exchange restrictions shall not be imposed by either Party in a manner unnecessarily detrimental or arbitrarily discriminatory to the claims, investments, trans-. port, trade, and other interests of the nationals and companies of the other Party, nor to the competitive position thereof."[13]

The aforementioned restrictions on the entry of capital included in the treaty formalized the treatment which foreign capital had been receiving since June 1950 when the Foreign Investment Law went into effect, and gave official recognition to the Japanese position that for some time Japan would find it necessary to impose exchange controls, particularly on capital transactions.

No other restrictions on the entry of capital are recognized in the treaty. According to the treaty provisions, United States nationals may organize wholly owned or joint companies under the commercial code of Japan and have the right to acquire majority interests in Japanese companies. The generally negative reception with which such requests have been received by Japanese Government officials has raised doubts as to whether there may be a conflict between the treaty provisions and the administration of the foreign investment program in Japan.

Japanese Government officials apparently do not agree that a conflict exists, since in their opinion, Japan imposes no restrictions as long as a guaranty is not requested. They contend that there is a clear distinction between the right to

invest and the guaranty of remittance and repatriation of capital as provided under the Foreign Investment Law, and that only in the latter case does the Government employ other qualifications in addition to balance of payments on the entry of capital.

Investment Guaranty Agreement

Pursuant to the provisions of section III (b) (3) of the Economic Cooperation Act of 1948, as amended, on March 8, 1954, the United States and Japan signed an agreement by which new private investment in Japan by United States nationals may be guaranteed against expropriation and inconvertibility of profits and capital. One provision of this agreement is that both parties upon the request of either Government will consult on projects in Japan proposed by United States citizens on which guaranties are under consideration or have been made.

As the result of an exchange of notes subsequent to the signing of the agreement, it is understood by both parties that specific approval by the Japanese Government of each investment to be guaranteed by the United States Government is required before the United States Government extends any guaranty. Moreover, "it is further understood that guaranties against inconvertibility covering investments qualifying under the Foreign Investment Law and the Foreign Exchange and Foreign Trade Control Law will be drawn with the intention of creating claims by guaranteed investors against the United States only upon presentation of evidence of refusal by the Japanese Government of applications for conversion of yen amounts which are eligible for conversion under the terms and conditions of the aforesaid laws."

---

[12] Article XII, paragraph 3, ibid.
[13] Article XII, paragraph 4, ibid.

CHAPTER IX

Taxation

In 1940, substantial revisions were made in the Japanese tax system whereby the income tax came to play a major role in total tax revenue in Japan. Since the end of World War II, further refinements have been made in the tax laws. Changes, not only in the basic laws but also in their administration, continue to be made periodically. There is no well-established, authoritative body of official rulings or procedures governing the administration of the tax system. Consequently it is not uncommon for the tax liability, particularly of individuals, to be determined on the basis of individual decisions of tax officials.

In general, foreign nationals—both individuals and business enterprises—are subject to the same national and local government taxation as is imposed upon Japanese nationals, with the exception that certain temporary measures (which are indicated in this chapter) provide special tax privileges for foreign nationals.

Some American investors and prospective investors consider that corporate and noncorporate taxes are a deterrent to foreign investment in Japan, particularly if the business is the family corporation type of organization. Others do not believe that these taxes have been a real deterrent, but agree that they may become so if tax officials persist in requiring voluminous information, adhering very strictly to the letter of the law, and—in the absence of a body of administrative rulings—making arbitrary decisions which tend to increase the possibilities for protracted negotiations and ultimately the total tax burden.

For example, they report that tax officials increasingly are requiring the submission of home office financial data, including balance sheets and profit-and-loss statements of the entire operations of the foreign company of which the Japan branch is a unit and that, in some instances, certified statements have been requested.

American firms also report that they must give much closer attention to the organization of their accounts in Japan than is necessary in the United States, because of the highly complex nature of the Japanese tax law and administrative practices. They find this to be particularly important with respect to calculating depreciation in Japan since the prescribed standards for this operation in Japan may differ from the procedure they follow in the United States.

CORPORATION TAXES

Under the current Corporation Tax Law and regulations, Japanese (domestic) corporations [1] are subject to taxes on all income earned or received. Foreign corporations [2] and branches are liable for Japanese taxes only on income accruing from business done or assets held in Japan, and such income is subject to taxation irrespective of where it is actually received. However, income of foreign corporations earned from activities outside of Japan or assets held in other countries are not subject to Japanese taxation. Consequently, in practice, the major elements involved in a determination of the tax status of a non-Japanese (foreign) corporation are whether assets are owned or business is conducted in Japan, and the level of income accruing from the ownership of such assets and conduct of business activities as well as the amount of expenses which can be deducted from such income.

There is no precise definition in Japanese tax laws and regulations as to what constitutes doing business in Japan. Considerable discretion is left to the tax administration officials, who frequently require submission of voluminous information and spend much time in negotiations.

American and other foreign enterprises have found that in actual administration a foreign corporation is not considered to be doing business in Japan when employees make infrequent visits merely to investigate business opportunities, or when it sells goods to Japanese importers or maintains an independent agent in Japan. However, the establishment of a branch office by an American company, the stationing in Japan of one or more full-time employees on a semipermanent or permanent basis, or the importation and sale of goods in Japan in contradistinction to the export of goods by the home office of the American company to a Japanese or foreign company or to an independent agent are considered as positive presumptions of "doing business in Japan."

Foreign investors also have found that the place where the income was received is not a particularly relevant factor in the determination of

[1] A domestic corporation is defined as one which has its head office or principal place of business in Japan.
[2] The Corporation Tax Law defines a foreign corporation as one "not having its head office or principal place of business within the enforcement area of this law but having its assets or business within the enforcement area . . . ."

income subject to taxation. When a foreign corporation has income from more than one source, Japanese officials frequently try to make a determination of the company's total income in order to decide what portion would be allocated for taxation purposes in Japan. This same procedure is frequently used when the foreign corporation deducts expenses from income.

American businessmen claim that in general the objective of the tax collector is to subject to taxation the largest possible portion of income and keep at a minimum permissible deductions from such income. They report that apparently foreigners' tax returns are investigated by special foreign taxation officials of the Japanese Government, and that foreigners often are required to appear for several personal conferences, submit detailed information, and engage in protracted negotiations. Theoretically, Japanese taxpayers are also subject to investigation, but this is said to be done on the basis of statistical sampling. Consequently, Americans and other foreign investors are of the opinion that they do not receive the liberal treatment with respect to deductions that is accorded to Japanese corporations.

American investors also state that it is customary for Japanese corporations to take full advantage of the formula provided under law to deduct the various emoluments extended to employees in lieu of cash wages. When American companies, and presumably other foreign firms, have considered it desirable and advantageous taxwise and for other reasons to provide employees with emoluments in lieu of cash wages, they have had difficulty in convincing tax officials that they should receive the same concessions that are given to Japanese nationals. For example, more and more American companies favor the practice of providing automobiles to their American employees without charge as an inducement to employment in Japan. No fixed policy has been adopted by tax officials concerning the acceptability of such an allowance as a deductible item for foreign taxpayers; rather, each case is subject to individual scrutiny and negotiation.

American businessmen feel that because of the nature of Japan's tax laws, a great deal of personal judgment on the part of tax officials is inevitable. Therefore, to assure a fair tax burden in Japan, American businessmen need to consider carefully the type of business organization and the other factors involved in order to keep to a minimum the possible area for personal judgment.

Taxes on Profits

The net profits of corporations are subject to three major taxes: (1) Corporation tax, (2) enterprise tax, and (3) inhabitants tax. The first is a national tax, the other two are local government taxes. The combined burden of these taxes on net profits, exclusive of taxes on income, is approximately 60 percent for the first year of business and between 52 and 58 percent (averaging about 54 percent) for the second and successive years, depending on the level of deductions of an individual company. The principal reason for the decrease of the tax burden after the first year is that the preceding year's enterprise tax is deductible as an allowable business expense in computing the corporation tax.

Corporation tax.—The corporation tax is a national levy on corporate profits. A flat rate of 35 percent is applied to net profits remaining after the deduction of authorized business expenses (including the enterprise tax paid in the preceding year) not exceeding 500,000 yen ($1,389), and 40 percent on amounts in excess of 500,000 yen. Japan does not have an excess profits tax. Unlike the corporate tax system in the United States, no preferred treatment is given to capital gains, which are taxed fully at the 35- or 40-percent rate. Ordinary, as well as capital, losses may be carried forward for 4 years and back for 1 year provided the corporation files its returns continuously over that period on a special form (known as "blue form") which entails the use of prescribed accounting methods. Reportedly, many of the American companies use this special form and, in general, have found it advantageous to do so.

Various exemptions and deductions are permitted in computing net profits subject to the corporation tax, the more important of which are depreciation of fixed assets, reserves for bad debts, and retirement allowances. When the special (blue) form is used, reserves for specified types of repairs and maintenance and inventory losses may be deducted. For calculating depreciation of fixed assets three types may be used, i. e., the straight line, declining balance, and product, the last named being applied only in mining. In some industries, such as certain utilities, the replacement method may be used in addition to the above three.

When a company acquires certain machinery and equipment, accelerated depreciation is sometimes allowable. Bad debt reserves, which may be used as a business expense, range from 0.7 to 2 percent of the total of accounts receivable, advances, and loans outstanding at the end of the period used for calculating the tax liability, or 20 percent of the company's adjusted net profit (35 percent in the case of banks and insurance companies), whichever is lower. When a corporation has actually transferred funds to a special retirement allowance account, a proportion of such transferred funds (established by a formula) may be deducted as a business expense in computing corporate income. Several methods are provided in the law for evaluating inventory and foreign investors have found it worthwhile to consider all of them thoroughly in order to obtain the largest possible deduction. Other, less important, allowances and deductions can result in moderate tax savings.

Careful study of the provisions and regulations of the Corporation Tax Law is essential because of their complexities, and many American businessmen have found it not only desirable but also necessary to seek the assistance of American tax attorneys and consultants, several of whom are practicing in Japan.

Enterprise tax.—This tax is levied and administered by the prefectures. It is levied on corporate net profits at the rate of 10 percent on the first 500,000 yen ($1,389) and 12 percent on all profits in excess of that amount. Thus, for all practical purposes, this tax, which in effect is the prefectural counterpart of the national corporation tax, amounts to a 12-percent levy on net profits (after deduction of allowable business expenses, including the amount of the enterprise tax paid in the preceding year).

Inhabitants tax.—This is a local levy assessed by prefectures and municipalities. For corporations, the prefectural tax is 600 yen ($1.67) on a per capita basis and a payment of 5 percent of the national corporation tax for the same year. The municipal tax on a per capita basis is 2,400 yen ($6.67) for corporations in cities with a population of 500,000 or more, 1,800 yen ($5) in cities with a population of 50,000 to 499,999, and 1,200 yen ($3.34) in cities with a population of less than 50,000. This tax is payable to each municipality in which an office or place of business is maintained. In addition, a charge of 7.5 percent of the national corporation tax for the same year is levied. In the city of Tokyo, for example, the combined inhabitants taxes are roughly 3,000 yen ($8.34) per capita, plus 12.5 percent of the national corporation tax.

When a corporation has offices in more than one jurisdiction, the accrued tax portion of the tax burden is distributed among the several municipalities roughly in proportion to the number of employees maintained by the company in each local jurisdiction. If a corporation finds that it does not earn net profits that are subject to the national corporation tax, only the per capita payment is required.

Miscellaneous Taxes

Various other taxes are assessed on corporations. The most important of these is the municipal property tax, which applies to all kinds of fixed assets, such as real estate, machinery, office furniture, fixtures, equipment (except automobiles), and other fixed assets used for business purposes. The tax rates range from 1.4 to 2.5 percent according to the municipality, with the standard being 1.4 percent of the asset's market value for the year.

Additional taxes include automobile, stamp, admission, bicycle, advertisement, and a host of others which are applicable to foreign as well as domestic corporations. However, American investors and others operating businesses in Japan have found that the average aggregate of these taxes does not add significantly to the costs of doing business.

Income Tax as Applicable to Corporations

Under certain circumstances the individual Income Tax Law is applicable to corporations. Since April 1, 1953, that law requires withholding at the source of 20 percent of payments of "royalties on industrial patent rights or other technological rights and special production formulas used in Japan by enterprises in Japan."

Dividends from securities or interest on loans or corporate debentures also are subject to the withholding tax under the Income Tax Law. Such payments to foreign corporations are subject to 10 percent withholding if the investment was approved by the Japanese Government (see chapter VIII). The 20-percent rate is applicable to foreign corporations on income from copyrights (including projection rights on films) and rentals and leases from real property and equipment.

In general, the withholding required under the Income Tax Law is applicable to foreign corporations. However, if the corporation or branch established in Japan is considered to be subject to the withholding tax and also has income from business activities or real property held in Japan which is subject to the Corporation Tax Law, the corporation or branch is required to aggregate all of its income in arriving at the amount of net income subject to taxation. The taxpayer is then given a tax credit for any taxes previously withheld under the Income Tax Law, except when income is derived from "dividends of profits or dividends during construction or distribution of surpluses, or profits from securities investment trust from a corporation having its head office or principal place of business within the enforcement area (Japan). . . ."[3]

Family Corporation Surcharge

The Corporation Tax Law embodies a special provision relating to so-called "family corporations."[4] This provision probably was included because of the importance in prewar years of this type of business organization in Japan and the

[3] Article 1, paragraph 2, item 4 of Income Tax Law.
[4] A family corporation is defined by Japanese law as a limited company in which stock ownership falls into any of the following categories: (1) The total of stocks of three stockholders or three partners or their relations is equal to 50 percent or more of all stock of the corporation, or of the entire amount invested in the corporation; (2) four stockholders or four relations and their relations own 60 percent or more; and (3) five stockholders or five partners and their relations own 70 percent or more.

advantageous position such businesses would have under the other provisions of the law. The family corporation provision, therefore, is designed to discourage the use of this type of business organization for the purpose of avoiding tax liability.

As applied to foreign corporations, the provisions governing family corporations are quite severe and result in the heaviest kind of tax burden. The tax authorities almost invariably have held that for tax purposes wholly owned subsidiaries and branches of foreign corporations fall under the category of family corporations.

In addition to the regular corporation tax rate, family corporations are subject to a special surcharge rate of 10 percent on current surplus if the total amount of retained surplus and accumulated reserves exceeds 25 percent of capital or 1 million yen (about $2,778), whichever is greater. The law states that this surcharge is applicable to a Japan branch of a foreign corporation and not to the reserves of the home corporation.

Under the law and enforcement regulations the tax authorities are provided with the legal authority to "make correction or determination without regard to the behavior or computation made by the family corporation in connection with its business, if such behavior or computation is considered likely to result in an improper reduction of corporation tax liability." Reports indicate that tax investigators customarily disallow all deductions of expenses on the arbitrary basis that the tax liability of a particular family corporation appears to be too low. Thus, from the standpoint of tax liability, many foreign businessmen are convinced that the family corporation type of organization is less advantageous than other types of business organizations.

NONCORPORATE BUSINESS TAXES

Noncorporate business profits are subject to payment of the income tax, the enterprise tax, and the inhabitants tax. Unlike corporate income, all income accruing to unincorporated businesses located in Japan is subject to Japanese taxes regardless of whether the income is from business transacted or assets held within or outside of Japan.

National Income Tax

The income tax is levied by the National Government on all net business profits, including commissions and professional fees accruing to unincorporated businesses located in Japan. The rates in late 1955 on annual taxable net income in yen (360 yen equal US$1) are as follows:

	Tax rate (percent)
Not more than 30,000	15
30,001 to 80,000	20
80,001 to 150,000	25
150,001 to 300,000	30
300,001 to 500,000	35
500,001 to 800,000	40
800,001 to 1,200,000	45
1,200,001 to 2,000,000	50
2,000,001 to 3,000,000	55
3,000,001 to 5,000,000	60
5,000,001 and higher	65

In computing the tax on a sliding-scale basis, each rate applies only to the portion of income falling within each income bracket. For example, assuming a net taxable income of 3.5 million yen, only the last 500,000 yen are taxed at the 60-percent rate. The previous 1 million yen in the amount is taxed at 55 percent and so on back, with the first 30,000 yen being taxed at 15 percent.

Local Government Taxes

Noncorporate business earnings are also subject to two local government taxes—the enterprise tax and the inhabitants tax.

The enterprise tax.—This tax is levied and administered by the prefectures. The rate on net profits of unincorporated businesses is 8 percent less 100,000 yen per annum. Professionals, such as attorneys, accountants, and similar technical persons, as well as physicians, dentists, midwives, masseurs, and similar practitioners, pay 6 percent less than 100,000 yen per annum.

The inhabitants tax.—This is levied by both the prefecture and the municipality in which the business has an office or maintains semipermanent or permanent employees. The municipal tax consists of a small per capita payment and a fixed rate on earned income. The maximum per capita payment is 600 yen in a city whose population exceeds 500,000. The prefectures and the municipalities divide the tax according to an agreed-upon proportion. In Tokyo and in most parts of the country the combined tax burden (municipal and prefectural) is 18 percent.

PERSONAL INCOME TAXATION

National Income Tax

For personal income tax purposes, foreigners in Japan fall into two general categories: (1) Nonresident taxpayers, or individuals who have been in Japan for less than 1 year and are subject to limited liability for taxes; and (2) resident taxpayers, or individuals who have been in Japan for 1 year or more and are subject to unlimited liability for taxes. Since the law is somewhat vague with respect to the terms of residence, foreigners often have found it difficult to determine the category in which they belong for income tax purposes, and it is not uncommon for the question of status to be a matter requiring the submission of various types of documentary evidence and considerable discussion and negotiation with tax officials.

Since April 1, 1952, nonresident taxpayers have been subject to a 20-percent tax on all salaries and wages earned in Japan regardless of whether they are paid in Japan or abroad. Prior to that date, nonresident taxpayers were liable for the 20-percent tax only on salaries actually paid to them in Japan. However, the Japanese Government recognized that this enabled foreigners in this category to avoid all Japanese personal income taxes. Nonresident taxpayers are not subject to taxes on any portion of income obtained from business or assets outside of Japan. No deductions are allowed for dependents, personal exemptions, or similar items.

The sliding-scale rates apply to income derived from property held or business done in Japan, including commissions and fees, and from interest, dividends, or royalty income obtained from sources within Japan, as on net profits of unincorporated businesses. The withholding rate on dividends is 10 percent; the dividend credit for an individual is 30 percent, based on the assumption that since the corporation already had paid a tax on the dividend the receiver of the dividend is entitled to claim credit for having paid a 30-percent tax on his dividend income.

In general, resident taxpayers are subject to taxes on all income from any source inside or outside of Japan. In theory, therefore, not only are salaries earned in Japan subject to full taxation, but also dividends from securities owned in the United States and income from real property. However, the Special Taxation Measures Law (law No. 61 of 1952), a revision of the earlier law of the same name, provided that salaries and wages earned in Japan but paid outside of Japan were exempt from taxation through December 31, 1955, the date on which this law expired. Under this special exemption provision, however, any portion of salaries or wages earned in Japan and paid outside of Japan but remitted back into Japan was taxed on the same basis as income actually paid in Japan.

To provide the tax collection authorities with a measure for ascertaining the amount of income on which the income tax should be levied, the law provided that the Minister of Finance designate as taxable income an amount which was judged to be the living expenses of the person taxed, with the upper limit the actual income received both in Japan and abroad.

A second feature of this same law allowed certain resident taxpayers a special deduction of 50 percent of their taxable salary income since January 1, 1952. This special exemption had been accorded only to specified classes of foreigners engaged in certain designated activities or employed by certain designated corporations. It was put into effect to encourage foreign investment in Japan and to assist in the development and improvement of industrial techniques.

The foreigners who were eligible for the special 50-percent exemption were: (1) Persons employed by a corporation having a foreign investment in Japan of not less than 100 million yen (about US$278,000) as of January 1 of any given year. These corporations must have been engaged in basic industries, such as mining, iron and steel, chemical, and shipbuilding, as specified by regulations issued by the Ministry of Finance; (2) certain specifically designated foreign technicians employed in basic manufacturing industries even though the corporation in which such persons were employed did not have any investment in Japan; (3) certain specified professional and technical individuals and service businesses, including attorneys, public accountants, technical consultants, newspapers and news syndicates, insurance companies, and banks; and (4) teachers in Japanese higher schools and colleges, and missionaries and other clergymen.

It was clear at the end of 1955 that this Special Taxation Measures Law would not be renewed. However, there were indications that some provision would be made to ameliorate the impact on foreigners of the termination of the Special Taxation Measures Law, perhaps by granting certain exclusions on income not received in Japan.

Standard deductions.—In computing net taxable income, resident taxpayers are entitled to certain standard exemptions and deductions, as follows:

Basic (personal) exemption__	¥80,000 per year.
Earned income exemption__	15 percent of taxable income to a maximum ¥60,000.
Deduction for dependents__	¥40,000 for first dependent, ¥25,000 for second and third dependents, ¥15,000 for each additional dependent.
Credit for life insurance____	¥15,000 maximum.

Other deductions are permitted for medical costs and miscellaneous expenses and special deductions are allowed for widows and persons over 65 years of age. Interest income, including loans, bank deposits, and bonds, is tax exempt.

After the foregoing deductions and exemptions have been taken, the income tax on earned income is computed on the basis of the same sliding scale of rates as are applicable to noncorporate income. An official tax table which sets forth the taxable amount for the various net income levels is available.

American businessmen often have commented that the individual income tax burden in the middle-income brackets is greater in Japan than in the United States and is, therefore, a deterrent to investment when employment of Americans is involved. They claim that under current Japanese tax law and administrative practice, gross salaries of American technical, managerial, and administrative personnel must be doubled to insure that the employees receive the agreed-upon net income.

Withholding.—The employer is required by law to withhold the tax and is charged with the responsibility of paying it to the Government. The income taxes withheld must be paid to the tax office by the 10th of the month following the month in which salaries or wages were paid to the employee. The employer also is required to make a year-end adjustment before the last payday of the year to indicate the amount actually due. This adjustment must be reported by the end of January of the following year. The employer also is obliged to provide his employees with a statement of total payments and withholdings.

Penalties.—For failure to comply with the withholding provisions, employers are liable for penalties which in theory are quite severe. However, according to reliable reports from various business sources the penalties are rarely assessed at the maximum. In the vast majority of cases involving foreigners the tax authorities have taken a rather sympathetic view, generally attributing the failures to comply as mistakes emanating from language difficulties or inability to understand fully the laws and regulations.

The penalties are as follows: (1) For failure to withhold taxes, a fine not to exceed 1 million yen and imprisonment not to exceed 3 years; and (2) for late payment of withholding taxes, interest charges of 14.6 percent per year for each day after the 10th of the month on which the payment becomes due, and taxes in addition to the interest charges ranging from 10 percent of the overdue tax for payments made within 1 month after the due date to 25 percent for a period exceeding 3 months. If fraud is involved in the employer's delinquency, the law provides a penalty of 50 percent of the amount of tax in arrears plus the interest charges and other penalties indicated above. Prospective American investors, in choosing the type of withholding payment arrangement best suited for their purposes, should take into account the heavy penalty charges exacted for failure to withhold. It has been found that, in actual administration of the penalty provisions affecting employers, interest charges are almost invariably imposed whereas a much more lenient attitude is taken regarding the other penalty provisions, with the exception that penalties are usually assessed for late payment.

For the self-assessed taxpayer the penalties for nonfiling range from 10 to 25 percent and for underdeclaration of income the penalty is 5 percent of the overdue tax.

Local Taxes

Inhabitants tax.—This tax is a levy imposed by both the municipality and the prefecture in which the individual resides. The municipal tax consists of a small per capita payment and a levy based on the amount of earned income. The maximum per capita payment is 600 yen in a city whose population exceeds 500,000, and the income tax rate varies by municipality. The per capita levy of the prefectural tax is a standard 100 yen, with the income tax rate also varying according to prefecture. In Tokyo and in most parts of Japan the tax rate is about 18 percent.

The employer is required to notify the municipality in which each employee has residence as of January 1 of each year of the amount of salary paid to him and the national income tax withheld during the preceding calendar year. Occasionally, the local government instructs the employer to withhold the inhabitants tax and specify the amounts for each employee; otherwise the taxpayer is billed direct by the local government tax office.

Other local taxes.—Individuals are subject to other minor taxes which generally do not increase the total tax burden substantially. Of these minor taxes, the municipal property tax, which is assessed on land, houses, and other depreciable assets is the most important. For 1955 and thereafter, this tax rate is 1.4 percent per year of the market value of the property concerned.

Other taxes are municipal registration and transfer taxes. The former is 5 percent of the registered value of real property, such value ranging from 25 to 35 percent of market value. The transfer tax is assessed on any transfer of real property at 3 percent of the market value thereof.

JAPAN-U. S. TAX CONVENTION

A Japan-United States tax convention became effective in March 1955 (see appendix H for complete text), under which United States investors will not be subject to the 10-percent income tax levied at the source in Japan on dividends received from Japanese corporations. In addition, the American citizen, resident, or corporate shareholder of a Japanese corporation is entitled to credit against his or its United States income tax 25 percent of the amount of the dividend if, and only if, he reports as income 125 percent of the dividend received. This credit, similar to that allowed the Japanese shareholder in reduction of Japanese income tax, reflects a part of the Japanese corporation tax on the profits from which the dividend was distributed. Thereafter, no Japanese tax other than that on the profits of the corporation shall be assessed upon stock dividends of an American national who possesses no permanent domicile within Japan.

Excepted from the exemption from the Japanese tax on dividends are United States citizens who are residents in Japan and United States corporations which have permanent establishments in Japan, such as branch offices or factories.

The convention is retroactive to January 1, 1955. Accordingly, Japanese taxes levied on dividends declared by Japanese corporations on or after January 1, 1955, and paid to American investors presumably are subject to refund. Moreover, the convention provides that the rate of tax on interest received by residents from bonds, securities, debentures, or other types of indebtedness and on income from technological assistance arrangements (royalties etc.) and from rights to use copyrights, trademarks, and other industrial property rights shall not exceed 15 percent.

As a result of the convention, new Japanese tax legislation and administrative rulings and a new set of administrative practices will be forthcoming. American businessmen will be well advised to follow such developments. For example, many businessmen are awaiting the interpretation which Japanese tax officials may give to article III–3 of the convention with respect to the allocation of profits received from imports, their interest being to learn what portion of total profits tax officials will be subject to Japanese taxation.

CHAPTER X

Business Organization and Management

THE NATURE OF BUSINESS

Japan's present business organization differs from both its prewar and early postwar counterparts. There are no Zaibatsu (powerful family holding companies) or Zaibatsu-type empires as in prewar years, nor are there as many small business units as there were in the early postwar years following the Occupation-sponsored and directed business democratization program.

In the prewar Japanese economy there was a high degree of concentrated control by the Zaibatsu in industry, finance, and commerce. The Zaibatsu had near-monopoly control over some sections of the economy and substantial control over other important sectors. The most important of these large combines were Mitsui, Mitsubishi, and Sumitomo. Additional control over the economic life of the country was exercised by these family groups through cartel arrangements, pyramids of operating and holding companies, and domination of banking, insurance, and shipping. Concomitant with the powerful combines and their substantial control over significant areas of the economy there were many small firms and family establishments engaged principally in the light and consumer goods industries and the distributive trades, primarily retailing.

Small-scale enterprises are more numerous than before the war as a result of the postwar economic deconcentration, but a substantial degree of concentration still exists in certain industries. For example, in the primary metals industry (iron, steel, smelting, and foundries), 8 percent of the firms employ more than 75 percent of the workers of the industry; and in the chemical field, about 7 percent of the firms employ more than 70 percent of the workers. In the textile industry, 90 percent of all of the firms each employ less than 100 workers, and the remaining 10 percent have more than 50 percent of the workers of the industry.

A considerable degree of reconcentration has taken place in trading since the early days of the dissolution program, but this concentration has not resulted in the same type or size of trading organizations as were in existence in prewar years, nor do the present large firms have the degree of influence enjoyed by the Zaibatsu in the 1930's. No trading firm in Japan today controls one-fifth of Japan's international trade or nearly 40 percent of domestic trade as did the Mitsui Trading Company before the war.

Nevertheless, the trend toward reconcentration is clear. Negotiations are proceeding apace among the larger ex-Zaibatsu companies for further mergers and amalgamations looking toward the establishment of larger, more powerful business organizations patterned on the prewar types. The modification of the Anti-Monopoly Law and other business legislation which has taken place will undoubtedly spark this movement.

Should the prewar pattern materialize it would have an important bearing on the outlook and conditions for private foreign investment. There is mounting evidence that side by side with mergers and amalgamations control is centering in the financial institutions of the country, which are using the credit structure as a powerful instrument of control; whereas prewar, Zaibatsu power revolved largely around control of hundreds of firms through holding companies which concentrated stock ownership in a relatively few hands.

The extreme shortage of capital has furthered the trend toward mergers and consolidation, since the ex-Zaibatsu banks, as well as others, have given preference in their loan policy to the ex-Zaibatsu companies and other large firms. As a matter of fact, credit has become the vehicle through which control is effected, inasmuch as financial companies are prohibited by the Anti-Monopoly Law from owning more than 10 percent of the stock in another company (prior to the September 1953 revision of the law, the ceiling was 5 percent). This control is manifested largely by the appointment of bank officials to executive positions in industrial and trading companies and effectively utilizing old personal relationships of the ex-Zaibatsu officials. With few exceptions, officers and directors in ex-Zaibatsu firms are former Zaibatsu officials.

There have been relatively few open cartel arrangements, such arrangements having been prohibited by the Anti-Monopoly Law until its revision in September 1953, but pressure for their use is mounting in business circles, and it is unlikely that the much weakened Fair Trade Commission will be able to do more than retard the rate of growth. Observers of the business scene hold the view that the 1953 revision of the Anti-Monopoly Law, which permits the establishment of cartels to prevent depression in an industry and to promote rationalization, legalized already existing cartels, as well as other practices prohibited under the old law.

Some of the cartels were instituted under other laws, such as the Smaller Enterprise Law and the Export-Import Trading Law. Unlike the prewar associations, membership in these cartels is voluntary. There is pressure for a return to the prewar type of association, which had far-reaching and compulsory powers, as being in the best interests of the country. Businessmen who favor this revival claim that the policing of unfair trade practices would be more effective than is now the case, and many in Government support this view.

Many Japanese businessmen and Government officials believe that the reconcentration of industry and trade has proceeded neither rapidly enough nor far enough, and there is increasing dissatisfaction in both the Japanese business community and Government with the restrictions of the Anti-Monopoly Law. They believe that large-scale business organizations and cartels are not only desirable but necessary, and that the dissolution program resulted in the creation of uneconomic business units.

They claim that additional mergers are necessary to (1) improve the capital structure of Japanese firms; (2) reduce operating costs; (3) eliminate cutthroat competition; (4) prevent unfair trade practices, such as selling at unduly low prices, quality adulteration, and infringement on foreign industrial property rights; and (5) increase the power and prestige of Japanese companies in international competition. To support their views, businessmen and Government officials point to the trading field, in which, they claim, the existence of a large number of firms operates to reduce the possibility of profitable operations, increases the cost of imports, and results in unfair trading practices.

The Government, therefore, is urging that further mergers be effected as soon as possible to enable Japanese companies to concentrate on competing against foreign companies rather than among themselves.

Financial Weakness

As a result of war losses and the serious postwar inflation, corporate savings were virtually wiped out in postwar Japan. Consequently, industrial and trading firms have been heavily dependent upon borrowed funds. Before World War II only about 20 percent of operating funds were borrowed from financial institutions, compared with nearly 80 percent in some recent postwar years. The demand is so great for short-term loans that most of the banks are heavily over-loaned; in 1953 the ratio of loans to deposits was nearly 100 percent. This shortage of capital has resulted in per annum interest rates starting at 8 percent—and usually much higher—adding considerably to costs. To attract equity capital business firms must pay dividends of 15 to 30 percent.

This is a continuing problem in postwar Japan despite the high rate of capital accumulation in recent years, which increased from 15 percent of the gross national product in fiscal year 1950 (ending March 31, 1951) to about 26 percent in fiscal year 1953. Japanese companies often have had difficulty in raising the capital needed in connection with a proposed foreign investment arrangement.

An even greater problem is the unavailability of long-term capital. In an attempt to alleviate this difficulty, the Government has established several long-term banking institutions, such as the Long-Term Credit Bank, the Industrial Bank of Japan, and the Export-Import Bank of Japan (see chapter V). These Government financing institutions also have tended to favor the old and large companies in extending loans, not necessarily on the basis of favoritism but because such firms are a sounder risk. The effect is obvious, however—the larger firms, a significant proportion of which are successor Zaibatsu companies, can wield considerable influence on the success of the smaller, financially weaker companies.

Those among the smaller firms which try to compete are dependent for success on their ability to establish good banking contacts, particularly with the smaller banks, or to affiliate with one of the larger companies as a supplier, subcontractor, or distributor. By these means, they are able to share in the limited supply of loanable funds.

Management Concepts and Practices

The difference between American and Japanese concepts and practices is considerably greater than that between techniques. Japanese businessmen are considerably more conservative than American businessmen in their approach to management problems, and they have been much slower in adopting scientific management principles and practices.

Utilization of labor is one of the primary differences. The attitude of Japanese management toward labor is basically paternalisitc despite the rise of trade unions and the increase in the number and scope of labor and social security legislation (see chapter XI), and employers seldom discharge workers even through their retention cannot be economically justified. This practice of spreading the work, coupled with the undermechanization in Japanese industry, undoubtedly is the underlying reason for the lower efficiency of Japanese labor as compared with American labor. Admittedly, this labor policy has limited the unemployment resulting from technological improvements in recent years, but unless there is a basic change in attitude it will continue to affect Japan's industrial progress.

Basic differences between American and Japanese management are evident also in other important aspects of business administration. In the majority of manufacturing firms, modern cost accounting is virtually nonexistent. One manifestation of the deep-rooted traditions of the Japanese is the essentially conservative attitude taken by some businessmen toward changed and changing market conditions both at home and abroad. As a consequence, there is a tendency to view the market as static and to resist innovations and the improvement of important business management practices such as inventory control, quality control, and market research.

In business relations it is often found that the traditional leader-follower relationship and desire for security and stability translates itself into narrow areas of responsibility with attendant overcentralization of authority. Another outgrowth of these same traditions is the overstratification in some sections of Japanese business. These manifestations tend to discourage the full exercise of individual initiative and reduce the possibilities for improved management concepts and practices. Still another factor hindering the adoption of scientific management practices is the low rate of mobility of management officials.

Despite these inhibiting factors, representatives of management, Government, and the public are showing an increasing awareness of the need to improve management practices and modernize production processes. This interest is a logical outgrowth of the various investment arrangements concluded in recent years under which there has been a flow of American management officials to Japan and of Japanese management officials to the United States and Europe to study and observe modern management practices.

The Japan-American Productivity Center [1] undoubtedly will provide further stimulus. Like similar centers in Europe, it (1) disseminates information on methods of increasing productivity, (2) sends teams to the United States and Europe and invites to Japan experts from the United States and Europe, (3) holds seminars on various aspects of scientific management theory and practice, (4) operates training and information centers, (5) provides counseling services on productivity improvement, and (6) provides liaison with other groups in Japan which may be interested in scientific management.

LAWS RELATING TO BUSINESS

Business Organization, Commercial Code

Under the Japanese Commercial Code,[2] it is permissible to establish a sole proprietorship, a partnership (limited or unlimited), or a joint-stock company (stock corporation). Foreign investors generally find that the stock corporation is the most advantageous type of business organization. A summary of the basic provisions of the Commercial Code, particularly as they apply to the stock corporation, follows:

The stock corporation.—A stock corporation (kabushiki-kaisha) must be composed of at least seven members, who must draw up, sign, and register articles of incorporation that give the following information: (1) Objective of the corporation; (2) trade name, which must contain the word "kabushiki-kaisha"; (3) total number of shares authorized to be issued; (4) par value of each share, if shares having par value are issued; (5) statement of the existence, restriction, or exclusion of the preemptive rights of shareholders, or the extension thereof to third persons; (6) total number of shares authorized to be issued at the time of incorporation, whether with or without par value, and the minimum issue price; (7) place of principal office and each branch office; (8) manner in which the company is to issue its public notices; and (9) full name and permanent residence of each promoter.

The following provisions relating to special benefits and contributions of promoters are not deemed valid unless included in the articles of incorporation: (1) Nature of special benefits received by promoters and full names of such promoters; (2) full names of promoters whose contributions are in the form of property other than money, the nature and value of such property, and the number, kind, and value of the shares given therefor; (3) expenses of incorporation which are to be borne by the company and the remuneration to be received by the promoters. Contributions in the form of property other than money can be made only by promoters.

Any alteration of the articles of incorporation requires a two-thirds vote of the shareholders

---

[1] Officially inaugurated on February 14, 1955.

[2] Adopted in 1898, and extensively revised by law No. 167 of May 10, 1950.

present at a general meeting who own more than one-half of the total shares issued.

A stock corporation must register at the place of its principal office and of each branch office. In general, the 2-week period within which registration is to be made begins from the day the general organization meeting of the company is held.

The total number of shares issued at the time of incorporation shall not be less than one-fourth of the total number of shares to be issued by the company. Public notices shall be issued by inserting such notices in the Official Gazette or a daily newspaper.

A stock corporation may issue par-value and/or non-par-value shares, and the liability of each shareholder is limited to the subscription price of his own shares. The value of all shares having par value must be equal and each par-value share must be not less than 500 yen (approximately US$1.40), and the issue price of a par-value share cannot be less than its face value. Co-owners of shares (two or more persons) are jointly and severally liable for payments to the company for the value of their shares. Shares may be assigned to other persons and cannot be restricted even by the articles of incorporation.

An important provision of the code is the introduction of authorized capital stock and non-par-value stock. The management of a stock corporation is authorized to issue the required amount of non-par-value stock to finance enterprises; the right to issue new shares, within the limits set forth in the articles of incorporation, rests with the board of directors.

Three directors must be elected at a general meeting of the shareholders for a term not exceeding 2 years.[3] The stock corporation may not require that the directors be shareholders. The corporation may provide in the articles of incorporation that the election of directors be made by the system of cumulative voting but, irrespective of such provision, any shareholder or shareholders having at least 25 percent of the total number issued may request election by cumulative voting.[4]

Provision is made for protection of the rights of minority shareholders in relation to the board of directors. Should a shareholder think that "irreparable damage may be caused to the company" when action is not taken within 30 days after the request is made by a shareholder to enforce the liability of directors, he is entitled to institute a suit demanding injunction against the company.[5] Should the shareholder lose the case, such shareholder would not be held liable for damage to the company unless ill intent has been involved.

A shareholder is also entitled to demand that the company suspend the issuance of shares if he believes it is carried out "in a grossly unfair manner or at a grossly unfair price." Further protection is provided minority shareholders in the grant of cumulative voting power so that they may select directors more of their own choice. Minority shareholders also are provided the opportunity of redeeming shares at fair value when such shareholders are opposed to amalgamation of the company or to transfer of the company's business to a third party, even though the decision to do so has been made at a shareholders' meeting.

Subscriptions for debentures may be invited on a resolution by the board of directors. The total amount of debentures may not exceed the stated capital and the reserve fund, except that, if the value of the property of the company as indicated in the last balance sheet is not equal to the stated capital and the reserve fund, the value of the debentures may not exceed the value of the property.

An increase in the capital of the company may not exceed four times the total number of issued shares. A reduction of capital may be voted in the same manner as an increase of capital. When the number of shares is to be reduced, the company must notify the shareholders and issue a public notice of such intention, indicating the period during which stock certificates must be surrendered.

Should the company be in danger of becoming insolvent, or under other special circumstances, the appropriate court, upon application of a director or a shareholder holding shares representing 3 percent of the total number of issued shares continuously for the 6 months preceding such application, may order the company to institute reorganization proceedings. Upon issuance of such an order, it shall be registered at the seat of the main office and each branch office of the company.

The Japanese Securities and Exchanges Law provides that no security shall be issued or sold by public offering unless the issuer files a registration certificate, in triplicate, with the Securities and Exchange Commission containing such data as the objective; trade name; matters pertaining to capital or subscription; names and addresses of officers, promoters, underwriters, and major stockholders; and description of the security concerned. The registration statement shall be signed by all of the promoters or officers, or, if the firm is a foreign company, by its representative in Japan. The registration statement shall be accompanied by the articles of incorporation, application for the acceptance of stocks or debentures, prospectus, financial statements, and other relevant documents.

The partnership.—The Commercial Code provides for two types of partnerships—unlimited (gomei-kaisha) and limited (goshi-kaisha).

To form an unlimited partnership, articles of

[3] The term of office of first directors may not exceed 1 year.
[4] Request for cumulative voting must be made in writing within 5 days of the date set for a general meeting at which election of not less than two directors is planned.
[5] In the district court at the seat of the principal office of the company. District courts have exclusive jurisdiction in such cases.

incorporation must be executed and signed by each member, and must contain the following information: (1) Objective of the business; (2) trade name, which must contain the words "gomei-kaisha"; (3) full name and permanent residence of each member; (4) place of head office and each branch office; and (5) the contribution to be made by each member.

Within 2 weeks after registration of the partnership's formation, the following particulars must be registered at the place of its principal office and each branch office: (1) Objective of the business; (2) the period of duration or the causes for dissolution, if such have been determined; (3) the contribution of each member (if in the form of property other than money, its value and the part already performed); and (4) provisions concerning representation in the event not all of the members are to represent the partnership.

The limited partnership is composed of some members with limited liability and others with unlimited liability. The provisions covering the unlimited partnership with respect to articles of incorporation and registration apply to the limited partnership, with the added provision that the articles of incorporation and other appropriate documents must specify the liability (limited or unlimited) of each member. Members of a limited partnership who have limited liability may make their contributions only in the form of money or other property. The trade name of the limited partnership must contain the word "goshi-kaisha."

The single entrepreneur.—Within the meaning of the code, a trader is a person who on his own behalf engages in commercial transactions as a business. He may use his surname, his full name, or any other designation as his trade name, except that the word "company" may not be used.

Provisions under the Civil Code also affect the establishment of business enterprises, but these generally are not as important or as advantageous to foreigners as are the provisions of the Commercial Code.

Branch of foreign corporation.—Branches of foreign corporations are subject to the same provisions of the Commercial Code as are companies formed in Japan. A foreign company which intends to engage in commercial transactions as a continuing business in Japan must appoint a representative in Japan and establish an office. A branch office of a foreign corporation may not engage in commercial transactions on a continuing basis in Japan until it has registered and given public notice of the formation of a branch office. As mentioned in chapter VIII, the Japanese Foreign Investment Law applies only to investment in Japanese corporations, and the remittance of profits and repatriation of capital of branch offices of foreign firms are not guaranteed at present.

Industrial Property Laws

Reference has been made to technological assistance as a type of investment, as defined in the Foreign Investment Law, and its widespread use during the past few years (see chapter VIII). In this connection, it is important that a foreign investor familiarize himself with the various Japanese laws which provide protection against unauthorized use of a valid industrial property right. Under Japanese law, industrial property rights receive maximum protection if registered in Japan.

Application for a patent, utility model, design, or trademark is made to the Japanese Patent Agency, Ministry of International Trade and Industry, in accordance with the Patent Law (law No. 96 of 1921, as amended), the Utility Model Law (law No. 97 of 1921, as amended), the Design Law (law No. 98 of 1921, as amended), the Trade Mark Law (law No. 96 of 1921, as amended), and various other applicable laws and regulations.[6]

Since Japan is a party to the Paris Convention for the Protection of Industrial Property concluded on March 20, 1883, and as amended at London, July 2, 1934,[7] it extends to American industrial property owners a priority period of 12 months in which to apply for registration in Japan with respect to patents for inventions and utility models, and 6 months on industrial designs, models, and trademarks and marks of manufacture.

The period of duration of a patent right is 15 years from the day of publication of the application. This period may be extended for 3 to 10 years as provided for by Cabinet order. The Japanese Patent Agency operates on a first-come-first-served principle, and a patent will be granted only to the first applicant.

A Provisional Copyright Agreement between the United States and Japan became effective April 28, 1952, and is valid for 4 years. American authors, composers, recording companies, motion-picture producers, and others receive the same copyright protection in Japan as is accorded by Japan to its nationals. Japanese nationals receive similar copyright protection under United States law.

If infringements of properly registered patents or trademarks occur, the laws of Japan are designed to adjudicate such cases, and there are many capable American and Japanese patent attorneys who are willing to represent the complainant.

The Japanese Government has taken legislative action to protect foreign industrial property rights properly registered in Japan and other countries. Under its Export Trade Control Order (Cabinet Order No. 378 of December 1, 1949, as amended), an exporter in Japan must obtain a license from

---

[6] These are available from the International Trade Development Division, Office of Intelligence and Services, Bureau of Foreign Commerce, Washington 25, D. C., or any of the Department's field offices.
[7] The Convention became effective in Japan on July 15, 1899.

the MITI for "all articles which infringe or are designated by the Ministry of International Trade and Industry as likely to infringe upon rights in patents, utility models, designs, trademarks and copyrights at the destination."[8]

Therefore, American patents and trademarks should be registered in Japan to guard against unauthorized export to the United States of the products covered. They should also be registered in other countries to prevent possible Japanese export to such markets.

When a complaint proving infringement at the country of destination is filed with the Export Section, International Trade Bureau, Ministry of International Trade and Industry, the Ministry will designate the article as coming under export control by printing a notice in its Official Bulletin. A direct warning will be sent to the exporter concerned (if the identity of the exporter is made known to the Ministry) stating that further export of the infringing articles will subject the exporter to penalties. Japanese export associations also attempt to police their members under the provisions of the Export-Import Trading Law.

Filing of an American patent in Japan does not afford protection against unauthorized manufacture and use of the product in Japan, however. To prevent manufacture in Japan of an article patented in the United States, a Japanese patent should be obtained.

On the basis of the Paris Convention for the Protection of Industrial Property, the Japanese Government enacted a Law for the Prevention of Unfair Competition.[9] With its latest amendment, this law provides that any person shall be liable for damages when he intentionally or through negligence commits any of the following acts: (1) Causes confusion by use of the same or similar trademarks, trade names, or other indications and selling, distributing, or exporting goods bearing such misleading markings; (2) creates misconceptions as to place of origin by using false names or other indications on merchandise or advertising; (3) includes markings on merchandise tending to create a false or misleading impression as to the quality, contents, or quantity of merchandise or to indicate that it was produced, manufactured, or processed in places other than the country of origin; and (4) makes or spreads false statements which are detrimental to the business reputation of another.

To obtain any action under this law, however, the foreign company must initiate the complaint.

Anti-Monopoly Law, Related Legislation

*The Law Relating to the Prohibition of Private Monopoly and Methods of Preserving Fair Trade, popularly known as the Anti-Monopoly Law, was enacted in 1947 [10] as a key measure for effecting the dissolution of the Zaibatsu business organizations and preventing their revival. The law as originally enacted prohibited one company from owning stock in another company, irrespective of amount and whether or not they were in competition with each other; banned ownership by financial companies of more than 5 percent of stock in operating companies; prohibited all interlocking directorates; placed severe restrictions on the conclusion of international contracts by Japanese companies; and prohibited virtually every type of concerted activity.

In August 1953 the law was revised significantly. While it was in process of the revision, there was great pressure for changes which would have given recognition to cartels as a general business practice.

There was some resistance to a major revision of the law, mainly from small and medium-sized business organizations and some of the larger prewar companies with no Zaibatsu connections who, because of the breaking up of the Zaibatsu firms (particularly in the trading field) were able to make gains during the postwar period and did not wish to lose their new and hard-won status. Certain sections of the labor movement, some consumer organizations, a relatively small group of intellectuals, certain of the cooperatives, the leadership of the left-wing political parties, and segments of the press also protested against a drastic revision.

This opposition was successful to the extent that it prevented repeal or complete emasculation of the law. However, important changes were made, which undoubtedly will have far-reaching effects on the future trend of the economy.

The principal changes in the law are as follows: (1) Concerted business activities (cartels) are permitted upon prior approval of the Fair Trade Commission when necessary "to cope with depression" and rationalize industry, even if competition is substantially restricted thereby; (2) possession of stock and the holding of concurrent positions in competing companies are permissible if competition is not substantially restrained thereby; (3) the amount of stock which financial institutions may acquire in nonfinancial business organizations is raised from 5 percent to 10 percent; (4) manufacturers have the right to compel distributors to maintain resale prices on certain trademarked products; and (6) mergers and amalgamations may be effected more easily.

Establishment and operation of holding companies in Japan are still prohibited under the Anti-Monopoly Law, but the definition of a holding company has been changed somewhat. In the old law it was recognized that a firm because of certain activities could in fact be classified as a holding company or become a holding company

---

[8] Attachment I to Cabinet Order 378 of December 1, 1949, item 30.
[9] Law No. 14 of 1934, as amended.

[10] Law No. 54 of 1947, as amended through September 1953 by law No. 259.

if not restrained. This has been eliminated in the new law.

The present law continues, in general terms, the prohibition against private monopolies and activities which result in a substantial restraint of competition. The use of unfair business practices is prohibited; these are defined by the Fair Trade Commission to include (1) boycotting or other unduly discriminatory treatment, (2) dumping or similar sales practices, (3) taking unfair advantage of one's economic position, and (4) unduly influencing customers.

Trade associations.—The revised Anti-Monopoly Law incorporates the Trade Association Law which was originally passed in 1948. The old Trade Association Law listed permitted activities for trade associations which, in general, were comparable with those permitted under United States laws. With the revision, trade associations may now engage in many activities which heretofore were considered inappropriate for such associations. The only limitations are that trade associations are prohibited from (1) substantially restricting competition, (2) entering into international agreements or contracts which unreasonably restrain trade or involve unfair business practices, (3) placing limitations on the number of entrepreneurs in any particular field, (4) unduly restricting the functions or activities of any member of the association, and (5) influencing members or others to engage in unfair business practices.

Smaller Enterprise Stabilization Law.—This law was originally enacted in August 1952 as an exception to the Anti-Monopoly Law, for the benefit of the small business enterprise, which is defined as a business which employs less than 300 workers and with less than 10 million yen (approximately $28,000) capital. Under its provisions producers may, with the approval of the Ministry of International Trade and Industry, establish associations to restrict production, curtail facilities, control prices, allocate markets, and institute other measures considered necessary to prevent or overcome protracted business depression in an industry. The MITI can force nonmembers of any association to adhere to the rules and regulations of the Smaller Enterprise Stabilization Law, if such action is deemed necessary to effect "stabilization" in an industry.

According to the Fair Trade Commission, by July 1954 the Government had approved the establishment of 117 associations covering 26 industries, including cotton and staple fiber, silk and rayon textile, and watch manufacturing.

Some observers favor the establishment of associations in the small and medium-sized industries in the belief that they tend to encourage a degree of stability and responsibility which otherwise could not be achieved because of the extremely weak position of many of the individual companies. Others believe that the associations are too restrictive and fear that abusive use of power may result.

Export-Import Trading Law.—The stated purpose of the Export-Import Law (law No. 299 of 1952) is to prevent unfair export practices, particularly as related to foreign industrial marks of origin. To accomplish this purpose in fulfillment of Japan's declared intention under the Peace Treaty (see chapter II) of conforming in public and private trade and commerce to internationally accepted fair trade practices, the law authorizes informal agreements among exporters, as well as the establishment of formal associations. It also gives authority to exporters—both individually and, under certain circumstances, in combination with producers—to conclude agreements, with the approval of the Ministry of International Trade and Industry, in order to prevent sales abroad at unduly low prices and, in other respects, reduce or eliminate what might be considered harmful and unnecessary competition in particular markets. Similarly, the law also permits importers to form associations to limit the degree of competition among Japanese importers in order to enhance their competitive position in world markets.

CHAPTER XI

Labor and Social Security

LABOR FORCE AND LABOR SUPPLY

The pressure of population—and its concomitant employment difficulty—is the key problem in Japan and, as stated in chapter II, it will continue to be serious for many years. On the other hand, the population is Japan's chief resource, since that country probably has the largest reservoir of skilled labor in Asia.

In mid-1955, estimates of the adult population (14 years of age and over) aggregated nearly 61 million. Of this total, approximately 44 million—about 25 million men and 19 million women—are considered to be in the labor force. About 20 million are engaged in agriculture and forestry. Of the 24 million in nonagricultural pursuits, about 7 million are in manufacturing; 6 million in trade and finance; 2 million in transportation, communications, and public utilities; and nearly 4 million in various service industries. An estimated 750,000 persons enter the labor force each year.

According to data compiled by the Ministry of Labor, the monthly average number of employed persons during the period January-June 1955 was more than 40 million; of this total 24.5 million were individual proprietors and family workers and 15.5 million were working for wages (see table 15). Upwards of 42 percent of those employed were engaged in agriculture and forestry.

In this same period about 695,000 were classified as unemployed (398,000 men and 297,000 women) —298,000 more than in the corresponding period a year earlier. Recent estimates indicate that the number of totally unemployed is increasing.

Unemployment figures do not present an accurate indication of the availability of labor at any given time, however. Better than one-half of the total labor force is composed of the self-employed, most of whom are engaged in agricultural pursuits. Many of these are underemployed as regards any reasonable definition of employment, the number engaged in agriculture being very high in relation to the acreage tilled. As a matter of fact, the farm traditionally has been the refuge of many who are unable to find jobs in industry. For this reason there is nearly always available in the rural areas a hidden reservoir of workers for industrial or other employment.

Some of these workers are skilled; however, even the unskilled can be trained relatively quickly, depending on the level of skill required. As a rule, the Japanese are hard-working and virtually all have the equivalent of an elementary school education. Many have a secondary education, and there are a large number of college-trained men and women.

The self-employed persons in nonagricultural enterprise, particularly those engaged in operating the many small specialized shops, also are significant as a source of labor. Another potential, but at present virtually unavailable, source consists of persons currently employed in nonagricultural pursuits but who are underutilized in various degrees. This practice of underutilizing labor stems from the long-established paternalistic relations between management and labor, the strong resistance of labor unions to rationalization and modernization, and the lack of any overall plan by the Government to cope with unemployment, with the result that all try to effect a compromise which, with few exceptions, continues the practice of uneconomic overstaffing in industry and Government.[1]

Table 15.—Average Monthly Employment, Agricultural and Nonagricultural, by Type of Worker, 1953–54 and January–June 1955

[In thousands of persons]

Item	1953	1954	1955 (Jan–June)
Agriculture and forestry			
Proprietors	5,513	5,386	5,413
Family workers	11,036	10,716	10,705
Employees	580	563	518
Total	17,129	16,665	16,636
Nonagricultural [1]			
Proprietors	4,750	4,906	5,047
Family workers	3,142	3,368	3,413
Employees	14,220	14,621	14,975
Unclassified or unknown		9	40
Total	22,112	22,904	23,475

[1] Includes fishing.

Source: Ministry of Labor.

[1] The role of the Government as an employer is not insignificant inasmuch as tobacco manufacturing and telegraph, telephone, and postal services are completely under public ownership. Moreover, most of the railroads are Government-owned and -operated. At the end of July 1954, more than 3.5 million workers, or about 37 percent of all persons working for wages, were employed by the Government, either directly or by the various Government corporations.

Foreign Personnel

The Japanese Government places no restrictions either by law or by actual practice against the employment of foreign nationals. As a matter of fact, since 1950 and until the end of 1955, special tax concessions were granted to foreign nationals employed by certain designated corporations.[2] Reportedly, however, many Japanese Government officials and others believe that Japan has achieved equality with the West in many fields from a technological standpoint as a result of 431 technical assistance agreements concluded since the end of the war (through December 1954) and that the need for special concessions to foreigners no longer exists. With increasing unemployment, there is also apprehension over the prospect of suitable jobs for the large number of people who have received technical training at Japanese institutions of higher education, on-the-job training by foreign technicians, and specialized education abroad.

Despite these developments it is unlikely that the Japanese Government will impose legislative restrictions on employment of foreign personnel. The Treaty of Friendship, Commerce and Navigation between Japan and the United States specifically provides that nationals of either party shall be permitted to enter each other's territory to engage in business operations in which they have made an investment (or are actively considering doing so), as well as to conduct trading activities. A trend toward increased use of Japanese personnel in all phases of industry and trade may be anticipated, however.

WAGES AND LABOR COST

Wages in Japan are low by Western standards, but because of the small ratio of industrial power and capital per worker, productivity of labor is generally much below that of many other industrialized countries and, as a result, unit labor costs in several important sectors of the economy are relatively high. Thus, the low wage rates in Japan do not necessarily mean low unit wage costs. As a matter of fact, owing to high production costs, of which high labor cost per unit is an important factor, many of Japan's export products in recent years have not been able to compete successfully in international markets.

The level of Japanese wages has increased sharply since the end of World War II. The index of average monthly cash wages in manufacturing (production workers only) for calendar year 1954 stood at 326 (1934–1936=1). Sex, age, length of service, number of dependents, and other factors affect the level of wages paid to workers. For example, the average monthly cash wage in manufacturing during January–June 1954 was the equivalent of $43.73 (see table 16); for a female production worker the average was about 40 percent of that amount, although in some industries tne ratio was as high as 60 percent.[3] The cash income of managerial, clerical, and technical workers is considerably higher; technicians and managerial employees, particularly, may often receive two to four times more than skilled production workers.

There are variations, sometimes large, in the wages paid for the same kind of work in different parts of the country; in recent years, however, the spread has narrowed, largely owing to increased unionization. During recent postwar years, wages in manufacturing industry having 30 or more workers rose from a monthly average equivalent to $25.37 in 1950 to $42.56 in 1953 and stood at nearly $44 in mid-1954 (see table 16). Through 1951, the increases in wages did little more than keep up with the rapid rise in prices; but in 1952 and, more particularly, in 1953, wages caught up, so that workers' real wages and living standards showed improvement when compared not only with prewar years but also with the earlier postwar period (see table 17). Since prices have leveled off as a result of the Government's deflationary program instituted in late 1953, it can be expectèd that wages will follow a similar trend.

Cash payments represent only a part of the total labor cost to an employer. In many industries employers customarily provide—without any cost to the employee or at a very reduced rate—transportation, housing, and various welfare activities, other than those required by law. In addition, employers frequently provide higher paid employees with expense accounts for entertainment. As an indication of the widespread use of special benefits, in 1953 approximately 77 percent of all enterprises employing 30 or more persons maintained welfare facilities in some form. Of this total, more than three-fourths provided employees with housing either free of charge or at rates far below the prevailing market rates. The increase to labor costs by reason of the various payments in kind and welfare benefits extended to employees varies considerably but is not inconsequential in any instance.

On the average, foreign firms include only bonuses, transportation allowances, and, in some cases, expense accounts in addition to regular cash wages. However, foreign companies, particularly those having joint Japanese-foreign management, are under pressure to conform more closely to the Japanese practice.

[2] The Ministry of Finance made the designation. It has included persons employed by corporations which have made an investment in Japan of a minimum of ¥100 million (US$278,778) and technicians—persons in the professions or educational or similar categories contributing desired techniques to Japan.

[3] The big difference in earnings between male and female workers is related primarily to type of work and not to discrimination because of sex. As noted in another section of this chapter the Labor Standards Law prohibits such discrimination.

Table 16.—Average Monthly Total Cash Wages, by Industry (Establishments Employing 30 or More Persons), 1953 and January–July 1954

Industry	1953				January–July 1954			
	Total		Contract earnings (yen)	Special payments (yen)	Total		Contract earnings (yen)	Special payments (yen)
	Dollars	Yen			Dollars	Yen		
All selected groups	46.50	16,741	14,358	2,383	47.48	17,093	15,285	1,808
Mining	47.68	17,165	15,359	1,807	46.51	16,744	15,629	1,115
Manufacturing	42.56	15,322	13,349	1,973	43.73	15,743	14,224	1,519
Food and kindred products	39.39	14,181	11,631	2,550	40.82	14,696	12,494	2,203
Tobacco manufactures	51.04	18,373	14,030	4,343	52.11	18,758	15,589	3,169
Textile mill products	26.75	9,630	8,383	1,247	26.67	9,602	8,978	624
Apparel and other finished textile products	21.98	7,913	7,153	760	21.98	7,912	7,356	556
Lumber and wood products	27.28	9,820	9,084	737	28.22	10,162	9,739	423
Furniture and fixtures	29.53	10,630	10,138	491	31.75	11,429	11,138	291
Paper and allied products	56.92	20,490	16,486	4,005	57.53	20,710	17,590	3,120
Printing and publishing	47.81	17,213	15,061	2,152	48.72	17,538	15,928	1,610
Chemical products	48.55	17,479	14,751	2,729	50.68	18,244	15,907	2,336
Petroleum and coal products	57.50	20,699	16,283	4,416	64.94	23,380	18,429	4,950
Rubber products	37.96	13,667	11,955	1,712	36.63	13,185	12,053	1,132
Leather and leather products	39.22	14,119	12,499	1,620	39.08	14,067	12,927	1,140
Stone, clay, and glass products	44.58	16,050	13,676	2,374	47.01	16,924	14,916	2,008
Primary metal industries	56.95	20,501	18,065	2,435	59.33	21,360	19,147	2,213
Fabricated metal products	41.44	14,918	13,566	1,352	41.89	15,081	14,220	861
Machinery, except electrical	44.53	16,029	14,636	1,394	44.74	16,108	15,196	912
Electrical machinery and supplies	48.43	17,434	15,337	2,097	48.39	17,421	15,724	1,696
Transportation equipment	55.29	19,905	17,587	2,318	57.21	20,597	18,782	1,815
Precision instruments	45.86	16,509	14,508	2,001	47.02	16,926	15,431	1,495
Miscellaneous industries	29.71	10,694	9,901	793	32.92	11,851	10,807	1,045
Wholesale and retail trade	49.09	17,673	14,637	3,036	49.47	17,810	15,481	2,329
Finance and insurance	63.02	22,687	17,324	5,362	63.36	22,808	18,555	4,254
Transportation	48.89	17,600	15,107	2,493	49.97	17,988	16,222	1,766
Communications	50.37	18,134	15,229	2,905	54.11	19,479	17,454	2,024
Public utilities	65.78	23,681	19,038	4,642	67.23	24,202	19,370	4,473

Source: Monthly Labor Survey, Ministry of Labor.

Table 17.—Indexes of Consumer Prices in Urban Japan, Calendar Years 1950–55 [1]

[1951=100]

Year	Food	Clothing	Fuel and light	Housing	Miscellaneous	All items
1950	86.8	78.5	86.6	80.2	86.1	85.9
1952	103.8	85.5	118.3	109.2	116.8	105.0
1953	110.0	85.2	132.7	120.7	127.5	111.9
1954	119.0	86.1	136.3	127.5	135.5	119.1
1955:						
January	116.7	83.7	140.0	129.4	139.6	118.7
February	117.6	83.4	139.3	129.6	139.0	119.0
March	116.6	82.9	138.0	129.9	139.6	118.4
April	117.9	82.8	136.1	131.1	139.5	119.1
May	116.4	82.9	134.9	131.5	139.6	118.2
June	115.3	82.6	133.9	131.7	140.2	117.6

[1] Index weights vary by city and 28 cities were used in computing the indexes. To illustrate, the index weights used for Tokyo were as follows: Food, 56.2; clothing, 12.8; fuel and light, 4.9; housing, 4.6; and miscellaneous, 21.5.

Source: Statistics Bureau, Prime Minister's Office.

Wage Payment Systems and Regulations

Minimum wages have not been legally set, except for seamen, but the Labor Standards Law establishes the principle that minimum wages may be fixed by Government-established wage boards. Japanese law does not require mandatory salary increases for any reason. Wages may be set on a piece or time basis, and incentive systems have proved successful in many industries.

For overtime work, Japanese law requires that the employer pay full time plus 25 percent for any work in excess of the legal workweek of 48 hours.

If the employee works overtime between 10 p. m. and 5 a. m., the law requires payment of regular wages plus 50 percent.

In general the unit of work on which wages are based is the month, and the average number of hours worked monthly per worker ranged from 189 in 1950 to about 200 in June 1954. According to the law, cash wages must be paid at least once a month, a practice which has become customary among Japanese and foreign employers.

Special money grants frequently are made to employees on specific occasions, such as the birth of a child or the death of a member of a family. In addition, cash bonuses are paid at the end of the year and sometimes at midyear. The practice of paying bonuses has for so long been the custom that labor now regards it as a right and it is not unusual for the amount to be a subject of negotiation between management and labor, with the bonus equaling 1 month's wages minimum and in many cases 1½ to 2 months' wages. Foreign firms generally follow the Japanese practice and pay year-end bonuses equaling 1 month's wages; a large proportion also pay a midyear bonus equivalent to that amount.

Productivity

Despite the fact that the individual Japanese worker is industrious and relatively efficient, the productivity of labor is low. Manpower is plentiful and employers tend to use labor as a substitute

87

for increased mechanization, principally because capital is scarce and consequently very expensive. Many industries, therefore, are undermechanized or equipped with obsolete machinery. Moreover, as already indicated, a large segment of the working population is engaged in primary industries— farming, forestry, and marine—where the degree of mechanization is extremely low and where there is a preponderance of individual proprietors and family workers.

The degree of productivity varies from industry to industry, and from plant to plant within an industry, depending on the degree of mechaniza-.ion, the level of training of the workers, availability and quality of materials and power, working conditions, quality of management, and other variables which directly or indirectly affect output per worker. However, it is generally conceded that improvement in working conditions and greater application of scientific management principles can contribute substantially to the improvement of productivity. Management is slowly increasing its receptivity to scientific management techniques as evidenced by the establishment of a productivity center in Japan.[4] The degree of success which may be forthcoming is dependent upon many factors not the least of which is the extent of understanding and cooperative effort by labor.

Productivity in Japan after World War II did not reach even the low prewar level (average of 1934–36) until 1952. By that year, according to various studies, productivity in the United States and the United Kingdom had advanced by 35 percent and 26 percent, respectively, over that of prewar.

Complete and accurate data on productivity in Japan are not readily available, but the limited studies which have been made indicate that in the coal mining industry—a key industry since coal is an important element of cost in many industries—the Japanese worker's productivity is about one-tenth that of an American coal miner and one-third that of a British miner. In the steel industry—also a key industry—the comparisons are more favorable, the corresponding figures being somewhat better than one-fourth and one-half, respectively. In the electric power industry, the Japanese worker's productivity is approximately one-third that of the worker in the United States. These three industries are among the most mechanized in Japan.

Because labor productivity is so much lower in Japan than in advanced Western countries, wage costs are considerably higher than is indicated by wage rates and total income (cash payments plus special benefits) of the individual worker. However, in certain industries, particularly the smaller industries and the numerous family establishments (cottage industries), where wages are the

lowest, the labor cost per unit of output is lower than in the United States and other Western countries.

It may be expected that there will be a continuing upward movement of wages as a result of increased unionization, Government regulations, further industrialization and rationalization, and modernization of existing industrial plants. This trend will be counterbalanced and partly offset by the abundance of low-priced labor resulting from the ever-present pressure of population and the scarcity and high cost of capital.

LABOR UNIONS

Labor unions existed in Japan prior to World War II, but the number of unions and the percentage of workers who were members were strikingly small. The prewar peak of union membership was reached in 1936 when members totaled about 421,000, less than 8 percent of the industrial labor force. During the war the trade unions were required to affiliate with two Government-sponsored and -controlled labor organizations to expedite the war effort. In effect, therefore, free trade unionism was nonexistent at the end of the war.

The occupation which began in August 1945 provided the catalyst for the reformation and expansion of trade unionism in Japan. Soon after the surrender, the Supreme Commander for the Allied Powers (SCAP) instructed the Japanese Government to take appropriate action to encourage the unionization of labor since it was felt that unionization would not only improve the lot of the worker, but also lead to organized participation by labor in building a democratic country— a basic objective of the occupation.

As a result of this encouragement, unions grew rapidly during the first 4 years after the war. By the end of 1946 there were approximately 17,000 unions with a membership of about 5 million. Two years later the number of unions had more than doubled and membership totaled 6,656,000, or roughly 55 percent of persons working for wages in industry. Following this rapid growth, a decline began and in 1950 there were 29,000 unions with slightly more than 5,750,000 members. Since then the number of unions and membership has fluctuated; by mid-1953 the number of trade unions totaled 30,129 and membership was almost 5,843,000 or 40 percent of all industrial employees working for wages (see table 18).

The transportation and communications field has the highest rate of union organization (80 percent), followed closely by mining (77.6 percent). The rate drops precipitously to 38.9 percent in manufacturing and is lowest, as might be expected, in agriculture and forestry (10.2 percent). In terms of volume, however, the largest number of

[4] See chapter **X**.

unions and union members are found in manufacturing—9,291 and 1,872,460, respectively—with the next largest in the transportation and communications industry (6,000 unions having upwards of 1,394,000 members); and these two major segments of the economy account for nearly 60 percent of all organized workers (table 18).

Table 18.—Number of Employees and Union Membership, by Major Groups, June 1953

Industry	Number of employees	Union membership	Rate of unionization (*percent*)
Agriculture, forestry, and hunting	650, 000	66, 360	10. 2
Fishing	190, 000	33, 895	17. 8
Mining	600, 000	465, 392	77. 6
Construction	910, 000	267, 890	29. 4
Manufacturing	4, 810, 000	1, 872, 460	38. 9
Trade, finance, real estate, and insurance	2, 180, 000	408, 981	18. 8
Transportation and communications	1, 740, 000	1, 394, 082	80. 1
Service industries	2, 140, 000	876, 010	40. 9
Government [1]	1, 070, 000	456, 869	42. 7
Total	14, 290, 000	5, 841, 939	40. 2

[1] Does not include employees of various public corporations, such as railroad, telephone and telegraph, and certain others which are included under the applicable industry groups.

Sources: Number of employees, Statistics Bureau, Prime Minister's Office; union membership, Ministry of Labor.

At the end of June 1953, more than 56 percent of the approximately 5,842,000 union members in Japan were organized into the General Council of Trade Unions of Japan (SOHYO); 4 percent in the Japan Federation of Labor Unions (SODOMEI); about 0.7 percent in the National Federation of Industrial Organization (SHIN SANBETSU); 0.2 percent in the Congress of Industrial Unions of Japan (SANBETSU); about 14 percent in national unions not affiliated with any national federation; and 26 percent in various unions not affiliated with national unions or federations. Following the organization in February 1954 of the All-Japan Congress of Trade Unions (ZENRO), which includes SODOMEI and several former SOHYO unions and accounts for 12 percent of Japanese union membership, SOHYO's membership is estimated to have fallen off to 49 percent of all organized workers.

SOHYO, the major national labor federation, was organized in July 1950 with the assistance of Occupation authorities as an anticommunist labor organization dedicated to eliminating communist influence from the trade union movement. Until the Occupation ended in April 1952, this was, in general, SOHYO's position in the Japanese labor movement. Since then, it has moved to the left and now follows a leftist political line.

However, SOHYO's radicalism is chiefly the product of a few leaders. It apparently does not represent the real feelings of the workers, who are much more conservative than their leaders. Nearly two-thirds of the SOHYO membership is composed of Government workers—teachers, railway workers, and postal, telephone, and telegraph workers—who are forbidden by law to strike.

ZENRO, the second most influential labor federation, is composed of strongly anticommunist unions which bolted from SOHYO in protest against the leftist leadership. ZENRO follows the principles of modern trade unionism, with major emphasis on economic rather than political objectives. Strikes under the guidance of SOHYO's radical leadership ended disastrously in 1954, and there are indications of a gradual shift in membership from SOHYO to ZENRO.

INDUSTRIAL DISPUTES

The number of industrial disputes reached a peak in 1948 when there were more than 1,500 involving nearly 7 million workers. In the following year, the number of disputes declined slightly to 1,400, and the number of workers involved dropped sharply to 3.3 million. In 1950, the number of disputes recorded equaled that of 1948, but only about 2,350,000 workers were involved. During subsequent years there has been a downward trend in the number of disputes recorded but the number of workers involved was approximately at the 1949 level.

Only a portion of these disputes disrupted into work stoppages by strike action, lockouts, or slowdowns—many were settled amicably through the industrial relations machinery established after the war. Work stoppages declined from a high of 744 in 1948 involving 2.3 million workers with nearly 7 million man-days lost, to 576 stoppages in 1951 involving 1,163,000 workers and a loss in working days of slightly more than 6 million.

In 1952 the trend was reversed in both the number of stoppages—which increased to 590—and the number of workers involved—1,624,000—and there was an even sharper increase in the number of man-days lost, which rose to 15 million. This reversal resulted largely from the strike conducted by several large unions against the proposed revision of certain sections of postwar labor laws and the relatively lengthy strikes of the electrical workers and coal miners.

Data for 1953 indicate that there were 585 work stoppages in which 1,174,000 workers participated and that the number of man-days lost was the lowest in the postwar period. However, the number of days lost as a result of lockouts reached a postwar high.

The greatest incidence of work stoppages occurred in manufacturing—during the 5-year period 1949–53, at least 70 percent of all strikes, lockouts, and slowdowns took place in this segment of the economy. This partly reflects the fact that the largest number of union members are in the manufacturing field, but other important factors are involved.

During the 5-year period 1949–53, questions of wages and allowances were the cause of 70 percent of all labor disputes. Next in importance were opposition to discharge or demands for reinstatement of employees. Other principal issues resulting in disputes were working conditions, hours, vacations, and opposition to suspension, reduction, or shutdown of business activities.

Under the categories of opposition to discharge, demands for reinstatement of employees, and miscellaneous causes of disputes during 1953 and 1954, are included the actions by labor against the growing trend toward rationalization and modernization of industry. This was particularly evident in the iron and steel, coal, nonferrous metals, machinery, chemical, oil refinery, and shipbuilding industries and in the main was related directly to labor's dissatisfaction with the introduction of labor-saving machinery and equipment and more efficient managerial techniques and methods.

With employment prospects decreasing as hundreds of thousands of students enter the labor force each year, with many workers in both industry and agriculture underemployed, and with prospects not too bright for obtaining additional income-producing employment, labor in general opposes rationalization and may be expected to increase its resistance when the dismissal of employees is involved. In some instances management was forced to yield to labor's demands and withdraw dismissals.

LABOR LEGISLATION

Since the end of the war in 1945, Japan's labor legislation has been completely revamped. It now compares favorably with the labor legislation of most of the advanced industrialized countries of the free world and meets the standards of the International Labor Organization (ILO), of which Japan is a member. The principal laws currently in effect and important to those contemplating making an investment in Japan are the Trade Union Law, the Labor Standards Law, the Labor Relations Adjustment Law, Unemployment and Health Insurance Laws, the Workmen's Accident Compensation Law, and the Welfare Pension Law.

Labor Standards Law

The Labor Standards Law, which affects various aspects of employment, was enacted on April 5, 1947,[5] in accordance with the provisions of article 27 of the new Constitution of Japan [6] which provides that ". . . standards for wages, hours, rest and other working conditions shall be fixed by law . . ." The law is very broad in scope, being applicable to all types of enterprises except those employing only members of the family or relations living with the employer. It sets forth what has become known as the Labor Charter, i. e., general principles of the dignity of labor; equal treatment of the sexes, creeds, and nationalities in all matters relating to employment; guaranty of time off by employers for workers to exercise the franchise guaranteed by the Constitution; and prohibition of forced labor and the prewar labor boss system.[7]

The Labor Standards Law prescribes in detail minimum working conditions; the working day is 8 hours and the workweek 48 hours, with 1 day of rest weekly or, in exceptional cases, 4 days every 4 weeks. Vacations with pay are required and rules governing overtime and night work are set at the minimum of a 25-percent increase over the normal wage rate.

Five principles concerning payment of wages are prescribed, as follows: (1) Wages must be paid direct to the employee in cash and in full at least monthly at a specified time (no deductions from cash wages accrued may be made by the employer and no wages in kind may be paid unless specifically provided for by agreement); (2) the employer must pay the equivalent of 60 percent of a worker's average wages as "nonduty" compensation in the event the worker cannot work because of some reason connected with the employer; (3) if wages are paid on a piecework basis, the employer is obligated to guarantee a worker an income from wages equivalent to what he would have earned at the contract rate for the given number of hours; (4) minimum wages are not prescribed, but the law provides that they may be set by wage boards representing labor, management, and the public at public hearings, and (5) if minimum wages have been prescribed in accordance with the law, the employer may not pay wages less than the established minimum.

Other important provisions of the Labor Standards Law and applicable administrative regulations are concerned with minimum health and safety measures; special protection for women and minors; accident compensation; and responsibility of employers for formulating, filing, and displaying, in the place of employment, rules governing employment and inspection of places of employment. In general, the minimum age for employment is 15 years and limitations are placed on the amount of overtime which women and minors are permitted.

Also important are the provisions regarding accident compensation and the regulations governing illness of employees. If an employee has an

---

[5] Law No. 49 of 1947.
[6] See chapter II.

[7] Under this system, which was fairly widespread, particularly among day laborers, workers were paid less than the prevailing wages in the particular job category with the difference going to the boss as consideration for locating the jobs. This practice has been largely eliminated during the past few years as the use of employment exchanges established under the provisions of the Employment Security Law of 1947 has become more widespread.

accident or develops an illness in connection with his work, the employer must provide compensation for the accident, free medical treatment, and the necessary amount of sick leave with 60 percent of his pay. This liability can be covered by workmen's accident compensation insurance which guarantees 60 percent of the employee's base pay for 3 years. Such insurance can be obtained either through the Government or from private insurance companies. When illness is not attributable to the employee's duties, the employer has no legal liability.

Trade Union Law

The Trade Union Law [8] is designed to "protect the exercise by workers of autonomous self-organization and association in trade unions and encourage the practice and procedures of collective bargaining." Its various provisions detail the basic right of workers in private industry to organize into unions of their own choice, to engage in collective bargaining, and to strike. It provides for democratic procedures in union activities and places obligations on unions to register with the Government, keep a list of its membership at its head office, and acquire status as a legal person.

The law also provides for the exemption of unions from income and other taxes applicable to legal persons except when a union engages in profit-making activities.

Other important sections of the Trade Union Law deal with the establishing of labor relations commissions (consisting of an equal number of representatives of employers, employees, and the public) to enforce the provisions of the law and to perform conciliation, mediation, and arbitration services; and the prohibiting of unfair labor practices by employers.[9]

Labor Relations Adjustment Law

The Labor Relations Adjustment Law [10] was put into effect in the fall of 1946 to provide procedures for conciliation, mediation, and arbitration of labor disputes in private industry. The legal responsibility for performing these functions rests with the labor relations commissions established under the provisions of the Trade Union Law. The Labor Relations Adjustment Law provides for cooling-off periods to permit the machinery of conciliation, mediation, and arbitration to operate in order to prevent strikes and lockouts.

It does not prohibit strikes except in public utilities and certain other industries affecting the health and welfare of the people.

Social Insurance Legislation

The present social insurance system of Japan is an outgrowth of various laws and regulations put into effect before World War II. However, great strides forward in all aspects of social and welfare legislation were made after the war by means of extensive revision of some of the older laws and enactment of several new laws. The most important social insurance laws are those governing health insurance, the welfare pension plan, unemployment insurance, and workmen's accident compensation insurance.[11] Under these laws all companies, domestic or foreign, with more than five employees are required to participate in these programs.

National Health Insurance

The premium for national health insurance is 6 percent of the declared income up to a maximum income of ¥36,000 (US$100) monthly. The entire premium is shared equally by the employee and the employer, the Government's contribution being limited to payment of administrative costs. Benefits under this system are relatively few. The insurance does not cover the more expensive medicines and covers only about one-third of the cost of hospitalization and extensive and expensive medical treatment. As of 1953 approximately 25 million persons were covered under this program.

Welfare Pension Plan

The basic law covering the welfare pension plan was enacted in 1941, but the program did not become really operative on a broad scale until the complete revision of the law in mid-1954. The premium is shared equally by the employer and the employee, with the Government paying the administrative costs. The present premium rate is 3 percent of the declared income, with ¥18,000 (US$50) being the maximum monthly income on which premiums can be assessed. Benefits are provided in the form of old-age pensions, survivors' pensions, retirement allowances, and allowances and pensions for disability. The Ministry of Welfare estimates that in 1954

---

[8] Law No. 51 of December 22, 1945, as amended.
[9] These are defined to include discharge or discrimination because of membership in a trade union or because of intention to join a union, arbitrary refusal to bargain collectively with representatives of the workers employed, and control over or interference with the formation or management of a union.
[10] Law No. 25 of September 27, 1946, as amended.

[11] The basic laws governing these programs are: National Health Insurance Law (law No. 60 of 1938, as amended); Welfare Pension Insurance Law (law No. 60 enacted in March 1941 and completely revised by law No. 115 of May 1954); Unemployment Insurance Law (law No. 146 of November 1947, as amended); and Workmen's Accident Compensation Insurance Law (law No. 50 of April 1947, as amended).

nearly 8 million persons were covered under the welfare pension plan.

Unemployment Insurance

The premium for unemployment insurance is shared by the employer, the employee, and the Government; the Government also bears all costs of administering the program. The premium varies in accordance with the status of the worker, i. e., regular or casual. The rate for regular workers is 1.6 percent of all wages paid to the insured each month and this sum is borne about equally by the employer and the employee. At the end of 1953, the Ministry of Labor estimated that nearly 226,000 establishments having about 7.7 million employees were covered by unemployment insurance.

Workmen's Accident Compensation

The entire cost of workmen's accident compensation insurance is borne by the employer except for administrative expenses which are paid by the Government. The premium rate is based on the amount of wages paid to a worker and the accident record of the company. As a general rule the employer is required to make payment in advance for 1 year, and necessary adjustments are made at the end of the fiscal year. Benefit payments are made for medical expenses, permanent or extended disability, funeral expenses, and compensation to survivors. At the end of 1953 more than 431,000 enterprises and nearly 9 million employees were covered under workmen's accident compensation insurance.

Selected Economic Statistics

The data on foreign trade in tables I through VIII are for postwar years. All of the values have been converted to dollars on the basis of 360 yen to US$1. Export values are f. o. b. and import values c. i. f. The source for all the foreign trade statistics is the Bureau of Customs, Japanese Ministry of Finance.

Table I.—Exports of Principal Commodities, Calendar Years 1953–54 and January–June 1955

[Quantity in units indicated; value in thousands of dollars]

Commodity	Quantity			Value		
	1953	1954	1955 (Jan.–June)	1953	1954	1955 (Jan.–June)
Total				1,274,945	1,629,367	892,187
Food				123,848	130,532	55,311
Fish and fish preparations ... metric tons	121,281	140,727	67,184	60,708	74,235	29,939
Tea ... 1,000 lb	29,191	37,872	7,495	8,774	13,556	2,844
Meal and wheat flour ... metric tons	114,646	28,738	5,564	15,115	2,908	531
Seasoning, mostly monosodium glutamate ... do	2,813	2,943	1,228	9,949	10,031	3,479
Beverages and tobacco				7,559	4,146	1,479
Crude materials, inedible, except fuel				69,555	83,279	38,267
Wood				13,299	21,029	11,434
Silk, raw ... 1,000 lb	63,859	76,229	30,747	42,828	46,890	17,781
Mineral fuels, lubricants, and related materials				9,074	5,670	3,613
Animal and vegetable oils and fats				11,543	12,996	12,652
Fish and marine animal oils ... metric tons	17,743	18,861	43,627	8,080	9,346	11,009
Chemicals				62,275	78,908	47,836
Fertilizers, manufactured ... metric tons	613,568	664,737	455,372	32,940	36,978	23,904
Manufactured goods				664,321	942,408	519,939
Plywood ... 1,000 sq. meters	14,576	41,209	29,880	9,513	25,519	18,553
Yarn of wool and hair ... 1,000 lb	3,546	11,862	3,418	7,719	26,322	7,268
Cotton yarn and thread ... do	21,201	29,547	12,087	15,908	23,591	11,339
Cotton fabrics ... 1,000 sq. yd	914,009	1,278,075	498,009	179,174	252,319	98,905
Silk fabrics ... do	17,892	25,911	13,146	8,697	13,640	6,903
Woolen and worsted fabrics ... do	4,981	12,051	8,216	6,826	16,815	12,612
Rayon filament fabrics ... do	228,445	263,720	144,315	43,314	49,570	24,885
Rayon spun fabrics ... do	144,946	202,542	228,026	29,224	53,148	35,606
Cement ... metric tons	795,324	904,568	428,538	17,013	19,035	8,256
Pottery				28,320	34,847	18,919
Iron and steel ... metric tons	843,471	1,183,019	719,755	139,545	166,424	86,983
Ingots, blooms, and slabs ... do	119,428	133,611	152,306	11,372	9,597	11,424
Joints, girders, and angles ... do	88,153	195,872	186,526	9,970	19,474	18,260
Universal plates and sheets, uncoated ... do	241,708	311,303	180,678	32,713	43,257	22,130
Plates and sheets, coated ... do	226,817	272,336	138,435	51,210	56,687	27,267
Railway rails ... do	15,873	88,039	81,619	2,041	7,760	7,339
Wire and wire rods ... do	25,730	67,572	63,623	3,592	8,972	8,273
Tubes, pipes, and fittings ... do	85,922	56,400	71,366	21,827	13,129	11,781
Copper ... do	5,981	30,194	24,578	5,649	23,141	20,174
Machinery and transportation equipment				188,727	202,308	107,544
Textile machinery and parts				16,530	45,494	16,859
Sewing machines ... number	818,350	1,215,058	700,386	20,348	28,174	15,935
Electrical machinery and parts				14,933	22,988	14,246
Railway vehicles and parts				9,318	8,017	8,232
Bicycles and parts				6,454	6,899	3,589
Ships and boats, over 250 gross tons ... number	28	25	12	93,351	46,473	28,084
Miscellaneous manufactured articles				126,124	165,860	102,202
Clothing				37,552	56,000	40,227
Optical and photographic instruments, appliances, and parts				13,715	15,409	8,628
Toys				23,557	32,147	17,862
Miscellaneous transactions and commodities, n. e. s.				596	656	495
Reexports				11,323	2,604	2,849

n. e. s.—Not elsewhere specified.

Table II.—Imports of Principal Commodities, Calendar Years 1953–54 and January–June 1955

[Quantity in units indicated; value in thousands of dollars]

Commodity	Quantity			Value		
	1953	1954	1955 (Jan.-June)	1953	1954	1955 (Jan.-June)
Total				2,409,830	2,399,596	1,222,167
Food				604,141	643,378	296,103
Rice, unmilled_____metric tons__	1,079,088	1,432,283	666,657	214,753	250,852	104,600
Barley, unmilled_____do____	705,931	763,799	275,536	60,558	51,104	19,749
Wheat, unmilled_____do____	1,686,500	2,187,090	971,708	139,035	168,040	71,943
Maize (corn), unmilled_____do____	186,696	194,895	189,463	14,641	14,359	14,163
Sugar_____do____	1,094,321	1,013,832	506,967	121,466	107,912	56,010
Beverages and tobacco				20,948	10,459	6,613
Crude materials, inedible, except fuels				1,154,293	1,125,970	621,686
Hides and skins, undressed_____metric tons__	59,022	46,911	30,197	30,640	19,805	10,712
Soybeans_____do____	448,407	507,765	467,085	55,636	66,492	58,915
Rubber, crude, excluding latex_____do____	91,091	81,472	43,193	46,053	38,476	28,988
Wood_____cubic meters__	1,643,290	1,869,020	981,353	44,525	48,044	30,007
Logs, lauans and apitongs_____do____	1,282,678	1,458,495	877,397	31,925	36,257	25,223
Wool, raw_____1,000 lb__	217,205	155,712	110,965	211,279	147,077	90,867
Cotton, raw except linters_____do____	1,066,619	1,078,856	538,577	373,805	409,417	207,516
Cotton mill waste, deviled cotton waste, and cotton shoddy, not further manufactured_____1,000 lb__	82,455	77,420	42,850	20,329	20,667	10,441
Jute, flax, hemp, ramie, and manila fibers_____do____	176,152	150,075	73,690	24,339	19,512	9,889
Jute_____do____	70,903	59,580	35,103	6,364	5,850	3,958
Manila_____do____	70,231	60,182	32,298	11,387	8,410	4,079
Phosphate rock_____metric tons__	1,059,503	1,383,673	783,639	17,894	24,472	15,136
Potash salts, crude_____do____	519,135	653,446	391,302	23,922	29,082	17,491
Salt_____do____	1,384,139	1,743,530	875,647	12,956	16,050	8,868
Iron ore and concentrates_____do____	4,290,202	5,004,787	2,156,829	61,283	66,235	30,327
Iron and steel scrap_____do____	1,140,766	978,130	414,166	62,772	43,878	18,072
Nonferrous metal scrap_____do____	51,693	73,828	8,384	25,355	35,808	3,220
Mineral fuels, lubricants and related materials				288,836	267,371	137,173
Anthracite coal_____metric tons__	414,794	368,221	218,682	7,825	6,516	3,920
Bituminous coal (for coking)_____do____	3,651,151	3,072,011	1,147,942	66,529	53,995	22,104
Petroleum, crude_____kiloliters__	5,927,041	7,415,984	3,922,148	120,471	134,029	68,657
Motor spirits_____do____	372,783	570,244	190,982	13,501	14,027	7,198
Gas oil, diesel oil, and other fuel oils_____do____	2,820,735	2,513,003	1,573,890	54,294	46,086	28,222
Animal and vegetable oils and fats				19,508	23,931	16,667
Beef tallow_____metric tons__	100,363	95,007	55,447	15,638	18,821	12,210
Chemicals (includes drugs)				69,172	63,862	37,383
Coal-tar dyestuffs and natural indigo_____metric tons__	1,461	1,030	768	7,544	5,941	4,861
Manufactured goods				65,492	61,305	26,363
Tin and tin alloys_____metric tons__	5,057	5,128	2,909	10,813	9,995	5,877
Machinery and transportation equipment				160,755	177,088	67,828
Metalworking machinery				17,420	25,160	11,633
Passenger automobiles_____number__	25,929	14,976	3,015	35,510	18,176	3,820
Aircraft and parts				11,134	12,771	1,468
Ships and boats_____number__	76	76	36	13,184	10,053	1,986
Miscellaneous manufactured articles				23,771	23,163	11,303
Miscellaneous transactions and commodities, n. e. s.				1,180	628	207
Reimports				1,734	2,441	841

n. e. s.—Not elsewhere specified.

Table III.—Exports to Major Countries, Calendar Years 1953–54 and January–June 1955

[In thousands of dollars]

Country	1953	1954	1955 (Jan.–June)
Total	1,274,945	1,629,367	892,187
North America	293,159	348,412	220,036
United States [1]	226,859	276,766	184,876
Canada	15,107	21,047	17,239
Cuba	1,872	3,034	2,258
Mexico	12,013	28,789	3,012
Other North and Central American countries including West Indies	37,308	18,776	12,651
South America	58,256	158,171	61,283
Argentina	15,623	48,869	35,063
Brazil	21,740	78,250	12,395
Other countries	20,893	31,052	13,825
Europe	118,754	146,309	106,809
Belgium-Luxembourg	6,017	8,045	3,887
France	11,776	11,636	4,923
Germany, Western	15,827	18,190	13,944
Italy	4,168	5,390	3,440
Netherlands	13,998	21,823	15,180
Sweden	9,624	8,420	7,210
Switzerland	4,557	4,745	2,597
United Kingdom	33,144	51,129	32,653
Other countries	19,643	17,021	22,975
Asia	654,581	796,876	385,916
Arabia	6,291	9,051	6,158
Burma	33,072	45,607	20,003
Ceylon	13,886	17,297	8,180
China	4,546	19,112	14,593
Formosa (Taiwan)	60,970	65,943	26,712
Hong Kong	62,226	77,271	39,315
India	27,422	43,860	38,020
Indonesia	105,444	119,725	30,463
Iran	14,672	23,463	13,248
Iraq	14,330	16,975	12,517
South Korea	106,839	68,573	22,569
Malaya and Singapore	39,488	47,618	35,207
Pakistan	14,911	56,005	24,469
Philippines	27,547	31,194	24,108
Ryukyu Islands	47,421	43,140	21,440
Thailand (Siam)	52,554	65,112	23,082
Other countries	22,962	46,930	25,832
Africa	128,792	138,502	84,740
Belgian Africa	8,622	13,047	1,931
British East Africa	903	3,445	6,616
British West Africa	22,803	43,437	25,893
Egypt	3,015	6,422	7,043
Liberia	53,553	25,154	19,775
Union of South Africa and territories	28,256	30,652	13,137
Other countries	11,635	16,345	10,345
Australia and Oceania	21,403	41,097	33,403
Australia	9,026	28,210	25,458
New Zealand	1,365	2,627	3,227
Other countries	11,012	10,260	4,718

[1] Excludes territories and possessions.

Table IV.—Imports From Major Countries, Calendar Years 1953–54 and January–June 1955

[In thousands of dollars]

Country	1953	1954	1955 (Jan.–June)
Total	2,409,830	2,399,596	1,222,167
North America	1,025,581	1,102,472	506,773
United States [1]	757,867	847,009	390,525
Canada	127,705	122,557	52,649
Cuba	48,600	24,277	10,290
Mexico	84,144	92,283	47,478
Other North and Central American countries, including West Indies	7,265	16,346	5,831
South America	125,835	177,315	62,405
Argentina	51,608	60,782	14,732
Brazil	39,118	73,838	35,321
Other countries	35,109	42,695	12,352
Europe	200,834	193,143	81,656
Belgium-Luxembourg	8,711	13,764	4,398
France	26,745	20,557	8,300
Germany, Western	37,858	44,107	24,738
Italy	8,492	17,487	3,354
Netherlands	16,197	11,744	5,694
Sweden	12,965	9,079	2,393
Switzerland	8,057	10,903	6,243
United Kingdom	48,828	37,108	15,851
Other countries	32,981	28,394	10,685
Asia	798,842	736,891	441,845
Arabia	110,915	124,098	56,453
Burma	50,253	63,098	31,220
Ceylon	2,201	2,639	1,206
China	29,702	40,774	39,883
Formosa (Taiwan)	64,045	57,092	41,257
Hong Kong	8,002	3,961	2,485
India	75,147	51,564	28,885
Indonesia	48,852	60,177	36,084
Iran	14,930	21,451	11,578
Iraq	872	603	2,777
South Korea	8,567	8,177	4,772
Malaya and Singapore	63,428	63,821	41,534
Pakistan	108,040	36,192	28,508
Philippines	62,733	67,134	42,531
Ryukyu Islands	14,183	10,126	8,260
Thailand (Siam)	84,655	69,175	42,745
Other countries	52,317	56,809	21,667
Africa	55,873	51,287	29,610
Belgian Africa	171	70	54
British East Africa	4,724	6,036	2,443
British West Africa	1,276	309	97
Egypt	22,828	28,018	14,583
Liberia	(2)	241	5
Union of South Africa and territories	19,579	10,585	9,070
Other countries	7,295	6,028	3,358
Australia and Oceania	202,865	138,259	99,835
Australia	172,339	117,119	87,810
New Zealand	9,762	4,504	3,070
Other countries	20,764	16,636	8,955
Special areas	----------	229	43

[1] Excludes territories and possessions.
[2] Less than $500.

Table V.—Imports of Principal Commodities, by Major Sources, Calendar Years 1953–54 and January–June 1955

[Quantity in units indicated; value in thousands of dollars]

Commodity and source	Quantity			Value		
	1953	1954	1955 (Jan.–June)	1953	1954	1955 (Jan.–June)
Rice, unmilled_____metric tons__	1,079,088	1,432,283	666,657	214,753	250,852	104,600
Thailand (Siam)_____do__	423,893	379,648	254,364	75,264	58,766	37,163
Burma_____do__	199,739	326,914	155,846	39,781	51,228	23,358
United States_____do__	177,672	345,718	113,131	38,874	68,123	19,872
China_____do__		75,213	78,050	_____	12,523	13,651
Formosa (Taiwan)_____do__	54,031	43,357	49,629	12,733	9,306	7,863
Italy_____do__	27,465	67,356	15,632	6,170	13,450	2,687
Indochina_____do__	37,918	46,231	(1)	7,919	9,096	(1)
Others_____do__	158,370	147,846	5	34,012	28,360	6
Barley, unmilled_____do__	705,931	763,799	275,536	60,558	51,104	19,749
Canada_____do__	274,270	332,795	63,443	22,154	22,758	3,973
United States_____do__	211,138	204,999	116,200	16,889	13,648	8,336
Australia_____do__	210,585	216,557	95,893	20,444	13,992	7,440
Others_____do__	9,938	9,448	_____	1,071	706	_____
Wheat, unmilled_____do__	1,686,500	2,187,090	971,708	139,035	168,040	71,943
United States_____do__	927,450	1,094,659	482,765	77,332	83,082	34,900
Canada_____do__	685,550	807,552	387,183	55,180	59,352	29,118
Argentina_____do__	32,725	264,515	78,850	3,385	24,266	6,344
Australia_____do__	40,375	20,064	22,910	3,138	1,318	1,581
Others_____do__	_____	300	_____	_____	22	_____
Sugar_____do__	1,094,321	1,013,832	506,967	121,466	107,912	56,010
Formosa (Taiwan)_____do__	336,714	332,962	195,161	40,198	38,201	22,180
Cuba_____do__	500,330	264,003	111,588	48,412	23,795	10,275
Peru_____do__	99,454	114,050	6,185	10,790	9,931	497
Ryukyu Islands_____do__	18,147	18,273	20,564	3,906	4,432	4,758
Indonesia_____do__	11,905	158,800	14,618	1,464	18,734	1,688
Others_____do__	127,771	125,744	158,851	16,696	12,819	16,612
Wool, raw_____1,000 lb__	217,205	155,712	110,965	211,279	147,077	90,867
Australia_____do__	131,785	98,705	80,184	128,229	92,059	65,344
Union of South Africa_____do__	15,127	6,321	9,382	14,527	6,072	7,063
Argentina_____do__	31,432	26,746	8,322	26,009	20,738	5,802
Brazil_____do__	15,862	11,431	2,345	14,156	11,724	2,129
Others_____do__	22,999	12,509	10,732	28,358	16,484	10,529
Cotton, raw_____do__	1,066,619	1,078,856	538,577	373,805	409,417	207,516
United States_____do__	324,034	445,469	211,929	122,009	170,527	81,845
Mexico_____do__	219,903	226,568	117,282	81,925	87,528	46,364
Pakistan_____do__	280,143	73,293	67,537	88,424	24,653	23,816
Egypt_____do__	38,865	42,476	19,942	16,936	21,469	10,728
Brazil_____do__	31,018	130,847	52,163	11,147	47,557	19,802
India_____do__	47,937	33,388	22,850	11,146	10,581	7,293
Others_____do__	124,719	126,815	46,874	42,218	47,102	17,668
Iron ore and concentrates_____metric tons__	4,290,202	5,004,787	2,156,829	61,283	66,235	30,327
Philippines_____do__	1,205,220	1,479,885	853,004	15,366	17,305	10,170
Malaya and Singapore_____do__	863,589	1,119,405	349,933	10,897	13,813	5,284
India_____do__	455,237	757,999	380,807	7,637	12,595	6,313
Canada_____do__	908,803	556,785	255,861	13,109	7,527	4,288
United States_____do__	463,578	421,529	71,462	8,699	6,345	1,085
Portuguese India_____do__	251,823	491,866	182,455	3,549	6,485	2,544
Others_____do__	141,952	167,318	63,307	2,026	2,165	643
Iron and steel scrap_____do__	1,140,766	978,130	414,166	62,772	43,878	18,072
United States_____do__	101,314	403,485	152,688	5,614	17,755	7,103
India_____do__	346,242	152,803	47,235	20,151	6,812	1,916
Ryukyu Islands_____do__	140,732	70,382	55,320	6,464	2,835	2,315
Hong Kong_____do__	38,414	31,024	27,429	2,188	1,071	1,148
Indonesia_____do__	163,949	21,077	23,382	9,178	1,142	1,102
Australia_____do__	83,655	68,981	22,066	4,599	3,349	997
Malaya and Singapore_____do__	63,947	41,587	10,143	3,693	1,914	412
Others_____do__	202,513	188,791	75,903	10,885	9,000	3,079
Phosphate rock_____do__	1,059,503	1,383,673	783,639	17,804	24,472	15,136
United States_____do__	471,928	803,247	450,971	7,033	13,481	8,470
Egypt_____do__	201,328	210,664	133,034	3,099	3,393	2,229
French Oceania_____do__	198,138	166,099	88,497	4,212	3,669	2,110
Others_____do__	188,109	203,663	111,137	3,550	3,929	2,227
Potash salts, crude_____do__	519,135	653,446	391,302	23,922	29,082	17,491
Germany, Western_____do__	179,736	251,277	154,858	8,877	11,621	7,197
France_____do__	156,675	191,942	86,852	7,823	9,517	4,254
Germany, Eastern_____do__	132,733	141,576	84,026	5,390	5,242	3,232
Others_____do__	49,991	68,651	65,566	1,832	2,702	2,808
Salt_____do__	1,384,139	1,743,530	875,647	12,956	16,050	8,868
India_____do__	248,344	210,257	65,423	2,447	1,944	662
Arabia_____do__	186,125	214,861	161,147	1,783	2,044	1,695
Spain_____do__	103,628	134,520	80,160	996	1,396	974
Egypt_____do__	252,371	278,074	128,943	2,259	2,660	1,419
China_____do__	197,686	428,498	186,175	1,616	3,414	1,620
Formosa (Taiwan)_____do__	132,155	80,869	94,470	1,220	703	823
Others_____do__	263,830	396,451	159,329	2,635	3,889	1,675
Coal, all kinds_____do__	4,920,864	3,607,889	1,367,667	89,804	63,060	26,045
United States_____do__	3,474,830	2,935,979	1,111,720	65,750	52,422	21,626
Indochina_____do__	265,050	194,382	170,074	5,267	3,699	3,198
Others_____do__	1,180,984	477,528	85,873	18,787	6,939	1,221

1 Less than one-half the unit of quantity or value.

Table V.—Imports of Principal Commodities, by Major Sources, Calendar Years 1953–54 and January–June 1955—Continued

[Quantity in units indicated; value in thousands of dollars]

Commodity and source	Quantity			Value		
	1953	1954	1955 (Jan.–June)	1953	1954	1955 (Jan.–June)
Petroleum, crude_____kiloliters__	5,927,041	7,415,984	3,922,148	120,471	134,029	68,657
Arabia_____do____	4,443,925	5,663,869	2,785,927	90,088	100,818	48,256
British Borneo_____do____	283,193	110,141	428,167	5,725	2,047	8,103
Indonesia_____do____	239,501	489,441	477,120	4,754	8,878	7,915
Others_____do____	960,422	1,152,533	230,934	19,904	22,286	4,383
Gas oil, diesel oil, and other fuel oil_____do____	2,820,735	2,513,003	1,573,890	54,294	46,086	28,222
United States_____do____	1,334,155	930,065	812,049	25,942	15,947	13,871
Arabia_____do____	1,036,313	1,146,513	369,885	19,858	21,805	7,286
Iran_____do____	46,228	286,264	189,622	992	5,724	3,526
Malaya and Singapore_____do____	292,348	130,089	198,770	5,342	2,220	3,462
Others_____do____	111,691	20,072	3,564	2,160	390	77
Hides and skins_____metric tons__	59,022	46,911	30,197	30,640	19,805	10,712
United States_____do____	33,612	32,340	23,729	16,242	12,557	8,042
Australia_____do____	3,227	1,762	796	1,491	646	263
New Zealand_____do____	4,197	1,585	399	2,263	752	150
Thailand (Siam)_____do____	1,120	1,125	1,445	535	580	712
Others_____do____	16,866	10,099	3,828	10,109	5,270	1,545
Soybeans_____do____	448,407	507,765	467,085	55,636	66,492	58,915
United States_____do____	408,704	442,874	338,877	49,929	56,232	40,855
China_____do____	24,420	45,864	115,253	3,495	7,413	16,152
Others_____do____	15,283	19,027	12,955	2,212	2,847	1,908
Rubber, crude, excluding latex_____1,000 lb__	91,091	81,472	43,193	46,053	38,476	28,988
Malaya and Singapore_____do____	48,364	65,615	34,178	24,205	30,650	22,600
Indonesia_____do____	41,785	13,442	8,901	21,386	6,790	6,314
Others_____do____	942	2,415	114	462	1,036	74
Wood_____cubic meters__	1,643,290	1,869,020	981,353	44,525	48,044	30,007
Philippines_____do____	1,245,454	1,312,318	794,907	31,054	33,124	23,292
United States_____do____	288,830	378,198	88,624	10,182	10,360	3,927
Others_____do____	109,006	178,504	97,822	3,289	4,560	2,788
Passenger automobiles_____number__	25,929	14,976	3,015	35,510	18,176	3,820
United States_____do____	20,299	8,485	2,678	27,753	14,367	3,497
Germany, Western_____do____	1,311	1,614	91	1,970	1,984	103
United Kingdom_____do____	3,043	986	225	4,093	1,121	195
Others_____do____	1,276	3,891	21	1,694	704	25

Table VI.—Exports of Principal Commodities, by Major Markets, Calendar Years 1953–54 and January–June 1955

[Quantity in units indicated; value in thousands of dollars]

Commodity and market	Quantity			Value		
	1953	1954	1955 (Jan.–June)	1953	1954	1955 (Jan.–June)
Fish and fish preparations_____metric tons__	121,281	140,727	67,184	60,708	74,235	29,939
United States_____do____	63,662	69,369	38,671	38,186	39,879	18,897
Formosa (Taiwan)_____do____	16,173	17,114	3,461	4,136	4,081	630
Hong Kong_____do____	8,846	5,529	2,750	3,890	1,777	831
Burma_____do____	4,730	5,981	3,234	1,848	2,059	902
Malaya and Singapore_____do____	7,501	6,163	2,555	2,523	2,115	950
United Kingdom_____do____	(1)	5,993	429	(1)	8,023	673
Egypt_____do____	2,342	3,549	3,025	1,019	1,401	1,185
Others_____do____	18,027	27,029	13,059	9,106	14,900	5,871
Tea_____1,000 lb__	29,191	37,872	7,495	8,774	13,556	2,844
United States_____do____	3,928	5,792	915	1,499	2,301	391
Algeria_____do____	7,269	8,018	2,142	2,002	2,918	793
United Kingdom_____do____	230	6,168	761	42	1,938	253
French Morocco_____do____	8,304	4,738	876	2,600	1,746	360
Chile_____do____	490	2,928	50	172	1,110	27
Indochina_____do____	1,728	1,827	_____	443	724	_____
Others_____do____	7,242	8,401	2,751	2,016	2,819	1,020
Silk, raw_____do____	63,859	76,229	30,747	42,828	46,890	17,781
United States_____do____	15,248	46,086	18,526	9,953	27,510	10,533
France_____do____	10,640	9,159	5,211	7,508	5,798	3,120
Netherlands_____do____	7,868	1,081	15	5,017	757	9
United Kingdom_____do____	4,285	5,006	1,141	2,970	3,134	633
Germany, Western_____do____	454	283	226	2,374	1,360	1,021
Indochina_____do____	3,070	3,282	1,314	1,980	2,071	780
Brazil_____do____	767	225	_____	3,843	1,198	_____
Others_____do____	21,527	11,107	4,314	9,183	5,062	1,685
Cotton yarn and thread_____do____	21,201	29,547	12,087	15,908	23,591	11,339
Indonesia_____do____	4,786	11,146	4,020	3,314	7,930	2,830
Burma_____do____	6,410	6,048	1,523	5,193	4,565	1,371
Pakistan_____do____	4,171	3,198	2,523	3,268	2,602	2,105
Hong Kong_____do____	1,256	3,575	692	921	2,449	539
Germany, Eastern_____do____		1,559	n. a.	_____	2,445	n. a.
Others_____do____	4,578	4,021	3,329	3,212	3,600	4,494

See footnote at end of table.

Table VI.—Exports of Principal Commodities, by Major Markets, Calendar Years 1953–54 and January–June 1955—Continued

[Quantity in units indicated; value in thousands of dollars]

Commodity and market	Quantity			Value		
	1953	1954	1955 (Jan.-June)	1953	1954	1955 (Jan.-June)
Cotton fabrics_____1,000 sq. yd__	914, 009	1, 278, 075	498, 009	179, 174	252, 319	98, 905
Indonesia_____do___	303, 851	282, 509	44, 650	58, 202	54, 179	8, 916
Thailand (Siam)_____do___	83, 162	109, 192	31, 919	16, 639	21, 409	5, 749
United States_____do___	33, 600	50, 049	45, 149	5, 946	10, 701	9, 646
Australia_____do___	21, 949	57, 591	35, 864	4, 851	13, 702	8, 520
Hong Kong_____do___	48, 466	54, 352	17, 350	8, 959	10, 057	3, 585
Malaya and Singapore_____do___	35, 841	53, 241	29, 008	7, 830	10, 756	5, 865
Burma_____do___	40, 665	68, 240	30, 415	7, 943	13, 611	5, 727
Iran_____do___	43, 513	42, 941	25, 947	8, 409	8, 837	5, 258
British West Africa_____do___	29, 305	61, 253	28, 640	6, 834	13, 866	6, 247
Netherlands_____do___	17, 420	36, 622	25, 213	2, 603	5, 494	3, 757
United Kingdom_____do___	32, 702	66, 491	30, 783	4, 712	10, 212	4, 659
Pakistan_____do___	382	84, 926	6, 313	141	16, 475	1, 300
Others_____do___	223, 153	310, 668	146, 758	46, 105	63, 020	29, 676
Silk fabrics_____do___	17, 892	25, 911	13, 146	8, 697	13, 640	6, 903
United States_____do___	6, 476	9, 056	6, 838	3, 342	5, 272	3, 832
France_____do___	1, 626	1, 521	1, 001	668	662	437
Brazil_____do___	411	3, 419	2	250	1, 823	3
Canada_____do___	1, 350	998	458	490	554	342
Others_____do___	8, 029	10, 917	4, 847	3, 947	5, 329	2, 289
Rayon filament fabrics_____do___	228, 445	263, 720	144, 315	43, 314	49, 570	24, 885
Hong Kong_____do___	29, 241	29, 729	15, 981	4, 915	4, 580	2, 208
Malaya and Singapore_____do___	19, 096	26, 925	32, 174	3, 268	4, 628	5, 269
Indonesia_____do___	55, 766	26, 977	8, 949	9, 867	4, 931	1, 612
Ceylon_____do___	15, 604	20, 692	6, 716	3, 239	4, 178	1, 216
Union of South Africa and territories_____do___	29, 878	35, 797	8, 134	6, 206	7, 222	1, 465
Burma_____do___	7, 948	8, 941	2, 180	1, 569	1, 823	418
Iraq_____do___	8, 970	9, 030	7, 354	1, 654	1, 638	1, 200
Arabia_____do___	9, 695	13, 162	9, 344	1, 897	2, 493	1, 709
British West Africa_____do___	6, 447	13, 037	7, 835	1, 495	2, 706	1, 551
Others_____do___	45, 800	79, 430	45, 648	9, 204	15, 371	8, 237
Spun rayon fabrics_____do___	144, 946	302, 542	228, 026	29, 224	53, 148	35, 606
Hong Kong_____do___	9, 800	19, 023	13, 411	2, 106	3, 432	2, 058
Malaya and Singapore_____do___	8, 511	24, 096	24, 913	1, 495	3, 966	4, 062
Iraq_____do___	21, 677	29, 497	26, 847	4, 595	5, 781	4, 336
British West Africa_____do___	6, 314	27, 229	29, 193	1, 351	4, 913	5, 487
Union of South Africa and territories_____do___	17, 615	27, 351	12, 319	3, 828	5, 897	2, 661
Belgian Africa_____do___	4, 551	19, 327	3, 355	1, 117	3, 759	570
Philippines_____do___	737	11, 883	20, 244	119	1, 703	2, 421
Others_____do___	75, 741	144, 136	97, 744	14, 613	23, 697	14, 011
Fertilizers, manufactured_____metric tons__	613, 568	714, 737	455, 622	32, 937	36, 975	23, 904
South Korea_____do___	350, 962	295, 388	175, 100	19, 385	14, 268	9, 511
Formosa (Taiwan)_____do___	153, 683	273, 673	168, 874	7, 793	15, 168	9, 110
China_____do___	27, 876	105, 546	96, 142	1, 047	5, 121	4, 600
Others_____do___	81, 047	40, 130	15, 506	4, 712	2, 418	683
Cement_____do___	795, 324	904, 568	428, 538	17, 013	19, 035	8, 256
South Korea_____do___	184, 650	157, 223	61, 260	4, 037	3, 294	1, 144
Ryukyu Islands_____do___	155, 128	118, 481	69, 246	3, 308	2, 530	1, 348
Hong Kong_____do___	103, 320	136, 027	80, 510	2, 192	2, 864	1, 509
Malaya and Singapore_____do___	88, 377	99, 065	49, 048	1, 869	2, 070	919
Indonesia_____do___	58, 959	122, 341	10, 580	1, 270	2, 569	223
Others_____do___	204, 890	271, 431	157, 894	4, 337	5, 708	3, 113
Pottery_____do___				28, 320	34, 847	18, 919
United States_____				12, 950	16, 422	9, 286
Indonesia_____				1, 011	1, 131	209
Iran_____				1, 129	1, 197	607
Union of South Africa and territories_____				847	1, 094	752
Canada_____				1, 087	1, 124	553
Indochina_____				446	710	310
Thailand (Siam)_____				463	606	211
Malaya and Singapore_____				948	879	610
Philippines_____				877	630	560
Burma_____				1, 222	701	353
Others_____				7, 340	10, 353	5, 468
Iron and steel_____metric tons__	843, 471	1, 183, 019	719, 755	139, 545	166, 424	86, 983
Argentina_____do___	90, 993	306, 201	188, 191	11, 298	37, 463	18, 161
India_____do___	66, 062	138, 736	121, 701	9, 587	14, 890	13, 418
Indonesia_____do___	28, 315	62, 746	18, 565	6, 160	13, 345	3, 518
Philippines_____do___	72, 326	52, 170	40, 336	12, 664	9, 030	5, 862
United States_____do___	89, 077	21, 755	11, 260	18, 047	2, 700	1, 020
Thailand (Siam)_____do___	69, 235	6, 154	25, 122	12, 785	724	3, 752
United Kingdom_____do___	47, 039	1, 230	9, 182	4, 634	342	880
Germany, Western_____do___	40, 721	(¹)	1, 997	5, 073	(¹)	230
Malaya and Singapore_____do___	44, 750	7, 746	31, 739	8, 840	633	4, 392
Pakistan_____do___	19, 343	54, 103	26, 683	2, 336	3, 672	3, 743
Others_____do___	275, 610	532, 178	244, 979	48, 121	83, 625	32, 007
Copper and alloys of copper_____do___	5, 981	30, 194	24, 578	5, 649	23, 141	20, 174
Brazil_____do___	2, 294	6, 294	1, 544	2, 275	5, 515	1, 313
Argentina_____do___	1, 516	1, 092	908	1, 206	967	786
Netherlands_____do___		8, 367	6, 819	----------	5, 841	5, 650
India_____do___	4	2, 067	1, 164	8	1, 443	944
Formosa (Taiwan)_____do___	752	1, 411	496	817	1, 244	405
Others_____do___	1, 415	10, 963	13, 647	1, 343	8, 131	11, 076

See footnote at end of table.

Table VI.—Exports of Principal Commodities, by Major Markets, Calendar Years 1953–54 and January–June 1955—Continued

[Quantity in units indicated; value in thousands of dollars]

Commodity and market	Quantity			Value		
	1953	1954	1955 (Jan.–June)	1953	1954	1955 (Jan.–June)
Textile machinery and parts_____	_____	_____	_____	16,530	45,494	6,859
Pakistan_____	_____	_____	_____	4,526	22,797	6,056
South Korea_____	_____	_____	_____	2,997	7,334	946
Brazil_____	_____	_____	_____	1,591	5,154	555
Formosa (Taiwan)_____	_____	_____	_____	2,684	1,908	513
India_____	_____	_____	_____	1,709	1,933	893
Yugoslavia_____	_____	_____	_____		691	5,433
Others_____	_____	_____	_____	3,023	5,677	2,463
Sewing machines_____number__	818,350	1,215,058	700,386	20,348	28,174	15,935
United States_____do____	375,693	333,539	292,852	7,184	6,128	5,692
Brazil_____do____	38,053	180,935	35,774	678	3,071	538
Colombia_____do____	34,949	65,927	22,616	1,111	1,849	662
Indonesia_____do____	1,764	68,171	28,274	71	1,601	652
Malaya and Singapore_____do____	25,946	43,612	20,304	903	1,323	544
South Korea_____do____	2,255	52,863	12,452	134	1,053	238
Peru_____do____	36,033	27,342	13,337	905	1,050	414
Hong Kong_____do____	35,301	39,351	20,009	1,160	905	410
Venezuela_____do____	35,332	24,567	6,973	1,340	926	238
Others_____do____	233,024	378,751	247,795	6,862	10,268	6,547
Ships and boats, over 250 gross tons_____do____	28	25	12	93,351	46,473	28,084
Liberia_____do____	12	6	6	48,970	24,633	19,536
Indonesia_____do____		2	_____		6,099	
United States_____do____	1	4		1,176	13,623	_____
Panama_____do____	5		1	23,405		2,483
Denmark_____do____	1	_____	1	3,852		2,269
United Kingdom_____do____	2			11,000		
Others_____do____	7	13	4	4,948	2,118	3,796
Plywood_____1,000 sq. meters__	14,576	41,209	29,880	9,513	25,519	18,553
United States_____do____	10,125	24,538	20,361	7,122	16,406	13,600
United Kingdom_____do____	1,621	8,574	6,495	716	4,108	2,992
Canada_____do____	211	1,243	1,124	194	838	732
Others_____do____	2,619	6,854	1,900	1,481	4,167	1,229

¹ Less than one-half the unit.
n. a.—Not available.

Table VII.—Imports From the United States, Territories, and Possessions, by Principal Commodities, Calendar Years 1953–54 and January–June 1955

[Quantity in units indicated; value in thousands of dollars]

Commodity	Quantity			Value		
	1953	1954	1955 (Jan.–June)	1953	1954	1955 (Jan.–June)
Total_____	_____	_____	_____	761,304	851,129	391,731
Foodstuffs_____	_____	_____	_____	159,148	179,927	n. a.
Wheat, unmilled_____1,000 metric tons__	928	1,095	483	77,332	83,082	34,900
Rice, unmilled_____do____	178	346	113	38,874	68,123	19,872
Barley, unmilled_____do____	211	205	116	16,889	13,648	8,336
Maize (corn), unmilled_____do____	164	76	153	12,832	5,799	11,423
Beverages and tobacco_____	_____	_____	_____	11,922	8,089	n. a.
Crude materials, inedible, except fuels_____	_____	_____	_____	271,187	360,723	n. a.
Wood_____1,000 cubic meters__	289	378	89	10,182	10,360	3,927
Hides and skins_____1,000 metric tons__	34	32	24	16,242	12,557	8,042
Soybeans_____do____	409	443	339	49,929	56,232	40,855
Cotton, raw, except linters_____1,000 lb__	324,034	445,469	211,929	122,009	170,527	81,845
Cotton millwaste, deviled cotton waste, and cotton shoddy, not further manufactured_____1,000 lb__	53,500	42,344	15,314	15,650	13,061	4,406
Phosphate rock_____1,000 metric tons__	472	803	451	7,033	13,481	8,470
Iron ore and concentrates_____do____	464	422	71	8,699	6,345	1,085
Iron and steel scrap_____do____	101	403	153	5,614	17,755	7,103
Chemical woodpulp_____do____	13	31	18	2,058	5,770	4,101
Mineral fuels, lubricants, and related materials_____	_____	_____	_____	114,291	85,433	n. a.
Coal_____1,000 metric tons__	3,475	2,936	1,112	65,750	52,422	21,626
Petroleum, crude_____1,000 kiloliters__	198	159	45	4,828	3,373	842
Motor spirits_____do____	166	128	64	7,418	4,734	2,708
Gas oil, diesel oil, and other fuel oils_____do____	1,334	930	812	25,942	15,947	13,871
Lubricating oils and greases_____1,000 metric tons__	33	37	n. a.	3,901	4,010	n. a.
Animal and vegetable oils and fats_____	_____	_____	_____	15,479	18,973	n. a.
Beef tallow_____metric tons__	94,696	91,676	44,128	14,719	18,150	9,374
Chemicals_____	_____	_____	_____	37,329	36,547	n. a.
Medical and pharmaceutical products_____	_____	_____	_____	9,661	6,132	n. a.
Coal-tar dyestuffs and natural indigo_____metric tons__	192	213	111	836	857	549
Manufactured goods classified by material_____	_____	_____	_____	18,282	23,358	n. a.
Machinery and transportation equipment_____	_____	_____	_____	118,442	123,204	n. a.
Passenger automobiles_____number__	20,299	8,485	2,678	27,753	14,367	3,497
Aircraft_____	_____	_____	_____	8,428	7,078	n. a.
Metalworking machinery_____	_____	_____	_____	12,721	15,064	4,900
Miscellaneous manufactured articles_____	_____	_____	_____	14,856	14,751	n. a.
Miscellaneous transactions and commodities, n. e. s_____	_____	_____	_____	368	124	n. a.

n. a.—Not available.
n. e. s.—Not elsewhere specified.

99

Table VIII.—Exports to the United States, Territories, and Possessions, by Principal Commodities, Calendar Years 1953–54 and January–June 1955

[Quantity in units, indicated; value in thousands of dollars]

Commodity	Quantity			Value		
	1953	1954	1955 (Jan.–June)	1953	1954	1955 (Jan.–June)
Total				235,669	284,138	188,302
Foodstuffs				45,040	45,963	n. a.
Fish and fish preparations_____metric tons	63,662	69,369	38,671	38,186	39,879	18,897
Tuna, fresh, chilled, or frozen_____do	39,059	46,870	n. a.	15,446	19,369	n. a.
Tuna, canned_____do	10,932	6,738	n. a.	10,097	7,672	n. a.
Crabs, canned_____do	1,727	1,120	n. a.	4,061	2,486	n. a.
Other fish and fish preparations_____do	8,885	9,635	n. a.	5,963	7,449	n. a.
Tea_____1,000 lb	3,928	5,792	915	1,499	2,301	391
Seasoning, mostly monosodium glutamate_____metric tons	285	237	96	912	763	264
Beverages and tobacco				151	206	n. a.
Crude materials, inedible, except fuel				19,602	39,293	n. a.
Lumber, nonconiferous				2,399	5,010	n. a.
Silk, raw_____1,000 lb	15,248	46,086	18,526	9,953	27,510	10,533
Bristles_____metric tons	290	290	n. a.	1,565	1,434	n. a.
Mineral fuels, lubricants, and related materials				37	6	n. a.
Animal and vegetable oils and fats				4,262	3,332	n. a.
Fish and marine animal oils_____metric tons	5,019	4,584	6,685	3,382	3,158	3,219
Chemicals				4,832	3,804	n. a.
Manufactured goods classified by material				95,187	102,214	n. a.
Plywood_____1,000 sq. meters	10,125	24,538	20,361	7,122	16,406	13,600
Cotton fabrics_____1,000 sq. yd	33,600	50,049	45,149	5,946	10,701	9,646
Silk fabrics_____do	6,476	9,056	6,838	3,342	5,272	3,832
Woolen and worsted fabrics_____do	374	1,218	1,651	576	1,901	2,628
Bed linen, table linen, etc				4,659	4,342	3,412
Carpets				7,569	7,424	n. a.
Pottery				12,950	16,422	9,286
Pearls, natural and cultured				2,986	3,645	3,236
Iron and steel, including alloy steel_____metric tons	89,077	21,755	11,260	18,047	2,700	1,020
Machinery and transportation equipment				10,144	25,003	n. a.
Sewing machines_____number	375,693	333,539	292,852	7,184	6,128	5,692
Miscellaneous manufactured articles				55,912	63,759	n. a.
Clothing				14,910	18,441	n. a.
Optical and photographic instruments, appliances, and parts				4,631	5,067	3,822
Ornamental flowers, feathers, etc				4,269	4,354	n. a.
Toys				14,227	17,628	10,987
Miscellaneous transactions and commodities				502	558	n. a.

n. a.—Not available.

Table IX.—Estimated Value of Foreign Investments in Japan, End of Calendar Years 1953–54

[In millions of dollars]

Item	1953			1954		
	Pre-war	Post-war	Total	Pre-war	Post-war	Total
Equity investments	(1)			(1)		
Stocks and proprietary interests		32			37	
Technological assistance contracts		2 209			2 293	
Real estate		15			16	
Total	1 125	256	381	1 125	346	471
Loans:						
Public						
External bonds	3 406		406	3 376		376
International Bank for Reconstruction and Development		40	40		40	40
Private	(1)	47	47		61	61
Total	406	4 87	493	376	4 101	477
Grand total	531	343	874	501	447	948

1 The figure of $125 million used in this tabulation as representing the aggregate value of all types of prewar private foreign investment in Japan is an approximation derived from the estimated prewar value of these investments.
2 Represents capitalized value calculated by the Foreign Investment Section, Japanese Ministry of Finance.
3 Indicates estimated interest, as well as principal of issued bonds not due as of the end of the year, in accordance with the September 1952 agreement on the funding of dollar and sterling prewar bonds.
4 Accumulated total of private loans outstanding as of the end of the respective year.

Source: Data based on Japanese Government sources.

Table X.—Capitalized Value of Technological Assistance Contracts Approved by the Japanese Government,[1] by Country and Year, June 1950–December 1954 [2]

[In thousands of dollars]

Country	June–Dec. 1950	Calendar year— 1951	1952	1953	1954	Total	Per-cent of total
Total	12,404	80,181	60,495	55,047	84,803	292,930	100.0
Canada			204	702		906	(³)
Denmark	1,054			12	87	1,153	.4
United Kingdom			4,687	8,548	307	13,542	4.7
France		33,650	1,354	2,033	317	37,354	12.8
Germany, Western			3,605	6,175	1,264	11,043	3.8
Netherlands			2,626			2,626	1.0
Italy				581	12,829	13,410	4.6
Panama				3,051	8,220	11,271	3.9
Sweden		758	210	44	37	1,049	.3
Switzerland	709	6,349	446	7,199	4,001	18,704	6.4
United States	10,641	39,424	47,363	26,702	57,741	181,871	62.1

[1] Under the provisions of the Foreign Investment Law.
[2] Represents capitalized value calculated by the Foreign Investment Section, Ministry of Finance, on the basis of a 5-percent interest rate and individual tenure of contracts.
[3] Negligible.

Source: Japanese Ministry of Finance.

Table XI.—Classification of Technological Assistance Contracts Approved by the Japanese Government,[1] by Industry, as of December 31, 1954

Industry	Number of cases	Percent of total
Total	431	100
Machinery	237	55
Electrical	100	23
Transportation	25	6
Other	112	26
Metal and metal products	38	9
Chemical	77	18
Spinning and weaving	24	6
Petroleum	15	3
Rubber and feathers	12	3
Construction	7	2
Glass and stone	10	2
Pulp and paper	6	1
Electric power and gas	3	1
Recreation and amusement	1	(²)
Printing and publishing	1	(²)

[1] Under the provisions of the Foreign Investment Law.
[2] Negligible.

Source: Foreign Capital Research Society, c/o Bank of Japan.

Table XII.—Loans Extended to Japanese Companies by Foreign Investors, June 1950–December 1954 [1]

[Amount in U. S. dollars]

Industry and Japanese recipient	Foreign investor	Nationality	Amount	Term (years)	Rate of Interest (percent)
Paper, pulp, and related products— Nippon Pulptex Co., Ltd	I. Lawrence Lasavoy	United States	100,000	2	6.0
Chemical and related products— Japanese Geon Co., Ltd	B. F. Goodrich Chemical Co	do	175,000	5	7.0
Kyowa Fermentation Industrial Co., Ltd	Hongkong Transportation Co., Ltd	Hong Kong	138,889	5	5.0
Lederle (Japan), Ltd	American Cyanamid Co	United States	100,000	6	6.0
Takeda Pharmaceutical Co., Ltd	do	do	150,000	5½	4.0
Ciba Products Co., Ltd	Ciba, Ltd	Switzerland	83,600	6	0
Petroleum and coal products— Koa Oil Co., Ltd	Caltex Oil Products Co	United States	950,000	5	4.0
Do	do	do	1,300,000	8	4.0
Mitsubishi Oil Co., Ltd	Tide Water Associated Oil Co	do	333,333	1	5.0
Do	do	do	500,000	1	5.0
Nippon Petroleum Refining Co., Ltd	California-Texas Corp	do	[2] 1,234,810	13	4.0
Toa Fuel Processing Co., Ltd	Standard-Vacuum Oil Co	do	3,500,000	10	4.0
Mitsubishi Oil Co., Ltd	Tide Water Associated Oil Co	do	1,670,379	1	5.0
Nippon Petroleum Refining Co., Ltd	Caltex International, Ltd	do	[2] 17,765,019	11½	4.0
Koa Oil Co., Ltd	Caltex Oil Products Co	do	41,374	5	4.0
Iron, steel, nonferrous metals, and metal products— Nippon Light Metal Co., Ltd	Aluminium, Ltd	Canada	1,792,000	8	5.5
Machinery— Toyo Carrier Manufacturing Co., Ltd	Carrier Corp	United States	26,000	3	4.0
Gadelius & Co., Ltd	Gadelius & Co., A. B	Sweden	96,000	4	0
Toyo Carrier Manufacturing Co., Ltd	Carrier Corp	United States	26,000	3	4.0
Do	do	do	300,000	17	4.0
Construction— Electric Power Development Co	Bank of America	do	7,000,000	3	4.5
Do	do	do	2,000,000	2¼	4.5
Electric power and gas— Japan Development Bank	International Bank for Reconstruction and Development.		40,200,000	20	5.0
Tokyo Electric Power Co	International General Electric Co	United States	9,989,135	7½	5.0
Transportation— Mitsui Steamship Co., Ltd	Bank of America	do	2,800,000	1½	5.0
Nitto Merchant Shipping Co., Ltd	do	do	2,000,000	3	5.0
Iino Marine Transportation Co., Ltd	do	do	2,400,000	3	5.0
Mitsui Steamship Co., Ltd	do	do	2,800,000	3	5.0
Foreign trade and wholesale— Nippon Goodyear Co	Goodyear Tire & Rubber Co	do	500,000	5	5.0
Consolidated Oil Co., Ltd., of Japan	Consolidated Oil Co	do	100,000	15	4.75
Warehousing and storage— Showa Trading Co., Ltd	Hongkong Transportation Co., Ltd	Hong Kong	69,445	5	5.0
Akita Warehouse Co., Ltd	Credit Suisse	Switzerland	105,669	3	6.0
Spinning and weaving— Naigai Knitting Co., Ltd	Julius Kayser & Co	United States	80,000	4	6.0
Teikoku Rayon Co., Ltd	Ing. A. Maurer, S. A	Switzerland	375,276	3	5.5
Do	do	do	426,624	3	6.5

[1] In accordance with the provisions of the Foreign Investment Law which accounts for all but a minor fraction of the total.
[2] Original loan amounted to $19,000,000; on March 25, 1953, $17,765,019 of total outstanding at that time was taken over by Caltex International Ltd.

Source: Foreign Capital Research Society, c/o Bank of Japan.

Table XIII.—Japanese Companies in Which Foreigners Participate in Management, by Major Industry Groups,[1] as of December 1954

[Capital in millions of yen]

Contracting party	Capital	Foreign investor	Nationality	Percent of foreign ownership
Spinning and weaving—				
Teikoku Yarn Manufacturing Co., Ltd	191	J. & P. Coats, Ltd	England	60.0
Toyama Fishing Net Manufacturing Co., Ltd	50	Linen Thread Co	do	60.0
Naigai Knitting Co	120	Julius Kayser & Co	United States	25.0
Katakura Hudson Hosiery Co., Ltd	200	Hudson Hosiery Co	do	31.5
Lumber and wood products—				
Hida Manufacturing Co., Ltd	17	Stanley S. Slotkin	do	12.0
Shinmaru Hatch Board Co	5	I. J. Langleb	do	10.0
Paper and related products—				
Nippon Pulptex Co., Ltd	5	I. Lawrence Lasavoy and six others	do	99.7
Chemicals and related products—				
Ferro-Nippon Co., Ltd	54	Ferro Enamel Corp	do	10.0
Japanese Geon Co., Ltd	500	B. F. Goodrich Chemical Co	do	35.0
Japan Reichhold Chemicals, Inc	43	Reichhold Chemicals, Inc	do	45.0
Hokkaido Development Co., Ltd	33	International Engineers, Inc	do	18.0
Monsanto Chemical Manufacturing Co., Ltd	1,200	Monsanto Chemical Co	do	50.0
Tokyo Ink Manufacturing Co., Ltd	50	Interchemical Corp	do	23.1
Kyowa Fermentation Manufacturing Co., Ltd	1,120	Hongkong Transportation Co., Ltd	Hong Kong	11.0
Asahi-Dow, Ltd	400	Dow Chemical International, Ltd	United States	50.0
Nippon Titanium Co., Inc	200	R. S. Aries and Associates, Inc		75.0
Lederle (Japan), Ltd	70	American Cyanamid, Co	do	50.0
Pfizer-Tanabe Co., Ltd	100	Pfizer Corporation	Panama	50.0
Japan Merck Co., Ltd	25	Merck & Co., Inc	United States	50.0
Nippon Color Manufacturing Co., Ltd	30	Sinclair & Valentine Co., Ltd	do	20.0
Nippon Special Paint Co., Ltd	19	Yates & Smart Paint Co	do	35.0
Petroleum—				
Toa Fuel Manufacturing Co., Ltd	2,106	Standard-Vacuum Oil	do	55.0
Koa Oil Co., Ltd	660	Caltex Oil Products Co	do	50.0
Mitsubishi Oil Co., Ltd	2,400	Tide Water Associated Oil Co	do	50.0
Nippon Petroleum Refining Co., Ltd	4,000	California-Texas Corp	do	50.0
Showa Oil Co., Ltd	1,700	Anglo-Saxon Petroleum Co., Ltd	England	50.0
Rubber and leather products—				
Yokohama Rubber Co., Ltd	669	B. F. Goodrich Co	United States	35.0
Toyo Shoe Manufacturing Co., Ltd	20	Palama Shoe Co., Ltd	do	48.0
Dunlop Rubber Co. (Japan), Ltd	236	Dunlop Rubber Co., Ltd	England	100.0
Chiyoda Shoe Manufacturing Co., Ltd	70	Intercontinental Shoe Corp	United States	10.0
Paramount Shoe Co., Ltd	20	Palama Shoe Co., Ltd	do	50.0
Stone, clay, and glass products—				
Nippon Sheet Glass Co., Ltd	600	Libby-Owens-Ford Glass Co	do	14.0
American-Japanese Hollow Tile Co., Ltd	3	Saburo Fujimoto	do	70.0
Metals and metal products—				
Toyo Aluminum Co., Ltd	65	Aluminum, Ltd	Canada	51.0
Nippon Light Metals Co., Ltd	1,860	do	do	50.0
Japan Drive-It Co., Ltd	20	Daniel W. Clery and three others	United States	50.0
Shinko Pfaudler Co., Ltd	135	The Pfaudler Co	do	33.3
Electrical machinery, equipment, and supplies—				
Mitsubishi Electrical Manufacturing Co., Ltd	2,400	Westinghouse Electric International Co	do	4.0
Sumitomo Electrical Manufacturing Co., Ltd	2,000	International Standard Electric Corp	do	17.5
Furukawa Battery Co., Ltd	20	Gould-National Batteries, Inc	do	10.0
Fuji Electrical Manufacturing Co., Ltd	1,500	Siemens Schuckertwerke, A. G	Germany	3.0
Do	1,000	Siemens & Halske, A. G	do	3.0
Matsushita Electronics Corp	660	N. V. Philips Gloeilampenfabricken	Netherlands	30.0
Ray-O-Vac Co. (Japan), Ltd	180	Ray-O-Vac Co	United States	40.0
Nippon Electrical Equipment Co., Ltd	400	Robert Bosch G. m. b. H	Germany	10.0
Tokyo-Shibaura Electric Co., Ltd	4,000	International General Electric Co	United States	15.9
Nippon Electric Co., Ltd	1,000	International Standard Electric Co	do	32.7
Transportation machinery—				
Toyo Aircraft Manufacturing Co	400	Fletcher Aviation Corp	do	10.0
Other machinery—				
Babcock Hitachi, Ltd	360	Babcock & Wilcox, Ltd	England	50.0
International Business Machines Co. of Japan	30	International Business Machines Corp	United States	99.0
Japan Remington Rand, Inc	20	Remington Rand, Inc	do	70.0
National Cash Register Co. (Japan), Ltd	125	National Cash Register Co	do	70.0
Toyo Carrier Manufacturing Co., Ltd	2	Carrier Corp	do	75.0
Fuji Tablewares Co., Ltd	10	E. C., Ltd	do	50.0
Toyo-Otis Elevator Co., Ltd	73	Otis Elevator Co	do	99.9
Tokyo Precision Instrument Co., Ltd	160	Sperry Corp	do	25.0
Nihon Regulator Co., Ltd	18	Askania Regulator Co	do	33.0
Niigata Converter Co., Ltd	40	Twin Disc Clutch Co	do	25.0
Nippon Grinnell Sprinkler Co., Ltd	8	Mather & Plate, Ltd	England	100.0
Niigata Worthington Co., Ltd	26	Worthington Corp	United States	96.0
Construction—				
Ishikawajima Koehring Co	100	Koehring Co	do	25.0
Nippon Water Main Cleaning Co., Ltd	10	National Water Main Cleaning Co	do	25.0
Services—				
Japan Air Lines Equipment & Supplies Co., Ltd	200	Northwest Airlines, Inc	do	14.7
Do	200	Transocean Air Lines	do	14.5
American Electronics Enterprises Ltd	30	Radio Corporation of America	do	100.0
Foreign trade and wholesale—				
Shinozaki Produce Co., Ltd	30	Yan Yuan	China	90.0
Cyco, Ltd	4	Richard C. Scott and six others	United States	100.0
International Machinery Corp	36	Oscar Kohorn & Co., Ltd	do	70.0
Kyokko Trading Co., Ltd	10	East Asiatic Co	Denmark	60.0
Futehally Cotton Co., Ltd	10	Adnan N. Futehally	India	12.0
Do	10	Asad N. Futehally	do	13.0
Do	10	Mogbil N. Futehally	do	12.0
Do	10	Abu N. Futehally	do	13.0
Cosa Corporation of Japan, Ltd	30	Julius Mueller	United States	62.0
Wilbur-Ellis Co. (Japan), Ltd	1	Joseph M. Zimmerman	do	50.0
Do	1	Paul A. Oreally	do	30.0

See footnotes at end of table.

Table XIII—Japanese Companies in Which Foreigners Participate in Management, by Major Industry Groups,[1] as of December 1954—Continued

[Capital in millions of yen]

Contracting Party	Capital	Foreign investor	Nationality	Percent of foreign ownership
Foreign trade and wholesale—Continued				
Shell Co. of Japan	2,100	Shell Petroleum Co., Ltd	England	100.0
Asiatic Metals and Ore Corp	1	Frank Korn and seven others	United States	97.0
Nippon Goodyear Co., Ltd	4	Goodyear Tire & Rubber Co. and six others	----do	99.7
Daiichi Produce Co., Ltd	1,029	C. A. England & Co	----do	9.0
Frank Hacking (Japan), Ltd	2	Frank Hacking (Canada), Ltd	Canada	53.0
Shinko Raw Cotton Co., Ltd	20	Primura Corp., S. A	Panama	79.0
Keiko Produce Co., Ltd	12	A. Schulman, Inc	United States	50.0
Consolidated Oil Co., Ltd., of Japan	1.5	Consolidated Oil Co	----do	10.0
B. F. Goodrich of Japan, Ltd	27	B. F. Goodrich Co	----do	100.0
Chiyoda Building Co., Ltd	2	American International Underwriters	----do	100.0
Transportation—				
Taiheiyo Marine Transportation Co., Ltd	400	Wheelock Marden & Co., Ltd., and two others	England	13.0
Warehousing and storage—				
Showa Trading Co., Ltd	15	Hongkong Transportation Co., Ltd	Hong Kong	13.0

[1] As approved under the Foreign Investment Law.

Source: Foreign Capital Research Society, c/o Bank of Japan.

Table XIV.—Foreign Companies Which Have Concluded Technological Assistance Agreements With Japanese Firms, May 1950–December 1954 [1]

Date of validation	Foreign company	Nationality	Japanese recipient	Kind of technology	Term (years)
Spinning and Weaving					
May 23, 1951	Joseph Bancroft & Sons Co	United States	Takase Dyeing & Printing Works, Ltd.	Durable and washable finish of textiles by the use of resin.	15
Jan. 23, 1952	John B. Stetson Co	----do	Tokyo Hat Co., Ltd	Manufacture of felt hats	5
Mar. 19, 1952	Julius Kayser & Co., Ltd	----do	Naigai Amimono Co., Ltd	Manufacture of silk full-fashioned hosiery.	15
Mar. 27, 1952	Cluett Peabody & Co., Inc	----do	Toyo Spinning Co., Ltd	Shrinkproof finish of cotton textiles	5
June 25, 1952	----do	----do	Kanegafuchi Spinning Co., Ltd	----do	5
Nov. 18, 1952	Joseph Bancroft & Sons Co	----do	Frank Hacking (Canada), Ltd	Manufacture of crease-resistant "Everglaze" textiles.	15
Nov. 18, 1952	----do	----do	Daido Dyeing & Printing Works, Ltd.	----do	15
Nov. 18, 1952	----do	----do	Toyo Spinning Co., Ltd	----do	15
Mar. 31, 1953	Scholler Brothers, Inc	----do	Naigai Amimono Co., Ltd	Shrinkproofing wool and mixed wool products.	10
June 2, 1953	Cluett Peabody & Co., Inc	----do	Fuji Spinning Co., Ltd	"Sanforized" and "Sanfor" compressive shrinking of woven cotton, linen, and ramie fabrics.	5
June 2, 1953	----do	----do	Nisshin Cotton Spinning Co., Ltd	----do	5
June 2, 1953	----do	----do	Kureha Spinning Co., Ltd	----do	5
June 2, 1953	----do	----do	Toyo Sen-i Co., Ltd	----do	5
Dec. 15, 1953	----do	----do	Hamaguchi Dyeing Works, Ltd	----do	5
Dec. 15, 1953	----do	----do	Ichishin Bleaching Co., Ltd	----do	5
Dec. 15, 1953	----do	----do	Yamatogawa Dyeing Works, Ltd	----do	5
Apr. 20, 1954	American Viscose Corp	----do	Toyo Spinning Co., Ltd	Stabilization of cellulose	18
May 4, 1954	Pacific Mills	----do	Fuji Spinning Co., Ltd	Manufacture of bulk filament into staple.	14
June 15, 1954	----do	----do	Kanegafuchi Spinning Co., Ltd	----do	14
June 15, 1954	----do	----do	Nankai Woolen Yarn Spinning Co., Ltd.	----do	14
July 6, 1954	Cluett Peabody & Co., Inc	----do	Kurashiki Spinning Co., Ltd	Shrinkproof finish of fabrics	5
July 6, 1954	----do	----do	Daido Dyeing & Printing Works, Ltd.	----do	5
Oct. 19, 1954	Joseph Bancroft & Sons Co	----do	Nippon Cloth Manufacturing Co., Ltd.	Manufacture of "Everglaze" textiles	15
Dec. 7, 1954	Cluett Peabody & Co., Inc	----do	Nitto Spinning Co., Ltd	Shrinkproof finish of fabrics ("Sanforized").	5
Paper and Pulp					
Nov. 8, 1951	Dr. Oswald Wyss	Switzerland	Nikko Sangyo Co	Production of homogeneous soft and hard wooden fiberboards.	15
Nov. 21, 1951	----do	----do	Iwakuragumi Co., Ltd	----do	15
Mar. 17, 1953	C. T. Takahashi & Co	United States	Mitsui Mokuzai Manufacturing Co., Ltd.	Production of "Hardboard" by the Chapman wet process.	2
Aug. 23, 1951	Seaman & Seaman	----do	Sanyo Pulp Co., Ltd	Production of sulfite rayon pulp	2
Sept. 5, 1951	----do	----do	Dai-Nippon Celluloid Co., Ltd	Wood and cotton cellulose purification	1
June 11, 1952	Stainer Sales Co	----do	Nippon Pulptex Co., Ltd	Manufacture of paper towels and paper-towel dispensing cabinets.	5

See footnotes at end of table.

Table XIV.—Foreign Companies Which Have Concluded Technological Assistance Agreements With Japanese Firms, May 1950–December 1954 [1]—Continued

Date of validation	Foreign company	Nationality	Japanese recipient	Kind of technology	Term (years)
			Chemical Products, Pharmaceuticals		
Oct. 27, 1950	Ferro Enamel Corp	United States	Ferro-Nippon Co., Ltd	Production of porcelain enamel and ceramic glaze frits.	10
Dec. 7, 1950	American & Far Eastern Engineers, Inc.	----do	Mitsui Chemical Ind. Co., Ltd	Production of vinyl chloride	4
Dec. 21, 1950	----do	----do	Toyo Koatsu Manufacturing Co., Ltd.	Production of melamine resin	4
Jan. 9, 1951	B. F. Goodrich Chemical Co	----do	Japanese Geon Co., Ltd	Production of vinyl and vinylidene chloride.	15
Jan 20, 1951	Ciba, Limited	Switzerland	Takeda Pharmaceutical Co., Ltd	Production of sulfathiazole	5
Jan. 30, 1951	J. R. Geigy, S. A	----do	Nichizui Trading Co., Ltd	Production of DDT insecticides	9
Feb. 9, 1951	Reichhold Chemicals Inc	United States	Japan Reichhold Chemicals, Inc	Production of synthetic resins and pigments.	12
Feb. 12, 1951	Nichizui Trading Co., Ltd	Switzerland (Japanese ownership).	Nippon Soda Co., Ltd., and 33 others.	Production of DDT insecticides	9
Apr. 12, 1951	E. I. du Pont de Nemours & Co	United States	Toyo Rayon Co., Ltd	Production of nylon	15
Apr. 12, 1951	American Cyanimid Co	----do	Shin-etsu Chemical Manufacturing Co.	Production of granulated calcium cyanamide.	9
Apr. 25, 1951	----do	----do	Sumitomo Chemical Manufacturing Co., Ltd.	Production of melamine resin	15
Apr. 12, 1951	Merck & Co., Inc.	----do	Kyowa Fermentation Industrial Co., Ltd.	Production of streptomycin	15
Apr. 12, 1951	----do	----do	Meiji Seika Co., Ltd	----do	15
Apr. 12, 1951	American Chemical Paint Co	----do	Ishihara Sangyo Co., Ltd	Production of 2-4 D acetic acid	10
Apr. 12, 1951	----do	----do	Nissan Chemical Industries, Ltd	----do	10
Apr. 25, 1951	Les Usines de Melle, S. A	France	Kurashiki Rayon Co., Ltd	Continuous recovery and concentration of acetic acid from a dilute solution of sodium acetate.	15
June 20, 1951	E.I. duPont de Nemours &Co	United States	Osaka Kinzoku Manufacturing Co., Ltd.	Production of freon gas	6
June 20, 1951	Sapac Corp	----do	Yamanouchi Pharmaceutical Co., Ltd.	Production of pharmaceuticals	15
June 20, 1951	----do	----do	Shionogi & Co., Ltd	----do	15
June 23, 1951	Chemical Construction Corp	----do	Sumitomo Chemical Manufacturing Co., Ltd.	Production and use of methanol catalyst.	10
June 23, 1951	Nichizui Trading Co., Ltd	Switzerland (Japanese ownership).	Osaka Godo Co., Ltd	Production of DDT insecticides	9
June 23, 1951	----do	----do	Toyo Oil Co., Ltd	----do	10
July 18, 1951	Parke, Davis & Co	United States	Sankyo Co., Ltd	Production of chloromycetin (chloramphenical).	15
Aug. 1, 1951	Monsanto Chemical Co	----do	Monsanto-Kasei Manufacturing Co., Ltd.	Production of polyvinyl chloride and butyl benzyl phthalate.	(2)
Aug. 23, 1951	Ciba, Limited	Switzerland	Nippon Carbide Manufacturing Co., Inc.	Production of melamine resin	8
Aug. 23, 1951	----do	----do	Denki Kagaku Manufacturing Co., Ltd.	----do	8
Sept. 5, 1951	Nichizui Trading Co., Ltd	----do (Japanese ownership).	Hokkai Sankyo Co., Ltd	Production of DDT insecticides	10
Sept. 5, 1951	----do	----do	Hokushu Kagaku Kogyo Co., Ltd	----do	10
Sept. 5, 1951	Interchemical Corp	United States	Toyo Ink Mfg. Co., Ltd	Production of printing ink, and sale and use of Interchemical products.	10
Sept. 20, 1951	Hooker Electro-Chemical Co	----do	Nissan Chemical Industries, Ltd	Production of chlorous compounds	11
Sept. 20, 1951	Commercial Solvents Corp	----do	Kyowa Fermentation Industrial Co., Ltd.	Production of N-butyl alcohol and ethyl alcohol.	5
May 14, 1952	Montecatini Societa Generale Per l'Industria Mineraria e Chimica.	Italy	Nissan Chemical Industries, Ltd	(1) Production of liquefied CO_2 from converted winker gas; (2) production of granulate calurea and ammonization of superphosphate from urea ammonia liquor.	15
May 14, 1952	Dow Chemical International, Ltd.	United States	Asahi-Dow, Ltd	Production of vinyl chloride monomer, vinylidene chloride monomer, copolymers of vinyl chloride, and vinylidene chloride.	15
May 14, 1952	Master Builders Co	----do	Nippon Soda Co., Ltd	Production of "Pozzolith"	10
June 25, 1952	American Chemical Paint Co	----do	Pacific Projects Co	Production of "Rodiness"	10
Sept. 16, 1952	U. S. Vitamin Corp	----do	Takeda Pharmaceutical Co., Ltd	Processes for imparting solubility to vitamin mixtures.	5
Oct. 1, 1952	Glidden Co	----do	Ishihara Sangyo Co., Ltd	Production of titanium dioxide pigment.	7
Dec. 23, 1952	American Chemical Paint Co	----do	Nippon Paint Co., Ltd	Production of metal surface-treating chemicals, including anticorrosion, cleaning, rust-corrosion, rust-removing, paint-removing, and rust-preventing chemicals.	10
Feb. 3, 1953	Barsky & Strauss Inc	----do	Mitsubishi Chemical Industries, Ltd.	Production of various chemical products, including ammonium sulfate, dyestuffs, and pharmaceuticals.	1
Mar. 3, 1953	Parker Rust Proof Co	----do	Nihon Parkerizing Co., Ltd	Production of metal coatings	3
Mar. 17, 1953	Beaunit Mills Inc	----do	Asahi Chemical Manufacturing Co., Ltd.	Production of cuprammonium	10
Mar. 31, 1953	Pfizer Inter-American, S. A	Panama	Pfizer-Tanabe Co., Ltd	Production of terramycin	15
Mar. 31, 1953	International General Electric Co., Inc.	United States	Shin-etsu Chemical Manufacturing Co., Ltd.	Production of organic silicon products	7
Mar. 31, 1953	----do	----do	Tokyo-Shibaura Electric Co., Ltd.	----do	7
Mar. 31, 1953	Ciba, Ltd	Switzerland	Ciba Products, Ltd	Pharmaceutical products	5

See footnotes at end of table.

Table XIV.—Foreign Companies Which Have Concluded Technological Assistance Agreements With Japanese Firms, May 1950–
December 1954 [1]—Continued

Date of validation	Foreign company	Nationality	Japanese recipient	Kind of technology	Term (years)
Chemical Products, Pharmaceuticals—Continued					
Mar. 31, 1953	Wyeth International, Ltd	United States	Banyu Seiyaku Co., Ltd	Production of Bicillin	15
Mar. 31, 1953	R. S. Aries and Associates, Inc.	do	Nippon Titanium Co., Ltd	Production of titanium dioxide products.	8
Apr. 17, 1953	J. R. Geigy S. A	Switzerland	Fujisawa Pharmaceutical Co., Ltd.	Production of irgapyring, irgafen preparations.	3
May 6, 1953	American Cyanamid Co	United States	Lederle Laboratories (Japan), Ltd.	Production of aureomycin	15
June 2, 1953	Monsanto Chemical Co	do	Nissan Chemical Industries, Ltd	Techniques of applying silicic acid solution to fabrin.	15
July 21, 1953	American Cyanamid Co	do	Sumitomo Chemical Co., Ltd	Production of "Parathion" (agricultural insecticide).	15
Sept. 1, 1953	Glidden Co	do	Ishihara Sangyo Kaisha, Ltd	Production of latex emulsion paint and latex enamel paint products.	7
Sept. 1, 1953	Dow Chemical Co	do	do	Production of vegetable hormone with 4-chlorophenoxy acetic acid as its major component.	14
Sept. 1, 1953	do	do	Nissan Chemical Industries Ltd	do	14
Nov. 17, 1953	Montecatini Societa Generale Per l'Industria Mineraria e Chimica.	Italy	do	Fauser method for fuel oil gasification	15
Nov. 17, 1953	Farbenfabriken Bayer, A. G	West Germany	Sumitomo Chemical Co., Ltd	Production of "Parathion" (agricultural insecticide).	15
Dec. 1, 1953	Rowland S. Potter	United States	Fuji Photo Film Co., Ltd	Production of photographic papers and other materials.	2
Mar. 28, 1953	Falco Metal Products, Inc	do	Lederle Laboratories (Japan), Ltd.	Lending of "Accogel" machine and techniques on installment, operation, and maintenance thereof.	6
Mar. 2, 1954	American Cyanamid Co	do	do	Manufacture of "achromycin" (tetracyline products or products containing tetracycline).	15
Mar. 16, 1954	Lovens Kemiske Fabrik	Denmark	Sankyo Co., Ltd	Manufacture of penicillin aminoester ("Leocillin").	5
Mar. 16, 1954	Pfizer Corp	Panama	Pfizer-Tanabe Co., Ltd	Manufacture of tetracin (tetracycline products or products containing tetracycline).	15
Apr. 6, 1954	Bristol Laboratories, Inc	United States	Banyu Seiyaku Co., Ltd	Manufacturing techniques of procaine penicillin in oil.	15
Apr. 20, 1954	Dow Chemical Co	do	Taito Co., Ltd	Techniques relating to methods of use of dehydro acetic acid and sodium acetate as antiseptic for food.✝	13
July 20, 1954	Merck & Co., Inc	do	Japan Merck Banyu Seiyaku Co., Ltd.	Manufacture of cortisone and hydrocortisone.	1
Aug. 17, 1954	C. F. Boehringer & Soehne G. m. b. H.	West Germany	Yamanouchi Pharmaceutical Co., Ltd.	Manufacture of chloromphenicol	10
Apr. 6, 1954	{Farbenfabriken Bayer A. G {Ing. A. Maurer S. A	}West Germany	Teikoku Rayon Co., Ltd	{Techniques for manufacturing cellulose acetate, and dyeing and processing for finishing thereof.	5
May 4, 1954	Seaman & Seaman Robert P. King	United States	Asahi Chemical Industry Co., Ltd.	Techniques relating to continuous aging of alkali cellulose.	15
May 4, 1954	do	do	Nitto Spinning Co., Ltd	do	15
June 1, 1954	Inventa A. G	Switzerland	Nippon Rayon Co., Ltd	Manufacture of nylon 6 (Grillon)	15
July 20, 1954	Seaman & Seaman Robert P. King	United States	Teikoku Rayon Co., Ltd	Techniques relating to continuous aging of alkali cellulose.	15
May 18, 1954	Interchemical Corp	do	Toyo Ink Manufacturing Co., Ltd.	Manufacture of pigment for textile cloth and paint for industrial use.	10
Oct. 5, 1954	Sinclair & Valentine Co	do	Nippon Color Matters Industry Co., Ltd.	Manufacture of various kinds of printing ink, pigment, varnish, etc.	10
Oct. 19, 1954	St. Regis Paper Co	do	Matsushita Electric Industry Co., Ltd.	Manufacture of plastic injection molding products and laminated products.	5
Dec. 7, 1954	American Cyanamid Co	do	Sumitomo Chemical Industry Co., Ltd.	Manufacture of insecticide (Malathion).	12
Dec. 7, 1954	Dow Chemical Co	do	Nippon Soda Co., Ltd	Manufacture of insecticide	15
Dec. 10, 1954	Montecatini Societa Generale Per l'Industria Mineraria e Chimica	Italy	Shin-Nippon Nitrogenous Fertilizer Co., Ltd.	Manufacture of ammonia gas from heavy oil.	15
Dec. 21, 1954	Sun Chemical Corp	United States	Dai-Nippon Ink Manufacturing Co., Ltd.	Manufacture of various kinds of printing ink.	10
Petroleum and Products					
Oct. 3, 1951	Standard-Vacuum Oil Co	United States	Toa Nenryo Manufacturing Co., Ltd.	Petroleum-refining processes	5
June 11, 1952	Universal Oil Products Co	do	Nippon Kihatsuyu Co., Ltd	Techniques relating to platforming process, "Arosorb" process, fluid catalytic cracking process, hydrocatalytic reforming process, and UDEX "Unisol" process.	10
July 23, 1952	California Texas Oil Co., Ltd	do	Nippon Petroleum Refining Co., Ltd.	General technical assistance in workshop construction, and procurement of materials and machinery in U. S.	3½
July 23, 1952	Authur G. McKee & Co	do	do	Technical assistance in construction of oil-refining unit, and procurement of materials.	3½

See footnotes at end of table.

105

Table XIV.—Foreign Companies Which Have Concluded Technological Assistance Agreements With Japanese Firms, May 1950– December 1954 [1]*—Continued*

Date of validation	Foreign company	Nationality	Japanese recipient	Kind of technology	Term (years)
Petroleum and Products—Continued					
July 23, 1952	California Texas Oil Co., Ltd	United States	Koa Oil Co., Ltd	General technical assistance in workshop construction, and procurement of materials and machinery in U. S.	3½
July 23, 1952	Universal Oil Products Co	do	Nippon Petroleum Refining Co., Ltd.	Techniques relating to platforming process (process producing petroleum of high-octane value).	15
July 23, 1952	International Catalytic Oil Processes Corp.	do	do	Techniques relating to fluid catalytic cracking processes.	5
July 23, 1952	Standard Oil Development Co	do	do	Petroleum-refining process, including propane deasphalting and fluid catalytic cracking.	10
July 23, 1952	Universal Oil Products Co	do	Koa Oil Co., Ltd	Techniques relating to platforming process under UOP method.	15
Nov. 18, 1952	Houdry Process Corp	do	Daikyo Oil Co., Ltd	Techniques relating to catalytic cracking process and to construction of "Houdriflow" unit.	7
Dec. 16, 1952	Universal Oil Products Co	do	Maruzen Oil Co	Techniques relating to fluid catalytic cracking for the purpose of producing petroleum of high-octane value.	5
Dec. 16, 1952	California Research Corp	do	Daikyo Oil Co., Ltd	Techniques relating to acid film polymerization of hydrocarbon gas.	5
Dec. 23, 1952	Texas Development Corp	do	Nippon Petroleum Refining Co., Ltd.	Techniques relating to the dewaxing of hydrocarbon oil (crude oils).	15
Mar. 17, 1953	do	do	Mitsubishi Oil Co., Ltd	Furfural extraction process and wax fraction process as refining process for lubricating oils by use of solvents.	10
Mar. 17, 1953	Tide Water Associated Oil Co	do	do	Acetone benzene dewaxing process as refining process for lubricating oils by use of solvents.	10
Rubber and Leather Products					
Dec. 26, 1950	B. F. Goodrich Co	United States	Yokohama Rubber Co., Ltd	Manufacture of rubber products	14
Apr. 12, 1951	Palama Shoe Co	do	Toyo Shoe Manufacturing Co., Ltd.	Manufacture of shoes	5
Apr. 12, 1951	Andrews Alderfer Processing Co., Inc.	do	Bridgestone Tire Co., Inc	Production of rubber thread products.	15
Apr. 30, 1951	Dunlop Rubber Co., Ltd	England	Dunlop Rubber Co. (Japan), Ltd.	Production of rubber products	8
June 20, 1951	Goodyear Tire & Rubber Co	United States	Bridgestone Tire Co., Inc	Production of rubber products, including tires, tubes, hoses, conveyors, and transmission belts.	5
Feb. 6, 1952	Philip Tucker Gidley	do	Nikka Rubber Co., Ltd	Manufacture of rubber footwear and rubber foam products.	2
Mar. 5, 1952	Intercontinental Shoe Corp	do	Chiyoda Shoe Manufacturing Co., Ltd.	Manufacture of shoes by machines.	5
May 14, 1952	Selby Shoe Co	do	Nippon Rubber Co., Ltd	do	10
Dec. 2, 1952	Palama Shoe Co., Ltd	do	Paramount Shoe Co., Ltd	do	5
Mar. 17, 1953	Apex Tire & Rubber Co	do	Showa Rubber Co., Ltd	Production of shoe soling-material made of synthetic polymers.	5
Oct. 5, 1954	Pirelli Societa Per Azioni	Italy	Sumitomo Electric Manufacturing Co., Ltd. / Tokai Rubber Manufacturing Co., Ltd.	Manufacture of rubber hose, V-belt, floor cover, rubber lining, rubber thread, and sponge rubber.	5
Oct. 5, 1954	Societa Applicazioni Gomma Antivibranti.	do	do	Manufacture of shockproof rubber	
Glass and Stone Products					
Feb. 19, 1951	Russel P. Heuer	United States	Shinagawa Fire Brick Co., Ltd	Production of "Ritex," "Steelklad," and "Ferroclip" firebrick.	15
Apr. 12, 1951	Saburo Fujimoto	do	American-Japanese Hollow Tile Co., Ltd.	Production of cement blocks	3
Mar. 27, 1952	Corheart Refractories Co., Inc	do	Asahi Glass Co., Ltd	Production of electrically cast refractories.	10
July 9, 1952	Frazier-Simplex, Inc	do	do	Manufacture of "Simplex" suspended shadow wall and end wall, used in the tank furnace of glass products.	5
Feb. 17, 1953	Bigelow-Liptak Corp	do	Toyo Babcock Co., Ltd	Manufacture of Bigelow-Liptak fireproof suspended arches and walls.	2
Oct. 6, 1953	Frazier-Simplex, Inc	do	Asahi Glass Co., Ltd	Manufacture of "Helical Batch Charger."	5
Dec. 15, 1953	Corning Glass Works	do	do	Manufacture of television glassware	10
Aug. 17, 1954	Libbey-Owens-Ford Glass Co	do	Nippon Sheet Glass Co., Ltd	Manufacture of heatproofing and soundproofing sheet glass (double sheets).	2
Aug. 17, 1954	Pligrico Company	do	Nippon Refractory Co., Ltd	Manufacture of refractories in indeterminate form.	5
Sept. 7, 1954	La Compagnie des Manufacture des Glaces et Products Chimiques de St Gobain Channy & Ciry.	France	Asahi Glass Co., Ltd	Manufacture of foamed glass	6

See footnotes at end of table.

Table XIV.—Foreign Companies Which Have Concluded Technological Assistance Agreements With Japanese Firms, May 1950–December 1954[1]—Continued

Date of validation	Foreign company	Nationality	Japanese recipient	Kind of technology	Term (years)
			Metals and Metal Products		
Mar. 5, 1951	Resources and Facilities Corp	United States	Tsugami Manufacturing Co., Ltd	Manufacture of "Heli-Coil" screw and tools.	13
Apr. 12, 1951	Singmaster & Breyer	do	Mitsui Mining & Smelting Co., Ltd.	Supervision and guidance for the erection, heating up, and tuning up of vertical retort zinc distillation furnaces.	9
Apr. 30, 1951	Armco International Corp	do	Fuji Iron and Steel Co., Ltd	Production of flat-rolled products in strip mills.	10
May 16, 1951	do	do	Yawata Iron & Steel Co., Ltd	Installation of the "Sendzimir" galvanize coating unit for the purpose of galvanizing steel coils.	8
May 16, 1951	do	do	do	Production of silicon steel sheets by hot-rolled methods (including steel making).	12
May 23, 1951	Philips Screw Co., Inc	do	J. Osawa & Co., Ltd	Manufacture of cross recessed head screws and screw drivers.	5
June 20, 1951	Meehanite Metal Corp	do	Meehanite Metal Co. of Japan	Metallurgy and casting	10
June 23, 1951	William S. Vaughan	do	Fiji Iron and Steel Co., Ltd	Metallurgy of iron and steel	2
Jan. 23, 1952	Armco International Corp	do	Yawata Iron & Steel Co., Ltd	Production of flat-rolled products in strip mills.	10
May 28, 1952	{Charles B. Francis / Ralph B. Poter}	do	Nippon Steel Works, Ltd	Production of rolls of various mills and other large-size castings by "MFP casting method."	8
Oct. 1, 1952	Aluminium, Ltd	Canada	Nippon Light Metal Co., Ltd	Techniques relating to manufacture of alumina and aluminum ingot, and development of hydro power generation.	15
Nov. 4, 1952	Canadian Nickel Products, Ltd	do	Tokyo Shibaura Electric Co., Ltd	Production of cast iron containing magnesium.	15
Nov. 4, 1952	Powder Power Tool Corp	United States	Japan Drive-It Co., Ltd	Manufacture of special nail driving bolts called "Drive-It" and their accessories.	10
Dec. 23, 1952	Thoger G. Jungersen	do	Furukawa Electric Co., Ltd	Techniques and method relating to precision casting of metals and alloys.	15
Feb. 3, 1953	Aluminum Laboratories, Ltd	Canada	Toyo Aluminium K. K	Production of aluminum foil and sheet	10
Feb. 3, 1953	Canadian Nickel Products, Ltd	do	Kubota Iron & Machinery Works, Ltd.	Production of magnesium containing cast iron.	15
Mar. 3, 1953	do	do	Toyota Motor Co., Ltd	do	15
Mar. 3, 1953	do	do	Toyota Automatic Loom Works, Ltd.	do	15
Mar. 3, 1953	Tadeus Sendzimir	United States	Nippon Kinzoku Sangyo Co., Inc	Use of Sendzimir cold strip mills	10
Mar. 17, 1953	Canadian Nickel Products, Ltd	Canada	Hitachi, Ltd	Production of magnesium containing cast iron.	15
July 30, 1952	United Engineering and Foundry Co.	United States	Japan Steel Works, Ltd	Manufacturing techniques of cast steel rolls for rolling mills.	10
Oct. 14, 1952	Vereinigte Kessel Werke A. G	West Germany	Yokoyama Engineering Co., Ltd	Manufacture of boilers and apparatus, and project drawings for boilers.	5
Dec. 16, 1952	General American Transportation Corp.	United States	Tsukishima Machinery Co., Ltd	Manufacture of gas tanks, liquid tanks, and tank roofs.	3
Mar. 31, 1953	Canadian Nickel Products, Ltd	Canada	Sumitomo Metal Manufacturing Co., Ltd.	Production of cast iron containing magnesium.	15
Mar. 31, 1953	American Electro Metal Corp	United States	Nippon Electric Co., Ltd	Production of the following five items of powder metallurgy: (1) Molybdenum and tungsten, (2) structural parts and infiltrated structural parts, (3) hard materials, (4) contact materials, and (5) miscellaneous fields.	3
Mar. 31, 1953	Compagnie des Forges & Acieries de la Marine & de St. Etienne.	France	Kobe Steel Works, Ltd	Production of forgings by the special forging process of "fibrage integral" (complete grainflow).	10
April 21, 1953	Canadian Nickel Products, Ltd	Canada	Shin Mitsubishi Jukogyo Co., Ltd	Production of magnesium-containing cast iron.	15
May 8, 1953	do	do	Mitsubishi Shipbuilding & Engineering Co., Ltd.	do	15
Oct. 6, 1953	do	do	Kobe Cast Iron Works, Ltd	do	15
Oct. 6, 1953	do	do	Yanmar Diesel Engine Co., Ltd	do	15
Dec. 15, 1953	Western Electric Co., Inc	United States	Tohoku Metal Industries, Ltd	Production of magnetic alloys	4
Mar. 2, 1954	Société Centrale, D'echanges Techniques Internationaux.	France	Nippon Special Steel Mfg. Co., Ltd.	Iron sand refining by "Philipon" type furnace.	7
Mar. 16, 1954	Hammond Iron Works	United States	Toyo Heating Industry Co., Ltd	Manufacture of floating roof tank and other tanks.	2
Mar. 16, 1954	Irving Rossi	do	Sumitomo Metal Industries Co., Ltd.	Continuous casting of special steel	15
Sept. 7, 1954	Canadian Nickel Products, Ltd	Canada	Kawasaki Heavy Industry Co., Ltd.	Manufacture of magnesium containing cast iron.	15
Nov. 9, 1954	Continental Can Co., Inc	United States	Toyo Can Manufacturing Co., Ltd.	Manufacture of cans and crowns	5
Feb. 29, 1952	United States Pipe & Foundry Co.	do	Kubota Iron & Machinery Works, Ltd.	Manufacture of cast-iron pressure pipes and cast-iron soil pipes.	10

See footnotes at end of table.

Table XIV.—*Foreign Companies Which Have Concluded Technological Assistance Agreements With Japanese Firms, May 1950–December 1954* [1]—*Continued*

Date of validation	Foreign company	Nationality	Japanese recipient	Kind of technology	Term (years)
			Communication Equipment		
Sept. 21, 1950	International General Electric Co., Inc.	United States	Furukawa Electric Co., Ltd	Production of vinyl-acetal insulated wire.	6
Sept. 28, 1950	International Standard Electric Corp.	do	Sumitomo Electric Industries, Ltd.	Manufacture of plastic insulated wire, low-frequency toll cable, and carrier and coaxial cables.	8
Nov. 6, 1950	do	do	Nippon Electric Co., Ltd	Manufacture of machinery and equipment for telecommunication and radio broadcasting.	10
Mar. 29, 1951	Westinghouse Electric International Co.	do	Mitsubishi Electric Co., Ltd	Manufacture of electrical machinery and equipment.	5
Mar. 1, 1951	do	do	do	Manufacture of frequency modulation system of radio communication apparatus.	15
May 1, 1951	Western Electric Co., Inc.	do	Furukawa Electric Co., Ltd	Manufacture of land lines, coaxial and submarine cables, and accessories for communication purposes.	5
May 23, 1951	Chemical Construction Corp.	do	Mitsui Shipbuilding & Engineering Co., Ltd.	Manufacture of electrolytic hydrogen-oxygen cell.	15
June 23, 1951	Day-Brite Lighting, Inc.	do	Tokyo Shibaura Electric Co., Ltd	Manufacture of fluorescent lighting fixtures.	6
July 5, 1951	Gould-National Batteries, Inc.	do	Furukawa Battery Co., Ltd	Manufacture of storage batteries for automobiles and for industrial uses.	5
July 18, 1951	Radio Corporation of America	do	Kobe Kogyo Co., Ltd	Manufacture of radio receiving tubes and transistors, cathode ray tubes, and transmitting tubes for sound broadcast transmitters.	10
July 18, 1951	International General Electric Co., Inc.	do	Showa Electric Wire & Cable Co., Ltd.	Manufacture of vinyl-acetal insulated wires.	7
Aug. 1, 1951	do	do	do	Manufacture of solid-type power cables.	5
Aug. 23, 1951	Hogan Laboratories, Inc. / Faximile, Inc.	do	Jiji Press, Ltd	Manufacture of graphic communications, including facsimile transmitting and recording equipment known as "Hogan Fax System."	10
Sept. 19, 1951	Union Carbide & Carbon Corp	do	Osaka Transformer Co., Ltd	Manufacturing or assembling and operation or handling of submerged arc welder (trade name: "Union-melt"), which is used in electric welding process.	9
Feb. 20, 1952	Pittsburgh Lectromelt Furnace Corp.	do	Shin-Daido Steel Co., Ltd	Manufacture of arc furnaces, smelting furnaces, and accessories.	9
Mar. 27, 1952	Sperry Corp	do	Tokyo Keiki Seizosho Co., Ltd	Manufacture of Sperry marine radar	10
Apr. 16, 1952	Western Electric Co., Inc	do	Sumitomo Electric Ind., Ltd	Manufacture of land lines (wire and cable).	5
Apr. 16, 1952	Bendix Aviation Corp	do	Tokyo Kiki Seizoshs Co., Ltd	Manufacture of Bendix depth recorders	5
Apr. 16, 1952	Westinghouse Electric International Co.	do	Mitsubishi Electric Co., Ltd	Manufacture of marine radar equipment.	15
Apr. 30, 1952	Radio Corporation of America	do	Kobe Kogyo K. K.	Manufacture of electron tubes, television, and other electronic products.	10
May 14, 1952	do	do	Hitachi, Ltd	Manufacture of radio receiving tubes, transmitting tubes, and cathode ray tubes.	10
June 11, 1952	Siemens Schuckertwerke, A. G.	West Germany	Fuji Electric Manufacturing Co., Ltd.	Manufacture of electric power machinery (d. c. machine, transformer, mechanical rectifier) and integrating-type meter, etc.	14
June 11, 1952	Siemens & Halske, A. G.	do	do	Manufacture of communications equipment (communications equipment, radio communication equipment, and telephone switchboard).	14
June 11, 1952	Radio Corporation of America	United States	Tokyo Shibaura Electric Co., Ltd	Manufacture of electron tubes (receiving tube, transmitting tube, cathode ray tube, and transistor).	10
July 23, 1952	Western Electric Co., Inc.	do	do	Techniques relating to directional antenna systems known as "Metal Lens" for the purpose of concentrating and transmitting UHF waves.	2
July 23, 1952	International General Electric Co., Inc.	do	do	Fabrication of apparatus and equipment for electric power generation and distribution, and utilization for electricity of high voltage.	10
July 25, 1952	Duro Test Corp	do	Tokyo Duro Co., Ltd	Techniques relating to manufacture of fluorescent lamps.	12
Sept. 16, 1952	Radio Corporation of America	do	Hayakawa Electric Co., Ltd	Manufacture of radio, television, and other electronic equipment.	5
Nov. 18, 1952	Western Electric Co., Inc.	do	Shinko Seisakusho Co., Ltd	Techniques relating to telegraph stations and switching system.	3
Dec. 2, 1952	N. V. Philips Gloeilampenfabricken.	Netherlands	Matsushita Electronics Corp	Manufacture of fluorescent tubes, incandescent lamps, electron tubes, and glass used therefor.	15
Mar. 3, 1953	Radio Corporation of America	United States	Nippon Hoso Kyokai (N. H. K.)	Manufacture of television and radio broadcasting equipment.	5
Mar. 3, 1953	do	do	Yaou Radio Manufacturing Co., Ltd.	do	5
Mar. 3, 1953	do	do	Nippon Columbia Co., Ltd	do	5
Mar. 3, 1953	do	do	Nippon Electric Co., Ltd	do	5

See footnotes at end of table.

Table XIV.—Foreign Companies Which Have Concluded Technological Assistance Agreements With Japanese Firms, May 1950–December 1954 [1]—Continued

Date of validation	Foreign company	Nationality	Japanese recipient	Kind of technology	Term (years)
**Communication Equipment—Continued**

Date of validation	Foreign company	Nationality	Japanese recipient	Kind of technology	Term (years)
Mar. 17, 1953	International General Electric Co., Inc.	United States	Fujikura Cable Works, Ltd	Manufacture of gas-filled cables	2
Mar. 17, 1953	----do	----do	Showa Electric Wire & Cable Co., Ltd.	----do	2
Mar. 17, 1953	----do	----do	Sumitomo Electric Industries, Ltd.	----do	2
Mar. 17, 1953	----do	----do	Furukawa Electric Co., Ltd	----do	2
Mar. 31, 1953	Nordiska Kable-og Tradfabriker	Denmark	----do	Manufacture of "flat-type" cables	7
Mar. 31, 1953	Westinghouse Electric International Co.	United States	Mitsubishi Electric Co., Ltd	Manufacture of fluorescent lamps of the preheat, instant, and rapid start types, and slim line, circle arc, and circle varieties of the low-pressure mercury arc.	10
Apr. 21, 1953	Western Electric Co., Inc	----do	Oki Electric Industry Co., Ltd	Printing telegraph equipment (teletype).	3
May 6, 1953	Electric and Musical Industries, Ltd.	England	Nippon Electric Co., Ltd	Manufacture of beam tetrodes and television receivers.	5
May 19, 1953	Sangamo Electric Co	United States	Toko Seiki Co	Manufacture of parts of thermal demand meters.	3
June 16, 1953	Radio Corporation of America	----do	Ikegami Tsushinki Co., Ltd	Manufacture of television receivers	5
June 16, 1953	----do	----do	Chitose Television Co., Ltd	----do	5
June 16, 1953	----do	----do	Riken Television Industry Co., Ltd.	----do	5
June 16, 1953	----do	----do	Kyoritsu Dempa Co., Ltd	----do	5
June 16, 1953	----do	----do	Dempa-Do Co., Ltd	----do	5
June 16, 1953	----do	----do	Nippon Musen Electric Co	----do	5
June 16, 1953	----do	----do	Nippon Alpha Electric Co., Inc	----do	5
June 16, 1953	----do	----do	Nanao Radio Co., Ltd	----do	5
July 10, 1953	Western Electric Co., Inc	----do	Mitsubishi Electric Co., Ltd	Manufacture of wave refractors	4
July 7, 1953	Radio Corporation of America	----do	Yamanaka Electric Co., Ltd	Manufacture of television receivers	5
July 7, 1953	----do	----do	Mitaka Electric Co., Ltd	----do	5
July 7, 1953	----do	----do	Matsushita Electric Manufacturing Co., Ltd.	----do	5
July 7, 1953	----do	----do	Mitsuoka Denki Seisakusho Co	----do	5
July 21, 1953	----do	----do	Mitsubishi Electric Co., Ltd	----do	5
July 21, 1953	----do	----do	Sanyo Electric Co., Ltd	----do	5
Sept. 1, 1953	----do	----do	Victor Company of Japan, Ltd	----do	5
Oct. 6, 1953	----do	----do	Shin Nippon Television Industrial Co., Ltd.	----do	5
Oct. 6, 1953	----do	----do	Taiyo Musen Kogyo Co., Ltd	----do	5
Oct. 6, 1953	----do	----do	Fuji Seisakusho, Ltd	----do	5
Oct. 6, 1953	----do	----do	Minami Television Co., Ltd	----do	5
Oct. 6, 1953	----do	----do	Nichibei Television Co., Ltd	----do	5
Oct. 6, 1953	----do	----do	Fuji Zosen Sharyo Co., Ltd	----do	5
Oct. 6, 1953	----do	----do	Sankosha Co. Ltd	----do	5
Oct. 6, 1953	----do	----do	Daiho Electric Co., Ltd	----do	0
Oct. 6, 1953	----do	----do	Hope Television Co. Ltd	----do	5
Oct. 6, 1953	----do	----do	Fuji Onkyo Television Co., Ltd	----do	5
Oct. 6, 1953	----do	----do	Tama Electric Manufacturing Co., Ltd.	----do	5
Oct. 6, 1953	----do	----do	Chuo Musen Co., Ltd	----do	5
Dec. 15, 1953	Robert Bosch G. m. b. H	West Germany	Nippon Electrical Equipments Co.	Manufacture of automotive electrical equipment.	10
Dec. 4, 1953	Brown Boveri & Co., Ltd	Switzerland	Yasukawa Electric Manufacturing Co., Ltd.	Manufacture of direct current machines and control equipment therefor.	10
Oct. 6, 1953	Radio Corporation of America	United States	Nippon Denkyo Co., Ltd	Manufacture of television receivers	5
Jan. 19, 1954	Electric & Musical Industries, Ltd.	England	Tokyo Shibaura Electric Co., Ltd.	Manufacture of television transmitters	5
Jan. 19, 1954	----do	----do	Nippon Columbia Co., Ltd	Manufacture of television receivers and beam tetrodes.	5
Jan. 19, 1954	International General Electric Co., Inc.	United States	Tokyo Shibaura Electric Co., Ltd	Manufacture of electrical equipment for P. C. C. cars, etc.	7
Feb. 2, 1954	Western Electric Co., Inc	----do	Tokyo Communication Industry Co., Ltd.	Manufacture of transistors	10
Mar. 2, 1954	Ajax Electrothermic Corp	----do	Tokyo Shibaura Electric Co., Ltd	Manufacture of high-frequency induction electric furnaces.	5
Mar. 2, 1954	Raytheon Manufacturing Co., Inc.	----do	Nippon Machinery Trading Co., Ltd	Manufacture of marine radar and sounder.	5
Mar. 2, 1954	Compagnia Industrielle de Telepones.	France	Oki Electric Industry Co., Ltd	Manufacture of carrier equipment and fascimile telegraph equipment.	10
Mar. 2, 1954	International General Electric Co., nc.	United States	Tokyo Shibaura Electric Co., Ltd.	Manufacture of photo flash bulbs	9
Mar. 2, 1954	----do	----do	West Electric Co., Ltd	----do	9
June 15, 1954	Oerlikon Engineering Co	Switzerland	Kawasaki Heavy Industry Co., Ltd.	Manufacture of hydrogenerators and transformers.	15
June 15, 1954	Radio Corporation of America	United States	Matsushita Electron Industry Co., Ltd.	Manufacture of receiving tubes and transistors.	5
June 15, 1954	Western Electric Co., Inc	----do	Tokyo Shibaura Electric Co., Ltd.	Manufacture of transistors, photo transistors, etc.	10
June 15, 1954	Resources and Facilities Corp	----do	Tokyo Keiki Seizosho Co., Ltd	Manufacture of ultrasonics reflect scope.	10
July 20, 1954	Brown Boveri & Co., Ltd	Switzerland	Tokyo Shibaura Electric Co., Ltd	Manufacture of air blast circuit breakers.	10
July 20, 1954	Armour Research Foundation of Illinois Institute of Technology.	United States	Tokyo Communication Industry Co., Ltd.	Techniques relating to magnetic recorder.	15
July 20, 1954	Radio Corporation of America	----do	Toyo Wireless Co., Ltd	Manufacture of receiving tubes and cathode ray tubes.	5

See footnotes at end of table.

Table XIV—Foreign Companies Which Have Concluded Technological Assistance Agreements With Japanese Firms, May 1950–December 1954 [1]—Continued

Date of validation	Foreign company	Nationality	Japanese recipient	Kind of technology	Term (years)
Communication Equipment—Continued					
Aug. 17, 1954	Askania-Werke A. G	West Germany	Tokyo Kiki Engineering Co., Ltd	Manufacture of controlling equipment ("Askania" type) and accessory measuring apparatus.	6
Oct. 5, 1954	Radio Corporation of America	United States	Osaka Sound Co., Ltd	Manufacture of radio receivers	5
Oct. 5, 1954	___do___	___do___	Teikoku Electric Wave Co., Ltd	___do___	5
Oct. 5, 1954	___do___	___do___	Shirosuna Electric Machinery Co., Ltd.	___do___	5
Oct. 5, 1954	___do___	___do___	Standard Wireless Industry Co., Ltd.	___do___	5
Oct. 5, 1954	___do___	___do___	Nakajima Radio & Television Manufacturing Works Co., Ltd.	___do___	5
Oct. 19, 1954	Western Electric Co., Inc	___do___	Hitachi, Ltd	Manufacture of transistors	10
Oct. 19, 1954	___do___	___do___	Mitsubishi Electric Machinery Co., Ltd.	___do___	10
Nov. 9, 1954	___do___	___do___	Kobe Manufacturing Co., Ltd	Manufacture of transistors, photo transistors, etc.	10
Transportation Equipment					
Nov. 30, 1950	MacGregor-Comarain, Inc	United States	MacGregor Far East, Ltd	Manufacture of steel hatch covers for ships.	2
Apr. 12, 1951	Unit Truck Corp	___do___	Far East Enterprises, Ltd	Manufacture of braking equipment for railways.	5
Aug. 1, 1951	Westinghouse Air Brake Co	___do___	Mitsubishi Electric Co., Ltd	Manufacture of braking apparatus and parts for rolling stock.	5
Aug. 1, 1951	___do___	___do___	Nippon Air Brake Co., Ltd	___do___	5
Sept. 5, 1951	Bendix Aviation Corp	___do___	Diesel Kiki Co., Ltd	Manufacture of braking apparatus for automobiles.	5
Sept. 20, 1951	National Malleable & Steel Castings Co.	___do___	Hitachi, Ltd	Manufacture of trucks for freight service, railway car couplers, draft gears and buffing devices, yokes, journal boxes, and carry irons.	20
Sept. 20, 1951	International General Electric Co., Inc.	___do___	Tokyo Shibaura Electric Co., Ltd	Manufacture of diesel electric locomotives.	8½
Oct. 14, 1952	{Sanford Investment Co. / Sanford-Day Iron Works, Inc.	___do___	}Aetna Japan Co., Ltd	{Manufacture of automatic bottom-dumping mining cars.	5
Nov. 18, 1952	Fletcher Aviation Corp	___do___	Toyo Aircraft Manufacturing Co., Ltd.	Techniques relating to aircraft design and manufacture.	10
Dec. 23, 1952	Austin Motor Co., Ltd	England	Nissan Motor Co., Ltd	Manufacture of Austin motor vehicles (Austin A 40 Somerset, four-seater).	7
Dec. 23, 1952	Lohmann Werke A. G	West Germany	Aisan Kogyo Co., Ltd	Manufacture of engines for bicycles	14
Feb. 7, 1953	Bell Aircraft Corp	United States	Nippon Machinery Trading Co., Ltd.	Manufacture of Bell model 47D-1 200-hp. helicopter and wooden rotor blades.	7
Mar. 31, 1953	Transit Research Corp	___do___	Sumitomo Metal Industries, Ltd., and nine others.	Manufacture of P. C. C. cars (sound-prevented, friction-prevented, high-speed streetcars).	15
July 27, 1953	Swiss Car and Elevator Manufacturing Corp., Ltd.	Switzerland	Kinki Sharyo Co., Ltd	Manufacture of lightweight rolling stock.	8
Sept. 1, 1953	Willys-Overland Export Corp	United States	Mitsubishi Heavy Industries Reorganized, Ltd.	Manufacture of four-wheel-drive vehicles (especially Jeeps).	5
Oct. 6, 1953	United Aircraft Corporation	___do___	___do___	Manufacture of aircraft engine parts	5
Nov. 17, 1953	National Pneumatic Co., Inc.	___do___	Nippon Air Brake Co., Ltd	Manufacture of power-operated apparatus for the operation or control of doors and signals.	10
Nov. 17, 1953	Beech Aircraft Corporation	___do___	Fuji Heavy Industries, Ltd	Manufacture of Beechcraft model B-45 aircraft.	6
June 23, 1954	Continental Motors Corp	___do___	Fuji Motors Co., Ltd	Manufacture of small-size reciprocating engine.	10
Mar. 3, 1953	La Regie Nationale des Usines Renault.	France	Hino Diesel Industry Co., Ltd	Assembly and production of Renault-4CV small-size passenger car.	7
Mar. 3, 1953	Rootes Motors Ltd	England	Isuzu Motor Co., Ltd	Assembly of Hillman Minx cars and Commer delivery vans.	7
Oct. 5, 1954	North American Aviation, Inc.	United States	Mitsubishi Heavy Industries Reorganized, Ltd.	Overhaul of jet plane (F-86) and manufacture of its parts.	5
Nov. 9, 1954	Oerlikon Engineering Co	Switzerland	Kinki Rolling Stock Co., Ltd	Manufacture of driving equipment of motor for electric car (segment, coupling system).	5
Nov. 9, 1954	United Aircraft Corp	United States	Mitsubishi Heavy Industries Reorganized, Ltd.	Manufacture of helicopter parts and overhaul of helicopters.	5
Other Machinery and Equipment					
Aug. 29, 1950	Oscar Kohorn & Co., Ltd	United States	Kotobuki Industries Co	Manufacture of machinery for producing synthetic fibers.	10
Nov. 15, 1950	Rayon Consultants, Inc	___do___	Mitsubishi Heavy Industries Reorganized, Ltd.	Manufacture of machinery and equipment for the production of synthetic fibers and films.	10
Dec. 14, 1950	Remington Rand, Inc	___do___	Japan Remington Rand, Inc	Manufacture of typewriters and other business machines and equipment.	20
Dec. 29, 1950	Frank W. Young	___do___	Mitsubishi Chemical Machinery Manufacturing Co., Ltd.	Manufacture of vacuum filter	15
Jan. 24, 1951	National Cash Register Co	___do___	National Cash Register Co., (Japan) Ltd.	Manufacture of cash registers and other business machines and equipment.	5
Feb. 17, 1951	Escher Wyss, Ltd	Switzerland	Kawasaki Dockyard Co., Ltd	Manufacture of water-power turbines	15

See footnotes at end of table.

Table XIV.—Foreign Companies Which Have Concluded Technological Assistance Agreements With Japanese Firms, May 1950–December 1954 [1]—Continued

Date of validation	Foreign company	Nationality	Japanese recipient	Kind of technology	Term (years)
			Other Machinery and Equipment—Continued		
Mar. 3, 1951	Carrier Corp	United States	Toyo Carrier Kogyo Co., Ltd	Manufacture of air-conditioning machines, etc.	10
Apr. 5, 1951	Aktiebolaget Imo-Industry	Sweden	Kawasaki Dockyard Co., Ltd	Manufacture of Imo pumps and motors	9
Apr. 12, 1951	Sulzer Fréres S. A	Switzerland	Japan Steel Works, Ltd.	Manufacture of gas compressors	14
Apr. 12, 1951	Reliance Machine & Stamping Works.	United States	Far East Enterprises, Ltd	Manufacture of high-pressure grease guns and appliances relating thereto.	5
Apr. 12, 1951	American Cynamid Co	do	Mitsubishi Chemical Machinery Co., Ltd.	Manufacture of granular cyanamid	10
May 1, 1951	Sperry Corp	do	Tokyo Keiki Seizosho Co., Ltd	Manufacture of "Sperry marine magnetic compass pilot".	10
May 4, 1951	Les Usines de Melle S. A	France	Nippon Joryu Kogyo Co., Ltd	Manufacture of distillation equipment for extra pure alcohol.	2
Sept. 22, 1950	Sulzer Freres S. A	Switzerland	Uraga Dock Co Tamashima Diesel Kogyo Co., Ltd.	Manufacture of two-stroke and four-stroke internal combustion engines.	15
Nov. 18, 1950	Aktieselskabet Burmeister & Wain's Maskim-OG Skibsbyggeri.	Denmark	Mitsui Shipbuilding & Engineering Co., Ltd.	Manufacture of engines for merchant vessels, etc.	10
Apr. 12, 1951	Silzer Freres S. A	Switzerland	Harima Shipbuilding Works, Ltd.	Manufacture of two-stroke and four-stoke internal-combustion engines.	13
Apr. 18, 1951	do	do	Mitsubishi Shipbuilding & Engineering Co., Ltd.	Manufacture of diesel engines for vessels.	13
Apr. 18, 1951	do	do	Shin-Mitsubishi Heavy Industries Co., Ltd.	do	13
May 2, 1951	do	do	do	Manufacture of Sulzer traction diesel engines.	15
May 2, 1951	do	do	do	Manufacture of vibration damper for engines.	15
May 2, 1951	Aktiebolaget Liung-Stroms Angturbin.	Sweden	do	Manufacture of steam turbines	8
May 16, 1951	Combustion Engineering Superheater, Inc.	United States	Mitsubishi-Nippon Heavy Industries Co., Ltd.	Manufacture of equipment for steam generator and combustion.	15
May 1, 1951	Sperry Corp	do	Tokyo Keiko Seizosho Co., Ltd	Manufacture of "standard Sperry gyro compass" and "two-unit gyro pilot "for marine vessels.	10
May 1, 1951	do	do	do	Manufacture of "Sperry Loran receiving equipment."	10
June 20, 1951	Aktiebolaget Superior	Sweden	Gadelius & Co., Ltd	Manufacture of equipment for Superior automatic soot blower.	5
June 20, 1951	Aktiebolaget Arca Regulatorer	do	do	Manufacture of automatic pressure, temperature, and humidity regulators of steam, gas, and liquids.	5
June 20, 1951	Yarnall-Waring Co	United States	do	Manufacture of equipment for separation of steam and condensate.	5
June 20, 1951	Continental Foundry & Machine Co. of Chicago.	do	do	Manufacture of regulators of water in boilers.	10
June 23, 1951	Walter Kidde & Co., Inc	do	Tokyo Keiko Seizosho Co., Ltd	Manufacture of fire detecting and extinguishing systems.	10
July 18, 1951	H. W. Butterworth & Sons Co	do	Mitsubishi Heavy Industries Reorganized, Ltd.	Manufacture of rayon spinning and other textile finishing machines.	10
Aug. 2, 1951	Otis Elevator Co	do	Toyo Otis Elevator Co	Manufacture of modern elevator and escalator equipment.	10
Sept. 19, 1951	Allis Chalmers Manufacturing Co.	do	Kobe Steel Works, Ltd	Manufacture of industrial machines of various descriptions (crushing, grinding, and washing machinery; cement and lime machinery; pulp and paper machinery; and power transmission machinery).	5
Oct. 17, 1951	James T. Matsuoka & Co	do	Japan Steel Works, Ltd	Manufacture of "Intensive Mixer" for plastics.	5
Nov. 21, 1951	Aktiebolaget Kamyr	Sweden	Gadelius & Co., Ltd	Engineering and manufacture of pulp bleaching apparatus.	5
Nov. 21, 1951	Aktiebolaget Ljungstroms Angturbin.	do	do	Techniques relative to regenerative preheating of air for steam boilers and other furnaces by utilizing the heat in the flue gases.	5
Jan. 9, 1952	Escher Wyss, Ltd	Switzerland	Mitsubishi Shipbuilding & Engineering Co., Ltd.	Design, construction, and manufacture of water-power turbines.	15
Jan. 23, 1952	Dorr Co	United States	Sanki Engineering Co., Ltd	Handling of finely divided solids in fluids wherever found in chemical, metallurgical, and industrial processing; and consulting engineering and plant design in these fields.	10
Jan. 23, 1952	International General Electric Co., Inc.	do	Tokyo Shibaura Electric Co., Ltd.	Manufacture of apparatus and equipment for electric-power generation.	9
Feb. 6, 1952	United Engineering and Foundry Co.	do	Shibaura United Engineering Co., Ltd.	Design and manufacture of rolling mills.	
Feb. 20, 1952	Westinghouse Electric International Co.	do	Mitsubishi Heavy Industries Reorganized, Ltd.	Manufacture of axial flow steam turbines for use on land and vessels.	15
Mar. 5, 1952	Luwa A. G	Switzerland	Kanegafuchi Spinning Co.	Manufacture of pneumatic clearers on spinning machines.	15
Mar. 27, 1952	Askania Regulator Co	United States	Nippon Regulator Co., Ltd	Manufacture of regulators, industrial instruments, and self-control equipment.	10
Apr. 2, 1952	Foster Wheeler Corp	do	Ishikawajima Heavy Industries Co., Ltd.	Manufacture of stationary and marine steam-generating units.	10
Apr. 16, 1952	Les Usines de Melle S. A	France	Nippon Joryu Kogyo Co., Ltd	Manufacture of Mell system special acid-resisting pump.	5
Apr. 30, 1952	Cyclo Getriebebau K. G	West Germany	Sumitomo Machinery Co., Ltd	Design and manufacture of Cyclogears.	10

See footnotes at end of table.

111

Table XIV.—Foreign Companies Which Have Concluded Technological Assistance Agreements With Japanese Firms, May 1950 December 1954 [1]—Continued

Date of violation	Foreign Company	Nationality	Japanese recipient	Kind of technology	Term (years)
		Other Machinery and Equipment—Continued			
May 28, 1952	A. B. Kalle-Regulatorer	Sweden	Gadelius & Co., Ltd	Manufacture of automatic regulator of pressure, temperature, etc. of steam, gases, and liquids.	5
May 28, 1952	Ingenjorsfirman Wallquist & Co	___do	___do	Manufacture of pulp- and paper-making apparatus.	5
June 11, 1952	Yale & Towne Manufacturing Co.	United States	Kiichi Harada	Manufacture of tools known as "Pull-Lifts."	10
June 11, 1952	Stadtler, Hurter & Co	Canada	Japan Steel Works, Ltd	Manufacture of pulp- and paper-making machinery.	15
June 25, 1952	Southwestern Engineering Co	United States	Yokohama Engineering Co., Ltd	Manufacture of machinery and equipment for heavy media separation process known as "Sweco" process.	5
July 9. 1952	Laye and Thurne A. G	Sweden	Gadelius & Co., Ltd	Manufacture of apparatus for dissolving pulp, recovering fiber in waste water, etc.	5
July 9, 1952	John E. Greenawalt	United States	Sumitomo Machinery Co	Manufacture of Greenawalt sintering equipment.	15
July 9, 1952	S. A. Cridan	France	Tsugami Mfg. Co., Ltd	Manufacture of high-speed threading machines (screw-cutting lathe).	10
July 23, 1952	J. M. Voith G.m.b.H	West Germany	Fuji Electric Manufacturing Co., Ltd.	Manufacture of Francis, Pelton, Kaplan, and propeller turbines.	15
Nov. 4, 1952	S. Morgan Smith Co	United States	Dengyosha Prime Mover Works, Ltd.	Manufacture of hydraulic turbines of Kaplan type, and related apparatus.	15
Nov. 18, 1952	American Zinc Lead & Smelting Co.	___do	Mitsubishi Mining Co., Ltd	Separation of ores (heavy media separation process using magnetite).	15
Dec. 2, 1952	Minneapolis Honeywell Regulator Co.	___do	Yamatake Instruments Co., Ltd	Manufacture of industrial instruments, including thermocouple, resistance thermometer, and millivolt actuation.	6
Dec. 16, 1952	Twin Disc Clutch Co	___do	Niigata Converter Co., Ltd	Techniques relating to manufacture and installment of hydraulic torque converters and couplings.	15
Dec. 16, 1952	Walter Kidde & Co., Inc	___do	Tokyo Keiki Seizosho Co., Ltd	Manufacture of tension controllers and compensaters for spinning machines.	4
Dec. 16, 1952	Svenska Rotor Maskiner Aktiebolag.	Sweden	Kobe Steel Works, Ltd	Manufacture of hydraulic converters.	10
Jan. 20, 1953	Babcock & Wilcox, Ltd	England	Babcock Hitachi, Ltd	Construction of water-tube steam-raising plants.	14
Feb. 3, 1953	Christensen Diamond Product Co.	United States	Maikai Trading Co., Ltd. (Nippon Christensen Diamond Products Co., Ltd.).	Manufacture of diamond bits for mining and civil engineering uses.	10
Mar. 3, 1953	Escher Wyss, Ltd	Switzerland	Mitsubishi Shipbuilding & Engineering Co., Ltd.	Manufacture of closed-cycle, land-type gas turbines.	15
Mar. 3, 1953	___do	___do	Fuji Electric Manufacturing Co., Ltd.	___do	15
Mar. 17, 1953	___do	___do	Tsukishima Machinery Co	Manufacture of centrifugal separators	10
July 23, 1952	Koehring Co	United States	Ishikawajima Koehring Co	Manufacture of various machines for civil engineering works, including batcher plant and concrete mixer.	15
Feb. 3, 1953	Escher Wyss, Ltd	Switzerland	Mitsubishi Shipbuilding & Engineering Co., Ltd.	Manufacture of steam turbines for land and marine use.	15
Mar. 3, 1953	___do	___do	___do	Manufacture of gas turbines (closed-cycle, for marine use).	15
Mar. 3, 1953	International General Electric Co., Inc.	United States	Hitachi, Ltd	Manufacture of steam turbines and electric generators.	9
May 6, 1953	Apparatebau Rothemuehle, Dr. Brandt & Co.	West Germany	Nikko Trading Co., Inc	Manufacture of Rothemuehle dust collectors and delivery vans.	10
Mar. 17, 1953	Maschinenfabrik-A u g s b u r g-Nürnberg A. G.	___do	Mitsubishi Nippon Heavy Industry, Ltd.	Manufacture of M. A. N.-type diesel engines.	15
Mar. 17, 1953	___do	___do	Kawasaki Dockyard Co., Ltd	___do	15
Mar. 31, 1953	Aktiebolaget Gotaverken	Sweden	Mitsui Shipbuilding & Engineering Co., Ltd.	Manufacture of steam turbo-compressors for marine use.	10
Mar. 31, 1953	Maschinenfabrik Nusse & Grafer Hommandit-Gesellschaft.	West Germany	Eiwa Trading Co., Ltd	Manufacture of large hole-boring machines.	5
Mar. 31, 1953	Sulzer Freres S. A	Switzerland	Shin-Mitsubishi Heavy Industries Co., Ltd.	Design and engineering plan for the manufacture of stationary diesel engines.	12
Mar. 31, 1953	___do	___do	___do	Manufacture of vibration dampers for land-type diesel engines.	12
Mar. 31, 1953	Hazemag Hartzer Kleinerungs und Zementmaschinebau G.	West Germany	Yokohama Engineering Co., Ltd	Manufacture of repulsion-type crushing machines.	10
Mar. 31, 1953	Western Machinery Co	United States	Sumitomo-Machinery Co., Ltd	Manufacture of "Wemco" heavy media separation equipment.	13
Mar. 31, 1953	Gute Hoffnungshutte Oberhausen A. G.	West Germany	Mitsubishi Shipbuilding & Engineering Co., Ltd.	Manufacture of steel pillar "Cappe"	15
Mar. 31, 1953	___do	___do	Daido Steel Co., Ltd	___do	15
Mar. 31, 1953	E. I. du Pont de Nemours & Co	United States	Mitsubishi Heavy Industries Reorganized, Ltd.	Manufacture of continuous refining and bleaching devices.	15
Aug. 26, 1953	Les Usines de Melle S. A	France	Nippon Joryu Kogyo K. K	Manufacture of distillation equipment for extra pure alcohol.	2
Sept. 1, 1953	Pleuger & Co	West Germany	Suido Kiko Co., Ltd	Manufacture of Pleuger submersible pumping units.	10
Sept. 15, 1953	Escher Wyss, Ltd	Switzerland	Mitsui Shipbuilding & Engineering Co., Ltd.	Manufacture of Escher Wyss variable pitch propellers, and parts and accessories thereof.	15
Oct. 10, 1953	Sulzer Freres S. A	___do	Uraga Dock Co., Ltd, Uraga-Tamashima Diesel Works, Ltd.	Manufacture of the Sarazin-type vibration damper for stationary diesel engines.	12
Oct. 28, 1953	Sperry Corp	United States	Tokyo Keiki Seizosho Co., Ltd	Manufacture of Sperry aeronautical instruments and Sperry marine instruments."	10

See footnotes at end of table.

Table XIV.—Foreign Companies Which Have Concluded Technological Assistance Agreements With Japanese Firms, May 1950 December 1954[1]—Continued

Date of violation	Foreign Company	Nationality	Japanese recipent	Kind of technology	Term (years)
			Other Machinery and Equipment—Continued		
Oct. 20, 1953	Sulzer Freres S. A	Switzerland	Uraga Dock Co., Ltd / Uraga-Tamashima Diesel Works, Ltd.	Design and engineering plan for the manufacture of stationary diesel engines.	12
Oct. 10, 1953	do	do	Harima Shipbuilding & Engineering Co., Ltd.	do	10
Nov. 16, 1953	do	do	Uraga Dock Co., Ltd / Uraga-Tamashima Diesel Works, Ltd.	Manufacture of high-speed marine diesel engines.	12
Oct. 20, 1953	Worthington Corporation	United States	Niigata Worthington Co., Ltd	Manufacture of Worthington compressors and pumps.	15
Oct. 20, 1953	Les Etalissements A. Cazeneuve.	France	Sho-un Kosakusho Co., Ltd	Manufacture of ultra-high-speed lathes.	10
Oct. 20, 1953	Dmag A. G	West Germany	Fuji Electric Manufacturing Co., Ltd.	Manufacture of winder sets for mining use, and accessories thereof.	10
Nov. 17, 1953	Syntron Co	United States	Shinko Electric Co., Ltd	Manufacture of electromagnetic vibrators, vibratory feeders, and other equipment thereof.	5
Dec. 15, 1953	Michigan Tool Co	do	Fujikoshi Steel Manufacturing Co., Ltd.	Manufacture of gear-shaving cutters	3
Dec. 15, 1953	Isoflex Corp	do	Nippon Reizo Co., Ltd	Production of "Isoflex" (insulation materials formed from plastic compounds).	3
Dec. 15, 1953	E. I. du Pont de Nemours & Co	do	Kyoto Machinery Co., Ltd	Manufacture of continuous refining and bleaching devices.	14
Dec. 1, 1953	Escher Wyss, Ltd	Switzerland	Mitsubishi Shipbuilding & Engineering Co., Ltd.	Manufacture of Escher Wyss "Rotasco Compressors" (rotary piston compressors for refrigerating machinery and other heat pumps).	15
Jan. 19, 1954	Oerlikon Machine Tool Works Byhrle Co.	do	Mitsubishi Shipbuilding & Engineering Co., Ltd.	Manufacture of high-speed lathes and hydraulic copying attachments.	10
Feb. 2, 1954	Joy Manufacturing Co	United States	Ishikawajima Heavy Industry Co., Ltd.	Manufacture of compressors, drill leaders, etc.	10
Mar. 2, 1954	C. Plath Nautical Instrument Manufacturer.	West Germany	Hokushin Electric Machinery Works Co., Ltd.	Manufacture of C. Plath-type air-cooling gyro-compass.	5
Apr. 20, 1954	Pfaudler Co	United States	Shinko Pfaudler Co., Ltd	Manufacture of glass lining machine and apparatus.	15
May 18, 1954	Power-Gas Corp., Ltd	England	Mitsubishi Chemical Working Machinery Co., Ltd.	Manufacture of various kinds of "PGC"-type gas-producing equipment.	3
June 1, 1954	Karlstad Mekaniskawerksted A. G.	Sweden	Gadelius & Co., Ltd	Manufacture of Markila-Blax method washing machine for pulp.	3
July 6, 1954	Copes-Vulcan Division of Continental Foundry & Machine Company.	United States	Mitsubishi Shipbuilding & Engineering Co., Ltd.	Design and manufacture of soot-blowing equipment and its parts for boiler use.	5
July 6, 1954	Vickers Inc	do	Tokyo Keiki Seizosho Co., Ltd	Manufacture of Vickers oil hydraulic vane-type pump and controls.	10
July 6, 1954	Kennedy Van Saun Manufacturing and Engineering Corp.	do	Kubota Iron & Machinery Works, Ltd.	Manufacture of machinery for making cement.	10
July 6, 1954	Perspecta Sound Inc	do	Nippon Victor Co., Ltd	Manufacture of "Perspecta" sound apparatus of image reproduction equipment.	7
July 20, 1954	Sundstrand International Corp	do	Niigata Engineering Co., Ltd	Manufacture of milling machines	10
Sept. 7, 1954	Henry J. Hersey Jr	do	Sanko Seisakusho Co., Ltd	Techniques relating to Hersey filter manufacture.	10
Sept. 7, 1954	Surface Combustion Corp	do	Chugai Furnace Ind. Co., Ltd	Manufacture of various types of furnaces for industrial uses.	5
Nov. 9, 1954	Fuller Co	do	Babcock Hitachi Co., Ltd	Techniques relating to transportation of and cooling apparatus for cement and other powdery products.	10
Nov. 18, 1954	Siemens Schuckertwerke, A. G	West Germany	Yokohama Engineering Co., Ltd	Manufacture of forced circulation boiler equipment.	5
Nov. 18, 1954	International MacGregor Organization S. A.	French Morocco	Far East MacGregor Co., Ltd	Design and manufacture of steel hatch covers for vessels.	3
Dec. 21, 1954	Loeshe Harzerkleinerungs und Zementmachinen K. G.	West Germany	Ube Industries Co., Ltd	Manufacture of Laeshe-type crushers and vertical cement kilns.	5
Dec. 21, 1954	Graver Tank & Manufacturing Co., Inc.	United States	Ishii Iron Works Co., Ltd	Manufacture of floating roof tanks and other tanks.	4
Dec. 27, 1954	Kennedy Van Saun Manufacturing and Engineering Corp.	do	Kubota Iron Mfg. Works, Ltd / Hitachi Shipbuilding Co., Ltd	Manufacture of machinery for cement manufacturing, etc.	10
			Construction		
May 10, 1951	Eastern United Co., Inc	do	Ryohei Mitsudo	Airform construction engineering and introduction of new equipment.	
July 23, 1952	Societe Technique pour l'Utilisation de la Precontrainte.	France	Kyokuto Kogen Concrete Shinko Co., Ltd.	Theory, technique, and method of execution relating to prestressed concrete.	10
Mar. 31, 1953	C. S. Johnson Co	United States	Ishikawajima Koehring Co	Manufacture of York-Flake Ice DER-150 ice-making machines.	5
May 6, 1953	Durisol A. G. für Leechtbaustoffe.	Switzerland	Nippon Durisol Co., Ltd	Production of Durisol light construction materials and their application to construction.	10
June 26, 1953	Guy F. Atkinson Co	United States	Hazamagumi Co., Ltd / Kumagaigumi Co., Ltd	Techniques concerning construction of dams.	3
Aug. 4, 1953	National Water Main Cleaning Co.	do	Suikan Kosei Co., Ltd	Techniques concerning cleaning of inside of steel ducts.	10
Dec. 15, 1953	Prepact Concrete Co	do	Nishimatsu Kensetsu Co., Ltd / Shimizu Kensetsu Co., Ltd	Production of "Prepact" concrete	5½

See footnotes at end of table.

Table XIV.—Foreign Companies Which Have Concluded Technological Assistance Agreements With Japanese Firms, May 1950–December 1954 [1]—Continued

Date of validation	Foreign company	Nationality	Japanese recipient	Kind of technology	Terms (Years)
		Electric Power and Gas Supply			
Mar. 27, 1952	Overseas Consultants, Inc	United States	Kyushu Electric Power Co., Inc	Supervision of engineering, design, and construction of arch dam and spillway, including all structures appurtenant to these two.	[2] 2
Apr. 2, 1952	do	do	Tokyo Electric Power Co., Inc	do	3
July 25, 1952	do	do	Kyushu Electric Power Co., Ltd	Consulting service in engineering, design, and construction of arch dam and spillway, including all appurtenances.	3
		Printing and Publishing			
Apr. 16, 1952	Milprint Inc	United States	Toppan Printing Co., Ltd	Printing of merchandise packages, including cartons, wrappers, and bags made of pliofilm, cellophane, aluminum foil, glassine, and waxed paper.	5
		Recreation			
Mar. 27, 1951	Westrex Corp	United States	Dai-ei Motion Picture Co., Ltd	Use of method and equipment for recording and production of sound in a timed relation with motion pictures.	8

[1] Approved under the provisions of the Foreign Investment Law.
[2] Effective for duration of capital tie-up.
[3] Effective for duration of development work.

NOTE.—This list was compiled from Foreign Capital Research Society, c/o Bank of Japan data and official Japanese Government sources and is presumably complete as of the date indicated.

Table XV.—Foreign Currency Remittances Under the Foreign Investment Law, October 1950–December 1954

[In dollars]

Period	Payment for technical assistance	Dividends	Interest on loans	Principal of loans	Principal of shares	Total
Oct. 1950–Mar. 1951	500, 656. 87					500, 656. 87
Apr. 1951–Mar. 1952	4, 842, 029. 06	734, 043. 29	23, 442. 12			5, 599, 514. 47
Apr. 1952–Mar. 1953	8, 156, 499. 27	1, 806, 088. 79	138, 037. 44	700, 048. 00		10, 800, 673. 50
Apr. 1953–Mar. 1954	11, 430, 857. 31	2, 900, 145. 52	628, 380. 66	2, 942, 324. 19		17, 901, 707. 68
1954—						
April	1, 061, 093. 17	20, 016. 56	46, 455. 49	289, 064. 00		1, 416, 629. 22
May	655, 719. 63	33, 658. 56	94, 677. 46	400, 638. 27		1, 184, 693. 92
June	679, 130. 25	797, 393. 86	251, 465. 94	279, 064. 00		2, 007, 054. 05
July	1, 088, 518. 92	41, 903. 62	27, 863. 68	903, 384. 94	114, 848. 68	2, 176, 519. 84
August	1, 386, 657. 54	86, 798. 39	22, 279. 15	350, 814. 00	10, 693. 72	1, 857, 242. 80
September	738, 188. 68	919, 959. 17	43, 057. 38	330, 314. 00	7, 290. 66	2, 038, 809. 89
October	940, 083. 07	4, 526. 82	89, 388. 30	274, 851. 93	49, 131. 34	1, 357, 981. 46
November	1, 285, 041. 31	156, 899. 44	81, 310. 16	999, 762. 20	38, 132. 82	2, 561, 145. 93
December	1, 050, 533. 25	646, 296. 02	376, 922. 77	284, 609. 32	28, 020. 18	2, 386, 381. 54
Total, April–Dec. 1954	8, 884, 965. 82	2, 707, 452. 44	1, 033, 420. 33	4, 112, 502. 66	248, 117. 40	16, 986, 458. 65
Total, Oct. 1950–Dec. 1954	33, 815, 008. 33	8, 147, 730. 04	1, 823, 280. 55	7, 754, 874. 85	248, 117. 40	51, 789, 011. 17

Source: Japanese Ministry of Finance.

Table XVI.—Government Receipts and Expenditures, General Account, Japanese Fiscal Years 1953–54

[In millions of yen]

Revenue	1953	1954	Expenditures	1953	1954
Taxes and stamps, total	756.7	778.3	Public works	175.0	163.3
Individual income tax	292.0	287.6	Education	99.6	113.4
Corporation income tax	176.8	202.6	Public investment	42.9	20.0
Revaluation tax	13.7	5.9	Housing	13.7	12.6
Liquor tax	146.2	140.8	Social insurance	73.7	89.3
Sugar tax	33.9	38.1	Veterans' pensions and related items	50.0	68.8
Gasoline tax	18.7	23.8	Police	21.6	14.8
Commodity taxes	24.2	24.4	Local equalization grants	137.6	137.0
Other taxes	8.0	6.9	Maritime Safety Agency	6.0	5.9
Customs and tonnage duties	26.1	25.2	National debt service	44.8	40.3
Stamp revenues	17.1	23.0	Agricultural insurance	19.4	17.3
Government enterprise receipts	16.6	13.3	Imported food subsidy	30.0	0
Monopoly revenue	150.7	125.2	Contribution to U. S. security forces	62.0	58.5
Sales of Government property	13.8	8.4	Japan Defense Agency	61.3	74.3
Miscellaneous revenue	43.8	34.4	Civil service pensions	11.5	14.6
Surplus carryover	45.6	40.3	Miscellaneous expenditures	9.8	25.5
			Reserve	17.5	8.0
			Departmental administration	150.8	136.3
Total revenue	1,027.2	999.9	Total expenditure	1,027.2	999.9

Source: Japanese Ministry of Finance.

Table XVII.—National Income and Gross National Product, by Distributive Shares, Japanese Fiscal Years 1934–36 (Average) and 1952–53 [1]

[Value in billions of yen]

Item	Value			Distribution—percent		
	1934–36 average	1952	1953	1934–36 average	1952	1953
National income	14.4	5,195.4	5,964.9	86.2 *(100.0)*	84.0 *(100.0)*	83.4 *(100.0)*
Compensation of employees	5.6	2,431.7	2,844.7	*(38.9)*	*(46.8)*	*(47.7)*
Proprietors' income	4.5	2,186.0	2,374.6	*(31.3)*	*(42.1)*	*(39.8)*
Personal rental income	1.3	48.5	65.4	*(9.0)*	*(.9)*	*(1.1)*
Personal interest income	1.3	80.0	109.3	*(9.0)*	*(1.5)*	*(1.8)*
Corporate income	1.3	473.0	577.3	*(9.0)*	*(9.1)*	*(9.7)*
Surplus of Government enterprises, etc	.4	35.9	73.2	*(2.8)*	*(.7)*	*(1.2)*
Net receipts from abroad	0	−11.0	−19.1	0	*(−.2)*	*(−.3)*
Interest on Government and consumer debts		−48.7	−60.5	*(−)*	*(−.9)*	*(−1.0)*
Reconciliation items	2.6	950.9	1,124.1	15.6	15.4	15.7
Plus: Indirect business tax	1.4	626.6	681.7	8.4	10.1	9.5
Less: Subsidies	0	−50.7	−41.6	0	−.8	−.6
Plus: Capital consumption allowances	1.2	375.0	484.0	7.2	6.1	6.8
Statistical discrepancy	−.3	36.0	67.2	−1.8	.6	.9
Gross national product	16.7	6,182.3	7,156.2	100.0	100.0	100.0
National expenditure:						
Personal consumption expenditure	11.0	3,762.9	4,415.1	65.9	60.9	61.7
Gross private domestic capital formation	2.6	1,187.0	1,361.5	15.6 *(100.0)*	19.2 *(100.0)*	19.0 *(100.0)*
Private dwelling house construction	.2	75.9	102.6	*(7.7)*	*(6.4)*	*(7.5)*
Producers' durable equipment	1.7	726.3	822.3	*(65.4)*	*(61.2)*	*(60.4)*
Changes in business inventories	.7	384.8	436.6	*(26.9)*	*(32.4)*	*(32.1)*
Net foreign investment	0	79.5	−11.6	0	1.3	−.1
Government purchase of goods and services	3.1	1,152.9	1,391.2	18.5	18.6	19.4
Government finance	1.9	519.3	680.2	11.3	8.4	9.5
Local finance	1.2	633.6	711.0	7.2	10.2	9.9
Gross national expenditure	16.7	6,182.3	7,156.2	100.0	100.0	100.0

[1] The Japanese fiscal year is from April 1 to March 31.

Source: Economic Counsel Board.

Table XVIII.—Assets and Liabilities of Eleven Principal Banks, Calendar Years 1952–54

[In millions of yen]

Item	1952	1953	1954
Assets, total	1,892,855	2,319,092	2,420,101
Cash, checks, and bills	235,548	248,296	257,066
Deposits with other banks	14,909	18,079	22,499
Securities	111,797	165,469	208,357
Loans and discounts	1,169,175	1,437,767	1,531,469
Foreign exchange [1]	105,023	115,747	54,522
Real and other property	26,293	34,491	47,428
Other	230,110	299,243	298,760
Liabilities, total	1,892,855	2,319,092	2,420,101
Deposits	1,259,949	1,521,861	1,687,553
Accounts payable	190,138	261,653	215,656
Foreign exchange [2]	93,594	85,058	25,961
Acceptances and guaranties	195,252	247,782	241,986
Capital	11,647	23,270	23,270
Reserves	21,221	33,117	46,752
Other	121,054	146,351	178,923

[1] Holdings for its own account (see chapter VII).
[2] Holdings on Government account (see chapter VII).

Source: Bank of Japan.

Table XIX.—Balance of Payments, Calendar Years 1953–54

[In millions of U. S. dollars]

Item	1953	1954
Goods and services	−226.2	−80.2
Exports, f. o. b.[1]	1,257.8	1,611.3
Imports, f. o. b	2,049.6	2,040.6
Transportation and insurance (net)	−183.3	−177.5
Government, not included elsewhere (net)[1]	802.1	603.3
Other (net)	−53.2	−76.7
Private donations	21.1	29.4
Private capital	−17.8	13.4
Official and bank capital	221.3	24.7
Long-term capital	−12.0	−4.2
Short-term capital:		
Use of IMF [2] resources (net)	62.4	----------
Other liabilities	101.0	107.4
Sterling balances (increase−)	125.4	−106.6
U. S. dollar balances (increase−)	−29.7	129.9
Other foreign assets (increase−)	−23.4	−99.1
Monetary gold (increase−)	−2.4	−2.7
Net errors and omissions	1.6	12.7

[1] Goods purchased by United Nations forces under the special procurement program are included in "Government, not included elsewhere."
[2] International Monetary Fund.

Source: Ministry of Finance, Government of Japan.

Table XX.—Total Deposits and Loans of All Banks,[1] Calendar Years 1946–54

[In millions of yen]

Year	Deposits	Loans	Ratio of loans to deposits
1946	144,868	146,406	101.1
1947	234,375	168,243	71.8
1948	505,349	381,347	75.5
1949	792,018	679,051	85.7
1950	1,048,564	994,746	94.9
1951	1,506,308	1,517,813	100.8
1952	2,223,820	2,128,022	95.7
1953	2,707,612	2,671,286	98.7
1954	3,036,687	2,911,968	95.9

[1] Excludes Bank of Japan.

Source: Bank of Japan.

Table XXI.—Outstanding Loans and Discounts of All Banks, by Interest Rate, Calendar Years 1952–53

[In millions of yen]

Rates of interest (percent)	Loans on bills and and deeds		Bills discounted	
	1952	1953	1952	1953
Total	1,362,580	1,682,635	646,406	970,698
Less than 5.11	5,153	13,681	9	3
5.11–5.47	393	705	--------	30
5.48–5.83	1,934	6,888	1	162
5.84–6.20	2,896	4,384	10	3
6.21–6.56	3,532	4,745	1	65
6.57–6.93	8,824	16,762	124	187
6.94–7.29	133,760	255,779	2,466	3,585
7.30–7.66	58,825	31,276	858	695
7.67–8.02	15,473	8,669	22,520	41,643
8.03–8.39	38,316	14,594	10,833	15,374
8.40–8.75	66,132	69,638	9,867	26,110
8.76–9.12	469,321	603,882	124,572	227,947
9.13–9.48	149,309	151,446	172,986	272,705
9.49–9.85	61,807	58,993	63,167	111,572
9.86–10.21	33,570	40,842	69,427	99,658
10.22–10.58	62,772	90,468	144,256	138,904
10.59–10.94	17,185	29,212	9,535	14,456
10.95–11.31	100,883	118,340	12,273	13,965
11.32–11.67	67,535	97,417	205	230
11 68–12.04	49,080	49,549	1,389	1,679
12.05–12.40	9,074	8,913	839	703
12.41 and over	6,806	6,452	1,068	1,051

Source: Bank of Japan.

Table XXII.—Wholesale Price Indexes in Japan, by Major Commodity Groups, Calendar Years 1950–54 and January–June 1955

[1934–36 average=1]

Item	1950	1951	1952	1953	1954	1955 (Jan.–June)
All commodities	246.8	342.5	349.2	351.6	349.3	343.9
Edible farm products	210.3	262.4	290.9	311.1	347.9	351.6
Other foodstuffs	278.0	306.7	314.8	310.1	328.1	322.9
Textiles	371.1	514.6	410.4	407.1	374.5	356.9
Fuels	212.8	254.7	322.4	320.5	310.3	324.4
Metals and metal products	189.1	376.0	365.6	344.5	322.6	325.7
Building materials	218.3	321.6	351.6	419.5	438.4	409.4
Chemical products	206.3	285.4	307.0	280.7	259.8	250.8
Miscellaneous	199.0	295.6	264.6	252.5	247.5	246.6
Producer goods	222.1	341.6	350.6	354.6	342.3	335.9
Consumer goods	267.4	325.2	328.3	327.3	337.5	334.3

Source: Bank of Japan.

Table XXIII.—Export-Import Price Indexes, by Major Commodity Groups, Calendar Years 1950–54 and January–June 1955

[July 1949 to June 1950=100]

Item	1950	1951	1952	1953	1954	1955 (Jan.–June)
Export						
All commodities	115.6	165.5	134.9	127.9	123.0	122.7
Foodstuffs	93.2	99.1	99.2	102.2	110.8	108.2
Textiles	122.4	159.3	117.5	112.1	107.6	101.4
Metals and metal products	125.8	242.3	205.5	188.2	172.7	190.9
Machinery	102.0	157.6	135.9	131.2	127.3	121.7
Timber and wood products	95.6	139.0	133.9	131.3	138.5	149.5
Chemical products	90.2	105.5	105.5	99.6	104.0	99.6
Ceramics	95.9	115.7	114.1	105.7	105.8	104.5
Miscellaneous	104.0	134.2	124.9	121.2	119.3	121.6
Import						
All commodities	107.8	136.3	122.1	110.1	105.7	106.9
Foodstuffs	102.4	121.0	126.1	119.5	106.5	108.2
Textiles	122.9	151.5	125.7	111.8	116.6	110.9
Minerals	94.2	137.9	113.6	94.5	94.9	98.7
Metals and metal products	105.6	165.9	141.5	121.7	119.8	120.9
Timber and wood products	123.4	164.3	107.3	87.8	86.6	91.5
Animals, vegetables, and their products	155.3	224.2	141.4	114.7	113.8	138.1
Oils and fats	110.1	148.4	104.5	91.8	96.5	100.2
Chemical products	81.3	100.1	84.3	72.9	74.4	77.9

Source: Bank of Japan.

Trade and Payments Arrangements[1]

	Payments arrangement	Trade arrangement [2]
Argentina _____	United States dollar expressed open account effective for 1 year beginning May 1, 1954, with 1-year automatic extension. Swing ceiling, $20 million.	$90 million each way. Effective for 1 year beginning January 1, 1955.
Belgian monetary area _____	United States dollar cash arrangement. Effective June 1, 1950, and continuing indefinitely until conclusion of formal trade and payments arrangements. No swing ceiling.	No trade plan.
Brazil _____	United States dollar expressed open account. Effective for 1 year beginning July 1, 1952, with 1-year automatic extension. Swing ceiling, $10 million.	Japan's exports, $33.5 million; imports, $35.6 million. Effective for 1 year.
Burma _____	Sterling cash bilateral arrangement effective until March 31, 1955; provided for settlement under the Anglo-Japanese Sterling Payments Agreement (see entry, Sterling area).	No trade plan. Commodities in two-way trade are listed but specific values are not indicated.
Ceylon _____	Sterling cash bilateral arrangement, effective indefinitely beginning September 6, 1952; provides for settlement under the Anglo-Japanese Sterling Payments Agreement (see entry, Sterling area).	Do.
Egypt _____	United States dollar expressed open account. Effective for 1 year beginning November 28, 1953, with 1-year automatic extension. Swing ceiling, $5 million.	Do.
Finland _____	United States dollar expressed open account. Effective for 1 year beginning December 24, 1952, with 1-year automatic extension. Swing ceiling, $1 million.	No trade plan.
Formosa (Taiwan) _____	United States dollar expressed open account. Effective for indefinite period beginning April 1, 1953. Swing ceiling, $10 million.	$74.5 million each way.
French Union _____	United States dollar expressed open account. Effective for indefinite period beginning July 7, 1948. Swing ceiling, $8 million.	No trade plan.
Germany, Federal Rep. of_	Sterling cash or German mark convertible into sterling.	Do.
Greece _____	United States dollar expressed open account. Effective for 1 year beginning April 1, 1955. Swing ceiling, $250,000.	$2.5 million each way for 1 year beginning April 1, 1955.
Indonesia _____	United States dollar expressed open account. Effective for 1 year beginning July 1, 1952, with 1-year automatic extension. No fixed ceiling; cash payment up to $20 million, of which $15 million is switch trade. Any balance above $20 million is to be paid in installments in 2 years.	Japan's exports, $55 million; imports, $40 million. Balance of $15 million to be obtained through three-way transactions, particularly with the Federal Republic of Germany.
Italy _____	United States dollar expressed open account. Effective until January 14, 1956. It is agreed that thereafter trade will be conducted on a cash basis.	No trade plan.

---

[1] As of December 1955.
[2] In the absence of a stated period, the value of trade indicated is for a 12-month period.

117

	Payments arrangement	Trade arrangement [2]
Korea, South	United States dollar expressed open account. Effective for indefinite period beginning April 1, 1950. Swing ceiling $2 million.	Japan's exports, $32 million; imports, $16 million. These figures are based on trade plan established several years ago and renewed from year to year without further negotiations.
Netherlands	United States dollar expressed open account. Effective for indefinite period beginning April 1, 1951. Swing ceiling, $2 million.	$73 million each way. Extended for 1 year beginning January 1, 1955.
Pakistan	Sterling cash bilateral arrangement effective for 1 year beginning February 1, 1954; provides for settlement under Anglo-Japanese Sterling Payments Agreement (see entry, Sterling area).	28 million pounds sterling ($78.4 million) each way. Effective for 1 year beginning September 15, 1954.
Peru	United States cash arrangement (basically an undertaking to encourage trade). Effective for an indefinite period beginning June 30, 1949.	No trade plan.
Philippines	United States dollar expressed open account. Effective September 18, 1954, to May 31, 1955. Swing ceiling, $2.5 million.	$50 million each way. Effective for 1 year following the July 1, 1950, agreement, which has been automatically extended.
Ryukyu Islands	An understanding signed on July 10, 1952, effective October 10, 1952, to facilitate trade between Japan and the islands. It does not include a trade plan and provides for United States dollar cash payment for all balances. This is not considered by the Japanese as a true trade agreement.	No trade plan.
Spain	United States dollar cash arrangement to encourage trade. Effective for an indefinite period beginning June 30, 1951.	Provides for most-favored-nation treatment for shipping.
Sterling area	Sterling settlement under Anglo-Japanese Sterling Payments Agreement, including trade with Ceylon, Burma, and Pakistan. Effective until September 1956.	Trade plan covers the period October 1955–March 1956. However, following targets were set for the 12-month period October 1955–September 1956: Japan's exports to the United Kingdom, 22.6 million pounds sterling; Japan's imports from the United Kingdom, 18.8 million pounds sterling. Japan's exports to British colonies, 108.3 million pounds sterling; imports, 45.6 million pounds sterling. The excess of exports is to be balanced by imports from British Dominions.
Sweden	United States dollar expressed open account. Effective for an indefinite period beginning March 5, 1952.	Japan's exports, $12 million; imports, $8 million. Effective for 1 year beginning April 1, 1954. July 1955 plan extended until December 31, 1955.
Syria	An understanding concluded on August 15, 1953, to establish favorable conditions for expansion of trade, such as application of general tariff rates for Japanese products. All settlements are on United States dollar cash basis. Provides for 1-year automatic extension.	No trade plan.
Thailand (Siam)	United States dollar expressed open account. Effective for 1 year beginning September 1, 1954. Swing ceiling, $5 million.	$65 million each way. Effective until December 31, 1955.
Turkey	United States dollar expressed open account. Effective February 8, 1955, to July 31, 1956. Swing ceiling, $1.5 million.	3.55 million each way. Effective February 8, 1955, to July 31, 1956.
Uruguay	Tentative United States dollar cash arrangement. No swing ceiling.	No trade plan at present.

[2] In the absence of a stated period, the value of trade indicated is for a 12-month period.

Law Concerning Foreign Investment—Excerpts[1]

CHAPTER I. GENERAL PROVISIONS

Article 1. (Purpose.) The purpose of this law is to create a sound basis for foreign investment in Japan, by limiting the induction of foreign investment to that which will contribute to the self-support and sound development of the Japanese economy and to the improvement of the international balance of payments, by providing for remittances arising from foreign investment, and by providing for adequate protection for such investments.

Article 2. (Principle concerning foreign investment.) Foreign investment in Japan shall be permitted to be as free as possible, and the system of validation and filing of report pursuant to the provisions of this law shall be relaxed and eliminated gradually as the necessity for such measures decreases.

Article 3. (Definitions.) In order to make uniform the application of this law and orders issued thereunder, the following terminology shall be defined to mean:

(1) "Foreign investors" shall mean

a. "Exchange nonresidents" (excluding juridical persons), as defined in article 6 paragraph 1 of the Foreign Exchange and Foreign Trade Control Law (law No. 228 of 1949).

b. Any juridical person (corporate body, enterprise), established under foreign law, or having its seat or place of administration in foreign countries, except those designated by the Minister of Finance.

c. Any juridical person (corporate body, enterprise), the stock or proprietary interest of which is wholly owned, directly or indirectly, by a person or persons as specified in either item a. or b. above.

d. Any juridical person (corporate body, enterprise), which is in fact controlled by a person or persons as specified in either item a. or b. above.

e. In addition to those as specified in any one of the items a. through d., inclusive, any person as mentioned in article 2 paragraph 1 of the Cabinet order concerning the Acquisition of Property and/or Rights by Foreign Nationals (Cabinet order No. 51 of 1949).

(2) "Japan," "foreign countries," "national currency," "foreign currency," "exchange residents," "foreign means of payment," "domestic means of payment," and "property" shall mean "Japan," "foreign countries," "national currency," "foreign currency," "exchange residents," "foreign means of payment," "domestic means of payment," and "property" as defined in article 6 paragraph 1 of the Foreign Exchange and Foreign Trade Control Law.

(3) "Technological assistance contracts" shall mean contracts concerning the transfer of patent or utility model rights or technologies, license agreement thereof, assistance concerning technical and factory management, and others designated by the competent Minister (hereinafter referred to as "technological assistance").

[1] Based on official Japanese translation of law No. 163 of 1950, as amended.

(4) "Proprietary interest" shall mean the proprietary interest of the member of the gomei-kaisha, goshi-kaisha, or yugen-kaisha, and other proprietary interests of juridical persons as provided for by Cabinet order.

(5) "Beneficiary certificate" shall mean the beneficiary certificate of the securities investment trust as mentioned in article 2 of the Securities Investment Trust Law (law No. 198 of 1951), or of the loan trust as mentioned in article 2 of the Loan Trust Law (law No. 195 of 1952).

(6) "Fruit" shall mean the dividends arising from stock or proprietary interest, such income arising from the trust relative to the beneficiary ownership represented by the beneficiary certificate of the securities investment trust as is distributed in proportion to the number of the beneficiary ownership concerned, income arising from the trust relative to the beneficiary ownership represented by the beneficiary certificate of the loan trust, and interest arising from debentures (exclusive of those which are floated abroad and the payment of which may be made abroad, hereinafter the same), or from claimable assets arising from loans.

(7) "Principal withdrawn" shall mean the proceeds arising from the sale of stock or proprietary interest, money delivered to the stockholder as a result of the redemption of the stock by profits in case the stock concerned is issued in accordance with the provisions of article 222 paragraph 1 of the Commercial Code (law No. 48 of 1899) and has the statement of time of the redemption concerned (hereinafter to be referred to as "redeemable stock"), such corpus of trust redeemed relative to the beneficiary ownership represented by the beneficiary certificate of the securities investment trust as is distributed in proportion to the number of beneficiary ownership concerned, corpus of trust redeemed relative to the beneficiary ownership represented by the beneficiary certificate of the loan trust, and the principal amortized of debentures or claimable assets arising from loans.

2. In case of doubt as to whether or not a juridical person (corporate body, enterprise) comes under a juridical person stipulated in item (1) c. or d. of the preceding paragraph, it shall be determined by the Minister of Finance.

Article 4. (Balance of payments statement of external assets and liabilities.) The Minister of Finance shall, as provided for by Cabinet order, prepare and maintain a balance of payments statement of external assets and liabilities.

2. The Minister of Finance shall submit periodically to the Cabinet the statement prescribed in the preceding paragraph.

3. The Minister of Finance may, as provided for by Cabinet order, request the Government agencies and others concerned to submit data necessary for the drafting of the statement prescribed in paragraph 1.

Article 5. (Measures to be taken when external liabilities become excessive or when there is danger of default.) In the event that the amount of external liabilities against the amount of external assets has become excessive and as a consequence a danger exists that necessary payment to a foreign country (including payment by foreign means of payments, the same hereinafter) arising from new foreign investment cannot be made, the Minister of Finance shall report to the Cabinet.

2. In the event that the report mentioned in the preceding paragraph is made, the competent Minister shall not license, validate, approve, or take any other administrative action to cause new obligations to foreign investors or new payment to a foreign country arising from such new obligations, until the Cabinet decides the policy to be followed with regard to the said report.

3. In the event that the Cabinet has decided its policy based on the report prescribed in paragraph 1, the competent Minister shall follow such policy when licensing, validating, approving, or taking other administrative action to cause new obligations to foreign investors or new payment to a foreign country arising from such new obligations.

4. The provisions of the preceding two paragraphs shall not be construed to impair the rights acquired by the foreign investor on the basis of license, validation, approval, and/or other administrative action granted or taken by the competent Minister in accordance with the provisions of laws and regulations.

Article 6. (Measures regarding foreign exchange budget.) The Ministerial Council shall, upon consideration of the balance of payments statement prescribed in article 4, appropriate in the foreign exchange budget the amount within which payment to a foreign country may be made of obligations to foreign investors pursuant to the provisions of this law.

Article 7. (Announcement of technological assistance desired.) The Minister of Finance and Minister of International Trade and Industry shall, in accordance with the Ministry of Finance ordinance and the Ministry of International Trade and Industry ordinance, make public a list of the kinds of technologies concerning which technological assistance from foreign investors is desired.

2. The Minister of Finance and the Minister of International Trade and Industry may revise from time to time the list made public in accordance with the provisions of the preceding paragraph.

Article 8. (Standards of validation, designation, etc.) The competent Minister shall apply the following standards on validating contracts prescribed in this law, and priority shall be given to those which will most speedily and effectively contribute to an improvement of the international balance of payments.

(1) Directly or indirectly contributing to the improvement of the international balance of payments, or

(2) Directly or indirectly contributing to the development of essential industries or public enterprises, or

(3) Necessary for continuation of existing technological assistance contracts concerning essential industries or public enterprises or for the alteration of the articles of the contracts concerned, such as renewal.

2. The competent Minister shall not validate contracts prescribed in this law which fall under any one of the following paragraphs:

(1) Contracts the provisions of which are not fair, or are in contravention of laws and regulations.

(2) Contracts which are deemed to be concluded or the alteration of articles of which, such as renewal of the contracts, is deemed to be made in a manner not free from fraud, duress, or undue influence.

(3) When deemed to have an adverse effect on the rehabilitation of the Japanese economy.

(4) Unless as provided for by Cabinet order, in the event that the payment for the acquisition by a foreign investor of stock, proprietary interest, beneficiary certificate, debentures, or claimable assets arising from loans is not made with any of the below-mentioned items:

a. Domestic means of payment which have been legally obtained through exchange of foreign means of payment for the purpose of the acquisition concerned, or others equivalent to the foreign means of payments.

b. Domestic means of payment which have been obtained by the foreign investor concerned through the sale by him of stock, proprietary interest, or beneficiary certificate the payment to a foreign country of the fruit or the principal withdrawn of which is deemed to have been authorized pursuant to the provisions of article 15-(2) paragraph 1, exclusive of the domestic means of payment obtained through such sale as was made 1 month or more earlier than the day of filing an application for validation of the acquisition concerned.

c. Concerning stock or proprietary interest as mentioned in the preceding subitem b., domestic means of payment which have been obtained by the foreign investor concerned as surplus assets distributed, as money paid to the stockholder or the member in case of amalgamation, as money delivered to the stockholder or the member in case where the stock (exclusive of the redeemable stock) or the proprietary interest concerned is redeemed by profits, as money delivered to the stockholder or the member pursuant to the provisions of article 379 paragraph 1 of the Commercial Code (inclusive of the case where these provisions apply mutatis mutandis in article 379 paragraph 3 and article 416 paragraph 3 of the same code, and in articles 58 and 63 of the Yugen-kaisha Law (law No. 74 of 1938), as money paid in return for the rights to the allotment of new stock in case where the said rights are transferred to others in accordance with the provisions of article 17-(2), as money paid in return for the transfer of rights to the allotment of the new stocks in case where the issuing company of the said outstanding stock has issued new stock due to crediting the revaluation reserves to the stated capital as prescribed in the provisions of article 109 of the Assets Revaluation Law (law No. 110 of 1950), or as money delivered to the stockholder due to request as provided for by the provisions of article 10 of the Law Concerning Crediting Revaluation Reserves to the Stated Capital (law No. 143 of 1951), and as others as provided for by Cabinet order (hereinafter to be referred to as "surplus assets distributed, etc."); exclusive of the case where the day of payment of the said surplus assets distributed, etc., is 1 month or more earlier than the day of filing an application for the acquisition concerned.

d. Domestic means of payment which have been obtained by the foreign investor concerned as the principal withdrawn of the beneficiary certificate as provided for in subitem b., exclusive of the case where the day of payment of the said principal withdrawn is 1 month or more earlier than the day of filing an application for the acquisition concerned.

e. Such domestic means of payment which have been obtained by the foreign investor concerned due to inheritance, bequest, or amalgamation from another foreign investor as come under any of subitems b. to d., inclusive, in case where "the foreign investor concerned" in subitems b. to d., inclusive, reads "another foreign investor as mentioned in subitem e."

f. Domestic means of payment which have been withdrawn by the foreign investor concerned for the purpose of the acquisition concerned from the Foreign Investors Deposit Account as provided for in article 9-(2) paragraph 1 on or after the day of validation of the acquisition concerned.

3. The provisions of the preceding two paragraphs shall be applied mutatis mutandis in the event that the Minister of Finance designates pursuant to the provisions of this law, or that the Foreign Investment Council expresses its opinion advising to give license, validation, approval, or other administrative actions pursuant to the provisions of this law.

Article 9. (Statement concerning remittance stipulation.) In the event that a foreign investor desires to receive compensation for technological assistance, fruit, or principal withdrawn of debentures or claimable assets arising from loans, by way of payment to a foreign country, the said effect shall be so stated in the contracts concerning technological assistance, subscription to debentures, or loans.

2. In the event that a foreign investor desires to receive payment of fruit or principal withdrawn of stock, proprietary interest, beneficiary certificate, or debenture, by payment to a foreign country, the said effect shall be so stated in the applications to the competent Minister for validation of acquisition of stock, proprietary interest, beneficiary certificate, or debentures from which such fruit or principal withdrawn arises.

Article 9–(2). (Foreign Investors Deposit Account.) The Foreign Investors Deposit Account shall be a special deposit account with the authorized foreign exchange bank (meaning the authorized foreign bank as provided for in article 11 of the Foreign Exchange and Foreign Trade Control Law) expressed in national currency, and shall be established for the foreign investors.

2. Those which may be deposited by a foreign investor in the Foreign Investors Deposit Account of the foreign investor concerned shall be as follows:

(1) Such proceeds arising from the sale of the stock or the proprietary interest which has been legally owned by the foreign investor concerned as come under article 15–(2) paragraph 1 item (3) (exclusive of the proviso), and have not existed 3 months or more as from the day of the sale concerned.

(2) Such principal withdrawn of the beneficiary certificate which has been legally owned by the foreign investor concerned as comes under article 15–(2) paragraph 1 item (4) (exclusive of the proviso), and has not existed 3 months or more as from the day of payment of the said principal withdrawn.

(3) Such surplus assets distributed, etc., given to the foreign investor concerned on the strength of the stock or the proprietary interest which had been legally owned by the foreign investor concerned and the payment to a foreign country of the principal withdrawn of which was deemed to have been authorized pursuant to the provisions of article 15–(2) paragraph 1, as have not existed 3 months or more as from the day of payment thereof.

(4) Such proceeds arising from the sale of stock or proprietary interest, principal withdrawn of beneficiary certificate, or surplus assets distributed, etc., the confirmation concerning which was made on behalf of the foreign investor concerned pursuant to the provisions of article 13–(3) (hereinafter to be referred to as "proceeds, etc.," in this item), or such proceeds, etc., arising from the claimable assets the confirmation concerning which was made, as have not existed 3 months or more as from the day of the confirmation concerned, inclusive, in case where the acquisition by the foreign investor concerned of the said proceeds, etc., or the claimable assets the confirmation concerning which had been made 3 months or more as from the day of payment (the day of sale as regards the proceeds arising from the sale of the stock or the proprietary interest) of the proceeds, etc., concerned or the proceeds, etc., arising from the said claimable assets, of only those which have been legally deposited in the Foreign Investors Deposit Account by another foreign investor.

3. No one shall deposit, nor shall there be deposited, any item other than those which may be deposited pursuant to the provisions of the preceding paragraph, in the Foreign Investors Deposit Account.

4. Other than those as provided for by the preceding three paragraphs, necessary matters concerning the Foreign Investors Deposit Account, such as establishment of the account concerned, depositing in the account concerned, or withdrawal therefrom, shall be provided for by Cabinet order.

CHAPTER II. VALIDATION, FILING OF REPORT, AND DESIGNATION OF FOREIGN CAPITAL INVESTED, ETC.

Article 10. (Validation of technological assistance contracts.) In the event that a foreign investor and the other party desire to conclude such technological assistance contracts, the compensation for which he will receive by way of payment to a foreign country, with the period of contract or the period of payment in excess of 1 year (hereinafter to be referred to as "A-class technological assistance contracts"), or to alter the articles of the said A-class technological assistance contracts, such as renewing the contracts concerned, or in the event that they desire to alter the articles of the technological assistance contracts other than A-class technological assistance contracts (hereinafter to be referred to as "B-class technological assistance contracts"), such as renewing the contracts concerned, with a result that the B-class technological assistance contracts come to be A-class technological assistance contracts because of the said alteration of the articles of the contracts such as renewal of the contracts concerned, validation of the said conclusion of the technological assistance contracts or alteration of the articles of the contracts concerned shall be obtained from the competent Minister in accordance with the ordinance of the competent Ministry.

Article 11. (Validation or filing of report of acquisition of stock or proprietary interest.) A foreign investor desirous of acquiring stock or proprietary interest (exclusive of those which come within the purview of the following paragraph) in a juridical person established under Japanese laws and orders shall obtain validation of the acquisition concerned from the competent Minister in accordance with the ordinance of the competent Ministry.

2. A foreign investor shall, if he has acquired the stock or proprietary interest in a juridical person established under Japanese laws and orders, acquisition of which creates additional assets of the juridical person concerned and the fruit or the principal withdrawn of which he will not receive by way of payment to a foreign country, file a report thereof with the competent Minister in accordance with the ordinance of the competent Ministry.

3. The provisions of the preceding two paragraphs shall not apply to cases as provided for in each of the following items where:

(1) A foreign investor acquires stock or proprietary interest due to transfer from another foreign investor who has legally owned the said stock or proprietary interest.

(2) A foreign investor acquires stock or proprietary interest due to inheritance or bequest.

(3) Upon the amalgamation of the juridical person who has legally owned stock or proprietary interest, the foreign investor who is a juridical person continuously existing after the amalgamation or newly established with the amalgamation acquires the said stock or proprietary interest.

(4) A foreign investor who legally owns outstanding stock or proprietary interest of a juridical person acquires, upon the amalgamation of the said juridical person, new stock or proprietary interest of the juridical person continuously existing after the amalgamation or newly established due to amalgamation, allotted on the strength of the said outstanding stock or proprietary interest.

(5) A foreign investor who legally owns outstanding stock acquires new stock allotted on the strength of the said outstanding stock upon the issuance of the new stock due to crediting to the stated capital of the reserve fund of the issuing company of the said outstanding stock.

(6) A foreign investor who legally owns outstanding stock acquires new stock allotted on the strength of the said outstanding stock upon the issuance of the new stock (exclusive of the new stock concerning which the amount of payment therefor is provided for in article 4 paragraph 1 of the Law Concerning Crediting Revaluation Reserves to the Stated Capital) due to crediting to the stated capital of the revaluation reserves of the issuing company of the said outstanding stock.

(7) A foreign investor who legally owns outstanding stock acquires new stock issued due to the splitting up or consolidation of the said outstanding stock.

(8) A foreign investor who legally owns outstanding stock acquires new stock issued for the purpose of paying dividends of the said outstanding stock.

(9) A foreign investor who has legally owned outstanding convertible stock or convertible debentures acquires new stock due to conversion of the said convertible debentures.

(10) A foreign investor receives restoration of stock or proprietary interest pursuant to the provisions of the Cabinet Order Concerning Restoration of United Nations Shares (Cabinet order No. 310 of 1949), German Property Custody Order (Cabinet order No. 252 of 1950), or of the Cabinet Order Concerning the Restoration, Etc., of United Nations Property (Cabinet order No. 6 of 1951).

(11) Other case as provided for by Cabinet order.

4. The provisions of the preceding two paragraphs (exclusive of the preceding paragraph items (2) to (10), inclusive) shall not in any way affect restrictions pursuant to the provisions of the Foreign Exchange and Foreign Trade Control Law.

Article 12. (Validation of acquisition of beneficiary certificate.) In the event that a foreign investor desires to acquire the beneficiary certificate the fruit or the principal withdrawn of which he will receive by way of payment to a foreign country, validation of the acquisition concerned shall be obtained from the Minister of Finance in accordance with the Ministry of Finance ordinance.

2. The provisions of the preceding paragraph shall not apply to cases which come under the cases as provided for in the preceding article paragraph 3 items (1) to (3), inclusive where "stock or proprietary interest" in the said items reads "beneficiary certificate."

3. The parts of the preceeding paragraph which are covered by the preceding article paragraph 3 item (1) shall not in any way affect restrictions as provided for in the Foreign Exchange and Foreign Trade Control Law.

Article 13. (Validation of acquisition of debentures or claimable assets arising from loans.) In the event that a foreign investor desires to acquire debentures of a juridical person established under Japanese laws and orders, or to acquire claimable assets arising from loans, the fruit or the principal withdrawn of which he will receive by way of payment to a foreign country, validation of the acquisition concerned shall be obtained from the competent Minister in accordance with the ordinance of the competent Ministry. Provided, however, the same shall not apply in case where the period as from the day of acquisition of the said debentures or claimable assets arising from loans to the day of amortization of the principal thereof is not longer than 1 year, and in other cases where the acquisition concerned is deemed to be made for the purpose of settlement of short-term commercial transactions under the provisions of the order based on the Foreign Exchange and Foreign Trade Control Law.

2. The provisions of the preceding paragraph shall not apply to cases which come under those in article 11 paragraph 3 items (1) to (3), inclusive, in case where "stock or proprietary interest" in the said items reads "debentures or claimable assets arising from loans."

3. The provisions of paragraph 1 proviso and the parts of provisions of the preceding paragraph which are covered by article 11 paragraph 3 item (1) shall not in any way affect restrictions as provided for in the Foreign Exchange and Foreign Trade Control Law.

Article 13–(2). (Designation of foreign capital invested.) In the event that a foreign investor desires to receive, by way of payment to a foreign country, the fruit or principal withdrawn of any of the below-mentioned stock, proprietary interest, beneficiary certificate, debentures, or claimable assets arising from loans (hereinafter to be referred to as "stock, etc.," in this article) the day of payment of which is not earlier than the day of acquisition (in case where the acquisition concerned was made due to inheritance or bequest, the day when the foreign investor concerned came to know the commencement of the inheritance or the bequest concerned; hereinafter the same in this article) by the foreign investor concerned of the said stock, etc., designation of the said stock, etc., may be obtained through filing an application with the Minister of Finance in accordance with the Ministry of Finance ordinance within 3 months as from the day of acquisition of the said stock, etc.:

(1) In cases as provided for in article 11 paragraph 3 item (1) (inclusive which come under those provided for in the said item where "stock or proprietary interest" in the item reads "beneficiary certificate, debentures or claimable assets arising from loans"), the stock, etc., which have been acquired by the foreign investor concerned making payment for which with those as mentioned in article 8 paragraph 2 item (4) subitems a. to f. inclusive.

In this case, "1 month or more earlier than the day of filing an application for the acquisition concerned" in article 8 paragraph 2 item (4) subitems b. to d., inclusive, shall read "3 months or more earlier than the day of acquisition concerned"; "on or after the day of validation of the acquisition concerned in the same paragraph item (4) f. shall read "less than 1 month earlier than the day of acquisition concerned."

(2) In cases as provided for by article 11 paragraph 3 items (1) to (3), inclusive (inclusive of the case as provided for in these items in case where "stock or proprietary interest" in these items reads "beneficiary certificate, debentures, or claimable assets arising from loan"), stock, etc., acquired by the foreign investor concerned due to transfer from another foreign investor (exclusive of the transfer the payment for which was made with domestic means of payment) inheritance, bequest, or amalgamation, the payment to a foreign country of the fruit or principal withdrawn which was deemed to have been authorized to the said another foreign investor, successee, legator, or the juridical person dissolved due to amalgamation (inclusive of the persons as provided for by Cabinet order in case where the acquisition of the stock concerned was made by them due to inheritance, bequest, or amalgamation) in accordance with the provisions of article 15 or article 15–(2) paragraph 1.

(3) In cases as provided for by article 11 paragraph 3 items (4) to (8), inclusive, stock or proprietary interest acquired by the foreign investor concerned on the strength of the outstanding stock or proprietary interest legally owned by the foreign investor concerned, the payment to a foreign country of the fruit or principal withdrawn of which has been deemed to have been authorized in accordance with the provisions of article 15–(2) paragraph 1.

(4) In cases as provided for by article 11 paragraph 3 item (9), stock acquired by the foreign investor concerned due to conversion of the convertible debentures or convertible stock legally owned by the foreign investor concerned, the payment to a foreign country of the fruit or principal withdrawn which has been deemed to have been authorized in accordance with the provisions of article 15 or article 15–(2) paragraph 1.

(5) In cases as provided for by article 11 paragraph 3 item (10), stock restored by the foreign investor concerned making payment with those as mentioned in article 8 paragraph 2 item (4) subitems a. to f., inclusive, as a return for the restored stock or as the equivalent thereto. The provisions of the latter part of item (1) shall apply mutatis mutandis to this case.

(6) Stock or proprietary interest acquired by the foreign investor concerned in case as provided for by article 11 paragraph 3 item (11), and other stock, etc., as provided for by Cabinet order.

Article 13–(3). (Confirmation of inheritance, etc., of compensation for technological assistance, etc.) In the event that, when a foreign investor has acquired from another foreign investor due to inheritance, bequest, or amalgamation, the compensation for technological assistance, fruit, principal withdrawn, or surplus assets distributed, etc., of stock, proprietary interest, beneficiary certificate, debentures, or claimable assets arising from loans (hereinafter to be referred to as "compensation, etc.," in this article) or claimable assets on those as mentioned heretofore, and the payment to a foreign country of the said compensation, etc. (inclusive of the compensation, etc., arising from the said claimable assets), or of the principal withdrawn of the stock or the proprietary interest from which the said surplus assets distributed, etc. (inclusive of the surplus assets distributed, etc., arising from the claimable assets concerned) has been deemed to have been authorized to the said another foreign investor (inclusive of the foreign investor in case where the said compensation, etc., or the said claimable assets had been acquired by the said another foreign investor due to inheritance, bequest, or amalgamation), the foreign investor concerned desirous to receive payment of the said compensation etc., or compensation, etc., arising from the said claimable assets by way of payment to a foreign country, may obtain confirmation by the Minister of Finance, through filing an application therewith in accordance with the Ministry of Finance ordinance within 3 months as from the day of acquisition (in case where the acquisition concerned was made due to inheritance or bequest, the day when the foreign investor concerned came to know the commencement of the inheritance or the bequest concerned) by the foreign investor concerned of the said compensation, etc., or the said claimable assets, exclusive of the case where the provisions of the preceding article apply.

Article 14. (Conditions attached to validation, designation, or confirmation.) The competent Minister or the Minister of Finance may, on making validation, designation, or confirmation pursuant to the provisions of this law, stipulate necessary conditions upon which validation is based.

2. In the event that a foreign investor who was granted the validation, designation, or confirmation as prescribed in this law has filed an application with the competent Minister or the Minister of Finance in accordance with the ordinance of the competent Ministry or the Ministry of Finance ordinance for alteration of conditions as stipulated pursuant to the preceding paragraph, the competent Minister or the Minister of Finance may alter them only in case where the competent Minister or the Minister of Finance finds inevitable reasons concerning the application concerned.

CHAPTER III. REMITTANCES ARISING FROM FOREIGN INVESTMENT

Article 15. (Guaranty of remittance of compensation for technological assistance, fruit, or principal withdrawn of debentures or claimable assets arising from loans.) In the event that, when the desire to receive compensation for technological assistance, fruit, or principal withdrawn of debentures or claimable assets arising from loans by way of payment to a foreign country, is expressly stated in accordance with the provisions of article 9, validation is granted by the competent Minister pursuant to the provisions of this law, or in the event that, when a foreign investor desires to receive fruit or principal withdrawn of debentures or claimable assets arising from loans by way of payment to a foreign country, designation of the said debentures or claimable assets arising from loans is made by the Minister of Finance in accordance with the provisions of article 13–(2), the payment of the said compensation (in case where the validation concerned is granted on alteration of articles of the technological assistance contracts concerned, such as renewal of the contract, only those the day of payment of which is not earlier than the day of validation thereof), fruit or principal withdrawn (inclusive of only those the day of payment of which is not earlier than the day of acquisition (in case where the acquisition concerned was made due to inheritance or bequest, the day when the foreign investor concerned came to know the commencement of the inheritance or the bequest concerned) by the foreign investor concerned of the said debentures or claimable assets) by way of payment to a foreign country shall be deemed to have been authorized to the foreign investor concerned, who had the said validation granted or designation made, pursuant to the provisions of article 27 of the Foreign Exchange and Foreign Trade Control Law, subject to the conditions stipulated by the competent Minister or the Minister of Finance, if any, pursuant to the provisions of the preceding article.

Article 15–(2). (Guaranty of remittance of fruit or principal withdrawn, etc., of stock, proprietary interest, or beneficiary certificate.) In the event that, when the desire to receive fruit or principal withdrawn of stock, proprietary interest, or beneficiary certificate by way of payment to a foreign country, is expressly stated in accordance with the provisions of article 9, validation is granted by the competent Minister pursuant to the provisions of this law or in the event that, when a foreign investor desires to receive fruit or principal withdrawn of stock, proprietary interest, or beneficiary certificate by way of payment to a foreign country, designation of the said stock, proprietary interest, or beneficiary certificate is made by the Minister of Finance in accordance with the provisions of article 13–(2), the payment of those as provided for in the below-mentioned items, the day of payment of which is not earlier than the day of acquisition (in case where the acquisition concerned was made due to inheritance or bequest, the day when the foreign investor concerned came to know the commencement of the inheritance or the bequest concerned) by the foreign investor concerned of the said stock, proprietary interest, or beneficiary certificate by way of payment to a foreign country shall be deemed to have been authorized to the foreign investor concerned, who had the said validation granted or designation made, pursuant to the provisions of article 27 of the Foreign Exchange and Foreign Trade Control Law, subject to the conditions stipulated by the competent Minister or the Minister of Finance, if any, pursuant to the provisions of article 14:

(1) Fruit of the stock, proprietary interest, or of beneficiary certificate concerned.

(2) Money delivered to the stockholder due to redemption by profits of the stock concerned (inclusive of only the redeemable stock).

(3) Proceeds arising from such sale of the stock or proprietary interest concerned as was made after 2 years from the day of acquisition (in case where the said stock or proprietary interest was acquired by the foreign investor concerned due to inheritance, bequest, or amalgamation, the day as provided for by Cabinet order) by the foreign investor concerned of the said stock or proprietary interest which was sold (in case where the acquisition by the foreign investor concerned of the stock or proprietary interest concerned was the acquisition of stock or proprietary interest of a juridical person continuously existing after the amalgamation, or newly established due to amalgamation in case of amalgamation of juridical persons as provided for by article 11 paragraph 3 item (4), stock or proprietary interest of the juridical person dissolved due to amalgamation; in case where the acquisition by the foreign investor concerned of the said stock which was sold had been the acquisition of stock issued due to the splitting up, consolidation, or conversion of the outstanding

stock as mentioned in the same paragraph item (7) or (9), the said outstanding stock before the said splitting up, consolidation, or the conversion thereof; in case where the acquisition by the foreign investor concerned of the said stock which was sold had been the acquisition of the stock due to carrying over (to mean, as provided by Cabinet order, the legal acquisition after the allotment of the new stock in case where a company issues new stock, of the same kind of stock issued by the said company as the stock on the strength of which the new stock is issued, with the proceeds arising from the sale of the said old stock; hereinafter the same), in case of new stock issued by the issuing company of the said old stock, the stock which was sold due to the said carrying over (in case where the carrying over is done twice or more in continuous repetition, the first carrying over), only in case the number of the stock acquired is not more than the number of the stock due to carrying over (in case where the carrying over is done twice or more in continuous repetition, the carrying over the number of the stock sold due to which is the least); hereinafter the same in this item; inclusive of only those which have been deposited in the Foreign Investors Deposit Account as provided for in article 9–(2) paragraph 1 continuously as from any day that exists within 3 months as from the day of the sale concerned in case where the said payment to a foreign country is to be made after 3 months as from the day of the sale concerned.

(4) Principal withdrawn of the beneficiary certificate concerned, inclusive of only those which have been deposited in the Foreign Investors Deposit Account as provided for in article 9–(2) paragraph 1 continuously as from any day that exists within 3 months as from the day of payment of the principal withdrawn concerned, in case where the said payment to a foreign country is to be made after 3 months as from the said day of payment of the principal withdrawn concerned.

2. The payment to a foreign country of those as provided for in the below-mentioned items shall be deemed to have been authorized to the foreign investor concerned as specified in each item concerned pursuant to the provisions of article 27 of the Foreign Exchange and Foreign Trade Control Law, subject to the conditions stipulated by the competent Minister or the Minister of Finance, if any, pursuant to the provisions of article 14:

(1) Such surplus assets distributed, etc., delivered to a foreign investor on the strength of stock or proprietary interest the payment to a foreign country of the principal of which has been deemed to have been authorized pursuant to the provisions of the preceding paragraph as exist after 2 years as from the day of acquisition (in case where the said stock or proprietary interest was acquired by the foreign investor concerned due to inheritance, bequest, or amalgamation, the day as provided for by Cabinet order) by the foreign investor concerned of the said stock or proprietary interest (in case where the acquisition by the foreign investor concerned of the said stock or proprietary interest was the acquisition of stock or proprietary interest of a juridical person continuously existing after the amalgamation, or newly established due to amalgamation, in case of amalgamation of juridical persons as provided for by article 11 paragraph 3 item (4), stock or proprietary interest of the juridical person dissolved due to amalgamation; in case where the acquisition by the foreign investor concerned of the said stock the payment to a foreign country of the principal withdrawn of which is deemed to have been authorized was the acquisition of stock issued due to the splitting up, consolidation, or to the conversion of the outstanding stock as mentioned in the same paragraph item (7) or (9), the said outstanding stock before the said splitting up, consolidation, or the conversion thereof; in case where the acquisition by the foreign investor concerned of the said stock the payment to a foreign country of the principal withdrawn of which is deemed to have been authorized had been the acquisition of the stock due to carrying over in case of new stock issued by the issuing company of the said old stock, the stock which

was sold due to the said carrying over (in case where the carrying over is done twice in continuous repetition, the first carrying over), only in case the number of the stock acquired is not more than the number of the stock sold due to carrying over (in case where the carrying over is done twice or more in continuous repetition, the carrying over the number of the stock sold due to which is the least); hereinafter the same in this article; inclusive of only those which have been deposited in the Foreign Investors Deposit Account as provided for in article 9–(2) paragraph 1 continuously as from any day that exists within 3 months as from the day of payment of the said surplus assets distributed, etc., in case where the said payment to a foreign country is to be made after 3 months as from the said day of payment of the surplus assets distributed, etc.

(2) Interest arising from the Foreign Investors Deposit Account as provided for in article 9–(2) paragraph 1, which a foreign investor establishes.

Article 15–3. (Limitation on amount of remittance of principal withdrawn, etc., of remittance-guaranteed stock, proprietary interest, or beneficiary certificate.) In the event that, when a foreign investor makes such payment to a foreign country of proceeds arising from sale of stock or proprietary interest as is deemed to have been authorized pursuant to the provisions of the preceding article paragraph 1, the total amount of the said proceeds paid to a foreign country exceeds, in each period of 1 year as from the day when, or from the day corresponding to the day when, 2 years elapsed as from the day of acquisition (in case where the said stock or proprietary interest was acquired by the foreign investor concerned due to inheritance, bequest, or amalgamation, the day as provided for by Cabinet order) by the foreign investor concerned of the said stock or proprietary interest (in case where the acquisition by the foreign investor concerned of the said stock or proprietary interest was the acquisition of the stock or the proprietary interest of a juridical person continuously existing after the amalgamation, or newly established due to amalgamation, in case of amalgamation of juridical persons as provided for by article 11 paragraph 3 item (4), stock or proprietary interest of the juridical person dissolved due to amalgamation; in case where the acquisition by the foreign investor concerned of the said stock the payment to a foreign country of the principal withdrawn of which is deemed to have been authorized was the acquisition of stock issued due to the splitting up, consolidation, or to the conversion of the outstanding stock as mentioned in the same paragraph item (7) or (9), the said outstanding stock before the said splitting up, consolidation, or the conversion thereof; in case where the acquisition by the foreign investor concerned of the said stock the payment authorized had been the acquisition of the stock due to carrying over in case of new stock issued by the issuing company of the said old stock, the stock which was sold due to the said carrying over (in case where the carrying over is done twice or more in continuous repetition, the first carrying over), only in case the number of the stock acquired is not more than the number of the stock sold due to carrying over (in case where the carrying over is done twice or more in continuous repetition, the carrying over the number of the stock sold due to which is the least); hereinafter the same in the article; in each year as from the year to which the said day when the said 2 years elapsed belongs, the total amount of the proceeds, arising from the sale of such stock or proprietary interest the payment to a foreign country of which is deemed to have been authorized as were owned by the foreign investor concerned as of the day when the said 2 years elapsed (hereinafter to be referred to as "remittable stock, etc.," in this paragraph), the number of stock, or value of investment relative to the proprietary interest (number of investment in case of proprietary interest of yugen-kaisha), of which is equivalent to 20 percent of the number of stock, or of the total value of the investment relative to the proprietary interest (total number of investment in case of the proprietary interest of yugen-kaisha), of the said remittable stock, etc., the provisions of the preceding article paragraph 1 shall not apply to the proceeds equivalent to the amount in excess of 20 percent.

2. The amount of the principal withdrawn of the beneficiary certificate the payment to a foreign country of which is deemed to have been authorized to a foreign investor pursuant to the provisions of the preceding article paragraph 1, and of which the foreign investor may make payment to a foreign country within each period of 1 year as from the day of, or from the day corresponding to the day of payment of, the principal withdrawn concerned, in each year as from the year to which the said day of payment belongs, shall be the amount equivalent to not more than 20 percent of the amount of the principal withdrawn of the beneficiary certificate the payment to a foreign country of which is deemed to have been authorized, and the provisions of the preceding article paragraph 1 shall not apply to the principal withdrawn equivalent to the amount in excess of the said 20 percent.

3. The amount of the surplus assets distributed, etc., arising from stock or proprietary interest the payment to a foreign country of which is deemed to have been authorized to a foreign investor pursuant to the provisions of the preceding article paragraph 2, and of which the foreign investor concerned may make payment to a foreign country in each period of 1 year as from the day when, or from the day corresponding to the day when, 2 years elapsed as from the day of acquisition (in case where the said stock or proprietary interest was acquired by the foreign investor concerned due to inheritance, bequest, or amalgamation, the day as provided for by Cabinet order) by the foreign investor concerned of the said stock or proprietary interest (in case where the acquisition by the foreign investor concerned of the said stock or proprietary interest was the acquisition of the stock or the proprietary interest of a juridical person continuously existing after the amalgamation, or newly established due to amalgamation, in case of amalgamation of juridical persons as provided for by article 11 paragraph 3 item (4), stock or proprietary interest of the juridical person dissolved due to amalgamation; in case where the acquisition by the foreign investor concerned of the said stock the payment to a foreign country of the principal withdrawn of which is deemed to have been authorized, was the acquisition of stock issued due to the splitting up, consolidation, or to the conversion of the outstanding stock as mentioned in the same paragraph item (7) or (9), the said outstanding stock before the said splitting up, consolidation, or the conversion thereof; in case where the acquisition by the foreign investor concerned of the said stock the payment to a foreign country of the principal withdrawn of which is deemed to have been authorized, had been the acquisition of the stock due to carrying over in case of new stock issued by the issuing company of the said old stock, the stock which was sold due to the said carrying over (in case where the carrying over is done twice or more in continuous repetition, the first carrying over), only in case the number of the stock acquired is not more than the number of the stock sold due to carrying over (in case where the carrying over is done twice or more in continuous repetition, the carrying over the number of the stock sold due to which is the least), hereinafter the same in this article; in each year as from the year to which the said day when the said 2 years elapsed belongs, shall be the amount equivalent to not more than 20 percent of the amount of the surplus assets distributed, etc., arising from the stock or the proprietary interest the payment to a foreign country of which is deemed to have been authorized, and the provisions of the preceding article paragraph 2 shall not apply to the surplus assets distributed, etc., equivalent to the amount in excess of the said 20 percent.

4. The provisions of paragraph 1 shall apply separately to each group of proceeds arising from the sale of the stock issued by the same juridical person or of the proprietary interest of members of the same juridical person; the provisions of the preceding paragraph shall apply separately to each group of surplus assets distributed, etc., of the stock issued by the same juridical person or the proprietary interest of the members of the same juridical person.

Article 16. (Guaranty of remittance of compensation for technological assistance, etc., accompanied by confirmation.) In the event that a foreign investor has obtained a confirmation concerning the compensation, etc., or claimable assets as provided for by article 13-(3) pursuant to the same article, the payment to a foreign country of the compensation, etc., concerned, compensation, etc., as provided for by the same article arising from the said claimable assets or interest arising from the compensation, etc., deposited in the Foreign Investors Deposit Account as provided for in article 9-(2) paragraph 1 shall be deemed to have been authorized pursuant to the provisions of article 27 of the Foreign Exchange and Foreign Trade Control Law, subject to conditions stipulated by the Minister of Finance, if any, pursuant to the provisions of article 14.

CHAPTER IV. PROTECTION OF FOREIGN CAPITAL

Article 17. (Protection of foreign capital.) In the event that the government, local public entities, or other duly authorized persons expropriate or compulsorily purchase, after the enforcement of this law, pursuant to procedures prescribed in a law other than the Foreign Exchange and Foreign Trade Control Law, the whole or a part of property legally owned in Japan by a foreign investor, the document indicating the said effect and matters as provided for by Cabinet order shall be submitted to the Minister of Finance in accordance with the provisions of Cabinet order, which the said foreign investor intends to make payment to a foreign country of the whole or a part of the corresponding amount receivable as the result of the said expropriation or compulsory purchase.

2. In the event that the document as prescribed in the preceding paragraph is filed, the Minister of Finance shall submit immediately data concerning necessary foreign exchange funds for the payment to a foreign country as stated therein to the Ministerial Council.

3. In the event that data as prescribed in the preceding paragraph are submitted, the Ministerial Council shall appropriate necessary funds in the foreign exchange budget in order to assure payment to a foreign country of the amount in return as stated therein for the period of 1 year from the day of the receipt of the said amount.

4. In the event that a foreign investor uses the funds appropriated in the foreign exchange budget pursuant to the provisions of the preceding paragraph, it shall be deemed that payment to a foreign country has been authorized pursuant to the provisions of article 27 of the Foreign Exchange and Foreign Trade Control Law.

5. In the event that the whole or a part of the assets of a juridical person which is in fact controlled by a foreign investor through ownership of stock or proprietary interest is expropriated or compulsorily purchased as prescribed in paragraph 1 above, similar treatment to those prescribed in the provisions of the preceding four paragraphs shall be extended to the stock or proprietary interest involved pursuant to the provisions of a law to be enacted separately.

Article 17-(2). In cases where a foreign investor (exclusive of exchange residents) has new stock allotted on the strength of the outstanding stock he owns based on the right to the allotment of new stock, the right to the allotment of new stock may be transferred to others.

2. The transfer of the right to the allotment of new stock as provided for in the preceding paragraph is not valid with regard to the company and other third parties without a written consent of the company.

CHAPTER V. ADJUSTMENT OF INVEST-MENTS AND BUSINESS ACTIVITIES BY FOREIGN INVESTORS

Article 18. (Reference to Cabinet.) In case of requesting Cabinet decision concerning important matters regarding investments or business activities by foreign investors, the government agencies (government agencies other than the Fair Trade Commission, as defined in article 3 paragraph 2 and article 24 of the National Government Organization Law (law No. 120 of 1948); hereinafter the same shall ask for the opinion of the Foreign Investment Council entrusting the Minister of Finance.

2. The Minister of Finance shall, in cases as provided for in the preceding paragraph, transmit the opinion of the Foreign Investment Council on the said matters to the Cabinet.

Article 18–(2). (Opinion of the Foreign Investment Council.) In case of granting the validation, designation or confirmation in accordance with the provisions of this Law, the Minister of Finance shall ask for the opinion of the Foreign Investment Council in advance, except for matters of minor importance.

2. In case of granting the validation in accordance with the provisions of this law, the Competent Minister shall respect the opinion of the Foreign Investment Council as prescribed in the preceding paragraph.

Article 18–(3). In case of licensing the payment to a foreign country of profits arising from legitimate business activities in Japan of the exchange residents in accordance with other laws and orders, the Minister of Finance shall ask for the opinion of the Foreign Investment Council in advance, except for the cases of minor importance.

Article 19. Except for the cases as provided for in the preceding paragraph, in the event that the government agencies propose to license, validate, approve, or take other administrative actions with regard to investments or business activities of foreign investors in accordance with the provisions of other laws and orders, they shall ask in advance for the opinion of the Foreign Investment Council entrusting the Minister of Finance, except for the cases of minor importance.

2. Government agencies, in taking administrative actions as mentioned in the preceding paragraph, shall respect the opinion of the Foreign Investment Council.

CHAPTER V–(2). FOREIGN INVESTMENT COUNCIL

Article 19–(2). (Establishment.) For the purpose of research and deliberation of the important matters concerning foreign investment in Japan, the Foreign Investment Council shall be established as an attached organization to the Ministry of Finance.

Article 19–(3). (Structure and operation.) The Foreign Investment Council shall consist of the Minister of Finance and nine or less commissioners.

2. The Minister of Finance shall command the business in charge of the Foreign Investment Council as the director thereof.

3. The commissioner of the Foreign Investment Council shall be appointed by the Minister of Finance out of the personnel of the relevant administrative agencies and men of knowledge and experience.

4. The term of service of the commissioner shall be 2 years. Provided, however, the term of service of the commissioner who fills up the vacancy shall be the term left for the former commissioner.

5. The commissioner of the Foreign Investment Council may be reappointed.

6. The commissioner of the Foreign Investment Council shall serve part time.

7. Necessary matters concerning the structure and operation of the Foreign Investment Council other than those as provided for in the preceding six paragraphs shall be provided for by the Cabinet order.

Application and Report Forms for Foreign Investment

Form 1.—Application for Validation of Conclusion (Alteration) of Technological Assistance Contract

Date:_____

To: Mr_____, Competent Minister

Applicant:[1]_____
Signature or seal

In accordance with the provisions of article 10 of the Law Concerning Foreign Investment, an application is hereby made on the subject matter of which particulars are described hereunder:

1. FOREIGN INVESTOR:
   - Name [2]   Referential address in Japan
   - Address [3]   Tel. No.
   - Nationality [4] Person in charge
   - Occupation [5]
2. OPPOSITE PARTY:
   - Name [2]   Referential address in Japan
   - Address [3]   Tel. No.
   - Occupation [5] Person in charge
3. TECHNOLOGICAL ASSISTANCE CONTRACT:
   - (a) Kind of technology.
   - (b) Contents of technological assistance.[6]
   - (c) Period of contract.
   - (d) Contents of alteration of articles of contract, if so.
4. REMITTANCE OF COMPENSATION FOR TECHNOLOGICAL ASSISTANCE:

   Kind   Amount or rate and   Currency   Time
           method of its com-
           putation

5. REFERENCE:
   - (a) Benefit of subject matter, if realized, to the opposite party of the foreign investor.
   - (b) Benefit of subject matter, if realized, to Japanese national economy.[7]
   - (c) Anticipated amount of remittance.
   - (d) Other matters necessitating detailed explanations.

Remarks:
[1] If incorporated, names of applicant and its representative or agent.
[2] If incorporated, trade name and name of representative.
[3] If incorporated, address of head office.
[4] In case the foreign investor is a juridical person established under Japanese laws and orders, address, nationality, and manner and grade of control of its substantial controller shall be entered.
[5] If incorporated, purpose of business and amount of capital.
[6] Concerning license, additionally state whether or not the patent right is registered in Japan, sublicense is expected, and license is exclusive.
[7] Especially prospective effects on the international trade and balance of payments.

FORM 2—FOOTNOTES

Remarks:
[1] If incorporated, names of applicant and its representative or agent.
[2] If incorporated, trade name and name of representative.
[3] If incorporated, address of head office.
[4] In case the foreign investor is a juridical person established under Japanese laws and orders, address, nationality, and manner and grade of control of its substantial controller shall be entered.
[5] If incorporated, purpose of business and amount of capital.
[6] Entry not required in case of acquisition of stock or proprietary interest

Form 2.—Application for Validation of Acquisition of Stock (Proprietary Interest)

Date:_____

To: Mr_____, Competent Minister

Applicant:[1]_____
Signature or seal

In accordance with the provisions of article 11 paragraph 1 of the Law Concerning Foreign Investment, an application is hereby made on the subject matter of which particulars are described hereunder:

1. FOREIGN INVESTOR:
   - Name [2]   Referential address in Japan
   - Address [3]   Tel. No.
   - Nationality [4] Person in charge
   - Occupation [5]
2. OPPOSITE PARTY:[6]
   - Name [2]   Referential address in Japan
   - Address [3]   Tel. No.
   - Occupation [5] Person in charge
3. ACQUISITION OF STOCK (PROPRIETARY INTEREST
   - Issuing company.[7]
   - Kind, amount, total face value, price of acquisition, etc.
   - Number of stock (proprietary interest), total face value, etc. of the same company held at the time of this application.
   - Manner of acquisition.[8]
   - Relevant investment plan.
   - Benefit to issuing company.[9]
4. KIND OF CURRENCY AND METHOD OF PAYMENT:[10]
5. REMITTANCE:

   Kind [11]   Amount desired   Currency   Time

6. OTHER RELEVANT MATTERS:

which creates additional assets to the issuing company. Just referential address, etc., shall be entered in "Issuing company."
[7] Trade name, name of representative, address of head office, purpose of business and amount of capital (in case of capital increase, the amount of capital after its increase shall be additionally entered).
[8] Statement shall be made on whether or not the acquisition creates additional assets to the issuing company, the acquisition is made due to the establishment of new company, to the capital increase, or to right to subscribe the new stock, etc.
[9] In case of capital increase, the contents of the plan for capital increase.
[10] The details as to the kind of currency shall be stated in the following manner pursuant to the classification as itemized in article 8 paragraph 2 item 4 of the Law Concerning Foreign Investment.
   (1) Item 4 a.—Kind of foreign means of payment or equivalent thereto.
   (2) Item 4 b.—Day of sale of the stock, proprietary interest, or beneficiary certificate sold, or concerning acquisition, number of validation, day of acquisition, manner of acquisition, and other matters necessary for acquisition, such as matters concerning carrying over.
   (3) Item 4 c.—Classification of the surplus assets, etc., day of payment, manner of acquisition, and other matters necessary for acquisition.
   (4) Item 4 d.—Day of payment, and as to beneficiary certificate relative to the principal withdrawn concerned, the number of validation, day of acquisition, manner of acquisition, and other matters necessary for acquisition.
   (5) Item 4 e.—Day of acquisition due to inheritance, bequest, or amalgamation, and matters shown in one of the above 2 through 4.
   (6) Item 4 f.—Day of sale or payment of stock, proprietary interest, or beneficiary certificate relative to the proceeds, etc., deposited.
[11] Distinction of dividend, proceeds, or principal withdrawn of redeemable stock shall be clarified.

Form 3.—Application for Validation of Acquisition of Stock

Date: _____

To: Mr. —————————, Competent Minister

Applicant:[1] _____
Signature or seal

In accordance with the provisions of article 11 paragraph 1 of the Law Concerning Foreign Investment, an application is hereby made on the subject matter of which particulars are described hereunder:

1. FOREIGN INVESTOR:
   Name[2]   Referential address in
   Address[3]   Japan
   Nationality[4]   Tel. No.
   Occupation[5]   Person in charge
2. SECURITIES DEALER:
   Trade name   Referential address in
   Address of head office   Japan
   Amount of capital and name   Tel. No.
   of representative   Person in charge
3. STOCKS TO BE ACQUIRED:
   Issuing company.
   Kind.[6]
   Face value per stock.[7]
   Number of stock.
   Total face value.
   Number and total value etc. of stock of the same
     company held at the time of this application.
4. KIND OF CURRENCY AND METHOD OF PAYMENT:[8]
5. REMITTANCE:

   Kind[9]   Amount desired   Currency   Time

6. OTHER RELEVANT MATTERS:

Remarks:
[1] If incorporated, name of applicant and its representative or agent.
[2] If incorporated, trade name and name of representative.
[3] If incorporated, address of head office.
[4] In case the foreign investor is a juridical person established under Japanese laws and orders, address, nationality, and manner and grade of control of its substantial controller shall be entered.
[5] If incorporated, purpose of business and amount of capital.
[6] In case of non-face-value stock, the effect shall be additionally stated.
[7] In case of non-face-value stock, issuing price shall be regarded as face value.
[8] The details as to the kind of currency shall be stated in the following manner pursuant to the classification as itemized in article 8 paragraph 2 item 4 of the Law Concerning Foreign Investment.
   (1) Item 4 a.—Kind of foreign means of payment or equivalent thereto.
   (2) Item 4 b.—Day of sale of the stock, proprietary interest or beneficiary certificate sold, or concerning acquisition, number of validation, day of acquisition, manner of acquisition, and other matters necessary for acquisition, such as matters concerning carrying over.
   (3) Item 4 c.—Classification of the surplus assets, etc., day of payment, manner of acquisition, and other matters necessary for acquisition.
   (4) Item 4 d.—Day of payment, and as to beneficiary certificate relative to the principal withdrawn concerned, the number of validation, day of acquisition, manner of acquisition, and other matters necessary for acquisition.
   (5) Item 4 e.—Day of acquisition due to inheritance, bequest, or amalgamation, and matters shown in one of the above 2 through 4.
   (6) Item 4 f.—Day of sale or payment of stock, proprietary interest, or beneficiary certificate relative to the proceeds, etc., deposited.
[9] Distinction of dividend, proceeds, or principal withdrawn of redeemable stock shall be clarified.

Form 4.—Application for Validation of Acquisition of Beneficiary Certificate

Date: _____

To: Mr. _____, Competent Minister

Applicant:[1] _____
Signature or seal

In accordance with the provisions of article 12 paragraph 1 of the Law Concerning Foreign Investment, an application is hereby made on the subject matter of which particulars are described hereunder:

1. FOREIGN INVESTOR:
   Name[2]   Referential address in
   Address[3]   Japan
   Nationality[4]   Tel. No.
   Occupation[5]   Person in charge
2. OPPOSITE PARTY:[6]
   Name[2]   Referential address in
   Address[3]   Japan
   Occupation[5]   Tel. No.
                        Person in charge
3. MANNER OF ACQUISITION:[7]
4. BENEFICIARY CERTIFICATE TO BE ACQUIRED:
   Kind.[8]
   Date of issue.
   Value per unit.
   Number of units.
   Face value (initial principal) and total value to be
     acquired.
   Period of trust contract, times of redemption and
     distribution of income.
   Total number of units and total value of initial
     principal.
5. KIND OF CURRENCY AND METHOD OF PAYMENT:[9]
6. REMITTANCE:

   Kind[10]   Amount desired   Currency   Time

7. OTHER RELEVANT MATTERS:

Remarks:
[1] If incorporated, names of applicant and its representative or agent.
[2] If incorporated, trade name and name of representative.
[3] If incorporated, address of head office.
[4] In case the foreign investor is a juridical person established under Japanese laws and orders, address, nationality, and manner and grade of control of its substantial controller shall be entered.
[5] If incorporated, purpose of business and amount of capital.
[6] In case of acquisition of beneficiary certificate on the day of issue thereof, the name of security dealer or trust company shall be entered.
[7] Classification of acquisition of beneficiary certificate on the day of issue, or after the day of issue, etc.
[8] Name of trusting company (trusted company in case of loan trust), serial number of issue, etc.
[9] The details as to the kind of currency shall be stated in a following manner pursuant to the classification as itemized in article 8 paragraph 2 item 4 of the Law Concerning Foreign Investment.
   (1) Item 4 a.—Kind of foreign means of payment or equivalent thereto.
   (2) Item 4 b.—Day of sale of the stock, proprietary interest or beneficiary certificate sold, or concerning acquisition, number of validation, day of acquisition, manner of validation, and other matters necessary for acquisition.
   (3) Item 4 c.—Classification of the surplus assets, etc., day of payment, manner of acquisition, and other matters necessary for acquisition.
   (4) Item 4 d.—Day of payment, and as to beneficiary certificate relative to the principal withdrawn concerned, the number of validation, day of acquisition, manner of acquisition, and other matters necessary for acquisition.
   (5) Item 4 e.—Day of acquisition due to inheritance, bequest, or amalgamation, and matters shown in one of the above 2 through 4.
   (6) Item 4 f.—Day of sale or payment of stock, proprietary interest, or beneficiary certificate relative to the proceeds, etc., deposited.
[10] Distinction of dividend, proceeds, or principal withdrawn of redeemable stock shall be clarified.

Form 5.—Application for Validation of Acquisition of Debentures

Date: _____

To: Mr. _____, Competent Minister

Applicant: [1] _____

In accordance with the provisions of article 13 paragraph 1 of the Law Concerning Foreign Investment, an application is made on the subject matter of which particulars are described hereunder:

1. FOREIGN INVESTOR:

   Name [2]   Referential address in Japan

   Address [3]   Tel. No.

   Nationality [4]   Person in charge

   Occupation [5]

2. OPPOSITE PARTY:

   Name [2]   Referential address in Japan

   Address [3]   Tel. No.

   Occupation [5]   Person in charge

3. MANNER OF ACQUISITION: [6]

4. MATTERS CONCERNING ACQUISITION OF DEBENTURES:

Kind (name of issuing company, number, etc.)	Total value (yen)	Interest rate, day and method of payment of interest and principal	Mortgage and other conditions	Total value of debentures issued

5. KIND OF CURRENCY OF AND METHOD OF PAYMENT: [7]

6. REMITTANCE:

   Kind [8]   Amount desired   Currency   Time

7. OTHER RELEVANT MATTERS:

Remarks:

[1] If incorporated, name of applicant and its representative or agent.

[2] If incorporated, trade name and name of representative.

[3] If incorporated, address of head office.

[4] In case the foreign investor is a juridical person established under Japanese laws and orders, address, nationality, and manner and grade of control of its substantial controller shall be entered.

[5] If incorporated, purpose of business and amount of capital.

[6] Distinction of subscription of debentures, purchase through securities exchange, or bilateral transaction.

[7] The details as to the kind of currency shall be stated in a following manner pursuant to the classification as itemized in article 8 paragraph 2 item 4 of the Law Concerning Foreign Investment (see application form 4, item 9).

[8] Distinction of interest or the principal withdrawn shall also be entered.

Form 6.—Application for Validation of Acquisition of Claimable Assets Arising From Loans

Date: _____

To: Mr. _____, Competent Minister

Applicant: [1] _____

Signature or seal

In accordance with the provisions of article 13 paragraph 1 of the Law Concerning Foreign Investment, an application is hereby made on the subject matter of which particulars are described hereunder:

1. FOREIGN INVESTOR:

   Name [2]   Referential address in Japan

   Address [3]   Tel. No.

   Nationality [4]   Person in charge

   Occupation [5]

2. OPPOSITE PARTY:

   Name [2]   Referential address in Japan

   Address [3]   Tel. No.

   Occupation [5]   Person in charge

3. MATTERS CONCERNING ACQUISITION OF CLAIMABLE ASSETS:

   Amount of loan, kind of currency, etc.

   Interest rate and day of payment of interest.

   Time of maturity and method of redemption.

   Mortgage and other conditions.

4. KIND OF CURRENCY AND METHOD OF PAYMENT: [6]

5. REMITTANCE:

   Kind [7]   Amount desired   Currency   Time

6. OTHER RELEVANT MATTERS:

Remarks:

[1] If incorporated, name of applicant and its representative or agent.

[2] If incorporated, trade name and name of representative.

[3] If incorporated, address of head office.

[4] In case the foreign investor is a juridical person, established under Japanese laws and orders, address, nationality, and manner and grade of control of its substantial controller shall be entered.

[5] If incorporated, purpose of business and amount of capital.

[6] The details as to the kind of currency shall be stated in a following manner pursuant to the classification as itemized in article 8 paragraph 2 item 4 of the Law Concerning Foreign Investment (see application form 4, item 9).

[7] Distinction of interest or the principal withdrawn shall also be entered.

Form 7.—Application for Designation of Foreign Capital Invested

Date: --------------------
To: Mr. --------------, Competent Minister
Applicant: [1] --------------
Signature or seal

In accordance with the provisions of article 13–(2) of the Law Concerning Foreign Investment, an application is hereby made on the subject matter of which particulars are described hereunder:

1. FOREIGN INVESTOR:
   Name [2]   Referential address in Japan
   Address [3]   Tel. No.
   Nationality [4]   Person in charge
   Occupation [5]

2. FOREIGN CAPITAL INVESTED:

Kind [6]	Amount	Total face value, etc.	Day of acqui- sition. [7]	Total amount of the same kind of in- vested for- eign capital held at the time of this application.

3. MANNER OF ACQUISITION: [8]

4. FOUNDATION OF DESIGNATION: [9]

5. REMITTANCE:

Kind [10]	Amount desired	Currency	Time

6. OTHER RELEVANT MATTERS:

Remarks:
[1] If incorporated, name of applicant and its representative or agent.
[2] If incorporated, trade name and name of representative.
[3] If incorporated, address of head office.
[4] In case the foreign investor is a juridical person established under Japanese laws and orders, address, nationality, and manner and grade of control of its substantial controller shall be entered.
[5] If incorporated, purpose of business and amount of capital.
[6] Distinction of stock, proprietary interest, beneficiary certificate, debentures or claimable assets arising from loans shall be clarified.
[7] In case of inheritance or bequest, the day when the applicant came to know the commencement of the inheritance or bequest.
[8] Which of the items of article 13–(2) of the Law Concerning Foreign Investment to be applied and which of the items of article 11 paragraph 3 of the same Law (inclusive of the case where these provisions apply mutatis mutandis in article 12 paragraph 2 and article 13 paragraph 2) to be applied shall be explained in full detail. If article 13–(2) item 1 or 2 is to be applied, the same statements as those in the above remarks (4) (nationality) shall be made concerning the other foreign investor (transferer), successee, legatee, and the juridical person dissolved due to amalgamation. In case of application made pursuant to Supplementary Provisions paragraph 3 of the Law for Partial Amendments to the Law Concerning Foreign Investment, the said effect and the details thereof shall be mentioned.
[9] Entry shall be made on the matters authenticating that the acquisition by the applicant was made with those as mentioned in article 8 paragraph 2 item 4, subitems a. to e. of the Law Concerning Foreign Investment, on the details of the validation which shows that the guaranty of remittance had been granted to the other foreign investor, successee, legatee, or juridical person dissolved due to amalgamation, on the day of acquisition thereof, as well as on the details of the validation which shows that the guaranty of remittance had been granted to the applicant relative to the stock, proprietary interest, or debentures concerning which the stock, proprietary interest, or debentures were acquired, and on the day of acquisition of stock, proprietary interest, or debentures. Further, in case the application is made in accordance with the provisions of the Supplementary Provisions paragraph 3 of the Law for Partial Amendments to the Law Concerning Foreign Investment, the said effect and the details thereof (in case where the guaranty of remittance has been given to the dividends, that effect) shall be entered too.
[10] Distinction of returns or the principal withdrawn shall be entered.

Form 8.—Application for Confirmation of Compensation, etc.

Date: --------------------
To: Mr. --------------, Competent Minister
Applicant: [1] --------------
Signature or seal

In accordance with the provisions of article 13–(3) of the Law Concerning Foreign Investment, an application is hereby made on the subject matter of which particulars are described hereunder:

1. FOREIGN INVESTOR (SUCCESSOR):
   Name [2]   Referential address in Japan
   Address [3]   Tel. No.
   Nationality [4]   Person in charge
   Occupation [5]

2. OPPOSITE PARTY (SUCCESSEE):
   Name [2]   Referential address in Japan
   Address [3]   Tel. No.
   Occupation [5]   Person in charge

3. MANNER AND CLASSIFICATION OF SUCCESSION OF COMPENSATION, ETC. [6]

4. REMITTANCE:

Kind of com- pensation, etc. [7]	Date of ac- quisition. [8]	Amount (yen).	Currency	Time

5. GUARANTY OF REMITTANCE CONCERNING TECHNOLOGICAL ASSISTANCE CONTRACT OR INVESTED CAPITAL FROM WHICH COMPENSATION, ETC. AROSE:

   a. Validation or designation:
      Number
      Date
      Summarized contents
   b. Foreign investor with guaranty of remittance granted:
      Name [2]
      Address [3]
      Nationality [4]
      Relation to successee

6. OTHER RELEVANT MATTERS:

Remarks:
[1] If incorporated, name of applicant and its representative or agent.
[2] If incorporated, trade name and name of representative.
[3] If incorporated, address of head office.
[4] In case the foreign investor is a juridical person established under the Japanese laws and orders, address, nationality, manner and grade of control of its substantial controller shall be additionally entered.
[5] If incorporated, purpose of business and amount of capital.
[6] Entry shall be made of the inheritance, bequest, or amalgamation, the acquisition effected as compensation for technological assistance, fruit or principal withdrawn of stock, proprietary interest, beneficiary certificate, debentures, claimable assets arising from loans, or of surplus assets distributed, etc. (inclusive of the claims thereof). Further, in case the application is made in accordance with the provisions of the Supplementary Provisions paragraph 3 of the Law for Partial Amendments to the Law Concerning Foreign Investment, the said effect shall be additionally entered.
[7] Classification of compensation, etc., of which confirmation is desired.
[8] In case of inheritance or bequest, the day when the applicant came to know the commencement thereof.

Form 9.—Application for Alteration of Conditions Attached to Validation

Date: --------------------

To: Mr. --------------, Competent Minister

Applicant: [1] ----------------
Signature or seal

In accordance with the provisions of article 14 paragraph 2 of the Law Concerning Foreign Investment, an application is hereby made on the subject matter of which particulars are described hereunder:

1. FOREIGN INVESTOR:

Name [2]	Referential address in
Address [3]	Japan
Nationality [4]	Tel. No.
Occupation [5]	Person in charge

2. OPPOSITE PARTY:

Name [2]	Referential address in
Address [3]	Japan
Occupation [5]	Tel. No.
	Person in charge

3. CLASSIFICATION OF VALIDATION, DESIGNATION, OR CONFIRMATION, ITS DATE AND NUMBER:

4. SUMMARIZED CONTENTS OF VALIDATION, DESIGNATION OR CONFIRMATION, THE ALTERATION OF CONDITIONS ATTACHED TO WHICH THE APPLICANT DESIRES:

5. CONTENTS OF ALTERATION OF CONDITIONS:

6. REASON FOR ALTERATION:

7. OTHER RELEVANT MATTERS:

Remarks:
[1] If incorporated, name of applicant and its representative or agent.
[2] If incorporated, trade name and name of representative.
[3] If incorporated, address of head office.
[4] In case the foreign investor is a juridical person established under the Japanese laws and orders, address, nationality, and manner and grade of control of its substantial controller shall be additionally entered.
[5] If incorporated, purpose of business and amount of capital.

Form 10.—Report on Acquisition of Stock (Proprietary Interest)

Date: -------------------

To: Mr. -----------------, Competent Minister

Reporter: [1] --------------
Signature or seal

In accordance with the provisions of article 11 paragraph 2 of the Law Concerning Foreign Investment, a report is hereby made on the subject matter of which particulars are described hereunder:

1. FOREIGN INVESTOR:

Name [2]	Referential address in
Address [3]	Japan
Nationality [4]	Tel. No.
Occupation [5]	Person in charge

2. OPPOSITE PARTY: [6]

Name [2]	Referential address in
Address [3]	Japan
Occupation [5]	Tel. No.
	Person in charge

3. STOCK (PROPRIETARY INTEREST) ACQUIRED:
Date of acquisition.
Issuing company. [7]
Kind, amount, total face value of stock (proprietary interest) held at the time of making this report.

4. OTHER RELEVANT MATTERS:

Remarks:
[1] If incorporated, name of reporter and its representative or agent.
[2] If incorporated, trade name and name of representative.
[3] If incorporated, address of head office.
[4] In case the foreign investor is a juridical person established under the Japanese laws and orders, address, nationality, and manner and grade of control of its substantial controller shall be additionally entered.
[5] If incorporated, purpose of business and amount of capital.
[6] Entry not required in case the acquisition of stock or proprietary interest creates additional assets to the issuing company. Just the referential address, etc., shall be entered in "Issuing company."
[7] Trade name, name of representative, address of head office, purpose of business, and amount of capital (in case of capital increase, the amount of capital after its increase shall be additionally entered).

Form 11.—Report on Conclusion (Alteration) of Technological Assistance Contract

Date: _____

To: Mr. _____, Competent Minister

Reporter:[1] _____
Signature or seal

In accordance with the provisions of article 10 of the Law Concerning Foreign Investment, a report is hereby made on the subject of which particulars are described hereunder:

1. FOREIGN INVESTOR:

Name [2]
Address [3]
Nationality [4]
Occupation [5]

Referential address in Japan
Tel. No.
Person in charge

2. OPPOSITE PARTY:

Name [2]
Address [3]
Occupation [5]

Referential address in Japan
Tel. No.
Person in charge

3. DATE AND NUMBER OF VALIDATION GRANTED RELATIVE TO THE REPORTED MATTERS:

4. DATE OF PUTTING THE REPORTED MATTERS INTO PRACTICE:

5. OTHER RELEVANT MATTERS:

Remarks:
[1] If incorporated, name of reporter and its representative or agent.
[2] If incorporated, trade name and name of representative.
[3] If incorporated, address of head office.
[4] In case the foreign investor is a juridical person established under Japanese laws and orders, address, nationality, and manner and grade of control of its substantial controller shall be entered.
[5] If incorporated, purpose of business and amount of capital.

Form 12.—Report on Acquisition of Stock (Proprietary Interest, Beneficiary Certificate, Debentures, or Claimable Assets Arising From Loans)

Date: _____

To: Mr. _____, Competent Minister

Reporter:[1] _____
Signature or seal

In accordance with the provisions of article 24 paragraph 1 of the Law Concerning Foreign Investment, a report is hereby made on the subject matter of which particulars are described hereunder:

1. FOREIGN INVESTOR:

Name [2]
Address [3]
Nationality [4]
Occupation [5]

Referential address in Japan
Tel. No.
Person in charge

2. KIND:

3. CONTENTS OF VALIDATION:

Date and number of validation.
Amount and value validated.

4. CONTENTS OF ACQUISITION:

Date of acquisition.
Amount and value acquired.

5. OTHER RELEVANT MATTERS:

Remarks:
[1] If incorporated, name of reporter and its representative or agent.
[2] If incorporated, trade name and name of representative.
[3] If incorporated, address of head office.
[4] In case the foreign investor is a juridical person established under the Japanese laws and orders, address, nationality, and manner and grade of control of its substantial controller shall be additionally entered.
[5] If incorporated, purpose of business and amount of capital.

Treaty of Friendship, Commerce and Navigation[1]

The United States of America and Japan, desirous of strengthening the bonds of peace and friendship traditionally existing between them and of encouraging closer economic and cultural relations between their peoples, and being cognizant of the contributions which may be made toward these ends by arrangements promoting mutually advantageous commercial intercourse, encouraging mutually beneficial investments, and establishing mutual rights and privileges, have resolved to conclude a Treaty of Friendship, Commerce and Navigation, based in general upon the principles of national and most-favored-nation treatment unconditionally accorded, and for that purpose have appointed as their Plenipotentiaries,

The United States of America:
  Robert D. Murphy, Ambassador Extraordinary and Plenipotentiary of the United States of America to Japan; and
Japan:
  Katsuo Okazaki, Minister for Foreign Affairs,

Who, having communicated to each other their full powers found to be in due form, have agreed upon the following Articles:

ARTICLE I

1. Nationals of either Party shall be permitted to enter the territories of the other Party and to remain therein: (a) for the purpose of carrying on trade between the territories of the two Parties and engaging in related commercial activities; (b) for the purpose of developing and directing the operations of an enterprise in which they have invested, or in which they are actively in the process of investing, a substantial amount of capital; and (c) for other purposes subject to the laws relating to the entry and sojourn of aliens.
2. Nationals of either Party, within the territories of the other Party, shall be permitted: (a) to travel therein freely, and to reside at places of their choice; (b) to enjoy liberty of conscience; (c) to hold both private and public religious services; (d) to gather and to transmit material for dissemination to the public abroad; and (e) to communicate with other persons inside and outside such territories by mail, telegraph and other means open to general public use.
3. The provisions of the present Article shall be subject to the right of either Party to apply measures that are necessary to maintain public order and protect the public health, morals and safety.

ARTICLE II

1. Nationals of either Party within the territories of the other Party shall be free from unlawful molestations of

[1] Signed at Tokyo, April 2, 1953.

every kind, and shall receive the most constant protection and security, in no case less than that required by international law.
2. If, within the territories of either Party, a national of the other Party is taken into custody, the nearest consular representative of his country shall on the demand of such national be immediately notified. Such national shall: (a) receive reasonable and humane treatment; (b) be formally and immediately informed of the accusations against him; (c) be brought to trial as promptly as is consistent with the proper preparation of his defense; and (d) enjoy all means reasonably necessary to his defense, including the services of competent counsel of his choice.

ARTICLE III

1. Nationals of either Party shall be accorded national treatment in the application of laws and regulations within the territories of the other Party that establish a pecuniary compensation, or other benefit or service, on account of disease, injury or death arising out of and in the course of employment or due to the nature of employment.
2. In addition to the rights and privileges provided in paragraph 1 of the present Article, nationals of either Party shall, within the territories of the other Party, be accorded national treatment in the application of laws and regulations establishing compulsory systems of social security, under which benefits are paid without an individual test of financial need: (a) against loss of wages or earnings due to old age, unemployment, sickness or disability, or (b) against loss of financial support due to the death of father, husband or other person on whom such support had depended.

ARTICLE IV

1. Nationals and companies of either Party shall be accorded national treatment and most-favored-nation treatment with respect to access to the courts of justice and to administrative tribunals and agencies within the territories of the other Party, in all degrees of jurisdiction, both in pursuit and in defense of their rights. It is understood that companies of either Party not engaged in activities within the territories of the other Party shall enjoy access therein without registration or similar requirements.
2. Contracts entered into between nationals and companies of either Party and nationals and companies of the other Party, that provide for the settlement by arbitration of controversies, shall not be deemed unenforceable within the territories of such other Party merely on the grounds that the place designated for the arbitration proceedings is outside such territories or that the nationality of one or

more of the arbitrators is not that of such other Party. Awards duly rendered pursuant to any such contracts, which are final and enforceable under the laws of the place where rendered, shall be deemed conclusive in enforcement proceedings brought before the courts of competent jurisdiction of either Party, and shall be entitled to be declared enforceable by such courts, except where found contrary to public policy. When so declared, such awards shall be entitled to privileges and measures of enforcement appertaining to awards rendered locally. It is understood, however, that awards rendered outside the United States of America shall be entitled in any court in any State thereof only to the same measure of recognition as awards rendered in other States thereof.

ARTICLE V

1. Neither Party shall take unreasonable or discriminatory measures that would impair the legally acquired rights or interests within its territories of nationals and companies of the other Party in the enterprises which they have established, in their capital, or in the skills, arts or technology which they have supplied; nor shall either Party unreasonably impede nationals and companies of the other Party from obtaining on equitable terms the capital, skills, arts and technology it needs for its economic development.
2. The Parties undertake to cooperate in furthering the interchange and use of scientific and technical knowledge, particularly in the interests of increasing productivity and improving standards of living within their respective territories.

ARTICLE VI

1. Property of nationals and companies of either Party shall receive the most constant protection and security within the territories of the other Party.
2. The dwellings, offices, warehouses, factories and other premises of nationals and companies of the other Party located within the territories of the other Party shall not be subject to unlawful entry or molestation. Official searches and examinations of such premises and their contents, when necessary, shall be made only according to law and with careful regard for the convenience of the occupants and the conduct of business.
3. Property of nationals and companies of either Party shall not be taken within the territories of the other Party except for public purpose, nor shall it be taken without the prompt payment of just compensation. Such compensation shall be in an effectively realizable form and shall represent the full equivalent of the property taken; and adequate provision shall have been made at or prior to the time of taking for the determination and payment thereof.
4. Nationals and companies of either Party shall in no case be accorded, within the territories of the other Party, less than national treatment and most-favored-nation treatment with respect to the matters set forth in paragraphs 2 and 3 of the present Article. Moreover, enterprises in which nationals and companies of either Party have a substantial interest shall be accorded, within the territories of the other Party, not less than national treatment and most-favored-nation treatment in all matters relating to the taking of privately owned enterprises into public ownership and to the placing of such enterprises under public control.

ARTICLE VII

1. Nationals and companies of either Party shall be accorded national treatment with respect to engaging in

all types of commercial, industrial, financial and other business activities within the territories of the other Party, whether directly or by agent or through the medium of any form of lawful juridical entity. Accordingly, such nationals and companies shall be permitted within such territories: (a) to establish and maintain branches, agencies, offices, factories and other establishments appropriate to the conduct of their business; (b) to organize companies under the general company laws of such other Party, and to acquire majority interests in companies of such other Party; and (c) to control and manage enterprises which they have established or acquired. Moreover, enterprises which they control, whether in the form of individual proprietorships, companies or otherwise, shall, in all that relates to the conduct of the activities thereof, be accorded treatment no less favorable than that accorded like enterprises controlled by nationals and companies of such other Party.
2. Each Party reserves the right to limit the extent to which aliens may within its territories establish, acquire interests in, or carry on public utilities enterprises or enterprises engaged in shipbuilding, air or water transport, banking involving depository or fiduciary functions, or the exploitation of land or other natural resources. However, new limitations imposed by either Party upon the extent to which aliens are accorded national treatment with respect to carrying on such activities within its territories, shall not be applied as against enterprises which are engaged in such activities therein at the time such new limitations are adopted and which are owned or controlled by nationals and companies of the other Party. Moreover, neither Party shall deny to transportation, communications and banking companies of the other Party the right to maintain branches and agencies to perform functions necessary for essentially international operations in which they are permitted to engage.
3. The provisions of paragraph 1 of the present Article shall not prevent either Party from prescribing special formalities in connection with the establishment of alien-controlled enterprises within its territories; but such formalities may not impair the substance of the rights set forth in said paragraph.
4. Nationals and companies of either Party, as well as enterprises controlled by such nationals and companies, shall in any event be accorded most-favored-nation treatment with reference to the matters treated in the present Article.

ARTICLE VIII

1. Nationals and companies of either Party shall be permitted to engage, within the territories of the other Party, accountants, and other technical experts, executive personnel, attorneys, agents and other specialists of their choice. Moreover, such nationals and companies shall be permitted to engage accountants and other technical experts regardless of the extent to which they may have qualified for the practice of a profession within the territories of such other Party, for the particular purpose of making examinations, audits and technical investigations exclusively for, and rendering reports to, such nationals and companies in connection with the planning and operation of their enterprises, and enterprises in which they have a financial interest, within such territories.
2. Nationals of either Party shall not be barred from practicing the professions within the territories of the other Party merely by reason of their alienage; but they shall be permitted to engage in professional activities therein upon compliance with the requirements regarding qualifications, residence and competence that are applicable to nationals of such other Party.
3. Nationals and companies of either Party shall be accorded national treatment and most-favored-nation treatment with respect to engaging in scientific, educational, religious and philanthropic activities within the

territories of the other Party, and shall be accorded the right to form associations for that purpose under the laws of such other Party.

ARTICLE IX

1. Nationals and companies of either Party shall be accorded within the territories of the other Party: (a) national treatment with respect to leasing land, buildings and other immovable property appropriate to the conduct of activities in which they are permitted to engage pursuant to Articles VII and VIII and for residential purposes, and with respect to occupying and using such property; and (b) other rights in immovable property permitted by the applicable laws of the other Party.

2. Nationals and companies of either Party shall be accorded within the territories of the other Party national treatment and most-favored-nation treatment with respect to acquiring, by purchase, lease, or otherwise, and with respect to owning and possessing, movable property of all kinds, both tangible and intangible. However, either Party may impose restrictions on alien ownership of materials dangerous from the standpoint of public safety and alien ownership of interests in enterprises carrying on the activities listed in the first sentence of paragraph 2 of Article VII, but only to the extent that this can be done without impairing the rights and privileges secured by Article VII or by other provisions of the present Treaty.

3. Nationals and companies of either Party shall be permitted freely to dispose of property within the territories of the other Party with respect to the acquisition of which through testate or intestate succession their alienage has prevented them from receiving national treatment, and they shall be permitted a term of at least five years in which to effect such disposition.

4. Nationals and companies of either Party shall be accorded within the territories of the other Party national treatment and most-favored-nation treatment with respect to disposing of property of all kinds.

ARTICLE X

Nationals and companies of either Party shall be accorded, within the territories of the other Party, national treatment and most-favored-nation treatment with respect to obtaining and maintaining patents of invention, and with respect to rights in trade marks, trade names, trade labels and industrial property of every kind.

ARTICLE XI

1. Nationals of either Party residing within the territories of the other Party, and nationals and companies of either Party engaged in trade or other gainful pursuit or in scientific, educational, religious or philanthropic activities within the territories of the other Party, shall not be subject to the payment of taxes, fees or charges imposed upon or applied to income, capital, transactions, activities or any other object, or to requirements with respect to the levy and collection thereof, within the territories of such other Party, more burdensome than those borne by nationals and companies of such other Party.

2. With respect to nationals of either Party who are neither resident nor engaged in trade or other gainful pursuit within the territories of the other Party, and with respect to companies of either Party which are not engaged in trade or other gainful pursuit within the territories of the other Party, it shall be the aim of such other Party to apply in general the principle set forth in paragraph 1 of the present Article.

3. Nationals and companies of either Party shall in no case be subject, within the territories of the other Party, to the payment of taxes, fees or charges imposed upon or applied to income, capital, transactions, activities or any other object, or to requirements with respect to the levy and collection thereof, more burdensome than those borne by nationals, residents and companies of any third country.

4. In the case of companies of either Party engaged in trade or other gainful pursuit within the territories of the other Party, and in the case of nationals of either Party engaged in trade or other gainful pursuit within the territories of the other Party but not resident therein, such other Party shall not impose or apply any tax, fee or charge upon any income, capital or other basis in excess of that reasonably allocable or apportionable to its territories, nor grant deductions and exemptions less than those reasonably allocable or apportionable to its territories. A comparable rule shall apply also in the case of companies organized and operated exclusively for scientific, educational, religious or philanthropic purposes.

5. Each Party reserves the right to: (a) extend specific tax advantages on the basis of reciprocity; (b) accord special tax advantages by virtue of agreements for the avoidance of double taxation or the mutual protection of revenue; and (c) accord to its own nationals and to residents of contiguous countries more favorable exemptions of a personal nature with respect to income taxes and inheritance taxes than are accorded to other non-resident persons.

ARTICLE XII

1. Nationals and companies of either Party shall be accorded by the other Party national treatment and most-favored-nation treatment with respect to payments, remittances and transfers of funds or financial instruments between the territories of the two Parties as well as between the territories of such other Party and of any third country.

2. Neither Party shall impose exchange restrictions as defined in paragraph 5 of the present Article except to the extent necessary to prevent its monetary reserves from falling to a very low level or to effect a moderate increase in very low monetary reserves. It is understood that the provisions of the present Article do not alter the obligations either Party may have to the International Monetary Fund or preclude imposition of particular restrictions whenever the Fund specifically authorizes or requests a Party to impose such particular restrictions.

3. If either Party imposes exchange restrictions in accordance with paragraph 2 above, it shall, after making whatever provision may be necessary to assure the availability of foreign exchange for goods and services essential to the health and welfare of its people, make reasonable provision for the withdrawal, in foreign exchange in the currency of the other Party, of: (a) the compensation referred to in Article VI, paragraph 3, of the present Treaty; (b) earnings, whether in the form of salaries, interest, dividends, commissions, royalties, payments for technical services, or otherwise; and (c) amounts for amortization of loans, depreciation of direct investments, and capital transfers, giving consideration to special needs for other transactions. If more than one rate of exchange is in force, the rate applicable to such withdrawals shall be a rate which is specifically approved by the International Monetary Fund for such transactions or, in the absence of a rate so approved, an effective rate which, inclusive of any taxes or surcharges on exchange transfers, is just and reasonable.

4. Exchange restrictions shall not be imposed by either Party in a manner unnecessarily detrimental or arbitrarily discriminatory to the claims, investments, transport, trade, and other interests of the nationals and companies of the other Party, nor to the competitive position thereof.

5. The term "exchange restrictions" as used in the

present Article includes all restrictions, regulations, charges, taxes, or other requirements imposed by either Party which burden or interfere with payments, remittances, or transfers of funds or of financial instruments between the territories of the two Parties.

ARTICLE XIII

Commercial travelers representing nationals and companies of either Party engaged in business within the territories thereof shall, upon their entry into and departure from the territories of the other Party and during their sojourn therein, be accorded most-favored-nation treatment in respect of the customs and other matters, including, subject to the exceptions in paragraph 5 of Article XI, taxes and charges applicable to them, their samples and the taking of orders, and regulations governing the exercise of their functions.

ARTICLE XIV

1. Each Party shall accord most-favored-nation treatment to products of the other Party, from whatever place and by whatever type of carrier arriving, and to products destined for exportation to the territories of such other Party, by whatever route and by whatever type of carrier, with respect to customs duties and charges of any kind imposed on or in connection with importation or exportation or imposed on the international transfer of payments for imports or exports, and with respect to the method of levying such duties and charges, and with respect to all rules and formalities in connection with importation and exportation.
2. Neither Party shall impose restrictions or prohibitions on the importation of any product of the other Party, or on the exportation of any product to the territories of the other Party, unless the importation of the like product of, or the exportation of the like product to, all third countries is similarly restricted or prohibited.
3. If either Party imposes quantitative restrictions on the importation or exportation of any product in which the other Party has an important interest:
(a) It shall as a general rule give prior public notice of the total amount of the product, by quantity or value, that may be imported or exported during a specified period, and of any change in such amount or period; and
(b) If it makes allotments to any third country, it shall afford such other Party a share proportionate to the amount of the product, by quantity or value, supplied by or to it during a previous representative period, due consideration being given to any special factors affecting the trade in such product.
4. Either Party may impose prohibitions or restrictions on sanitary or other customary grounds of a non-commercial nature, or in the interest of preventing deceptive or unfair practices, provided such prohibitions or restrictions do not arbitrarily discriminate against the commerce of the other Party.
5. Nationals and companies of either Party shall be accorded national treatment and most-favored-nation treatment by the other Party with respect to all matters relating to importation and exportation.
6. The provisions of the present Article shall not apply to advantages accorded by either Party:
(a) to products of its national fisheries;
(b) to adjacent countries in order to facilitate frontier traffic; or
(c) by virtue of a customs union or free-trade area of which it may become a member, so long as it informs the other Party of its plans and affords such other Party adequate opportunity for consultation.
7. Notwithstanding the provisions of paragraphs 2 and

3 (b) of the present Article, a Party may apply restrictions or controls on importation and exportation of goods that have effect equivalent to, or which are necessary to make effective, exchange restrictions or controls applied pursuant to Article XII. However, such restrictions shall depart no more than necessary from the aforesaid paragraphs and shall be conformable with a policy designed to promote the maximum development of non-discriminatory foreign trade and to expedite the attainment both of a balance-of-payments position and of monetary reserves which will obviate the necessity of such restrictions.

ARTICLE XV

1. Each Party shall promptly publish laws, regulations and administrative rulings of general application pertaining to rates of duty, taxes or other charges, to the classification of articles for customs purposes, and to requirements or restrictions on imports and exports or the transfer of payments therefor, or affecting their sale, distribution or use; and shall administer such laws, regulations and rulings in a uniform, impartial and reasonable manner. As a general practice, new administrative requirements or restrictions affecting imports, with the exception of those imposed on sanitary grounds or for reasons of public safety, shall not go into effect before the expiration of 30 days after publication, or alternatively, shall not apply to products en route at time of publication.
2. Each Party shall provide an appeals procedure under which nationals and companies of the other Party, and importers of products of such other Party, shall be able to obtain prompt and impartial review, and correction when warranted, of administrative action relating to customs matters, including the imposition of fines and penalties, confiscations, and rulings on questions of customs classification and valuation by the administrative authorities. Penalties imposed for infractions of the customs and shipping laws and regulations concerning documentation shall, in cases resulting from clerical errors or when good faith can be demonstrated, be no greater than necessary to serve merely as a warning.
3. Neither Party shall impose any measure of a discriminatory nature that hinders or prevents the importer or exporter of products of either country from obtaining marine insurance on such products in companies of either Party. The present paragraph is subject to the provisions of Article XII.

ARTICLE XVI

1. Products of either Party shall be accorded, within the territories of the other Party, national treatment and most-favored-nation treatment in all matters affecting internal taxation, sale, distribution, storage and use.
2. Articles produced by nationals and companies of either Party within the territories of the other Party, or by companies of the latter Party controlled by such nationals and companies, shall be accorded therein treatment no less favorable than that accorded to like articles of national origin by whatever person or company produced, in all matters affecting exportation, taxation, sale, distribution, storage and use.

ARTICLE XVII

1. Each Party undertakes (a) that enterprises owned or controlled by its Government, and that monopolies or agencies granted exclusive or special privileges within its territories, shall make their purchases and sales involving either imports or exports affecting the commerce of the other Party solely in accordance with commercial con-

siderations, including price, quality, availability, marketability, transportation and other conditions of purchase or sale; and (b) that the nationals, companies and commerce of such other Party shall be afforded adequate opportunity, in accordance with customary business practice, to compete for participation in such purchases and sales.

2. Each Party shall accord to the nationals, companies and commerce of the other Party fair and equitable treatment, as compared with that accorded to the nationals, companies and commerce of any third country, with respect to: (a) the governmental purchase of supplies, (b) the awarding of concessions and other government contracts, and (c) the sale of any service sold by the Government or by any monopoly or agency granted exclusive or special privileges.

ARTICLE XVIII

1. The two Parties agree that business practices which restrain competition, limit access to markets or foster monopolistic control, and which are engaged in or made effective by one or more private or public commercial enterprises or by combination, agreement or other arrangement among such enterprises, may have harmful effects upon commerce between their respective territories. Accordingly, each Party agrees upon the request of the other Party to consult with respect to any such practices and to take such measures as it deems appropriate with a view to eliminating such harmful effects.

2. No enterprise of either Party, including corporations, associations, and government agencies and instrumentalities, which is publicly owned or controlled shall, if it engages in commercial, industrial, shipping or other business activities within the territories of the other Party, claim or enjoy, either for itself or for its property, immunity therein from taxation, suit, execution of judgment or other liability to which privately owned and controlled enterprises are subject therein.

ARTICLE XIX

1. Between the territories of the two Parties there shall be freedom of commerce and navigation.

2. Vessels under the flag of either Party, and carrying the papers required by its law in proof of nationality, shall be deemed to be vessels of that Party both on the high seas and within the ports, places and waters of the other Party.

3. Vessels of either Party shall have liberty, on equal terms with vessels of the other Party and on equal terms with vessels of any third country, to come with their cargoes to all ports, places and waters of such other Party open to foreign commerce and navigation. Such vessels and cargoes shall in all respects be accorded national treatment and most-favored-nation treatment within the ports, places and waters of such other Party.

4. Vessels of either Party shall be accorded national treatment and most-favored-nation treatment by the other Party with respect to the right to carry all products that may be carried by vessel to or from the territories of such other Party; and such products shall be accorded treatment no less favorable than that accorded to like products carried in vessels of such other Party, with respect to: (a) duties and charges of all kinds, (b) the administration of the customs, and (c) bounties, drawbacks and other privileges of this nature.

5. Vessels of either Party, in case of shipwreck, stranding, or of being forced to put into the ports, places and waters of the other Party, whether or not open to foreign commerce and navigation, shall enjoy the same assistance and protection as are in like cases enjoyed by vessels of such other Party or of any third country, and shall not be subject to any duties or charges other than those which would be payable in like circumstances by vessels of such other Party or of any third country. The cargoes of such vessels of either Party and all articles salvaged from them shall be exempt from customs duties unless entered for consumption within the territories of the other Party; but articles not entered for consumption may be subject to measures for the protection of the revenue pending their exit from the country.

6. Notwithstanding any other provision of the present Treaty, each Party may reserve exclusive rights and privileges to its own vessels with respect to the coasting trade, national fisheries and inland navigation, or may admit foreign vessels thereto only on a reciprocity basis.

7. The term "vessels", as used herein, means all types of vessels, whether privately owned or operated, or publicly owned or operated; but this term does not, except with reference to paragraphs 2 and 5 of the present Article, include fishing vessels or vessels of war.

ARTICLE XX

There shall be freedom of transit through the territories of each Party by the routes most convenient for international transit:

(a) for nationals of the other Party, together with their baggage;

(b) for other persons, together with their baggage, en route to or from the territories of such other Party; and

(c) for products of any origin en route to or from the territories of such other Party.

Such persons and things in transit shall be exempt from customs duties, from duties imposed by reason of transit, and from unreasonable charges and requirements; and shall be free from unnecessary delays and restrictions. They shall, however, be subject to measures referred to in paragraph 3 of Article I, and to nondiscriminatory regulations necessary to prevent abuse of the transit privilege.

ARTICLE XXI

1. The present Treaty shall not preclude the application of measures:

(a) regulating the importation or exportation of gold or silver;

(b) relating to fissionable materials, to radioactive by-products of the utilization or processing thereof, or to materials that are the source of fissionable materials;

(c) regulating the production of or traffic in arms, ammunition and implements of war, or traffic in other materials carried on directly or indirectly for the purpose of supplying a military establishment;

(d) necessary to fulfill the obligations of a Party for the maintenance or restoration of international peace and security, or necessary to protect its essential security interests; and

(e) denying to any company in the ownership or direction of which nationals of any third country or countries have directly or indirectly the controlling interest, the advantages of the present Treaty, except with respect to recognition of juridical status and with respect to access to courts of justice and to administrative tribunals and agencies.

2. The most-favored-nation provisions of the present Treaty relating to the treatment of goods shall not apply to advantages accorded by the United States of America or its territories and possessions to one another, to the Republic of Cuba, to the Republic of the Philippines, to the Trust Territory of the Pacific Islands or to the Panama Canal Zone.

3. The provisions of the present Treaty relating to the treatment of goods shall not preclude action by either Party which is required or specifically permitted by the

General Agreement on Tariffs and Trade during such time as such Party is a contracting party to the General Agreement. Moreover, either Party may withhold advantages negotiated under the aforesaid Agreement from those countries which by their own choice are not contracting parties thereto.

4. Nationals of either Party admitted into the territories of the other Party for limited purposes shall not enjoy rights to engage in gainful occupations in contravention of limitations expressly imposed, according to law, as a condition of their admittance.

5. Nothing in the present Treaty shall be deemed to grant or imply any right to engage in political activities.

ARTICLE XXII

1. The term "national treatment" means treatment accorded within the territories of a Party upon terms no less favorable than the treatment accorded therein, in like situations, to nationals, companies, products, vessels or other objects, as the case may be, of such Party.

2. The term "most-favored-nation treatment" means treatment accorded within the territories of a Party upon terms no less favorable than the treatment accorded therein, in like situations, to nationals, companies, products, vessels or other objects, as the case may be, of any third country.

3. As used in the present Treaty, the term "companies" means corporations, partnerships, companies, and other associations, whether or not with limited liability and whether or not for pecuniary profit. Companies constituted under the applicable laws and regulations within the territories of either Party shall be deemed companies thereof and shall have their juridical status recognized within the territories of the other Party.

4. National treatment accorded under the provisions of the present Treaty to companies of Japan shall, in any State, Territory or possession of the United States of America, be the treatment accorded therein to companies created or organized in other States, Territories, and possessions of the United States of America.

ARTICLE XXIII

The territories to which the present Treaty extends shall comprise all areas of land and water under the sovereignty or authority of each Party, other than the Panama Canal Zone and the Trust Territory of the Pacific Islands, except to the extent that the President of the United States of America shall by proclamation extend provisions of the Treaty to such Trust Territory.

ARTICLE XXIV

1. Each Party shall accord sympathetic consideration to, and shall afford adequate opportunity for consultation regarding, such representations as the other Party may make with respect to any matter affecting the operation of the present Treaty.

2. Any dispute between the Parties as to the interpretation or application of the present Treaty, not satisfactorily adjusted by diplomacy, shall be submitted to the International Court of Justice, unless the Parties agree to settlement by some other pacific means.

ARTICLE XXV

1. The present Treaty shall be ratified, and the ratifications thereof shall be exchanged at Washington as soon as possible.

2. The present Treaty shall enter into force one month after the day of exchange of ratifications. It shall remain in force for ten years and shall continue in force thereafter until terminated as provided herein.

3. Either Party may, by giving one year's written notice to the other Party, terminate the present Treaty at the end of the initial ten-year period or at any time thereafter.

IN WITNESS WHEREOF the respective Plenipotentiaries have signed the present Treaty and have affixed hereunto their seals.

DONE in duplicate, in the English and Japanese languages, both equally authentic, at Tokyo, this second day of April, one thousand nine hundred fifty three.

PROTOCOL

At the time of signing the Treaty of Friendship, Commerce and Navigation between the United States of America and Japan, the undersigned Plenipotentiaries, duly authorized by their respective Governments, have further agreed on the following provisions, which shall be considered integral parts of the aforesaid Treaty:

1. The term "access to the courts of justice and to administrative tribunals and agencies" as used in Article IV, paragraph 1, comprehends, among other things, legal aid and security for costs and judgment.

2. The provisions of Article VI, paragraph 3, providing for the payment of compensation shall extend to interests held directly or indirectly by nationals and companies of either Party in property which is taken within the territories of the other Party.

3. The term "public utility enterprises" as used in Article VII, paragraph 2, is deemed to include enterprises engaged in furnishing communications services, water supplies, transportation by bus, truck or rail, or in manufacturing and distributing gas or electricity, to the general public.

4. With reference to Article VII, paragraph 4, either Party may require that rights to engage in mining shall be dependent on reciprocity. Furthermore, Japan shall not be obligated by the terms of that paragraph to accord to enterprises of nationals and companies of the United States of America of the types mentioned in the first sentence of paragraph 2 of Article VII more favorable treatment than that accorded by the State or Territory of the United States of America in which such national is domiciled, or pursuant to the laws of which such company is organized, or in which, if such company is organized under federal law, such company has its principal office, to the enterprises of nationals and companies of Japan.

5. The provisions of Article VIII, paragraph 2, shall not extend to the professions of notary public and port pilot.

6. Either Party may impose restrictions on the introduction of foreign capital as may be necessary to protect its monetary reserves as provided in Article XII, paragraph 2.

7. With reference to Article XIV, paragraph 4, it is understood that either Party, acting in accordance with its laws, may prohibit the importation into its territory, or seize, or otherwise restrict or regulate the sale of any goods with respect to which there has been failure to comply

with marking requirements established to assure that the true geographic or commercial origin of such goods is correctly represented. Furthermore, each Party agrees to take appropriate steps to prevent misrepresentations, direct or indirect, that goods produced or sold in or exported from its territory originate within the territory of the other Party or any distinctive place within such territory.

8. During periods of emergency resulting in reduced availabilities of industrial raw materials and basic food-stuffs, the provisions of Article XVI, paragraph 1, of the present Treaty shall not prevent the application by either Party of needed controls over the internal sale, distribution or use of imported articles of categories which may be in short supply, other than or different from controls applied with respect to like articles of national origin. If imposed, such controls shall be applied by either Party in such a manner as to minimize injury to the competitive position within its territories of the commerce of the other Party, and shall be continued no longer than required by the supply situation.

9. Notwithstanding the national treatment provisions of Article XVI, paragraph 1, a Party may maintain screen quota regulations that require the exhibition of cinematograph films of national origin during a specified minimum portion of the screen time actually utilized by exhibitors for the commercial exhibition of all films. Screen quotas shall be computed on the basis of screen time per theatre per year or the equivalent thereof, and shall be subject to consultation.

10. It is understood that for the purposes of Article XVII, paragraph 1, availability of means of payment is considered to be a commercial consideration.

11. The provisions of Article XVII, paragraph 2(b) and (c), and of Article XIX, paragraph 4, shall not apply to postal services.

12. The provisions of Article XXI, paragraph 2, shall apply in the case of Puerto Rico regardless of any change that may take place in its political status.

13. Article XXIII does not apply to territories under the authority of either Party solely as a military base or by reason of temporary military occupation, or to Nansei Shoto south of 29 degrees north latitude (including the Ryukyu Islands and the Daito Islands), the Nanpo Shoto south of Sofu Gan (including the Bonin Islands, Rosario Island and the Volcano Islands) and Parece Vela and Marcus Island, the status of which is provided for in Article 3 of the Treaty of Peace with Japan signed at San Francisco on September 8, 1951.

14. The most-favored-nation treatment provisions of the present Treaty shall not apply with respect to those rights and privileges which may be accorded by Japan to (a) persons who originated in the territories to which all right, title and claim were renounced by Japan in accordance with Article 2 of the Treaty of Peace with Japan signed at San Francisco on September 8, 1951, or (b) the native inhabitants and vessels of, and trade with, the islands mentioned in Article 3 of the said Treaty of Peace.

15. During a transitional period of three years from the date of the coming into force of the present Treaty, Japan may continue to apply existing restrictions on the purchase by aliens, with yen, of outstanding shares in Japanese enterprises.

IN WITNESS WHEREOF the respective Plenipotentiaries have signed this Protocol and have affixed hereunto their seals.

DONE in duplicate, in the English and Japanese languages, both equally authentic, at Tokyo, this second day of April, one thousand nine hundred fifty three.

Foreign Exchange and Trade Control Law——Excerpts[1]

CHAPTER I. GENERAL PROVISIONS

Article 1. The purpose of this law is to provide for the control of foreign exchange, foreign trade and other foreign transactions, necessary for the proper development of foreign trade and for the safeguarding of the balance of international payments and the stability of the currency, as well as the most economic and beneficial use of foreign currency funds, for the sake of the rehabilitation and the expansion of the national economy.

Article 5. This law shall apply also to acts performed outside Japan by representatives, agents, employees and other persons engaged by juridical persons having their head offices or main places of business in Japan, in regard to the property or business of such juridical persons. The same shall apply to acts performed outside Japan by persons domiciled in Japan, their representatives, employees and other persons engaged by them, in regard to their property or business.

Article 6. Definitions of 16 terms used in this law are included under this article. Only the following are given in full since they are particularly pertinent to a prospective investor's understanding of the other provisions which follow.

(5) "Exchange residents" shall mean all natural persons who have their permanent place of abode or who customarily live in Japan, and also juridical persons (corporate bodies, enterprises), having their seat or place of administration in Japan. The branches in Japan (agencies, establishments, etc.) of exchange nonresidents are considered to be exchange residents irrespective of whether they are independent in law or not and even if the place of their administration or their headquarters is located abroad.

(6) "Exchange nonresidents" shall mean all persons, natural or juridical, other than those falling under the meaning of exchange residents.

(7) "Means of payment" shall mean bank notes, Treasury notes, small paper money, coins, checks, bills of exchange, money orders, letters of credit, and other orders for payment.

(8) "Foreign means of payment" shall mean money in foreign currency and other means of payment as specified in the preceding item which are expressed in foreign currency or payable abroad irrespective of the currency in which they are expressed.

(11) "Securities" shall mean entries in debt and stock registers, bonds, shares, certificates giving title to bonds or shares, debentures, corporate debentures, Treasury bills, mortgage bonds, scrips, profit certificates and similar documents, as well as interest and dividend coupons and talons.

(12) "Foreign securities" shall mean securities which are payable abroad or expressed in foreign currency value which are abroad.

(13) "Claimable assets" shall mean time deposits, demand deposits, insurance policies and claims, balances in current account, any claims to be paid such as arising out of loans or bids or any other claims, expressed in terms of money insofar as they are not embodied within the meaning of other items of this article.

(14) "Foreign claimable assets" shall mean those payable abroad or in foreign currency.

(15) "Goods" shall mean movable goods, with the exception of gold and other precious metals, means of payment, securities and documents in which claimable assets are embodied.

CHAPTER V. RESTRICTIONS AND PROHIBITIONS

Section I. Payments

Article 27. (Restriction and prohibition of payment.) Unless authorized as provided for in this law or in Cabinet order, no person shall in Japan:

(1) Make any payment to a foreign country;

(2) Make any payment to an exchange nonresident or receive any payment from an exchange nonresident;

(3) Make any payment to an exchange resident on behalf of an exchange nonresident or receive such payment;

(4) Place any sum to the credit of an exchange nonresident or receive any sum for credit from an exchange nonresident;

2. The provisions of items 2 through 4 of the preceding paragraph shall not apply:

(1) To payments made in national currency for settlement of expenditures arising in connection with an exchange nonresident's sojourn in Japan such as those covering cost of living or normal purchases of commodities or services;

(2) To payments in national currency made in the course of domestic business in Japan to which the exchange nonresident is authorized.

Article 28. Unless authorized as provided for in this law or in Cabinet order, no person shall in Japan and no exchange resident abroad shall make any payment to or for the credit of an exchange resident as a consideration or association with payment or other benefit accruing to anyone abroad or acquisition of property abroad.

Article 29. Unless authorized as provided for in this law or in Cabinet order, no person shall in Japan and no exchange resident abroad receive any payment from or on behalf of an exchange resident as a consideration or association with surrender of any value abroad.

---

[1] Law No. 228 of December 1, 1949, as amended to June 1, 1954.

Section II. Claimable Assets

Article 30. (Restriction and prohibition concerning claimable assets.) No person may be a party to creation, modification, liquidation, settlement, or direct or indirect transfer of the following items or to any other transaction of the same, unless authorized as provided for by Cabinet order:

(1) Claimable assets expressed in national currency between exchange nonresidents;

(2) Foreign claimable assets between exchange residents;

(3) Claimable assets between an exchange resident and an exchange nonresident.

Section III. Securities

Article 31. (Securities located in Japan.) No person may sell, buy, donate, exchange, lend, borrow, deposit, pledge, or transfer in any way securities located in Japan or transfer any rights to such securities without being duly authorized or obtaining a license under provisions of Ministry of Finance ordinance.

2. The provisions of the preceding paragraph shall not apply to transactions of domestic securities between exchange residents.

Article 32. (Securities located abroad.) No exchange resident may sell, buy, donate, exchange, lend, borrow, deposit, pledge, or transfer in any way securities located abroad or transfer any rights to such securities without being duly authorized or obtaining a license under the provisions of Ministry of Finance ordinance.

2. The provisions of the preceding paragraph shall apply to non-Japanese exchange residents only insofar as they pertain to securities which may have accrued to such non-Japanese exchange residents as a result of transactions which are governed by the provisions of this Law and the orders and ordinances thereunder.

Article 33. (Safekeeping of securities.) No person may, unless authorized as provided for by Ministry of Finance ordinance, be a party to an arrangement of safekeeping of a security, other than pertaining to domestic securities for safekeeping in Japan in favor of an exchange resident, or to foreign securities for safekeeping abroad in favor of an exchange nonresident, if such arrangement is made between exchange nonresidents.

Article 34. (Flotation of securities.) Unless being duly authorized or obtaining a license under the Ministry of Finance ordinance:

(1) No person may float abroad securities payable in national currency;

(2) No exchange resident may float any securities abroad;

(3) No exchange nonresident may float foreign securities in Japan.

Article 35. (Subscription of securities.) Without being duly authorized or obtaining a license as provided for by Cabinet order:

(1) No exchange resident shall subscribe to foreign securities;

(2) No exchange nonresident shall subscribe to domestic securities.

Section IV. Immovables

Article 36. (Immovables located abroad.) Unless authorized as provided for by Ministry of Finance ordinance, no exchange resident shall acquire foreign immovable property or right thereto.

Article 37. Unless authorized as provided for by Ministry of Finance ordinance, no exchange resident shall dispose of his foreign immovable property or give up or surrender any part of his right thereto.

Article 38. (Immovables located in Japan.) Unless authorized as provided for by Cabinet order, no exchange resident shall dispose of immovable property in Japan or any right pertaining to it in favor of an exchange nonresident.

Article 39. Unless authorized as provided for by Cabinet order, no exchange nonresident shall acquire immovable property in Japan or right thereto from an exchange nonresident.

Article 40. Unless authorized as provided for by Cabinet order, no exchange nonresident shall dispose of immovable property situated in Japan or give up or surrender any part of his right thereto.

Article 41. (Exceptions.) The provisions of articles 36 and 37 shall apply to non-Japanese exchange residents only insofar as they pertain to immovable properties specified therein which may have accrued to such non-Japanese exchange residents as a result of transactions which are governed by the provisions of this law and order and ordinances thereunder.

Section V. Others

Article 42. (Services.) Unless authorized as provided for by Cabinet order, no person shall contract for services involving payment, settlement or any other transaction governed by the provisions of this law.

Article 43. Unless authorized as provided for by Cabinet order, no exchange resident shall render services to an exchange nonresident unless an adequate payment is provided in accordance with the provisions of this law.

Article 44. Any person or exchange nonresident as specified in the preceding two articles may be required to obtain prior approval from or present certification of adequate payment to the competent Minister as provided for by Cabinet order.

Article 45. (Export or import of means of payment, etc.) Unless authorized as provided for by Cabinet order, no person may export or import means of payment, precious metals, securities, or documents embodying rights to claimable assets.

Article 46. The Cabinet order specified in the preceding article shall prescribe the manner and the degree to which the provisions of the preceding article shall apply to persons entering or leaving Japan.

CHAPTER VI. FOREIGN TRADE

Article 47. (Principle of export.) Export goods from Japan will be permitted with the minimum restrictions thereon consistent with the purpose of this law.

Article 48. (Approval of export.) Any person desiring to export goods from Japan may be required to obtain the approval of the Minister of International Trade and Industry for those types of export goods and/or method of transactions or payments as provided for by Cabinet order.

2. The restrictions provided for by Cabinet order specified in the preceding paragraph shall be within the limit of necessity for the maintenance of the balance of international payment and sound development of international trade or national economy.

Article 49. (Certification of payment method.) The Minister of International Trade and Industry may by ordinance require from any person desiring to export goods an adequate certification that satisfactory payment is provided as provided for by Cabinet order.

Article 51. (Emergency suspension of shipment.) The Minister of International Trade and Industry may suspend by ordinance the shipment of export goods, designating the articles and/or destination for a period not exceeding 1 month, when he deems it necessary as a matter of grave emergency.

Article 52. (Approval of import.) In order to ensure the most economic and beneficial imports of goods within the scope of foreign exchange budget any person desiring to effect import may be required to obtain approval therefor as provided for by Cabinet order.

Article 53. (Sanction.) The Minister of International Trade and Industry may prohibit any person who, in connection with the export or import of goods has violated the provisions of this law, ordinances or measures based thereon, from engaging in export or import transactions for a period not exceeding 1 year.

Article 54. (Direction and supervision to customs chief.) The Minister of International Trade and Industry shall direct and supervise the customs chief regarding the export and import of goods under his jurisdiction as provided for by Cabinet order.

2. The Minister of International Trade and Industry may delegate to the customs chief a part of his power based on this law as provided for by Cabinet order.

Article 55. (Presentation of collateral.) Any person desiring to import goods may, as provided for by Cabinet order, be required to furnish deposit or securities, or collateral in order to assure the effectuation of import concerned.

2. In case the person who obtained an import license did not effectuate such import the deposit, securities, or collateral under the preceding paragraph may be forfeit to the National Treasury in accordance with provisions of Cabinet order.

143

Techniques Japan Seeks To Import

This list was released by the Japanese Government in June 1955 in accordance with the provisions of the Law Concerning Foreign Investment (law No. 163 of May 10, 1950, as amended) and implementing regulations.

Textile Industry

Production of various synthetic fibers.

Chemical Industry

Production of synthetic resins and solvents from gases produced by distillation or cracking of petroleum.
Production of hexogen and composition B.
Production of synthetic phenol.

Petroleum Industry

Methods of olefin gas separation produced by catalytic cracking.
Utilization of olefin gas produced by cracking.
Production of catalyzer for reforming of petroleum.

Metal Industry

Production of metallic titanium.
Production of metallic magnesium.

Refining of copper, zinc, and sulfur.
Melting and processing of metallic titanium and production of alloys thereof.
Production of heatproof steel alloys.
Production of cold-drawn steel pipes.
Extrusion of steel at low or high temperatures.

Machinery Industry

Production of high-performance machine tools.

Aircraft Industry

Production of propellers, aviation radio equipment, and control system.
Production of jet planes, including engine and auxiliary apparatus.

Electrical Machinery Industry

Production of automatic controlling machine for combustion processes.

Pharmaceutical Industry

Production of ACTH
Production of banthine.

Japan-United States Tax Convention[1]

The Government of the United States of America and the Government of Japan, desiring to conclude a Convention for the avoidance of double taxation and the prevention of fiscal evasion with respect to taxes on income, have appointed for that purpose as their respective Plenipotentiaries:

The Government of the United States of America:
Mr. Walter Bedell Smith, Acting Secretary of State of the United States of America, and

The Government of Japan:
Mr. Sadao Iguchi, Ambassador Extraordinary and Plenipotentiary of Japan to the United States of America,

who, having communicated to one another their respective full powers, found in good and due form, have agreed upon the following Articles:

Article I

(1) The taxes referred to in the present Convention are:
(a) In the case of the United States of America: The Federal income taxes, including surtaxes.
(b) In the case of Japan: The income tax and the corporation tax.

(2) The present Convention shall also apply to any other tax on income or profits which has a character substantially similar to those referred to in paragraph (1) of this Article and which may be imposed by either contracting State after the date of signature of the present Convention.

Article II

(1) As used in the present Convention:
(a) The term "United States" means the United States of America, and when used in a geographical sense means the States, the Territories of Alaska and Hawaii, and the District of Columbia.

(b) The term "Japan," when used in a geographical sense, means all the territory in which the laws relating to the taxes referred to in paragraph (1) (b) of Article I are enforced.

(c) The term "permanent establishment" means an office, factory, workshop, branch, warehouse or other fixed place of business, but does not include the casual and temporary use of merely storage facilities. It also includes an agency if the agent has and habitually exercises a general authority to negotiate and conclude contracts on behalf of an enterprise or has a stock of mer-

chandise from which he regularly fills orders on its behalf. An enterprise of one of the contracting States shall not be deemed to have a permanent establishment in the other contracting State merely because it carried on business dealings in such other State through a bona fide commission agent, broker, custodian or other independent agent acting in the ordinary course of his business as such. The fact than an enterprise of one of the contracting States maintains in the other contracting State a fixed place of business exclusively for the purchase for such enterprise of goods or merchandise shall not of itself constitute such fixed place of business a permanent establishment of such enterprise. The fact that a corporation of one of the contracting States has a subsidiary corporation which is a corporation of the other contracting State or which is engaged in trade or business in the other contracting State shall not of itself constitute that subsidiary corporation a permanent establishment of its parent corporation.

(d) The term "enterprise of one of the contracting States" means, as the case may be, Japanese enterprise or United States enterprise.

(e) The term "United States enterprise" means an industrial or commercial enterprise or undertaking carried on in the United States by a resident (including an individual, a fiduciary and partnership) of the United States or by a United States corporation or other entity; and the term "United States corporation or other entity" means a corporation or other entity created or organized under the law of the United States or of any State or Territory of the United States.

(f) The term "Japanese enterprise" means an industrial or commercial enterprise or undertaking carried on in Japan by an individual resident in Japan or by a Japanese corporation or other entity; and the term "Japanese corporation or other entity" means a corporation or other association having juridical personality, or a partnership or other association without juridical personality, created or organized under the laws of Japan.

(g) The term "tax" means those taxes referred to in paragraph (1) (a) or (b) of Article I, as the context requires.

(h) The term "competent authorities" means, in the case of the United States, the Commissioner of Internal Revenue as authorized by the Secretary of the Treasury; and, in the case of Japan, the Minister of Finance or his authorized representative.

(i) The term "industrial or commercial profits" includes manufacturing, mercantile, agricultural, fishing, mining, financial and insurance profits, but does not include income in the form of dividends, interest, rents or royalties, or remuneration for personal services.

(2) In the application of the provisions of the present Convention by either contracting State any term not otherwise defined shall, unless the context otherwise requires, have the meaning which such term has under the laws of such State relating to the tax.

[1] Convention between the United States of America and Japan for the avoidance of double taxation and the prevention of fiscal evasion with respect to taxes on income.

147

Article III

(1) An enterprise of one of the contracting States shall not be subject to the tax of the other contracting State in respect of its industrial or commercial profits unless it has a permanent establishment situated in such other State. If it has such permanent establishment such other State may impose its tax upon the entire income of such enterprise from sources within such other State.

(2) In determining the tax of one of the contracting States no account shall be taken of the mere purchase of merchandise therein by an enterprise of the other contracting State.

(3) Where an enterprise of one of the contracting States has a permanent establishment situated in the other contracting State, there shall be attributed to such permanent establishment the industrial or commercial profits which it might be expected to derive if it were an independent enterprise engaged in the same or similar activities under the same or similar conditions and dealing on an independent basis with the enterprise of which it is a permanent establishment.

(4) In determining the industrial or commercial profits of a permanent establishment there shall be allowed as deductions all expenses wherever incurred, reasonably allocable to such permanent establishment, including executive and general administrative expenses so allocable.

(5) The competent authorities of both contracting States may, consistent with other provisions of the present Convention, arrange details for the apportionment of industrial or commercial profits.

Article IV

Where an enterprise of one of the contracting States, by reason of its participation in the management or the financial structure of an enterprise of the other contracting State, makes with or imposes on the latter enterprise, in their commercial or financial relations, conditions different from those which would be made with an independent enterprise, any profits which would normally have been allocable to one of the enterprises, but by reason of such conditions have not been so allocated, may be included in the profits of such enterprise and taxed accordingly.

Article V

(1) Notwithstanding the provisions of Article III and Article IV of the present Convention, income which an enterprise of one of the contracting States derives from the operation of ships or aircraft registered

(a) in such State, or

(b) in a third country which exempts (A) such enterprise and (B) an enterprise of the other contracting State, from its tax on earnings derived from the operation of ships or aircraft, as the case may be, registered in the respective States shall be exempt from the tax of such other contracting State.

(2) The present Convention shall not be construed to affect the arrangement between the Government of Japan and the Government of the United States providing for relief from double taxation on shipping profits effected by the exchange of notes at Washington dated March 31, 1926 and June 8, 1926.

Article VI

The rate of tax imposed by one of the contracting States on interest on bonds, securities, notes, debentures or any other form of indebtedness (including mortgages or bonds secured by real property) received from sources within such State by a resident or corporation or other entity of the other contracting State not having a permanent establishment in the former State shall not exceed 15 percent.

Article VII

The rate of tax imposed by one of the contracting States on royalties and other amounts received as consideration for the right to use copyrights, artistic and scientific works, patents, designs, secret processes and formulae, trade-marks and other like property (including in such royalties and other amounts, rentals and like payments in respect of motion-picture films or for the use of industrial, commercial, or scientific equipment) from sources within such State by a resident or corporation or other entity of the other contracting State not having a permanent establishment in the former State shall not exceed 15 percent.

Article VIII

A resident or corporation or other entity of one of the contracting States deriving

(a) income from real property (including gains derived from the sale or exchange of such property, but not including interest from mortgages or bonds secured by real property), or

(b) royalties in respect of the operation of mines, quarries or other natural resources situated within the other contracting State may elect, for any taxable year, to be subject to the tax of such other State on a net basis as if such resident or corporation or other entity had a permanent establishment in such other State during such taxable year.

Article IX

An individual resident of one of the contracting States shall be exempt from the tax of the other contracting State upon compensation for labor or personal services (including the practice of liberal professions) performed in such other State in any taxable year if such resident is temporarily present in such other State:

(a) For a period or periods not exceeding a total of 180 days during such taxable year and his compensation is received for such labor or personal services performed as an officer or employee of a resident or corporation or other entity of the former State, or

(b) For a period or periods not exceeding a total of 90 days during such taxable year and his compensation received for such labor or personal services does not exceed 3,000 United States dollars, or the equivalent sum in yen as computed at the official basic rate of exchange in effect at the time such compensation is paid.

Article X

(1) (a) Salaries, wages, and similar compensation paid by the United States to an individual who is a citizen of the United States (other than an individual who has been admitted to Japan for permanent residence therein) shall be exempt from tax by Japan.

(b) Salaries, wages and similar compensation paid by Japan to an individual who is a national of Japan (other than an individual who has been admitted to the United States for permanent residence therein) shall be exempt from tax by the United States.

(2) The provisions of this Article shall not apply to salaries, wages or similar compensation paid in respect of

services rendered in connection with any trade or business carried on by either of the contracting States for purposes of profit.

Article XI

A resident of one of the contracting States, who, in accordance with agreements between the Governments of the contracting States or between educational establishments in the contracting States for the exchange of professors and teachers, or at the invitation of the Government of the other contracting State or of an educational establishment in such other State, temporarily visits such other State for the purpose of teaching for a period not exceeding two years at a university, college, school or other educational institution in such other State, shall be exempt from the tax of such other State on his remuneration for such teaching for such period.

Article XII

(1) A resident of one of the contracting States who is temporarily present in the other contracting State solely as a student at a recognized university, college or school in such other State, shall be exempt from the tax of such other State with respect to remittances from abroad (including payments, if any, by his employer abroad).

(2) A resident of one of the contracting States who is a recipient of a grant, allowance or award from a religious, charitable, scientific, literary or educational organization of such other State and who is temporarily present in the other contracting State, shall be exempt from the tax of such other State on such grant, allowance or award remitted from abroad (other than compensation for personal services).

(3) A resident of one of the contracting States who is an employee of, or under contract with, an enterprise of such State or an organization referred to in paragraph 2 of this Article, and who is temporarily present in the other contracting State for a period not exceeding one year solely to acquire technical, professional or business experience from a person other than such enterprise or organization, shall be exempt from the tax of such other State on compensation from abroad paid by such enterprise or organization for his services rendered during such period, if the amount of compensation paid by such enterprise or organization for his services during such period, when computed on the annual basis, does not exceed 6,000 United States dollars, or the equivalent sum in yen as computed at the official basic rate of exchange in effect at the time such compensation is paid.

Article XIII

For the purpose of the present Convention:

(a) Dividends paid by a corporation of one of the contracting States shall be treated as income from sources within such State.

(b) Interest paid by one of the contracting States, including local Government thereof, or by an enterprise of one of the contracting States not having a permanent establishment in the other contracting State shall be treated as income from sources within the former State.

(c) Gains, profits and income derived from the purchase and sale of personal property shall be treated as derived from the country in which such property is sold.

(d) Gains, profits and income derived from the sale by a taxpayer in one of the contracting States of goods manufactured in the other contracting State in whole or in part by such taxpayer shall be treated as derived in part from the country in which manufactured and in part from the country in which sold, and to the extent such gains, profits

and income are not allocable under other provisions of the present Convention they shall be allocated between both contracting States in accordance with such taxpayer's relative sales and property in the respective countries.

(e) Income from real property (including gains derived from the sale or exchange of such property, but not including interest from mortgages or bonds secured by real property) and royalties in respect of the operation of mines, quarries, or other natural resources shall be treated as income derived from the country in which such real property, mines, quarries or other natural resources are situated.

(f) Compensation for labor or personal services (including the practice of liberal professions) shall be treated as income from sources within the country where are rendered the services for which such compensation is paid.

(g) Royalties for using, or for the right to use, in one of the contracting States, patents, copyrights, designs, trademarks and like property shall be treated as income from sources within such State.

Article XIV

It is agreed that double taxation shall be avoided in the following manner:

(a) The United States, in determining the tax of its citizens, residents or corporations or other entities may, regardless of any other provision of the present Convention, include in the basis upon which such tax is imposed all items of income taxable under the revenue laws of the United States as if the present Convention had not come into effect. The United States shall, however, subject to the provisions of section 131 of the Internal Revenue Code as in effect on the first day of January 1954, deduct from its tax the amount of the tax of Japan. In determining the credit under the said section 131 of the Internal Revenue Code, any interest received from an enterprise of the United States with a permanent establishment in Japan shall be treated as income from sources within Japan to the extent so treated under the laws of Japan, if the debt with respect to which such interest is paid is made in connection with the business of such permanent establishment of such enterprise.

(b) Japan, in determining the tax of its residents or corporations or other entities may, regardless of any other provision of the present Convention, include in the basis upon which such tax is imposed all items of income taxable under the tax laws of Japan as if the present Convention had not come into effect. Japan shall, however, deduct from its tax so calculated the amount of the tax of the United States upon income from sources within the United States and included for the taxes of both contracting States, but in an amount not exceeding that proportion of the tax of Japan which such income bears to the entire income subject to the tax of Japan.

(c) In determining the taxes of the contracting States of a recipient, who is a citizen, resident or corporation or other entity of the United States, of a dividend from a Japanese corporation, in so far as the tax of Japan imposed on income or profits of a corporation out of which a dividend is paid is deemed under the tax laws of Japan to have been imposed on a recipient of such dividend:

(i) The United States shall deem that such recipient has paid with respect to such dividend the tax of Japan in an amount equal to 25 percent of the amount of such dividend, and deduct, under the provisions of paragraph (a) of this Article, from its tax the amount of the tax of Japan so deemed to have been paid provided the recipient includes in gross income the amount of tax thus deemed to have been paid, and

(ii) Japan shall impose with respect to such dividend received by such recipient (except as such recipient is a resident of or has a permanent establishment in Japan) no tax other than the tax imposed on income or profits of the corporation out of which such dividend is paid.

149

Article XV

(1) Organizations organized under the laws of Japan and operated exclusively for religious, charitable, scientific, literary or educational purposes shall, to the extent and subject to conditions provided in the United States Internal Revenue Code, be exempt from the tax of the United States.

(2) Organizations organized under the laws of the United States and operated exclusively for religious, charitable, scientific, literary or educational purposes shall, to the extent and subject to conditions provided in the tax laws of Japan, be exempt from the tax of Japan.

Article XVI

(1) There shall be allowed, for the purposes of the tax of the United States, in the case of a resident of Japan who is a nonresident of the United States (other than an officer or employee of the Government of Japan), in addition to the exemption provided in section 214 of the United States Internal Revenue Code as in effect on the first day of January 1954, a credit against net income, subject to the conditions prescribed in section 25 of the Internal Revenue Code as in effect on the said date, for the spouse of the taxpayer and for each child of the taxpayer who are present in the United States and residing with him in the United States at any time during the taxable year, but such additional credit shall not exceed that proportion thereof which the taxpayer's gross income from sources within the United States for the taxpayer's taxable year bears to his entire income from all sources for the fiscal or calendar year in which ends such taxable year.

(2) For the purposes of the tax of Japan, there shall be allowed in the case of a citizen of the United States who is a resident of Japan the same exemptions for a dependent or dependents as those granted to a national of Japan who is a resident of Japan.

Article XVII

(1) The competent authorities of both contracting States shall exchange such information available under the respective tax laws of both contracting States as is necessary for carrying out the provisions of the present Convention or for the prevention of fraud or for the administration of statutory provisions against tax avoidance in relation to the tax. Any information so exchanged shall be treated as secret and shall not be disclosed to any person other than those, including a court, concerned with the assessment and collection of the tax or the determination of appeals in relation thereto. No information shall be exchanged which would disclose any trade, business, industrial or professional secret or any trade process.

(2) Each of the contracting States may collect the tax imposed by the other contracting State (as though such tax were the tax of the former State) as will ensure that the exemptions, reduced rates of tax or any other benefit granted under the present Convention by such other State shall not be enjoyed by persons not entitled to such benefits.

Article XVIII

Where a taxpayer shows proof that the action of the tax authorities of either contracting State has resulted, or will result, in double taxation contrary to the provisions of the present Convention, he shall be entitled to present the facts to the competent authorities of the contracting State of which he is a national or a resident, or, if the taxpayer is a corporation or other entity, to those of the contracting State under the laws of which it is created or organized. Should the taxpayer's claim be deemed worthy of consideration, the competent authorities of such State to which the facts are so presented shall undertake to come to an agreement with the competent authorities of the other contracting State with a view to equitable avoidance of the double taxation in question.

Article XIX

(1) The provisions of the present Convention shall not be construed to deny or affect in any manner the right of diplomatic and consular officers to other or additional exemptions now enjoyed or which may hereafter be granted to such officers.

(2) The provisions of the present Convention shall not be construed to restrict in any manner any exemption, deduction, credit or other allowance now or hereafter accorded by the laws of one of the contracting States in determining the tax of such State.

(3) Should any difficulty or doubt arise as to the interpretation or application of the present Convention, or its relationship to Conventions between one of the contracting States and any other State, the competent authorities of the contracting States may settle the question by mutual agreement; it being understood, however, that this provision shall not be construed to preclude the contracting States from settling by negotiation any dispute arising under the present Convention.

(4) The competent authorities of both contracting States may prescribe regulations necessary to interpret and carry out the provisions of the present Convention and may communicate with each other directly for the purpose of giving effect to the provisions of the present Convention.

Article XX

(1) The present Convention shall be ratified and the instruments of ratification shall be exchanged at Tokyo as soon as possible.

(2) The present Convention shall enter into force on the date of exchange of instruments of ratification and shall be applicable to income or profits derived during the taxable years beginning on or after the first day of January of the calendar year in which such exchange takes place.

(3) Either of the contracting States may terminate the present Convention at any time after a period of five years shall have expired from the date on which the present Convention enters into force, by giving to the other contracting State notice of termination, provided that such notice is given on or before the 30th day of June and, in such event, the present Convention shall cease to be effective for the taxable years beginning on or after the first day of January of the calendar year next following that in which such notice is given.

IN WITNESS WHEREOF, the undersigned Plenipotentiaries have signed the present Convention.

DONE at Washington, in duplicate, in the English and Japanese languages, each text having equal authenticity, this sixteenth day of April, 1954.

For the United States of America:
WALTER BEDELL SMITH

For Japan:
S. IGUCHI

C50625